WHEN
THE
NEWS
BROKE

HEATHER HENDERSHOT

WHEN THE NEWS BROKE

CHICAGO

1968 AND THE

POLARIZING

OF AMERICA

The University of Chicago Press

Chicago and London

The University of Chicago Press, Chicago 60637
The University of Chicago Press, Ltd., London
© 2022 by Heather Hendershot
Published 2022
Paperback edition 2024
Printed in the United States of America

33 32 31 30 29 28 27 26 25 24   1 2 3 4 5

ISBN-13: 978-0-226-76852-6 (cloth)
ISBN-13: 978-0-226-83328-6 (paper)
ISBN-13: 978-0-226-76866-3 (e-book)
DOI: https://doi.org/10.7208/chicago
/9780226768663.001.0001

Library of Congress Cataloging-in-Publication Data

Names: Hendershot, Heather, author.
Title: When the news broke : Chicago 1968 and the polarizing
    of America / Heather Hendershot.
Description: Chicago : The University of Chicago Press, 2022. |
    Includes bibliographical references and index.
Identifiers: LCCN 2022017164 | ISBN 9780226768526 (cloth) |
    ISBN 9780226768663 (ebook)
Subjects: LCSH: Democratic National Convention (1968 :
    Chicago, Ill.)—Press coverage. | Mass media—Political
    aspects—United States—History—20th century. | Riots—
    Illinois—Chicago—History—20th century.
Classification: LCC F548.52 .H46 2022 |
    DDC 977.3/11043—dc23/eng/20220420
LC record available at https://lccn.loc.gov/2022017164

♾ This paper meets the requirements of ANSI/NISO
Z39.48-1992 (Permanence of Paper).

Contents

Introduction Breaking the News, Chicago Style

Walter, your conscience must be bothering you, and indeed it should. . . . I heard you [on TV] defending the press. Why? Because the public blasted you and your colleagues for "one-sided" news coverage. . . . The ugly junk you report every night is not news because the same thing you talk about has been happening for the past ten or more years. Can you call that news? I, along with the majority of this USA, got sick of listening to your nightly reports many years ago. It just took the Chicago Convention to make us really blast you for your prejudiced and one-sided coverage. . . . Why satisfy the non-democratic, filthy, screaming minority groups with free TV coverage and at the same time subject millions of true American citizens with such sickening acts?

Letter from United Airlines pilot, New York City, January 2, 1969

Dear Mr. Cronkite, I was part of the demonstration at the Hilton Hotel Wednesday night. I am writing to thank you and CBS news for telling and showing the American people what happened to us. I know I for one was very glad to see the cameras and recorders on the street. I'm sure that many of the kids feel the same way. Last week they may have felt neutral or even hostile toward the press, but now that you too [the press] have been beaten they feel that you are now our allies. I am not a hippie, Yippie, or radical. I worked for McCarthy all spring and summer and I wanted to demonstrate against the war last night. . . . Last week I looked on the police as my friends. I don't hate them yet, but I do fear them now. Again, many thanks to you and your staff for telling the truth and standing up for us.

Letter from junior political science major at Loyola University, Chicago, August 29, 1968

Americans are bad at history, but good at nostalgia. It is tempting to look back to the pre-cable, pre-internet, network era of TV and conclude that political media must have been better back then—less contentious, less divisive, less polarizing. This view of the past requires some candy-coating: there was no "golden age" when political disagreements were polite and restrained on the air. And yet the broadcast era was, to some extent, a better (or at least a more dignified) time for news media. It was a time when Americans all watched the same stuff. Before the audience was fragmented by cable, beginning in the 1980s, network TV functioned as a "cultural forum," as TV historians have described it, offering a collective experience to be interpreted in different ways by individuals within a mass audience.[1] The notion of narrowcasting political reporting or opinion to small subgroups would have seemed farfetched back then. You had the option of subscribing to a journal of opinion like the *Nation* or the *National Review*, or to an underground, left-wing newspaper, or to a right-wing newsletter, but you had to actively seek out these specialized publications, and such alternatives did not exist on TV, outside of small-scale public access efforts and a few ambitious PBS oddities.

From the 1950s through the 1970s, Walter Cronkite, Dan Rather, and Mike Wallace on CBS and Chet Huntley and David Brinkley on NBC were the voices of reason, striving for even-handed analysis (figs. 1–2). It was so different from what we have now that even making the comparison is jarring. The changes in how news is produced, distributed, and consumed have been elemental, and it's hard to imagine how you could undo them. You'd have better luck unscrambling an egg. And even if you could, you'd want to consider the ramifications. What were the limitations of the network era?

With only three networks providing TV news, the gatekeeping was fierce; the objective was to stick to the facts and fulfill a public service. The transparent meaning of "the public" and "the greater good" was often taken for granted, and white, male, middle-class values mostly dominated. News was targeted to an imagined moderate, centrist viewer, and producers were anxious not to offend—notwithstanding coverage of civil rights, which consistently did anger white southern

FIGURE 1. Before Chicago, CBS anchorman Walter Cronkite—also known as "the most trusted man in America"—was widely understood as an objective voice striving for even-handed analysis. Most critical viewer mail sent to him charged that a particular story was incorrect or unbalanced. After Chicago, viewers wrote increasingly that the flaw lay not in individual stories but in Cronkite himself for exhibiting "liberal bias." CBS, 1968.

segregationists. It was virtually unheard-of for a national newscaster to disparage an elected official or a political candidate on air, outside of a closing segment in which such opinions were clearly stamped as "commentary" or "editorial." Before the rise of cable, a snarky laugh or an arched eyebrow, the kind of stylistic flourish regularly displayed by Tucker Carlson, Rachel Maddow, Sean Hannity, Don Lemon, or Laura

FIGURE 2. Like Cronkite, Chet Huntley (*left*) and David Brinkley (*right*) of NBC were widely considered "fair" before Chicago. When Goldwater supporters at the 1964 convention had worn "Stamp Out Huntley–Brinkley" buttons, it marked them as extremists. Even attendee Henry Kissinger was taken aback. Field Enterprises, Inc., 1968.

Ingraham, could get you fired. The approach to news was straight-forward, businesslike, and competent.

This insistent neutrality was aggressively un-flashy. Today viewers expect bells and whistles from CNN, Fox News, and MSNBC. Their "breaking news" chyrons are designed to excite and draw viewers in, which makes sense from a business perspective, but consider that in the network era "breaking news" was truly urgent. If an entertainment show was interrupted by news, or if, during a regular news broadcast, an anchor suddenly broke from his script, you had to wonder if the United States was at war or if someone had been assassinated. The words "we interrupt this program . . ." or "this just in . . ." pierced like a shot of adrenaline to the myocardium. By contrast, contemporary TV news is persistently labeled "breaking," regardless of the importance of the events reported. A story recycled and commented on throughout an eight-hour rotation hardly seems "breaking" at all, but this is how cable news outlets operate, to keep viewing interest up and costs down.

In the pre-cable era, the evening news ran at first for fifteen minutes; later, starting in 1963, it ran for half an hour.[2] Viewers expected a tidy distillation of facts, a supplement to the local newspaper, and a bit of analysis to make sense of it all. It was a healthy tonic to round off the day, packaged with enough storytelling to not completely bore the viewer. When the networks did long-form coverage, such as a week at a convention or covering a NASA launch, it was hyped as a special event on a par with the World Series.

The national news outlets may have seen themselves as performing a civic duty, but this duty had economic stakes. The executives of CBS, NBC, and ABC worried about costs and ratings, and their demands were conveyed to the directors of the news divisions. At the same time, the notion that TV news was a perpetual loss leader was promoted by the networks to convey their benevolence to both the FCC and the public. Yet, as media historian Michael Socolow has documented, ad sales for the news were robust throughout the network era, and "by the early 1960s, both NBC's *Huntley–Brinkley Report* and the *CBS Evening News* were earning enormous revenues."[3] (ABC consistently ran a distant third.) In 1965 *Huntley–Brinkley* was NBC's biggest annual moneymaker. Ads sold at $63,000 a minute during their hit show *Bonanza*. *Huntley–Brinkley* ads cost $21,000 per minute. But *Bonanza* ran only once a week, and it went into reruns during the summer, when TV viewing time decreased across the board. New episodes of *Huntley–Brinkley* aired five nights a week, every week.[4]

The CBS and NBC news divisions were in a perpetual ratings war, but that war was kept private, in a sort of gentleman's agreement, because to highlight ratings would undercut the public service function to which the news divisions were committed—a commitment underpinned by both idealism and pragmatism, depending on whether you were on the journalism side delivering stories or on the business side dealing with advertising and managing potential regulatory concerns. When CBS finally got solidly ahead of NBC in 1970, Dick Salant, the president of CBS news, sent a stern memo to his staff: "Fun's fun and I am sure everybody is just delighted with the current ratings of the *Evening News* compared to the *NBC Nightly News*. And I know it's mighty tempting to pump it out, loudly or quietly to the press. But once we start the rating game there is no end to it and particularly for journalism, it's not a healthy game. Therefore, I want to make sure that *nobody* in this shop and I mean nobody, directly or indirectly, over the table or under the table, feeds out our ratings to any part of the press."[5] This is strong stuff, highlighting not just issues of image but also issues of integrity.

In sum, the evening news was a profitable venture packaged and pursued as a neutral and benevolent one. This well-intentioned if imperfect effort to serve a broad national audience is worth valuing today, or even longing for, if one can do it without slipping into half-baked nostalgia. The notion of neutral, one-size-fits-all coverage seemed to slip away beginning with the rise of 24-hour news in the late 1990s, with specific cable channels arising (or evolving, like MSNBC) to target particular political perspectives, and culminating with the rise of social media in the 2000s.[6] These are key factors that have made the news seem "biased" and fragmented, but there are other ways to tell the story.[7]

One might look back to President Reagan's deregulation of the TV industry and elimination of the Fairness Doctrine, which had dictated that broadcasters had to give balanced coverage of controversial issues.[8] The end of the doctrine paved the way for the rise of Rush Limbaugh as a radio star and pundit.[9] But we could also narrate the history of political fragmentation on the airwaves by examining the rise of conservative watchdog groups like Reed Irvine's Accuracy in Media. Or through the story of how Roger Ailes began his career on *The Mike Douglas Show*, went to work for Richard Nixon, and eventually became CEO of Fox News. Or by revisiting the history of GOP efforts to cut off funding for public broadcasting. Or by recounting President Nixon's efforts to eliminate "biased" network news; Nixon's attacks were executed by his vice president, Spiro T. Agnew, who famously attacked East Coast, "elite" journalists as "nattering nabobs of negativitism."[10] That the "East Coast elite" Walter Cronkite was a University of Texas–Austin dropout, with family roots in Kansas City, or that Dan Rather struggled mightily to make tuition payments at Sam Houston State University, made no difference. Populism works less by facts than by declarations.

Ultimately, it is network TV coverage of the 1968 Chicago Democratic National Convention (DNC) and the fallout from that event that perhaps best illuminate how accusations of "liberal media bias" took root in the national political consciousness. During and following the convention, viewers across America decried TV coverage as slanted against the Chicago police, who—judging by all photographic evidence and firsthand accounts—had viciously teargassed and beaten protestors (and also journalists and bystanders) in the streets. But where was footage showing how the protestors had provoked the police, irate viewers asked, footage that would reveal that the protestors "got what they deserved"? And why, viewers wondered in thousands of letters and telegrams, sent during and after the convention, did newscasters sympathize with the beaten, calling them "kids" or "hippies" or "protestors" instead of "terrorists" or "communists"?

This anger was exhibited by a thirty-two-year-old airline pilot writing to Cronkite a few months after the convention. He complained about the news's "one-sided" reporting of "subversive acts and communist and non-communist demonstrations," in Chicago and elsewhere. He had long hated all the "ugly junk" on the news, but Chicago was the last straw for him. On the flip side there was the college junior who was attacked by police for demonstrating against the Vietnam War in front of the Hilton. The pilot seemed to have been pushed further right by convention coverage, while the college student had been a moderate who now felt herself tilting left, closing her thank-you letter to Cronkite with "I'll never forget what I learned last night on Michigan Avenue." She was in the minority as a Cronkite fan after Chicago, but there were as many responses to convention coverage as there were viewers—or in her case, participants.

In the weeks that followed, letters to CBS ran 11-to-1 against the network's coverage. This eruption of outrage was indisputably an organic one: viewers were not organized by the Republican National Committee or the John Birch Society or the *National Review* or Young Americans for Freedom to send telegrams to the networks. They simply picked up their phones and furiously dialed Western Union. The anger was often overtly right-wing or conservative, but not exclusively so. It would later be Nixon's genius to tap into this negative energy—to *weaponize* it—and motivate his "silent majority" to solidify their distrust of mainstream media.

After the convention, it seemed that Hubert Humphrey was doomed to lose the election at least in part because the chaos in Chicago had made the party look so bad on TV, so out of control. Mayor Richard J. Daley's nickname was "Mr. Democrat," but look what happened in Chicago, Republicans could say, driving home the idea that the Democrats were not the "law and order" party. Ironically, TV coverage was blasted by viewers for "liberal bias," yet that coverage ultimately served the Republican Party and, specifically, its candidate Richard Nixon.

There was incoherence here: those angry at the networks felt they got it wrong by showing so much violence and sympathizing with the protestors, and at the same time the very fact of massive protest against

President Johnson, embodied by those street demonstrators, showed that LBJ had failed and only Nixon could solve America's problems. Somehow, the complaint went, TV newsmen were hopelessly *liberal and subjective*, offering free publicity to the Chicago protestors and, at the same time, and presumably inadvertently, showing as an *objective fact* that Johnson and the Democratic Party had failed. This widespread disgust with the convention would confirm what Republican viewers already felt, but it might also speak to Democrats fed up with the war and wary of Humphrey. Indeed, Nixon held only a modest lead in the polls right up until the bitter end, when Humphrey finally declared some distance from LBJ's foreign policy, which edged up his numbers. Nixon barely won, and the crisis of the Democratic Party in Chicago—seen by millions on TV—was a key factor in nudging him over the finish line. As if to grind home the point that he had won the worst job in America, following his inauguration the Justice Department gave Nixon a packet of papers for declaring martial law, "with blanks to fill in the date and the name of the city."[11] This sort of preparedness was the legacy of Watts and Newark and Detroit and Chicago.

Notably, no one argued in the wake of the DNC that the networks had shown something "fake," to use twenty-first-century phrasing. Indisputably, protestors were beaten by Chicago police for seventeen minutes on Michigan Avenue on August 28, as the bloodied victims chanted, "The whole world is watching!"[12] Regardless of their feelings about "law and order" or police brutality, reasonable people would have to conclude that this was genuinely breaking news. That the news itself was broken was an altogether different kind of conclusion, though, and one that Nixon would amplify with all his might. This amplification continued after Nixon, accelerating in the Reagan years. It persevered in the George W. Bush years, and helped fuel the rise of the Tea Party following the election of Barack Obama. The attack on liberal media bias would reach a new peak in the Trump years of "fake news" (i.e., true news attacked as phony) with the president calling the press "the enemy of the people" and fostering violence against journalists. What had been experienced as a feeling in August 1968—that the mainstream media was infused with liberal bias—had for many become an ossified reality fifty years later.

The 1968 DNC was not only a key moment for the expression of concerns about liberal media bias but also a tipping point for the *nationalization* of the notion of such bias. Before this event, the idea that the mainstream media was tainted by a liberal perspective was widely considered marginal, or even extremist.[13] To be clear, before Chicago, hawks did not care for coverage of Vietnam that did not toe the government line. But for years such coverage was scant. The popular memory of that conflict is that it was a "television war" that played out in American living rooms; forces on the right have long contended that TV "lost the war for us." TV did show protest against the war, and it did air nightly body counts, but the news also dutifully reported the government line on Southeast Asia for years, turning more negative only in 1968, when Americans en masse had already started to sour on the war.[14]

Cronkite's famous 1968 report on Vietnam offers a case in point. Cronkite had earned his bona fides as a trustworthy news anchor for his coverage of the Kennedy assassination in 1963 and his uplifting coverage of the Gemini and Apollo space missions. His animus against right-wing senators Robert Taft in 1948 and Barry Goldwater in 1964 had caused friction, but he was generally seen by TV viewers as a moderate, establishment guy. He was "Uncle Walter," regularly rated in surveys as the most trusted man in America. Perplexed by hippies (including his own daughters), with their "indescribable" outfits that looked like they came from a "remnant sale," he recognized that the young generation no doubt saw him as "an old fuddy-duddy," as he put it.[15]

It was this middle-of-the-road squareness that had made his February 1968 *CBS News Special Report from Vietnam* so impactful. Like ABC and NBC, CBS had not previously made a hard pushback on official government statements on the war. In 1965, when Morley Safer covered a search-and-destroy mission in which American Marines torched 150 Vietnamese huts with flamethrowers and Zippo lighters, the president was outraged; with his typical bluntness, LBJ called CBS president Frank Stanton and accused him of shitting on the American flag. CBS management was not thrilled by the report, which included footage of crying women and children and concluded with Safer suggesting that the actions had been cruel and pointless, but this sort of controversial coverage was atypical. Unlike Safer, Cronkite had been suckered by the carefully managed press conferences and briefings he had attended in Saigon in 1965. At that point, he was, as biographer Douglas Brinkley put it, "a cautious hawk."[16] In 1965, CBS had aired a four-part *Special Report* on Vietnam, the transcript of which was printed shortly thereafter as a book with an introduction by Cronkite. There, Cronkite enthusiastically supported the US presence in Vietnam, which he described as "a commitment not for this year or next year but, most likely, for a generation. This is the way it must be if we are to fulfill our pledge to ourselves and to others to stop communist aggression wherever it raises its head."[17]

When the Tet Offensive erupted in early 1968, Cronkite traveled to Vietnam to make a new assessment, and upon his return stateside, he reluctantly reported that America was, at best, facing a stalemate in Southeast Asia. He insisted that his conclusions be marked as editorial evaluation and aired separately from the regular *CBS Evening News*. Johnson was agog, supposedly proclaiming, "If I've lost Cronkite, I've lost Middle America." It didn't matter if the statement was apocryphal, insofar as the sentiment was accurate: when the most middle-of-the-road guy turns on you, it's all over. Johnson's popularity ratings were already down, and a month after Cronkite's broadcast, the infinitely more popular Robert F. Kennedy declared his candidacy for president. LBJ announced he would not run for reelection.[18]

So heading into the Democratic National Convention in Chicago, Cronkite had already pointed out the elephant in the room: we were not winning in Vietnam. This may have been controversial for hawks, but CBS had not been deluged with angry viewer mail in the wake of the *Special Report*. Cronkite's broadcast was apparently more a wake-up call than an assault to most CBS viewers. As Douglas Brinkley put it, "The brand of CBS was impartiality," and this brand was not substantively undercut by Cronkite's assessment of the stalemate abroad.[19]

That said, it was not unusual for CBS to receive complaint letters. The network kept scrupulous records of pro and con mail, and a story was often judged successful if it received more or less equal amounts of negative and positive responses. In fact, each week the CBS research department created an internal scorecard. For the week of October 7, 1969, for example, "CBS News in general" received thirty positive letters and thirty-three negative letters.[20] That same week, fifty-nine requests for film and transcripts were made, a relic of the pre–VCR, DVD, and DVR era and obviously considered a sign of success for the news division. A report for the week of November 4, 1970, noted ten favorable responses to a feature on "Rock Music and Plants" ("ironic that rock music that killed plants was that of the late Jimi Hendrix") along with six critical letters ("Untrue! My son and I have identical plants. His plants . . . are beautiful. Mine are spare and anemic. Joe's stereo plays acid rock, mine Chopin.").[21]

The network's concern with viewer perceptions was more about professional standards of fairness and balance than about ratings. Many of the stories that provoked a reaction received roughly similar numbers of pro and con responses. Some stories elicited a severely skewed ratio of responses, but the network felt a good story *should* be provocative; strong responses were desired, and not just good ones. That may sound counterintuitive, but exclusively positive feedback might indicate bias just as much as the reverse.

The general public feeling (before Chicago, at least) was that Walter Cronkite and David Brinkley and Chet Huntley and their peers were neutral professionals, and that if they made mistakes, it was because they were human, not because they were pushing their own political perspectives. That said, there *were* some critics who saw the anchormen as incorrigible liberals or even communist sympathizers.

Goldwater, for example, was highly critical of how the media represented him throughout his presidential campaign. Journalist Theodore (Teddy) White evenhandedly noted that Goldwater was his own worst enemy. He might give a perfectly fine, even-keeled speech, but it would be sandwiched between provocative, impromptu press conferences where he made inflammatory off-the-cuff comments. The problem the press faced, then, was "How could one be fair to Goldwater—by quoting what he said or by explaining what he thought? To quote him directly was manifestly unfair, but if he insisted on speaking thus in public, how could one resist quoting him?"[22] It's unclear what would be "unfair" about quoting the awkward public utterances of a politician, but White's point was that you'd have to cover Goldwater selectively to avoid charges of "bias" from him. White was speaking primarily of the print press here, but Goldwater faced similar issues with TV coverage.

At the convention where he was nominated, TV viewers saw a wild frenzy of pro-Goldwater and anti-media sentiment. White notes that when Nelson Rockefeller made a strong statement against extremism's "strong-arm and goon tactics, bomb threats and bombings," he was viciously booed, but that the Goldwater team controlled the floor and the angry "kooks" were all up in the gallery. Regardless, the outrage against voices of moderation was deafening, and this is what viewers witnessed at home. When former President Eisenhower referred to "sensation-seeking columnists and commentators" in his address to the convention, there was a spontaneous explosion among the delegates, as they shouted at the press gallery. The moderate Eisenhower had not intended the line as a zinger and was perplexed.[23] Like all presidents, Eisenhower had had grievances with the press, but he didn't take such grievances as a militant rallying point.

The more right-wing delegates at the Cow Palace wore "Stamp Out Huntley–Brinkley" buttons and could be heard making comments like "You know, these nighttime news shows sound to me like they're being broadcast from Moscow."[24] Attendee Henry Kissinger noted that "the frenzy of cheering at the Cow Palace was reminiscent of Nazi times" and that the buttons "are a new phenomenon. The delegate who said to me, 'I am sorry the button is not big enough to include [ABC's] Howard K. Smith and all Eastern Newspapers' was a new form of delegate." The protean Kissinger was right on board with Nixon later when he attacked the news media, but at this earlier moment, the notion of a full-frontal assault on Huntley and Brinkley was strange enough— "extremist," if you will—to startle many conservatives.[25]

Political historian Nicole Hemmer has suggested that the notion of "liberal media bias" has its roots in Goldwater's complaints. Goldwater did give the notion a hard push, but the idea was seen as radical—it simply did not take root at that moment. Hemmer correctly adds that "future candidates would hone it into a brutally effective weapon."[26] It was the immediate aftermath of the DNC that first revealed the possibility of provoking mass hostility toward the mainstream media, and Nixon, of course, was the man who sharpened that brutally effective weapon to a fine point.

Another loud critic before Nixon's election was William F. Buckley, whose *National Review* magazine often made the case that the media had an anti-conservative slant.[27] Buckley sought to legitimate his brand of right-wing conservatism and to pull the GOP away from the moderate centrism that characterized it at the time. He also wanted to get the extremists out of the spotlight, a whack-a-mole endeavor. The most visible kooks were right-wing radio broadcasters like Dan Smoot and Carl McIntire who, in violation of FCC guidelines, used the airwaves to advance one-sided attacks on liberals and, by extension, on the "pro-communist" liberal media establishment.[28] Although the fanatics agreed with Buckley on numerous political points, they were adamant that the communists were behind everything from civil rights to the fluoridation of drinking water; their extremist style would hold back the movement as it sought mainstream legitimacy.

Some argue that Buckley's rejection of the extremists was all theater, and there is something to that perception; they were a large constituency, and their support for candidates like Goldwater and Reagan was desirable. That's why Buckley initially rejected John Birch Society founder Robert Welch but not the society's members, whose numbers he wanted to keep on his side. When JBS members reacted by pegging him as one of their elite enemies, he cut them loose too. Buckley had a genuine *distaste* for conspiratorial thinking and little patience for populism or demagoguery. (In 2000, he dismissed Donald Trump, who had made a feeble attempt to run for president, as a preening narcissist.) This made his concern about liberal bias especially notable:

it didn't come from a populist notion that the media needed to better serve the masses but, rather, from disgust with the premise—to his mind, phony—that Cronkite et al. offered neutral reporting. He was an early booster for cable because he thought the free market would solve the problem by providing conservative news. Obviously, he was half-right. Cable news struck a blow against the networks, while creating its own unique problems.

Southern segregationists were the other group (and one that clearly overlapped with the radio screwballs) who saw the national network news as hopelessly liberal-communist. Throughout the civil rights era, white southerners complained that the networks ignored their perspective and were manipulated by publicity-seeking integration-ists. The TV cameras were there when Eugene "Bull" Connor turned firehoses and attack dogs on Black children in Birmingham, Alabama. Likewise, when Governor George Wallace ordered police on horseback to trample and whip marchers on the Edmund Pettus Bridge in 1965, the networks recorded the event. (ABC famously interrupted *Judgment at Nuremberg*, a film about the trials of Nazi war criminals, to cut to the brutal footage.) Movement leaders knew that coverage was crucial to their cause, and segregationists weren't wrong to observe that the activists were using the media to their advantage. What was fishy was the implication that it was the mere presence of network cameras that caused violence, as if "Bombingham" would have been free of voter suppression and cross burning if not for visits from Dan Rather. Covering the civil rights movement in 1962, Rather recalls a sign in an Oxford, Mississippi, motel window reading "No Dogs, N*ggers, or Reporters Allowed."[29]

Bull Connor tidily concluded, "The trouble with this country is communism, socialism, and journalism."[30] By the late 1950s, many white southerners had taken to calling CBS the Communist, or Coon, or Colored Broadcasting Company. The same racist wordplay made NBC the "N*gger Broadcasting Company." Southerners compensated for what they saw as the flaws of the national news media by sticking to their guns on their own nightly, local news broadcasts, where they treated Black viewers with derision and defied any notion that such viewers were part of the "public" that they were duty-bound to serve by the terms of their FCC licenses.[31]

With a network affiliation came the contractual duty to air the national nightly news, but southern affiliates fought that obligation because they saw the national news as far too liberal. Jesse Helms offers a case in point. Before he became a senator, Helms wrote editorials for the White Citizens Council newsletter and ran a North Carolina TV-radio station, where he censored the national news to the best of his ability; "commentary" segments typically ran at the end of the network broadcasts, so you could lop them off without viewers being aware that a change had been made. Helms also regularly broadcast his own pro-segregation editorial segments. He was offended by *Huntley–Brinkley*'s coverage of the 1963 March on Washington, which had not a word to say about the movement's "communist ties" (plus Martin Luther King's associate Bayard Rustin was gay, and thus, according to Helms, a "moral degenerate").[32] Five years later, he seriously suggested that the *ABC Evening News* should substitute an inspirational story about Boy Scouts for coverage of King's Poor People's Campaign.[33]

One thing that made the backlash against network news coverage of the 1968 DNC unique was that it came not just from Helms or Connor supporters but from all over the country. The idea that the media had a liberal slant was suddenly drained of its extremist status, drained of its southern status, and, by extension, drained of explicit bigotry. Some disgruntled viewers who wrote to the networks did self-identify as conservative. These were the viewers who, in their letters and telegrams, explicitly vilified the hippies for their communist ideas and long hair—like that airline pilot. Some who hated the longhairs used nasty epithets and displayed their racism front and center; the Chicago protestors were virtually all white, but such viewers conflated them with African American rioters.

Others, however, self-identified as liberals and came across as desperate rather than as politically motivated: What has America come to? What would *you* do, Mr. Cronkite, if you were mayor of Chicago, and ten thousand people demanded to march in the streets? When will it end? This sense of anguish infuses the letters and telegrams, and clearly many of those who attacked the news for showing the violence and, they thought, getting it wrong were writing in frustration, struggling to convey their sadness, anger, or fatigue at the end of a long year of riots, assassinations, and Vietnam crises.

The question remains, What exactly made Chicago a tipping-point moment for viewers crying "bias"? The networks had shown all manner of domestic crises in the 1960s—the aftermath of the bombing of the Sixteenth Street Baptist Church in Birmingham, the integration of the University of Alabama in Tuscaloosa, rebellion in the streets of Watts, rioters protesting desegregation at Ole Miss. Only a year before the DNC, TV news had captured six days of looting and arson in Detroit, and a few months before the convention, the Black neighborhoods of Chicago had erupted in flames following Rev. King's assassination. Letters of both praise and complaint about coverage of all these events were sent to the networks as usual, but there was no nationwide groundswell of concern that the networks might have demonstrated a "bias" (liberal or otherwise) in their approach.

The DNC was a crisis, but not one categorically more dire than these earlier events. Chicago was not looted and burned in August 1968. There were no snipers. Enraged by petty misdemeanors, Mayor Daley complained that convention protestors *sat in the street and blocked traffic* and *broke curfew* in the cities' parks. Repeatedly denied permits to march by the city, they proceeded to do so anyway. As with earlier, more urgent urban protest actions, the situation was met with brutal law enforcement. The city was encased in barbed wire, its streets filled with military Jeeps and patrolled by National Guardsmen and police, most of whom struck first and asked questions later. Still, those four days in August couldn't compare to the six days of chaos in July 1967 in Detroit, and viewer complaints left the networks confused. They had covered the action in the streets of Chicago following their usual protocols. They made editorial choices, some good, such as letting long segments unroll with minimal editing and narration so viewers could take in a scene presented as "objectively" as possible, and some bad, such as holding off on showing pervasive street violence so that Wednesday night's altercation in front of the Hilton seemed like more of an aberration than an amplification of the preceding week. TV journalists' approach to fairness and objectivity had not changed. Yet viewers' responses had shifted.

Comparisons to other urban uprisings and riots put Chicago in perspective. Forty-three people died in Detroit, thirty-three of whom were Black. Thirty had died in Watts, of whom five were white, and twenty-six in Newark, again mostly Black. A National Guardsman declared upon arrival in Detroit, "I'm gonna shoot at anything that moves and that is Black."[34] Four Blacks had died in the uprising during the 1968 Republican convention in Miami, though it was underreported and mistakenly seen as completely unrelated to the GOP gathering. Following the Chicago DNC, a common refrain from authorities was that "nobody was killed," which was almost true. The Thursday before the convention, a visiting hippie, Dean Johnson, was shot dead by the police. He was a Native American from South Dakota, an "Indian" used as a "puppet" by the "crazies" of the National Mobilization Committee to End the War in Vietnam (the Mobe), according to Teddy White, a characterization worth singling out not only for its callousness but also because White was among the few to even note the incident.[35]

Still, the police had not opened fire in Chicago in August; they wielded nightsticks and tear gas rather than bullets. And yet, TV viewers reacted strongly, attacking not the police but the networks. To make sense of the uniqueness of the reaction to convention coverage, it helps to ask, who were these aggrieved "viewers"? The news divisions had high ideals about serving all, but it was the white middle-class audience that cried foul most loudly following Chicago.[36] To be blunt, Chicago was unique because of the race of those beaten and those doing the beating. White TV viewers had grown accustomed to seeing police and National Guardsmen brutalizing and arresting Black people, early on in Birmingham and later in Detroit and other northern cities. Some reacted in horror, whereas others cheered for the enforcement of "law and order." The point is not that all who were angry with the media following Chicago were reacting in a racist manner, but that the *context* for viewing urban altercations was that the norm on TV was to show Blacks looting or lobbing Molotov cocktails, and then being violently stopped by police. Daley had turned his town into a fortress specifically to preempt a Black uprising. He had been unable to control the revolt in April after King's death, but he would prevent another crisis in August, he reasoned, through a massive show of force.

The mayor failed to grasp that Black Chicagoans saw the DNC as a white event, and that the vast majority of protestors traveling to Chicago were white. Ralph Abernathy's Poor People's Campaign was there with two symbolic mules and a cart, and Bobby Seale and Dick Gregory made a few high-profile appearances, but the protest in the street was dominated by white hippies and Yippies, people whom the police viewed contemptuously as repellent draft dodgers, middle-class college students, and dropouts, potentially acting in solidarity with civil rights or Black Power activists. What viewers saw at home, then, was white police beating white protestors. It was not the kind of subjugation most often shown on the nightly news.

This might have produced a new kind of alarm in many white viewers, an intensified perception that America was falling apart at the seams. It wasn't just a question of "law and order" forces policing urban (poor, Black) America. If "normal" suburban, white, middle-class white kids could turn into hippies or join Students for a Democratic Society (SDS), drop out, and end up with their skulls cracked by the very men sworn to defend them, then the country was doomed. Since this couldn't be true, was *too horrible* to be true, the media must have told the story wrong, many white viewers concluded.

On the other hand, there were also white viewers who were fed up with campus radicalism and antiwar demonstrations, and who loathed the privileged, white college kids who dodged the draft and acted out by seizing buildings and staging sit-downs at elite institutions like Columbia and MIT. The only network coverage in Chicago that would have satisfied such viewers would have been full-throated attacks on the street demonstrators, just the sort of "advocacy reporting" against which the networks defined their efforts at fairness and neutrality. Viewers who felt that college kids were "spoiled" and "asking for trouble" brought their class antagonism to their interpretation of Chicago. These were the Americans who later approved of National Guard violence against students at Kent State in 1970, or who, that same year, sided with the construction workers who violently charged against peace protestors in the Hard Hat Riot in New York City. All of which is to say, race was a crucial issue in Chicago, but not the only one fueling anti-network antagonism amongst the "silent majority." Jesse Jackson had advised antiwar activist Rennie Davis that "if Blacks got whipped [in Chicago] nobody would pay attention, . . . but if whites got whipped, it would make the newspapers." Jackson was right, but the desired effect (mass sympathy) did not emerge. As one political analyst put it later, "America did not see itself in *these* white kids."[37]

When interviewed by journalists about what they thought of the DNC, Blacks responded that maybe now white people understood the reality of police brutality. The Kerner Commission's 1968 report, released just months before the Chicago convention, observed that "television newscasts during the periods of actual disorder in 1967 tended to emphasize law enforcement activities, thereby overshadowing underlying grievances and tensions. . . . Television coverage tended to give the impression that the riots were confrontations between Negroes and whites rather than responses by Negroes to underlying slum problems."[38] This description was correct, if limited. The CBS *Special Report*, "Watts: Riot or Revolt?," attempted to understand the frustrations of Watts residents, while also egregiously underplaying the racism and police brutality fostered by Los Angeles Chief of Police Bill Parker. In the name of "fairness," CBS showed both sides, ultimately arguing that the Black poor of Watts needed help, but also underplaying the systemic racism that they faced. Historian Rick Perlstein describes a program more in keeping with the Kerner Commission's analysis, a local TV production with the crude, B-movie title *Hell in the City of Angels*, which showed "war, breaking out in the streets of the United

States of America, as if out of nowhere."[39] If Watts was the preface to Nixon's political resurrection, as Perlstein suggests, Chicago helped propel that story toward its resolution.

In sum, Chicago was a tipping point for the mainstreaming and nationalization of the notion of "liberal media bias" for several reasons. First, because it showed police brutality in a way that should have hit home for white viewers, but that many rejected because it ran contrary to widely normalized, internalized notions of white supremacy and/or white privilege. There had to be another explanation, and they found it: TV missed something and told the story wrong. Second, the feeling that the media had exhibited bias might have dissipated after the convention, but for the fact that Daley kept the story alive for months, insisting that he and his police force had done nothing wrong. And finally, shortly thereafter, Nixon and Agnew applied the narrative of media failure in Chicago to coverage of Vietnam, and later Watergate. The Nixon-Agnew administration could have vilified the media without the events in Chicago, but convention fallout made it all easier. Nixon handily exploited the fact that most American TV viewers were convinced that the networks had misrepresented police violence in Chicago. Further, many Americans believed the police had the legitimate right to preserve "law and order," so the problem, from this perspective, was not whether the cops had used excessive force but that the networks did not go out of their way to advocate for that force.

The irony is that police violence was constant during convention week, and in the days leading up to it. Viewers accused the networks of showing *too much*, when they actually missed covering *most* of it. Some protestors cursed at police and threw projectiles at them, even bags of urine and feces. On the other hand, undercover agents provocateurs—later estimated as one-in-six of the protestors—also instigated violence.[40] A CBS special ten years later reported that at least two hundred people in the crowd in front of the Hilton on Wednesday night had been undercover agents.[41] Regardless of whether or not some genuine protestors might have acted violently, the federal government's aggressively (even exceedingly) neutral, nonpartisan *Walker Report* concluded that the Battle of Michigan Avenue had been a "police riot," and that police violence had been pervasive, and not just on Wednesday night. A reporter taking a photo or writing notes was likely to be hit repeatedly in the head with a nightstick. A driver stopped at a red light was likely to be maced by a cop through an open car window.[42] You didn't have to have long hair or carry a Vietcong flag to get your skull cracked in Chicago. Just being there was enough provocation to send the cops into a rage.

To put this in proper context, it helps to recall how truly shattering 1968 had been. In January and February, the Tet Offensive erupted in Vietnam; fighting lasted a month in Hue and two months in Khe Sanh. The series of battles were ultimately "won" by America, following which General William Westmoreland declared that he would need 206,000 more US soldiers to defeat the enemy. It was a spectacular setback: the narrative long spun by LBJ and the Pentagon—that we were finally just about to be victorious in Southeast Asia—literally crumbled before our eyes. The military victory was a political defeat.

The tone had been set for the year. On February 29, the Kerner Commission's report on civil disorders was released; it famously concluded that "our nation is moving toward two societies, one Black, one white— separate and unequal."[43] Also in February, there was a sanitation strike in New York City: apocalyptic images of mountains of garbage cluttered the nightly news, an obvious metaphor for the mounting American crisis. Later in 1968 the city would also endure a teacher's strike; New Yorkers were spared the gravediggers strike until 1970, a small mercy.[44] On March 16, Bobby Kennedy declared himself a presidential candidate. The My Lai Massacre—a war crime that would not be revealed until 1969—took place on the very same day. Later in March, six thousand Yippies congregated in Grand Central Terminal. Their plan was "to party all night then dance forth at dawn like bassarids up to the Sheep Meadow in Central Park 'to YIP up at the sun.'"[45] Unfortunately, a violent contingent set off some cherry bombs, at which point the police beat the crowd to a bloody pulp. To the Yippies already mobilizing for Chicago, it felt like a preview of coming attractions.

On April 4, King was assassinated. Riots followed in more than one hundred cities, including Chicago, Washington, DC, Baltimore, and Kansas City. On April 23, Columbia University students seized a campus building, taking several officials hostage. In May, the Catonsville Nine seized records from a Selective Service office in Maryland and burned them with napalm. In June, Bobby Kennedy was assassinated. In August, police beat thousands of protestors in the streets of Chicago. In October, American medalists at the Mexico City Olympics raised their fists in a Black Power salute during the playing of the national anthem; they were subjected to death threats upon their return to the United States. In November, the "law and order" candidate Nixon just barely squeaked by Hubert Humphrey to win the presidency. He might have done better if one of America's most famous segregationists, George Wallace, had not been running as a third-party candidate. Wallace seized votes across the nation, not just in the South, underscoring the pervasiveness of the racial crisis in 1968.

In late December, Apollo 8 entered its orbit around the moon, a shot in the arm for American morale, and seemingly the only thing America didn't flub this year. And yet this event offered little consolation to the down-and-out who wondered how such spending could be justified.[46] "I can't pay no doctor's bills. But Whitey's on the moon," Gil Scott-Heron observed one year later. To top it all off on the cultural front, 1968 was the year of a number of hopeless films—*Rosemary's Baby*, *Night of the Living Dead*, *Planet of the Apes*—and the year's highest grossing film, *2001: A Space Odyssey*, offered a perplexing, antiseptic, and ultimately psychedelic future, in which the Cold War simply never ended and people of color seemed to no longer exist. On New Year's Eve, CBS correspondent Harry Reasoner summarized the year as one of "horrors and failures."[47]

This was America in 1968. Chicago was its own microcosm of corruption, racism, and violence.

Richard J. Daley had won his first race for Chicago mayor in 1955. He died suddenly of a heart attack in 1976, one year into his sixth consecutive term. That Al Capone had voted for Daley in every election was the kind of cutesy joke you might hear from Johnny Carson on *The Tonight Show*. Everyone knew that corpses were voting in Chicago. Democrats were registered with addresses from psychiatric hospitals and vacant lots.[48] Winos were offered a bottle of Ripple in exchange for their vote—after all, the bars were closed when the polls were open. If you were poor, you might get a chicken for dinner. If you thought your vote was secret, you'd learn the truth when a poll worker entered the booth with you and watched you pull the "correct" lever, for the Democratic ticket. That practice was called "four-legged voting."[49] If you were an honest poll worker who made a fuss, you risked being beaten and then arrested for disorderly conduct. One crafty poll watcher who escaped injury observed a man entering a voting booth and pulling the lever seventy times.[50] After the polls closed, precincts reported votes carefully. It was best to see how many votes were *needed* to win before announcing your precinct's vote count. That way you could adjust up or down as necessary. This was known as "leveling the count."[51]

Daley managed the elections via his tightly controlled political machine. He had aldermen who did his bidding. He was chairman of the Cook County Democrats, which meant he put together the roster of Democratic nominees for office—tantamount to hand-picking winners. He had precinct captains who got the votes that he demanded, who sold tickets to fund-raising dinners (or paid for the tickets themselves if they could not find buyers), and who knocked on doors to get people registered.

The mayor had an army of patronage workers, and he could count on their votes as well. Automated elevators had "operators" earning fine salaries. A man who knew nothing about public health might find himself appointed city health commissioner, if he happened to be Mrs. Daley's obstetrician, and it didn't matter how many doctors complained when he denied the existence of high pollution, hunger, and even a flu epidemic.[52] Some people held two jobs on paper, were paid for both, but never showed up for either. Daley allies consistently won bids to provide city services, to build slum housing, or to insure, say, O'Hare Airport. A landlord or restaurateur who pushed back might suddenly find himself swarmed with inspections and fined huge sums for violations of health or building codes.

In 1971, *Chicago Daily News* columnist Mike Royko wrote *Boss*, a bestseller that excoriated Daley's corrupt regime, and he couldn't name half of his sources. It just wasn't safe to talk to a journalist about Daley if you wanted to keep your job, your home, or your welfare check. Mrs. Daley stomped into local bookstores and demanded that the book be removed, which ultimately helped Chicago sales enormously. *Boss* propelled Royko into the national spotlight; the reporting was tight, the style even tighter. It didn't exactly tell a *new* story. Daley's mania for forcing through his public works projects, his obstruction of desegregation, his disinterest in democracy, everyone knew all this. It was not an open secret. It was simply open. In a book review, though, longtime Daley foe Studs Terkel described what was new: "It has not been the 'astuteness' or 'shrewdness' of Richard J. Daley that has elected him four times. It is the 'pistol' in the hand of the precinct captain, who works among the dispossessed. It is the threat direct: loss of job, loss of welfare check, eviction from wretched project flat."[53] Daley was powerful not because he was a genius but because he was a bully.

Doesn't sound like the kind of person you'd want running the host city for a national political convention at a crisis moment, when the country was a political tinderbox, and the smallest spark could set off who-knows-what, does it? Why on earth would the Democrats make such a choice? The most concise explanation is that LBJ approved of Chicago, and he and Daley were tight. Further, the decision was made long before King's assassination, and up to that point Daley's city had mostly avoided the racial uprisings that other cities had faced in the 1960s. Chicago was considered an urban success story for having avoided financial problems and high crime rates, which further made it seem like an appealing place for the Democrats to meet. The DNC had also considered Miami, where the Republicans were convening, but the Democratic organizers worried that if there was a crisis during their convention, Florida's Republican governor might deliberately stall mobilization of the National Guard, to harm the Democrats. From

ective, Chicago might or might not have been the perfect
at Illinois's Democratic governor was appealing.

etworks wanted to stay in Miami to cover both conventions.
They'd have their infrastructure set up there, their equipment, and
so on. To move everything to Chicago after the GOP convention was
a huge waste of time, energy, and money. Well, inconveniencing the
networks was a plus as far as President Johnson was concerned. He
hated the way those sons-of-bitches were covering Vietnam. Although
not a booster for the war, Daley also hated the media. In a phone call
to the White House five weeks before the convention, Daley even suggested barring floor coverage of the convention; it would be better if
interviews were allowed only off-site. Interviews distracted both delegates and home viewers from the speeches on the dais, Daley complained, with reporters trying "to make it look as though we're all a lot
of goddamn fools." The mayor added that the convention "isn't about
this television hour, because what the hell? You and I know that it's
forgotten by the time the campaign is around in September and October, what happened at the convention, unless they catch you with a lot
of things that are bad."

Johnson agreed. And of course, Daley was right: the reason the floor
reporting mattered in 1968 was precisely because it unearthed "a lot
of things" that were "bad." This was an off-the-record moment for
Daley that revealed much: it wasn't doing bad things that concerned
him, it was getting caught. Johnson agreed and chuckled throughout
the conversation, conveying support for Daley's vision of a censored
convention. Daley closed by saying, "We can still win it, if we have the
right candidate, and I'm talking to the guy who's the right candidate."[54]
LBJ still hoped to show up in Chicago, drawn there by acclamation,
and Daley still hoped to get him nominated. He had already planned
a birthday party for Johnson on the second day of the convention. A
"Texas-sized birthday cake" had been baked.[55]

The looming political factor that brought the DNC to Chicago was
that Daley would ensure that "the right candidate" would be selected
there, and later in the general election. In 1960 Daley's machine had

been seen as a major player in the nomination and election of Kennedy. Ever since, there have been allegations that voter fraud in Illinois won the race for JFK.[56] Daley had a special affection for the fellow Catholic, and he was fiercely loyal to the Democratic Party in the way that only a certain kind of devoutly religious man could be. Seeking the mayor's endorsement in 1968, Bobby Kennedy said, "Daley means the ball-game." Asked about the comment, Daley slyly demurred, "he means I'm a great White Sox fan."[57] By the time of the convention, Daley was pegged as a kingmaker, the second most powerful Democrat after the president. It was perhaps an exaggeration: Illinois had twenty-six electoral votes, whereas California had forty, and New York had forty-three. But it was the perception, and at least half the time, perception is reality in politics. In sum, the Democratic National Committee couldn't say no to Chicago. It was, of course, an egregious mistake.

Perhaps the Democrats wanted to try to compete with the Republicans at being the law-and-order party, as if keeping it together in Chicago in August would demonstrate what a fine man their candidate was in November. But keeping the peace in Chicago was a tall order; it was a tall order in any city in 1968, especially in the summer, riot season. Following Rev. King's assassination, the Chicago police had been unable to seize control for two days. Black neighborhoods were devastated. Some 175 buildings were burned down, and eleven Blacks died, all male—at least seven of those at the hands of police. Nearly three thousand were arrested, and thousands became homeless.[58] Daley complained that the police superintendent should have ordered his men to "shoot to maim" looters and "shoot to kill" arsonists. When the press repeated what he said, Daley said they had distorted his words. They hadn't; it was all on film. But that was Daley's story, and he was sticking to it. His press secretary Earl Bush, unwittingly echoing Barry Goldwater's critique, declared that the media "should have printed what he meant, not what he said."[59]

Daley hated the print media just as much as he hated the TV people. The *Chicago Tribune* served conservative businessmen in particular and was delighted by Daley's building up of the downtown area, but the paper was also Republican and disgusted by the Democratic machine. Daley was contemptuous of the paper's beat reporters and, ever the champion of top-down power, didn't understand why the editors didn't clamp down on them. Daley showed up on the cover of *Time* magazine and was nationally portrayed as the man who had used his power to make Chicago better. Indeed, one of the city's nicknames was "the city that works." Daley had a deep understanding of Chicago's budgetary issues, and "the machine's clout in the state legislature enabled Chicago to . . . spread the fiscal burden of service delivery outside the city," which meant that it "avoided any budgetary responsibility for costly services like education, public welfare, hospitals, and transportation."[60] So, as other big cities struggled financially in the sixties and seventies, Chicago did comparatively well.

Daley seemed to be the opposite of New York's floundering Mayor John Lindsay. On a personal level, Daley could not have been impressed by Lindsay, who was so *soft* that he went on the *Tonight Show* and made jokes about all the mugging in his own city. What sort of a man made jokes at his own expense?[61] Obviously, the kind of man who didn't grow up next to the stockyards, who didn't go to church every day, who didn't have the unions in his back pocket or have the cojones to figure out how to stop a garbage strike dead in its tracks. Daley's national image was tougher: the national media said he ran his "machine" with an iron fist. He appreciated that, except he protested that it was simply "an organization," and not only a Democratic one but also a democratic one.

Ironically, Daley hated the media, but most of the time he didn't actually need it. Politicians in other cities might worry about name recognition or outdebating their opponents on radio or TV, but Daley had little investment in the kind of image building that increasingly propelled American politics following the rise of TV in the 1950s. When elections were coming up, the machine spent huge amounts of money on place-based advertising, such as billboards. Yes, there were also radio and TV ads, but the Daley machine broadcast ads during elections to ensure that people got to the polls to vote for the Democratic slate, not to convince people that their candidates were the best. They had already decided that for them. This attitude made Daley spectacularly inept when it came to preparing for the 1968 convention as a TV event. He could understand it only as a political event.

This was in part a generational issue. The earliest conventions covered by TV took place in 1948, when few people had sets. The convention halls were smoke-filled, the floors cluttered with used newspapers, which people read to pass the time during dull speeches. An auditorium full of chain smokers reading newspapers and ignoring the dais didn't play well on TV, but it didn't matter in 1948. Twenty years later, though, the televised event would be understood by most politicians as something that conveyed an *image* of the party. But not Daley. What did he care whether the cameras could make out a keynote speaker through clouds of tobacco, or whether CBS commentator Eric Sevareid had erudite thoughts to share? Daley was just there to get his guy nominated. Nixon had told *Mike Douglas Show* producer Roger Ailes in 1967 that TV was just a "gimmick." Ailes taught him that it was the most important gimmick, and thereby became his image consultant for the 1968 campaign.[62] Daley was more stubborn, an old man who expected the ways conventions and elections were run never to change.

TV was an unwanted interloper, and although he made a few last-minute beautification attempts before the TV cameras arrived in Chicago, he sunk most of his energy into converting his town into a fortress. He sealed the manhole covers with tar so protestors could not hide in the sewers. He installed a fence around the convention site and topped it with barbed wire. He put the entire police force of twelve thousand men on twelve-hour shifts. More than five thousand National Guardsmen had been called in, and about a thousand Secret Service and FBI agents. Ten thousand people protested in the streets and parks, and before arriving, they had worked for months to get permits for marches, which were systematically denied. They wanted to sleep in Lincoln Park, but the 11 p.m. curfew would not allow for it—though the city had authorized that curfew to be broken for other groups in the past. Protestors would be allowed near the delegates' hotels but kept miles away from the Amphitheatre, where the convention was being held. This was how Daley would maintain law and order in Chicago.

He even went out of his way to inconvenience the networks, making sure that they could not send out live images from anywhere but the convention hall, distributing half the usual number of floor passes, and making security at the Amphitheatre so restrictive that journalists and delegates felt manhandled and mistreated long before the opening pounding of the gavel. An anti-Vietnam or pro–Eugene McCarthy button was like a "kick me" sign to Amphitheatre security, but as one journalist on the scene observed, "a blind man—wearing huge black glasses with an enormous black cape, a shotgun under his arm, and a tall Afghan hound as a seeing-eye dog—could have negotiated the security and assassinated whomever he chose, if he also wore on his back and front a WE LOVE MAYOR DALEY sign."[63]

By the time the convention started on August 26, Daley had bent over backward to set everyone's teeth on edge. And to make them fear they'd get their teeth knocked out. What could go wrong?

Chapter One The Storm before the Storm

Imagine a network news correspondent arriving in Chicago in August 1968, one week before the Democratic National Convention. He's there to work the floor of the International Amphitheatre, maybe John Chancellor from NBC, or a lesser luminary like CBS newsman John Hart. Riding in from the airport, probably in transportation provided by the network—or at least not in a taxi, because there's a taxi driver's strike—he notices a few things right away.

As he gets closer to the hotel hub in the Chicago Loop, newly erected wooden fences block his view along the city streets. He would later learn that behind those fences were vacant lots, or rather the opposite, lots filled with garbage, beer cans, broken glass, and other urban effluvia. Some of Chicago's less pleasant sights have been hidden. Odors are more difficult to mask, as our newsman will discover soon enough: the convention is being held near the city's famous abattoirs. In 1914, Carl Sandburg described Chicago as "Hog Butcher for the World," and the nickname stuck. Pigs produce three times more excrement than humans do. So just two blocks from the building where more than five thousand delegates and alternates will attempt to decide the political future of the nation, a manure pile—presumably set aside to be sold for fertilizer—stands ten feet high and seventy feet wide. You don't have to see it to know it is there.

The other thing a new arrival to Chicago might notice on the way into town is the face of Richard J. Daley, literally everywhere. One sign screams "LADIES & GENTLEMEN WELCOME YOU HAVE ARRIVED IN DALEY COUNTRY." Another frequently repeated sign shows a hand lifting up a straw boater with a ribbon on it inscribed "Mayor Richard J. Daley," and beneath the hat "Hello Democrats! Welcome to Chicago!"

FIGURE 3.   Chicago was blanketed with welcome signs large and small, part of a campaign organized and executed by the Daley machine. The campaign also included hastily erected fences to hide ugly vacant lots and newly transplanted decorative flowers that had barely taken root by the time the convention began. David Douglas Duncan Papers and Photography Collection, © David Douglas Duncan, 1968, courtesy of Harry Ransom Center.

(fig. 3). There are even a few "Daley for President" and "Daley for Vice President" signs, which are flattering to the mayor, though Daley doesn't have those particular ambitions: he is already King of Chicago and has the ear of the White House. He doesn't need to be *in* the White House. The typography of all the signs is the same, as this is a welcome campaign organized and executed by the Daley machine, just like the hastily erected fences, and like the newly transplanted decorative flowers that have barely taken root around the city. One observer wrote that Daley had the attitude of a mortician who "wants his visitors to see nice colors in Chicago, smell nice things."[1] The awkward makeover reveals a mayor eager to show off his town by hiding its warts. And the use of the boater as a visual is a precise indicator of Daley's age and obliviousness to what might "play well" on national TV. It was a perfect hat to symbolize a nominating convention—if you were nominating Woodrow Wilson. To be fair, delegates *did* still wear such hats to conventions in the 1960s. Delegates had sported them at the Republican convention a few weeks earlier in Miami. But it was an old-fashioned gesture. The only other time viewers were likely to spot boaters on TV was when Maurice Chevalier made a guest appearance on a variety show, or when an old Harold Lloyd silent movie was broadcast.

When our newsman finally gets to the hotel, the clerk at the front desk warns him that electrical workers are on strike, so there won't be enough new telephone lines installed for the convention. That's going to make things tricky for journalists, whether they work for broadcast or print outlets. In fact, by the time the convention is underway, many payphones will be impossible to use because they are so jammed up with dimes, and there's simply no one available to empty them. Our man heads up to his room and picks up the phone to check the situation, maybe see if he can easily connect with an operator. Disconcertingly, a fresh sticker in the receiver cradle shows a picture of hizzoner himself, yet another welcoming message planted by Daley.

In his deluxe 1969 photo book chronicling both the Republican and Democratic conventions, David Douglas Duncan wrote that "the delegates were perhaps most unnerved—after seeing Big Brother's name splashed everywhere—to find his unblinking, plastic eyes waiting even under their hotel-room telephones. In all of Chicago there was no escape. Mayor Daley's fief, during nomination week, began to seem as unreal to some Americans as was that earlier, Republican, political-circus masquerade in Miami Beach."[2] Duncan was a combat photographer who had covered World War II and Korea, and he was just back from photographing the Battle of Khe Sanh in Vietnam. NBC had hired him to make nightly contributions to their convention coverage. Duncan would compile photomontages, crafting his own explanatory voice-over. After Vietnam, he probably anticipated this as a relatively easy assignment, even though he was new to TV and had to lean heavily on the NBC team's technical skills.

As a freelancer, he had the right to describe the Republican National Convention (RNC) as a "circus masquerade," but that's not how our newly arrived network correspondent talks. Or, rather, that's how he might talk over a tumbler of bourbon, with coworkers, but it's not the kind of thing he'd say on TV, where his job was to be objective, to re- port, to analyze perhaps, but not to use phrases like "circus masquer- ade." Still, he'd have to wonder if the mayor could be serious, telling delegates they have "arrived in Daley country" and posting that pro- Daley straw hat everywhere. And the signs are not just on lampposts and billboards but also in the windows of private businesses, ranging from Italian bakeries to Mexican tamale joints. This must be either the most popular mayor in America or the most megalomaniacal. Or both.

It was hard to believe the forced cheerfulness of all those welcom- ing signs. Before the convention even begins, it's clear that this will not be business as usual. To start with, Daley was going out of his way to stymie news coverage. That presented an ethical, professional problem for all the journalists who had flown in. The story was supposed to be the convention, not the challenges of covering the convention. TV news people had egos like anybody else, but everything about their profes- sional training told them that their objective was neutral invisibility. They considered news qua news only when censorship loomed; that was a story to be reported, because it indicated that someone in power had something to hide. The default presumption was that a journalist was supposed to *report* the story, not *be* the story. Daley and his police force would not make this easy. Anyway, it was time to get to work.

The week before the convention, Chicago reached its typical sum- mer high temperature of ninety degrees. This was when the Dem- ocratic credentials and platform committees met to do business, before the opening gavel on August 26. In that same time window, journalists and protestors arrived. A small army of laborers built those beauti- fying fences. Tavern keepers restocked top shelf, bottom shelf, and everything-in-between liquor, though less than usual in the vicinity of the convention, because Daley's policemen had "asked" all but two restaurant-bars near the Amphitheatre to close during the convention, as Walter Cronkite reported. "If Daley's men ask you to take a vacation, you take a vacation," Cronkite archly observed.

One of the places left open was the nearby Stockyard Inn, where the Sirloin Room restaurant had a gimmick: you could select your own steak, and they would brand it with your initials. This was an apt metaphor for the political deal-making and ego battles that took place there between (mostly) men who wanted to get their way: my name, my meat. The easily accessible on-site food at the Amphitheatre was no-frills. Hot dogs cost forty cents each, and you could buy pop in paper cups, without ice. Daley's team reasoned that ice cubes might be used as projectiles by angry delegates. This crackdown was a perfect synecdoche for Daley's approach to law and order. It's a wonder that he didn't confiscate the delegates' high heels and fountain pens, which might also make for handy weapons in a pinch. The ice situation was not as dire as one might have predicted; the mercury suddenly dropped twenty degrees on Sunday, August 25, the day before the convention started. This was perhaps the only stroke of good luck during that turbulent week.

The first bit of bad luck for the networks was the late-breaking crisis of last-minute restrictions. A few months later the *Walker Report* partially explained the situation: "The arrangements committee of the convention made an eleventh hour announcement limiting the three major TV networks to one mobile camera each on the floor of the convention and seven floor passes each. Convention Executive Director John Criswell countered news media complaints by saying that the committee had a strong inclination to eliminate floor cameras entirely." To give a sense of scale here, NBC had asked for fifteen passes for TV coverage alone—radio was a whole separate ask. NBC News president Reuven Frank despaired, "what faced us was the gutting of our system."[3] It was actually an improvement, because earlier Criswell had declared that only two floor reporters from each network would be allowed. As the *Walker Report* explains, "this was ostensibly done in the belief that too much floor coverage would add to the congestion of people (delegates, security people, and political guests) on the floor. But some newsmen charged that the convention committee wanted coverage to concentrate on the podium—a controlled show. Without floor passes, reporters felt they could not reach delegates to learn the real story of the moment."[4]

What the report misses is that Criswell was an operative for Johnson, and that the president was monitoring and manipulating convention proceedings from afar, with the notion that up until the last minute, he might still be drafted as the nominee. That's why organizers were so responsive to LBJ throughout the four-day event. The report likewise misses that Daley had a heavy hand in manipulating the mechanics of the convention and stymieing journalists with the president's tacit approval. One cannot overstate the connection between Daley and LBJ. On March 31, 1968, after he announced that he would not seek reelection, the first person the president chose to speak with on the phone was Daley. Texas Governor John Connally and Vice President Hubert Humphrey were left to twiddle their thumbs on hold.[5]

All of which is to say, the DNC arrangements committee was not the only enemy of free press coverage in Chicago, as the *Walker Report* implied. But what the report did precisely nail was that the DNC wanted a focus on the podium, a "controlled show" with cameras pointed at the dais rather than at delegates with microphones stuck in their faces. Further, Daley limited live coverage to the Amphitheatre, a restriction that also came at the eleventh hour, and which is a complicated story. To make sense of it, one must understand the procedures and technology of news-gathering, and also the professional valence of "liveness."

Network decision-making at a convention is hierarchical. A brief layout of how CBS worked in Chicago will convey the complexity of the system. Richard Salant was president of CBS News at the time; below him was *CBS Evening News* producer Ernest Leiser, who had gone to Vietnam with Cronkite earlier in 1968. Leiser and Salant, and CBS News vice president, Bill Leonard, would have consulted about big decisions at the convention, like approving Cronkite's interview with Daley. Don Hewitt, who later found fame producing *60 Minutes*, was institutionally below Leiser, but as a veteran on-site producer, he played a vital role in directing the coverage.

Sandy Socolow was Cronkite's direct producer and sat at his at elbow in the booth at the convention, just out of sight of the camera. Socolow later explained that he "was in touch with the control room and in touch with Hewitt, . . . with Hewitt kind of guiding the boat," an operation that was so complicated that, like guiding an aircraft carrier, "it takes five minutes to change course."[6] From there, he conferred with Cronkite or quietly slid notes across the anchor desk when Cronkite was on-air. He was literally and figuratively Cronkite's right-hand man. As the anchor, Cronkite made editorial decisions, but he didn't call the shots (in the literal sense) throughout the event.

And then there was CBS News producer Robert Wussler, a legend in the TV news business, who later became president of CBS Sports and of CBS Television, and went on to cofound CNN with Ted Turner. In Chicago, Wussler sat next to Hewitt in a remote-control room. There, Wussler supervised five "intermediate editors" who were responsible for curating multiple video transmissions ("feeds") arriving simultaneously from the anchor booth, floor cameras, remote cameras, and the basement analysis studio. As executive producer of the broadcast, Wussler monitored the incoming kaleidoscope of imagery and then rapidly selected the "final picture for air" that viewers saw at home. He was nominated for an Emmy for his work in Chicago.[7]

When all hell broke loose in the streets—every night, in different ways, not just on Wednesday night in front of the Hilton—this complicated hierarchy of players sorted out how much to show. Conventions always involved some material shot outside, for color or for context—in July, the networks had covered the arrival of Nixon at his Miami hotel—but the central focus of coverage was the convention itself, the politicians and the delegates.

The networks generally operated with tremendous fairness in Chicago, and attacks after the fact were unwarranted. At the same time, some errors were made, and one of those errors was under-reporting street violence. We'll probably never have exact documentation of who decided what in terms of that coverage, but it's important to understand that the decisions were both political and technical. On the technical front, the tremendous difficulty posed by Daley's prevention of live coverage outside the convention hall meant that the networks couldn't cut away at a moment's notice from the Amphitheatre to report on the streets. Further, as per Socolow's aircraft-carrier analogy, cutting away was never going to be easy; there were simply too many moving parts. Bill Leonard, who had been a floor reporter at earlier conventions, was on the management side of CBS by 1968. He assessed that "the real story was out there in the streets of Chicago, and we were forced to jackhammer into our live broadcast from the hall bits and pieces of it as tape and film filtered in."[8] This aggressive description is apt: there was too much material, it got to the Amphitheatre with great delay, and then the fragments were wedged into the show, with as much grace as possible, given the demands of keeping the "aircraft carrier" moving forward. On the political side, the network producers were keenly aware that there were activists in Chicago who *wanted* media coverage very badly. Their professional norms dictated that they constantly asked themselves if they were being manipulated, and this self-interrogation discouraged them from doing street coverage.[9]

Ultimately, it was a damned-if-you-do, damned-if-you-don't situation. Completely ignoring the streets would have been unconscionable, but showing *anything* in the streets would make the networks vulnerable to attack from those "law and order" Americans who were repulsed and angered by longhairs and antiwar protestors. The ferocity of this inevitable anger caught the networks by surprise.

The hierarchy of producers made the big decisions about what to show, but the floor reporters were also key players; their duty was to work the Amphitheatre for four days straight, searching for material, and then reporting what they had to the producers, who would decide where to turn the cameras. The job is not just a feat of interviewing, though; it's also a technological feat. A reporter might carry his own heavy sound device on a shoulder strap, or have a soundman trailing him. Men dominated, though Nancy Dickerson was a correspondent for CBS in 1960, and for NBC in 1964 and 1968. (Aline Saarinen reported for NBC in 1968, and Barbara Walters was in Chicago for NBC, anchoring *Today* with Hugh Downs but not appearing during Huntley–

Brinkley's coverage.) In 1960, the sound device had been called a transi-talkie, a cute name for a chunky and inelegant piece of equipment (fig. 4). Add to that a bulky headset equipped with FM transmitter-receiver and an antenna, which added a dash of Buck Rogers, and there was also a cameraman in tow. The TV video camera rigs were gigantic. The battery pack alone had to be mounted on the operator's back, onto a plastic harness molded to the upper body. Then the weighty camera was mounted on the operator's shoulder (fig. 5).[10] A lighter, more portable camera, the creepy-peepy (alternately "creepie-peepie," like "walkie-talkie") weighed in at sixty pounds. It was used alongside the regular, less portable TV cameras (fig. 6).[11] (These were all TV cameras, not film cameras.) The more of these awkward technological setups the networks had on the floor, the more interviews correspondents could get. Some stationary cameras were located higher up on a platform; these could seek out floor reporters and interviewees via telephoto lens. That wasn't as good as a floor camera, but it helped when the floor was too crowded for a cameraman to get a good shot.[12]

Each convention was a chance to show off the newest gizmo. In Chicago they had color for the first time, a big deal not because color TV was brand-new but because the color cameras used for shooting sitcoms or dramas were bulky monsters on wheels. For the conventions, the networks had to use more portable devices. The new color models were heavy as hell, but could still be hoisted onto an operator's back, and the harness was less bulky than the old molded-plastic model. The camera could be held in an operator's hand, but it was attached to his body by a stabilizing rod so that he did not constantly have to use his hand for support.

Each network used a different system, *Christian Science Monitor* reported at the time: "NBC is using its RCA Man-Pack portable color camera; ABC an Ampex radio-frequency color camera dubbed the Creepy-Peepy [updated from the 1964 black-and-white model]; and CBS its microwave Mini-Cam Mark VI, which weighs 51 pounds, about a quarter of the standard [non-portable] color-camera weight."[13] It's

FIGURE 4. At the 1960 convention, Nancy Dickerson poses with the transi-talkie sound transmitter, a cute name for a chunky and inelegant piece of equipment. Networks competed to outdo each other with the newest gadgets at each convention. Covering these events was expensive, but they brought prestige and demonstrated dedication to public service. CBS, 1960.

FIGURE 5. The TV video camera rigs used at conventions were gigantic. The battery pack alone had to be mounted on the operator's back, onto a molded upper-body plastic harness. Then the weighty camera was mounted on the operator's shoulder, as seen here in ABC's video rig from 1964. Field Enterprises, Inc., 1964.

fair to presume that ABC and CBS were shooting in color in part to keep up with NBC, whose parent company RCA manufactured TV sets and was promoting color to encourage people to buy new ones. NBC had originally gotten into the business of producing radio and later TV not because it was interested in the entertainment or news business but because it was in the business of *selling entertainment machines* for its parent company. The conventions offered another opportunity to promote color technology, which had already made substantial headway into American homes.[14] To this end, Walter Cronkite broke for every commercial with the phrase, "CBS News color coverage will continue in a moment." Viewers watching on an old black-and-white set were frequently reminded that they were missing out.

TV cameras had always needed a tremendous amount of light, and early test runs had left actors drenched in sweat, with mascara melt-

FIGURE 6.   A new portable camera, the creepy-peepy, weighing in at twenty-five pounds, would be shown off at the 1960 conventions. The 1968 color version weighed sixty pounds but was still small and considered portable. Cronkite referred to "CBS News color coverage" of the convention at every single commercial break point for four days. United Press International, 1960.

ing into starlets' eyes.[15] The light levels needed for black-and-white TV had come down, but color TV raised the ante right back up. In 1952, the Amphitheatre had hosted both political conventions, and had spent $500,000 on the installation of an air-conditioning system, perhaps an innovation that would have happened anyway (Chicago had long been ahead of the curve on air-conditioning because it was the center of the meatpacking industry), but one that could not have been unrelated to the demands of TV lighting. In 1968, another $400,000 would be sunk into air-conditioning, of which $100,000 went toward "*extra* air conditioning . . . installed in the Amphitheatre to offset the additional heat expected from the use of color-television equipment."[16] The system tempered the heat, though it did nothing to dampen the stench of the stockyards.[17] Delegates did not appear sweaty, and the lighting levels looked normal to home viewers, but it was obviously very bright on-site. It was disconcerting when cameras cut away from the dais for reaction shots at 1:00 a.m. and revealed a fair number of delegates wearing sunglasses.

If shooting in a convention hall was logistically and technically tricky, shooting outside was also a challenge, though one that the networks had also experienced in their field reporting, where 16mm cameras were the norm, and audio was a mix of synchronous (shot at the time) and postsynchronous (added later, such as voice-over or music). Civil rights coverage was always challenging, and when things turned violent, it was particularly difficult at night, because news crews had to turn on their lights to shoot. When white supremacists rioted to protest integration at Ole Miss in 1962, Dan Rather was on the scene with cameraman Dick Perez, who later filmed in Chicago. Rather said, "Whenever anyone turned on a light—which meant every time we needed to film—one or more bullets would attempt to knock it out. We had to film and move. Film and move. After a while we worked out a pattern: turn on our battery-powered, portable light, film for fifteen seconds by actual count, turn off the light—if we didn't get hit—and then run, because we were bound to catch gunfire or bricks or both."[18]

In the streets of Chicago, turning the networks' lights on was like painting a bullseye on reporters, spurring the police to attack. Conversely, the light was a signal to protestors that they were being recorded; critics said the lights and cameras made them act out, whereas demonstrators said those same lights and cameras enabled the documentation of police brutality. Sensitive film designed to shoot in low-level lighting was helpful, but not a problem solver. No one could have imagined a world in which everyone carries a tiny handheld camera, enabling the overt or discreet recording of police brutality, with synchronous sound, and even at night, as we saw in the case of George Floyd's murder and the uprisings that followed in 2020.

If civil rights was one key reference point for difficult field coverage, Vietnam was another. Combat footage was limited on American TV screens because it was difficult for a reporter and technical team to move through the jungles with troops—even though the 16mm film cameras used there were lighter and more portable than the TV cameras used on the convention floor. In Vietnam, cameramen worked with "lightweight" 16mm cameras, weighing twenty to thirty pounds, though one with a battery would be substantially heavier than the hand-cranked version. An accompanying soundman (or sometimes the reporter himself) would carry a Nagra magnetic tape recorder weighing around fifteen pounds. The footage would be shipped to Tokyo to be developed and then to New York for editing.[19] There was much TV footage during the Tet Offensive because the enemy hit Saigon, where the newsmen were stationed in hotels and ready to go. Viewers back home were disturbed not only because they had been given the impression that the enemy was just about to collapse but also because they had seen so much *coverage* of the war (body counts on the nightly news, accounts of battles won and lost) without actually seeing much *fighting*. It was more common to see interviews in camp, or the gathering of the wounded or delivery of supplies, than it was to see actual combat.

TV journalists knew that much of the visual problem (that is, a limited repertoire of visuals) was a technical one. Print journalists like Michael Herr, by contrast, were often able to report from right in the thick of things.[20] Photojournalists like David Douglas Duncan and Sean Flynn were likewise more able to get where the action was. This meant that Americans were more likely to see gruesome war images in print media such as magazines than on the nightly news. There were some network reporters like CBS's Jack Laurence who took great risks to get frontline coverage, but "in fact, only about 22 percent of all film reports from Southeast Asia in the period before the Tet Offensive showed actual combat, and often this was minimal."[21] Obviously, live images of Vietnam were not expected by Americans. But live images of political conventions—and of course, elections—were.

Liveness gave a sense of narrative urgency to events, an urgency especially coveted by producers during an event like a convention that was usually something like 10 percent breaking news, 20 percent speeches, and 70 percent interviewing, filling in context, and generally waiting for something exciting to happen. The high value placed on live coverage was not new. Many TV people were carryovers from radio, where for decades the fact that the medium was live had been understood as key to both its entertainment and its public service mission, a mission solidified (and later mythologized) via World War II reporting.

In the network era, live coverage was the gold standard for news, even if much televised imagery wasn't technically live. Studio shots of news anchors were always live, but it was often more difficult to show a story as it was unfurling. If reporters were on-site with a TV camera and a telephone-microwave hookup, they could transmit live from their news vans. Otherwise, they were likely to shoot on 16mm film and broadcast the developed and edited footage as soon as possible. What "liveness" meant depended on the situation. The launchings of Apollo 8 and Apollo 9 in 1968 and 1969 came pre-packaged as live media events. The networks set up camp in Florida to provide instant coverage. The "Bloody Sunday" footage of Alabama police beating civil rights marchers on the Edmund Pettus Bridge in 1965 was shot on 16mm, developed and edited, and shown shortly thereafter. The footage on the bridge *felt* live because it suddenly interrupted regularly scheduled programming. The interruption itself was live, of course, but the events had transpired earlier.

The conditions of perceived liveness may have varied widely, but liveness had become synonymous with quality where news was concerned. One iconic moment illustrates this precisely, and became a sort of touchstone for the competition between the network news divisions. ABC had blown it in 1963 when Jack Ruby assassinated Lee Harvey Oswald; their cameras weren't there, and they had been forced to report the story without images. NBC had shown the event as it transpired, and CBS had recorded it and shown the murder just a few moments after it happened. NBC won here by virtue of showing it live, CBS had come out in the middle, because at least they had footage, and ABC had further cemented its reputation as a "feckless news organization."[22]

If there was anything obvious about covering a political convention, it was that the whole thing would be arranged for live coverage, like a space launch or an election. As during those events, there were breaks for ads and long stretches when nothing happened, and anchormen, correspondents, and commentators had to fill time. If the networks managed to get millions of people to tune in for conventions, it was at least in part because TV offered little else to watch. Setting aside the question of whether or not viewers *enjoyed* the Chicago convention as a forced alternative to *Gunsmoke* or *Bonanza*, they did tune in. In fact, it was the top-rated TV event of 1968, with 90 percent of TV households tuning in, and an average of 9.5 hours of viewing per household.[23] There's no documentary record of how people felt about everything they saw, but we know that they were watching (or at least had their sets on) for hours, and extant viewer mail reveals some of the most emotional responses, ranging from pro and con responses to violence against journalists, to critiques of how the National Anthem was interpreted at the opening of each day.

The objective of a national political convention was for the party to nominate presidential and vice-presidential candidates and approve an official platform, and for the networks to show all of this as it was happening. Mixed in with this might be a few longer, pre-edited film reports following a story in depth, such as background on a particular candidate or issue. This was all standard operating procedure. Immediately, though, Chicago was a crisis for the networks not only because of the telephone problems and the reduced floor passes but also because live broadcasting would be limited to the convention hall and the parking lot outside. This situation was an insult to the professionalism of the TV newscasters. True, much convention coverage typically took place *inside* an arena, but it had been clear for months that *this* convention would be flooded with thousands of protestors outside, and they had made wild claims that they might infuse the city water supply with LSD or make love in the streets. The Yippies would have needed five tons of acid to spike the water supply, and city officials could not have truly believed the threat unless they were completely naive. But regardless of whether things turned bloody (or trippy or sexy) or the crowds were peacefully contained, there would be stories to cover in the streets. These stories would need to be live, because *that was how things were done.*

To limit such coverage, Daley would not give the networks the parking permits they needed for their news vans, or the hookups they needed for live transmission; they were finally able to park trucks outside delegates' hotels, across the street from Grant Park, a key area where protestors had gathered. The crisis was compounded by the most elemental problem, the electrical workers strike. Members of the International Brotherhood of Electrical Workers (IBEW) were in charge of installing telephones, key not only for voice communication but also for transmission of live images. NBC's Reuven Frank later noted, "We never knew if it was Daley or President Johnson for whom television was the enemy, but we had been singled out. The [telephone] installers' strike and the restrictions on mobile units were proof enough."[24] Without the necessary additional phone lines, plus properly placed trucks, live TV was severely curtailed, and Daley seemed pleased with this arrangement.

But Daley was *not* enthusiastic about any of the candidates—Hubert Humphrey, Eugene McCarthy, and, in faraway third place, George Mc-Govern. Daley wanted LBJ to be drafted at the last minute, or, alternatively, Ted Kennedy, each of whom had officially said he was out of the race. At first glance, an electrical workers strike might seem to have nothing to do with Daley's nomination preferences. But the McCarthy, Humphrey, and McGovern campaigns were hobbled by being pitifully short on phones to communicate with their delegates and staff. When Humphrey told Criswell that he needed more floor passes and phones (a request that Criswell passed along to the White House), he was told "to expect only two percent of what [he] wanted."[25] LBJ could have demanded more infrastructure support for Humphrey, but he did not. If it all sounds too petty to be true, then you have correctly understood the story.

There seems to be no paper trail proving that Daley encouraged the electrical workers strike, or slowed down its settlement. The IBEW "had been striking against Illinois Bell for over one hundred days [before the convention], and Daley was running out of time to convene them to put down their picket signs and wire the convention for television service. . . . He negotiated a temporary arrangement that allowed for 3,200 telephones and 200 teletypes to be installed at the Amphitheatre."[26] The notion that Daley was "running out of time" implies that he was genuinely displeased by the situation. And maybe he was. But the "temporary arrangement" was fishy. Unionized workers don't go on strike and then fortuitously volunteer to work anyway, unless some of them are, say, patronage hires, or otherwise indebted to city hall. In fact, there is good reason to believe that not everyone in the union was satisfied with the arrangement. In the weeks before the convention, as city workers toiled to prepare for delegates, telephone sabotage was common. On August 9, 1,000 telephones "in a downtown building were knocked out of commission when nearly 1,200 pairs of telephone wires were slashed in a closet that is kept locked." The day before, 2,400 wires had been cut. Both acts of sabotage seemed like inside jobs.[27]

One odd publicity image sent out before the convention nicely summarized the absurdity: a photo titled "Chicago Police Dept. Command Post" featured a large sign promoting the police, and a slightly smaller sign advertising the IBEW (fig. 7). There were three chairs, a radiator, a wall clock, and two trashcans, but no people in this bare-bones, electrically equipped command center, which appeared to offer little more than a switchboard and phones. The caption stated that this was an "independent switchboard" with "special hot lines." The photo seemed intended to show the modernity of the Chicago police, but the setup looked more like a cheap film-noir set.

Daley had at least made a pretense of trying to resolve the IBEW strike, but he had had less luck tackling the taxi driver strike. So rented buses shuttled the 5,244 delegates and alternates from their twenty-one hotels. Traveling those five or more miles was not swift, as the streets were crowded. Furthermore, the convention ran into the wee hours of the morning, which made it difficult for delegates to go out on the town. Obviously, the traffic congestion was due to all the people and police in the streets, and more taxis might not have helped get delegates back to their hotels, but in the rest of the city, traffic could move normally, and this made the taxi strike a thorn in Daley's side.

Chicago was a convention town, typically hosting more than one

FIGURE 7.   A press photo of a Chicago Police Department Command Post seemed intended to convey the technological sophistication of the police, but the setup looked more like a hold-over from a cheap film-noir set. As an image designed to promote Daley's convention preparation, it was a failure, inadvertently displaying his lack of sophistication in using mass media for public relations. Field Enterprises, Inc., 1968.

thousand of them each year, and the assumption was that the DNC would make money for local businesses, both the legit and the shady. A guide produced by Daley for delegates was all ads for fun times. At Frank & Marie's restaurant delegates could treat themselves to "a huge silver urn filled lazy Susan style with bowls of cottage, paté, pickled vegetables, spiced fruits, celery, radishes, and olives. The giant bowl is crowned with erect, crisp stalks of celery, topped with radishes—a sight to behold!"[28] Club Gi over on Ogden Avenue flaunted "Ultra-Psychedelic Lighting—a first in Chicago" plus Barbara "The Rubber Girl" and "Mr. Hypnosis," Nate Passaro.[29] Daley mistakenly assumed that delegates would have time to play, as was the convention norm. Let's not forget that *alternate* delegates might be less likely to stay put at the Amphitheatre during the convention if they had access to transportation. But the taxi strike inhibited everyone from freely visiting restaurants specializing in steaks and chops, cocktail lounges with go-go girls and billiards, and music clubs showcasing Buddy Rich and the Oscar Lindsay Trio.[30]

The networks didn't depend upon taxis to transport footage—they used motorcycle couriers—but the resulting increase in traffic congestion was an issue for them.[31] They had 16mm camera operators out in the streets several miles from the convention, following the police and the protestors. It was easier to shoot on 16mm than on video, which was still low resolution and difficult to edit, but unlike video, film had to be developed. The networks might use a local affiliate's film lab, or, more likely, a mobile van or trailer. Editing could also be done in a network trailer. With the taxi strike and a wildcat bus-driver strike (yes, another strike) increasing private car use, plus all the extra people in the streets, getting film back to headquarters at the Amphitheatre was harrowing.[32]

In the days leading up to the opening gavel, it was the technical limitations that preoccupied journalists. That the newsmen would also be singled out for beatings by the Chicago police had not occurred to anyone. Seasoned reporters and cameramen who had covered civil rights had come to expect violence from white locals, including (or even especially) the police, but that had never been a notable problem for journalists at a national political convention.

To make it all even more challenging, the anchors and newsmen had not really had time to recover from the Republican convention in Miami, just two weeks earlier. "Gavel-to-gavel" convention coverage is inevitably exhausting, whether things go well or not. In addition to doing all the work it takes to be ready to go live, the network reporters, anchors, technicians, managers, secretaries—the whole team—were facing eight or more hours of live coverage each day, and much of that was spent waiting for caucuses to sort things out, waiting for procedural votes to be completed, and waiting for vote counts to be tallied. Even a mildly interesting speech could be a relief: at last, something to cover on the dais!

Heading into the Chicago convention, there was a built-in narrative arc to the whole event, since at the end of it all, someone would be nominated, and the hawks or doves would prevail. Never forget: even if TV newsmen try to show only "what happens," they are obliged to tell it in some kind of narrative format. As Frank put it in a staff memo, "Every news story should have structure and conflict, problem and denouement, rising action and falling action, a beginning, a middle, and an end."[33] Of course, pre-prepared edited stories were different from live field reporting, where there were inevitable dead ends and dull interviews. But the drive was to find a story, to interview key characters, and, ideally, not to decide who were heroes or villains but to inquire of others who *they* thought were the heroes and villains.

Another way to manage the schedule was through extra filler material, such as political analysis, whether straightforward and relatively "objective" (Cronkite describing past conventions, for example) or analytical and labeled as such.[34] CBS had Eric Sevareid on staff for that, and they had procured Teddy White to bounce ideas off of him. White had won a Pulitzer Prize for *The Making of the President 1960*; he had followed up with *The Making of the President 1964*, and now he was working on his 1968 installment. His analytical credentials were airtight. NBC relied less on cutaways to commentators and more on the back-and-forth between co-anchors Chet Huntley and David Brinkley.

Meanwhile, ABC had broken with the gavel-to-gavel tradition by merely including a bit of convention overview in the nightly news and following later with a one-and-a-half-hour summary of the evening's events. For color commentary, they had hired William F. Buckley and Gore Vidal. The two men hated each other. Vidal was ultra-liberal and openly gay, and he had just written *Myra Breckinridge*, a scandalous best seller about a postoperative transsexual. Buckley was an ultra-conservative, devout Catholic—a founder of the modern conservative movement who was good friends with both Barry Goldwater and Ronald Reagan. Buckley was famous for his book attacking liberalism in higher education, *God and Man at Yale*. Both men were not only public intellectuals but also, more precisely, *celebrity* intellectuals. Vidal had once famously offered the advice, "Never miss an opportunity to have sex or appear on television." For his part, Buckley had his own TV show, *Firing Line*. Both had made guest appearances on *Rowan and Martin's Laugh-In*. When ABC approached Buckley about doing commentary with another guest at the conventions, he said he was game and would work with anyone but Vidal. Obviously, ABC's whole gimmick was to make sparks fly. It was a cost-effective way to boost ratings for the hopelessly third-place network. Eggheads might tune in for these intellectual cage fights, but the clever move did not demonstrate a commitment to elevating the level of television discourse.

Between all the network commentary, a few pre-prepared segments, speeches, floor votes, and delegate interviews, the four long nights of coverage would get filled up. This much was certain. In theory, what was most likely to be uncertain at a convention was: who would be the nominees, and what would be the party platform? In practice, these things often seemed clear before the convention. In that case, TV coverage might be little more than a free show promoting a political party and its candidate, the "controlled show" that Criswell, Johnson, and Daley had hoped for as they headed into Chicago.

Although much was unique about the 1968 Chicago convention, the desire of political parties to control the show was not new, though it had not been there from the very beginning. TV had first covered the national conventions in 1948, when four networks (ABC, CBS, NBC, and Dumont) aired their gavel-to-gavel coverage on just eighteen stations in nine cities.[35] Back in 1948, things were really happening, not simply being staged, at these conventions. With TV set ownership still low, the two major parties had no reason to seriously worry that TV might cause them embarrassment and had no incentive to stage-manage the entire affair, though of course the networks were doing their best to mold the whole thing into something attention-grabbing in order to boost the sale of sets. The hope in 1948 was that convention coverage would pique the curiosity of early adopters. By 1952, TV ownership had dramatically increased, and the Democrats and Republicans were acutely aware that a controlled show was ideal.

That was certainly how things had played out in Miami in 1968.

Norman Mailer's book on the conventions had many sharp political observations to make, but no surprises to report from the GOP convention. Even the baby elephant brought in to greet Nixon at the airport performed mostly on cue. When it "dropped a small turd," it still seemed to stay on message.[36] Nonetheless, throughout the rest of the Nixon campaign the pachyderm—known as Ana, from Anaheim—was subjected to an enema before every public event, just to play it safe.[37] Everyone predicted that Nixon would be the nominee in Miami. The RNC's only surprise was Spiro T. Agnew as vice-presidential nominee, because he was, as he himself acknowledged in his acceptance speech, "not a household name." Print journalists described the convention as dull and predictable. The day after the closing gavel, a *Washington Post* headline had declared "Boring Convention Ignored by Viewers."[38] Only one-third of American TV sets had been tuned in to the Republican convention during prime time.[39]

But to tell the story this way leaves out one crucial detail: there had been a riot. During the convention, a rally had been scheduled outside the Vote Power center in the Black neighborhood of Liberty City, an area already under high pressure because of the police force's heavy-handed stop-and-frisk policy. The police chief had flatly declared that he would use "shotguns and dogs" to deal with crime in "Negro" districts, adding, "When the looting starts, the shooting starts."[40] Activist Ralph Abernathy of the Southern Christian Leadership Conference was in town to demonstrate with his Poor People's Campaign Mule Train, and athlete Wilt Chamberlain was also there to campaign for Nixon; handbills promoting the Liberty City rally announced that the two Black men were scheduled to speak, though organizers had not confirmed this with either. Things turned sour when they did not arrive. Upon learning of the crisis, though, Abernathy rushed to the neighborhood to speak with residents, along with the Dade County mayor and the Florida governor, but tensions did not dissipate. By one account, the escalation specifically began when "a white *Miami Herald* reporter refused to leave the rally. Three men carried him out, and soon after, fifteen officers, mostly white, arrived and ordered protestors to disperse."

A few hours later a white man drove through the neighborhood in a car with a "Wallace for President" bumper sticker. The driver was forced to flee, his car was set aflame, looting broke out, tear gas followed, the police started shooting, and two days later, when the smoke and gas cleared, three African Americans were dead.[41] Chicago's Black newspaper, the *Daily Defender*, labeled this one of the "worst racial disorders" in the city's history.[42]

The disorder was not featured prominently in network-news convention coverage, however. Two years later, Frank explained that although "in terms of injuries and lives lost, the Miami incidents were more serious than the Chicago incidents," NBC News did not cover them. "The Miami demonstrations," he explained, "took place far from the widely known locations of our cameras, and we had no reason associated with covering convention activities for putting cameras there."[43] This attitude clearly points to some of the limits of the notion of "objective" political reporting. How were the events in Liberty City not seen as relevant to convention reporting, especially with a nominee positioning himself as a "law-and-order" candidate who would clamp down on peace demonstrations, looting, and rioting?

The events in Liberty City obviously bore a relationship to the Republican convention—the fact that Abernathy and Chamberlain were imagined as speakers confirmed that. Notably, the organizers of the rally had suggested that "if coverage of the Black mass rally is desired, you must send Black reporters only."[44] The networks employed hardly any Black correspondents (NBC had Bill Matney, and CBS had Hal Walker), so this was a challenging limitation. The publicity-seeking way to promote the civil rights rally would have been to openly invite network coverage and call it something like "Rally Against the Racist Republican Convention." But a civil rights rally outside Vote Power headquarters, to which only Black journalists were invited, was of little interest to the organizers of network convention coverage. When that rally unexpectedly—or predictably?—went very badly, the networks had no motivation to reconceive it as a "convention worthy" issue.

The Vote Power organizers had every reason to distrust white media coverage of their issues. The government's Kerner Report, released in March 1968, had emphasized, among other massive problems, flaws in mainstream (white) media coverage of Black uprisings throughout America. Of course, the citizens of Liberty City didn't need to read a government report to understand this, but the chronology bears emphasizing: the report had been released and received massive publicity six months before the political conventions. Both print and electronic news organizations were facing a moment of reckoning: What could they do to better cover racial issues? How could they increase the numbers of Black reporters in their ranks, a recommendation made in the report? These issues were not submerged; they were looming large. And the tipping point for the arrival of police in Liberty City—and the ensuing escalation—had involved a white *Miami Herald* reporter. Notably, the *Washington Post* had dispatched a Black reporter, Hollie West, from the convention floor to cover the crisis as it unfolded. He was wearing a suit and tie and sporting press credentials. He was arrested while trying to do his job. Or, more precisely, he was arrested *for* doing his job. This points to the gut-wrenching situation facing the Vote Power organizers. They wanted to control media coverage of their event, but every institutional force was aligned against them. The networks' disinterest in Liberty City as a "convention issue" should be understood in this context.

At the DNC, media coverage outside the convention hall played out very differently, for two reasons. First, the protestors were mostly white. The networks were already aware that they had been accused of giving "free publicity" to Black protestors and activists. They were wary about providing a platform for "radicals" in general, including whites in groups such as the Mobe, but racial tensions were so palpable in 1968, and concerns about amplifying the militant voices of Black Power ran high. In this context, it was simply more likely that white demonstrators in Chicago would get more media attention than would Black ones. However, to be clear, the networks still *under-covered* the street protest, in part out of the "free publicity" concern, and also because of the technical limitations Daley imposed.

A second key factor in coverage of street protest in Chicago was the media savvy of those under attack. Because the Chicago protestors loudly declared that they were part of the convention story, long before the event began, they became part of it. Tom Hayden and David Dellinger of SDS and the Mobe had sought out permits for marches for months before the convention, and when they didn't get them, they told the press. The Yippies, who also brought protestors to Chicago, were even more focused on getting media attention. In fact, the mass media was central to their project in a way that it was not for the political organizers of the New Left. As historian David Farber explains, the Yippies believed that "consciousness was created through cultural production" and that "by exploiting those forms of cultural production that they believed determined the consciousness of young people in particular—television, the music industry, FM radio stations, teen and youth magazines—they could subvert the ideology that gave credibility to America's entire pantheon of political symbols." Playfulness was central to their approach because they "believed they could make a revolution by simulating a revolution that looked like fun. The simulation would play to the mass media and through the mass media it would be made available to apolitical youth." The whole approach was wildly optimistic.[45]

And it depended on seizing the attention of the mainstream media—in particular the network news. Yippie cofounder Jerry Rubin later said, "the real drug was Walter Cronkite—it's hard to describe how excited we were when we realized how easy it was to get on those sign-off pieces at the end of the evening news broadcasts; . . . the more visual and surreal the stunts we could cook up, the easier it would be to get on the news, and the more weird and whimsical and provocative the theater, the better it would play."[46] Subpoenaed by the House Committee on Un-American Activities in 1968, Rubin displayed his taste for the theatrical by arriving dressed in an American Revolutionary War uniform . . . and later in a Santa Claus costume. So not surprisingly, in Chicago the Yippies pushed the visual and surreal stunts hard. They even nominated a pig (Pigasus) for president. Abbie Hoffman initially selected a cute pig, but Rubin insisted on an uglier one.[47] That sort of disagreement pointed to their commitment to performative specta-cle and was also the sort of thing that chafed more serious organizers looking to change policies and marshal systemic reform or revolution. The photo ops that the Yippies saw as central to their mission were, to many on the left, distractions from political work. As former SDS president Todd Gitlin pointedly remarked thirty years later, "Most of that decade's activists belonged to *less photogenic* civil rights, antiwar, and women's groups."[48]

When conservatives at the time attacked media coverage of the radi-cals and the counterculture, complaining that the dissenters were using the media, they were sometimes wrong and sometimes exactly right. The question should have been not simply whether the media were be-ing reactive (in effect, creating disturbances simply by being present), but whether the reactions were to genuinely newsworthy events that deserved coverage. And also, what positive purpose might that cover-age have? These had been crucial questions for the networks during their civil rights coverage. If those activists were "using" media cov-erage, it was to document injustice and also, though the presence of cameras often did *not* serve this purpose, to be protected from the even more extreme violence that might have occurred if the national news media had not been present. What conservative critics did not or would not see in the 1950s and beyond was that the networks were aware of the possibility of being manipulated, and that they tried to avoid that at all costs. That effort is repeatedly documented in numerous internal CBS staff memos, and has been attested to publicly as well. In a 1970 interview, Cronkite said point-blank, "I hate being used. I don't like reading in Jerry Rubin's book that he has used us. We're terribly aware of this. We're perfectly aware of it. But I don't see how we can refuse to cover something that is part of the social issue of the times simply because to do so would be to feed somebody else's propaganda."[49]

The Liberty City crisis seemed to illustrate the opposite: TV news being insufficiently reactive to protestors. There had been serious trou-ble in Miami, but the networks did not cover or interpret it in a way that negatively impacted the Republican convention, so the RNC mostly got the controlled show that they wanted. Asked about the crisis in Chicago as it unfurled, Daley pretended that no crisis existed while also insisting that the networks had no right to ask, because what about the violence they had ignored in Miami? Daley's attempts at redirection were disingenuous. With all the chaos in Chicago, the media could hardly be expected to pause to consider if they should be more "fair" to the mayor simply because they had underplayed the Liberty City crisis. But Daley was not incorrect to perceive the contrast. Before it even happened, broadcasters had been clear on the fact that the RNC would be a relatively staid and boring event—so that was how they covered it. It was, on the other hand, clear months ahead of time that Chicago would be dramatic. It was a question of *how* dramatic, and how the drama could be responsibly covered, without sensationalism.

And so at last on August 26, the futile attempts to gain march permits, the futile petitions to the police not to enforce the park curfew, the futile network efforts to get support from the mayor for proper live TV coverage, the futile attempts to settle all the strikes—none of it was resolved. The clock had run out. TV coverage started warming up at 6:30 p.m. Chicago time, with the opening gavel to be struck at 7:30.

Chapter Two   Day One

*"If the Democratic Party can't be democratic
. . . what hope is there for democracy?"*

The first day of the convention was an exercise in wishful thinking for both the Democratic Party and the network newsmen. The Democratic leadership wanted to portray the party as a force for progressive change, the party of civil rights, the party that would mend the fissures of 1968 America. They hoped the media would convey this picture. For their part, NBC and CBS hoped to accurately show the key events, offer helpful context and commentary, and beat out the other guy in the ratings. Both the politicos and the journalists hoped that the advance hype about potential violence had been exaggerated. Yes, there would be problems; you couldn't expect otherwise in 1968, but it might not be apocalyptic.

The convention was many things to many people. First, there were the organizers and chairmen of the party machine, team players who were devastated by Johnson's stepping down and were willing to support Hubert Humphrey without question. These were organizational supporters who wanted their party to look good on TV as a matter of principle, but also because they wanted to win the election. No one in this camp would expect Republicans to come over to their side as a result of positive TV coverage, but they hoped that a well-executed convention would help to keep Democratic voters and sway undecided ones. With public opinion turning against the war that Johnson had escalated, and Nixon promising to end it, there was reason to believe that party loyalty might not be enough to get the base out to the polls for Humphrey. From this organizational perspective, a strong convention followed by a strong campaign—all covered by TV—would boost the support of solid Democrats, reassure wavering ones, and hopefully pull in some unaffiliated, undecided voters. These were the realists.

Second, there were the upstart delegates, people like Donald Peterson and Allard Lowenstein who believed the party was faltering but could be saved. These were mostly Eugene McCarthy supporters, and many had participated in efforts to make the convention more "open"—that is, to get it out from under the control of the organizational team players. Some probably thought McCarthy could actually get the nomination, but most, more realistically, hoped his ideas would be shown to be popular enough that Humphrey would gravitate toward them and away from Johnson's policies. For this group, ideal convention TV coverage would show disagreement and even chaos, conveying dissension but also showing a happy ending. Humphrey would be nominated but with McCarthy's peace plank, and the country would be saved from Nixon. For this crowd, fighting shown on TV was desirable as a display of democracy in action, a party fighting for its life to stop both Nixon and Vietnam. Such a spectacle of dissension was what the realists wanted the TV cameras to ignore. For the upstarts, home TV viewers were voters but also witnesses to their struggles, as were the realists up on the platform, whom they wished to persuade. These were the idealists.

Third, there were the people of color—some among the delegates, and some seeking to become delegates, mostly Blacks, but some Latinos and Latinas among the Texans—who were demanding inclusion in the party. The Johnson administration had pushed through civil rights legislation, and yet segregationists still remained in power in the party, and people of color were underrepresented both at conventions and in voting booths. This group included some credentialed delegates who still felt disenfranchised or underappreciated by the party; some of them would convey those feelings by staging walkouts. This group also included challenging delegates who sought to displace regular delegates whom they said had been chosen unfairly. Like the McCarthyite idealists, this group would benefit from TV cameras covering dissension on the floor. The camera would reveal injustice, and in this way the media could potentially work to their advantage, as it had in the streets of Birmingham. But they weren't naive: TV wouldn't necessarily tell the story the way they wanted. These were the outsiders.

Fourth, there were the street demonstrators. Objectives were mixed among this group, from the "McCarthy kids," who were pro-peace college students, to the Mobe, an umbrella organization of more radical antiwar groups, to hippies and Yippies there to stage a radical protest against the mainstream. Some of these people were specifically protesting Johnson or Humphrey or the DNC, while others saw the party as so unreformable that the only cure was revolution. Some were very concerned about the convention itself, and others, as they put it, didn't give a fuck who was nominated. These are the groups that have been written about the most in the years following the Chicago convention. We'll just call them the protestors.

Each of these groups had a different stake in what TV convention coverage might mean, how it might benefit them, and how it might influence home viewers. And there was sometimes overlap among the groups—this is not a rigid taxonomy but rather a way to help us steer through the issues in play for the thousands who had gathered in Chicago. Meanwhile, the home viewing audience was huge, and though the ultimate fallout was clear—Nixon won, and notions of mainstream media's "liberal bias" took strong root—we have no empirical gauge of *exactly* how viewers received network TV coverage over the course of those four days. It nonetheless helps to head into our story considering these four groups. Every time the TV cameras showed delegates fighting or, conversely, toeing the line, or showed authoritarian or liberal attitudes from the speakers on the dais, or showed journalists or protestors being beaten by Chicago police, the first three groups, and elements of the fourth group, had a stake in asking, "will *showing this* (or not showing something else) help or hurt our cause?"

That said, heading into day one, the televisual stakes did not seem too high. There was every reason to believe that this would be a proforma session and that the fireworks would start on Tuesday. Monday's schedule started at 7:30 p.m. with the standard ceremonies and pomp and circumstance, followed by a welcome from the mayor of Chicago and a keynote speech from Hawaii Sen. Daniel K. Inouye. Next on the agenda were a few standard procedural issues, and then the schedule indicated early adjournment. The next day would open with the meatier stuff, such as debates over credentials challenges. There was reason to be guardedly optimistic that things would go smoothly the first day. They did not.

The networks started their coverage by going over the schedule and predicting how delegates would vote by state, based on their own research and number crunching. Early on, each network offered viewers a report on Mayor Daley. These segments neatly illustrate the differences among the approaches of the Big Three. They also show how the networks framed the tone for the day as one of "gloom and doom." Some home viewers watching over dinner might have wondered if this rhetoric was hyperbolic, but anyone who made it to the bitter end of the day's coverage, seven hours later, would probably conclude the opposite, that the networks' pessimistic opening rhetoric actually understated the situation in Chicago.

The Networks Compete and Set the Scene of "Doom and Gloom"

CBS built up a narrative of the environment created by Daley. Without mentioning the mayor, there was some prickly opening reporting. Cronkite reinforced the crisis of reduced live coverage, observing with restrained frustration that it meant it would take about an hour to report comments from the candidates, who were stationed at the Hilton. It was customary for candidates to remain off-site until one was nominated, another factor that made Daley's limits on live reporting onerous. He knew damn well that the candidates would not be at the Amphitheatre, and since he was still rooting for a last-minute LBJ or Ted Kennedy draft, he was happy for the other candidates to receive insufficient TV coverage.

Cronkite also reported the late-breaking news that the Democrats had that day "absolutely refused to give any student editors, mainly editors of college newspapers, the credentials for convention hall facilities." Cronkite was an ever-vigilant booster for both the First Amendment and the little guy, so this was just the kind of thing that got under his skin. He added archly that "the Republicans in Miami Beach did allow college students to watch and report on their convention." Although this blow to student newspapers was not directly relevant to CBS coverage per se, it was an early example of how the issue of news coverage itself became part of the story of the convention.

Cronkite next observed that "overall, the security around this International Amphitheatre has been worthy of an armed camp, a military installation." After more information on security protocols, Cronkite noted, "A Chicago newspaper man here this morning commented that there are so many troops in Chicago now that they're awaiting Bob Hope to come and entertain them." It was a cornball joke, and also one last poke at the military atmosphere that Daley had created. Cronkite finally offered this brief summary on Daley right before the opening invocation that officially kicked off the whole event: "And there is the mayor of this host city of Chicago, Richard Daley, one of the major powers in the Democratic Party, the head of one of the most powerful political organizations left in the United States, longtime mayor of this city, who has brought it to a new peak of greatness but runs it with an iron hand." The summary was brief, the reference to Daley's political machine as an "organization" (Daley's preferred term) conciliatory. Almost everything in the CBS coverage up to this point had been an elliptical criticism of the mayor, as Cronkite showed the negative results of conditions that Daley had orchestrated, without making any kind of personal attack. This was all as restrained, conscientious, and objective as possible, even as Cronkite and his team did feel a direct undercutting of their professional duties that could be traced to both Daley and the DNC, with whom Daley was clearly working in concert to restrict proper news coverage.

Half an hour later, CBS correspondent Roger Mudd gave a more pointed analysis: "I think the chaos and the destruction [among delegates] are not because of tradition or a desire to put on a good TV show. They're going to be there because the Democratic Party is in trouble. You can forget the bubbling 'politics of joy' from the vice president and Mayor Daley's omnipresent flower posters and his welcome signs. The dominant mood here in Chicago is one of gloom. . . . As one Democrat said today, Walter, for every cop and soldier the people see on TV guarding us, you can count one more vote for Richard Nixon." Mudd presented a tough analysis of the problems facing the Democrats. Democrats were *upset* about being in Daley's Chicago, he emphasized, because they were well aware that the mayor's version of "law and order" would harm them politically. Although Daley was likely enraged (and Nixon delighted) by Mudd's analysis, it was even-handed, tight, and professional. If anything, Mudd had held back. A tougher analysis would have drilled down on how Daley's rhetoric echoed Nixon's and on the fact that everyone knew that calls for "law and order" were implicitly calls to suppress both Black political action and the antiwar demonstrations raging across college campuses. What was startling was less the fact that Mr. Democrat had threatened violence against protestors—that was the Daley way—but that he had used language widely associated with the GOP.

ABC's coverage struck a different tone, unrestrained in its jabs at both Daley and the party. This underscored ABC's third-class status; attempting to boost its ratings, it would sometimes stretch the limits of collegial, fair news coverage. The ABC evening newscast included a Daley profile that opened by noting that opponents called him "King Richard." ABC next commented on Daley's "failure to communicate with the Negro ghetto. He's had two major riots in three years" and showed footage of him complaining that he had been misunderstood about his shoot-to-kill comments. He also stated that he didn't care about "intellectuals and university professors," a category that seemed to encompass most of his critics. One could imagine similar boiler-plate populism coming from George Wallace, with a heavy twang but the same amount of disgust.

Toward the end of the ABC lead-in to their truncated convention coverage, commentator Ralph Schoenstein delivered a caustic segment attacking Daley for his fences hiding the slums, his beautifying posters of flowers posted around town ("a nice concession to hay fever victims"), and his vendetta against "liberals, Negroes, Czecho-slovakians, and anchormen. Daley has suppressed freedom but has made the trains run on time," a not-so-subtle reference to Mussolini. Daley was a "foe of unemployment," a joke about his patronage hires, and was "holding the line for nineteenth-century government." CBS and NBC commentators were critical of Daley but would not have gone this far. Notably, ABC mentioned the reduced number of floor passes but did not dwell on the issue of live coverage, as Cronkite had. Since they were barely covering the convention anyway, the restrictions were less pressing for them.

ABC anchorman Frank Reynolds closed the newscast with a blistering analysis, explicitly labeled "commentary," as was then the norm: "It is painful to say this about a national convention of either major party, but this gathering of the Democrats in the stockyards has about it an air of *doom* that seems unhappily appropriate to the surroundings [the slaughterhouses]. . . . Division and disunity are mild terms to be applied to this convention. . . . The balloons and the funny hats are here, of course, and there is the usual collection of kooks and oddballs who turn up at any convention, but the Democrats this year have lost the knack of disagreeing without being disagreeable. And in that sense they are perhaps representative of the rest of the country. I'm Frank Reynolds. Good night." Cut to Lemon Pledge commercial.

ABC attacks were not so hardball that they would violate the Fairness Doctrine, and as for offending viewers, they had absolutely nothing to lose. The *CBS Evening News* was in first place, having been neck-and-neck with NBC's *Huntley–Brinkley Report* for some time and finally having gained the lead in 1967.[1] (NBC had trounced CBS at the 1964 conventions.[2]) ABC had been the last of the networks to be created, in 1945, when NBC had been forced out of its near-monopoly by the FCC. There had been two NBC networks, NBC Red and NBC Blue, until NBC divested itself of the lesser Blue, which was purchased by the American Broadcasting Corporation (ABC). ABC took decades to catch up in the ratings, and it was still in a distant third place in 1968.[3]

That year, ABC was also the network with the most low-budget, lowest-common-denominator programming: not trash, but not upscale either. Their highest-rated show was *Bewitched*, tied at number eleven with two CBS shows, *Mission: Impossible* and *The Red Skelton Hour*. On the first night in Chicago, they promoted clunkers such as the spooky *Journey to the Unknown* and *Here Come the Brides*, a Western comedy about randy lumberjacks. A quick look at advertising support during the DNC brings home the point about relative prestige: the main sponsor of CBS convention coverage was the petroleum company Esso; NBC's biggest sponsor was Gulf. ABC promoted its own TV programs, and also aired ads for cigarettes, brassieres (*padded* brassieres, at that), and Goodrich Tires, a more upscale sponsor, except the ads featured a gigantic woman in a miniskirt toying with a car à la *Attack of the Fifty Foot Woman*. These tires apparently had "knee-action sidewalls."

When ABC decided to include nightly convention commentary by Gore Vidal and William F. Buckley, everyone knew it was an economical gimmick to compensate for scant convention coverage. They had been sniping at each other nonstop, first in Miami and now in Chicago, so it was not surprising (though it was bracing) when the two men famously almost came to blows on day three, when Vidal called Buckley a "crypto-Nazi" and Buckley threatened to "sock" Vidal in his "goddamn nose." Their lively debate drew intellectual viewers who usually avoided the "boob tube," and also a wider audience, because you didn't have to get all (or even any) of the political nuances to understand that it was fun to watch.[4] On their second day in Chicago, Buckley said he had received a letter from Bobby Kennedy six months earlier in which RFK wrote, "I have changed my platform for 1968 from 'let's give blood to the Vietcong' to 'let's give Gore Vidal to the Vietcong.'" Vidal suggested that this sounded fishy and that a graphologist should examine the letter.

In his definitive study of CBS News a decade later, Gary Paul Gates stated the common perception in the media industry that the ABC news department "was notoriously lacking in class and tradition."[5] The evaluation was both unkind and accurate. Out of context, the Buckley and Vidal segments might seem like an attempt at class, but when you factor in the quality of the editorial material around it (a correspondent jokes about *diaper rash* in his Daley profile?), the novelty value becomes more obvious. On Monday in Chicago, the Buckley/Vidal segment was immediately preceded by an ad for the Playtex Firm 'n' Flatter girdle. To be fair, CBS and NBC also ran ads for foundation garments and cigarettes during the DNC, as well as commercials for artificial sweeteners, stereo cabinets, dog food, ballpoint pens, and all kinds of banal items. But their main sponsors were upscale outfits like oil and insurance companies, which brought gravitas to their coverage. Gulf and Esso were not interested in ABC.

ABC was ahead of the other networks on one count on Monday, though: they reported early on that their cameraman Charles Pharris had been attempting to film in the street when Chicago police broke his camera lens. A soundman working with Pharris had also been "roughed up," ABC revealed. As the *Walker Report* described it in more detail a few months later, an ABC crew was trying to film the arrest of activists Tom Hayden and Wolfe Lowenthal when "a policeman whacked soundman Walter James in the back with a nightstick and smashed a $900 [over $7,000 in 2022 dollars] lens belonging to Charles Pharris."[6] Generally, the three networks soft-pedaled police brutality in Chicago until they simply could not avoid it. The mild phrase "roughed up" is used an alarming number of times by CBS, NBC, and ABC as a euphemism for being beaten in the face, head, or back by a policeman's nightstick. The fact that police were bludgeoning soundmen for the crime of being soundmen was a deferred story, a point worth reinforcing because, as the convention progressed, TV viewers became more and more enraged that too much police brutality was being covered, when the hard truth was that relatively little of it was shown.

CBS and NBC got to the Pharris news, but they avoided covering street violence until very late the first day of the convention, when it finally seemed unavoidable. This was also when they finally had been able to get their hands on edited segments shot far from the Amphitheatre. ABC broke the story of the broken camera lens not because they were the best investigative reporters but because they were more likely to be sensationalist, and also because Pharris was one of their own. They had done the right thing in this instance but, since they ran only ninety-minute daily summaries, ABC convention coverage ultimately made little impact. They opened with the most obvious animus toward both Daley and the Democrats, but too few tuned in to cry foul.

NBC managed to strike the middle ground between CBS's guarded criticism of Daley and ABC's outright snark. Two moments best illustrate this. First, there was David Brinkley's opening salvo:

> In Chicago tonight, there is a bus strike, a taxi strike, and a telephone strike. Any other city with half of those troubles would have lost the Democratic convention a long time ago. But the fact it is still here and beginning in about a half an hour is due entirely to one man who the Democrats dare not offend, Mayor Richard Daley. The convention is being held in the *seedy* part of Mayor Daley's Chicago, which he has ordered dressed up with signs bearing his name. And temporary fences along the streets to hide the vacant lots and other sites the mayor doesn't want the delegates to see. And some barbed wire around the Amphitheatre to keep the delegates in and the demonstrators and almost everybody out. In spite of all the troubles, the Democrats insisted on coming here, thinking Mayor Daley could keep order, if anyone could. With all the police and military manpower and barbed wire, he may prove them right.

Brinkley ended by passing to his co-anchor Chet Huntley who would also, throughout the night, tell it like it was. Their coverage was serious, but NBC's anchors did lean toward trying to entertain, during a long, long event that often ground to a halt for floor votes and caucusing. Cronkite's strictly-facts approach was sometimes less engaging but more informative.

In letters to the networks, viewers regularly declared their allegiance to either Cronkite or Huntley and Brinkley. For those in the latter camp, the duo's banter and the contrast of styles made all the difference. Brinkley was seen as the one with the sense of humor; Huntley, as the one with more gravitas. (Cronkite and his crew saw this as a bit gimmicky.)[7] In 1956, CBS had led in convention ratings, but *New York Times*

TV critic Jack Gould wrote that Huntley-Brinkley had "injected the much needed note of humor in commentary" and suggested that "the CBS News department needs to cheer up."[8] Frank Sinatra and Milton Berle once sang a duet to the tune of "Love and Marriage" that went "Huntley-Brinkley, Huntley-Brinkley / One is glum the other quite twinkly . . ." Both anchors leaned more toward glum than usual in Chicago.

Glummest of all—and also quite brilliant—was the Daley segment created by David Douglas Duncan for NBC's day one coverage. Consider that each of the networks had a sort of "guest gimmick" for the convention. ABC had Buckley and Vidal; CBS had Pulitzer Prize-winner Teddy White in conversation with regular Eric Sevareid; and NBC had Duncan. Each gimmick matched its network's identity. Arguably, the Duncan gimmick was the most successful. The idea was that this famous war photographer would document both conventions, and each day he would compile a montage sequence of photos with an explanatory voice-over. At the RNC, Duncan had been a rarity, a photojournalist with whom Nixon felt relatively comfortable. Nixon had allowed Duncan to snap shots of him as he privately composed his nomination acceptance speech.

In introducing Duncan in Chicago, Brinkley explains that he had been instructed to take photos of "whatever pleases him." Duncan's photomontage opens with a shot of welcoming signs Daley had put up with butterflies and flowers painted on them. You might think Chicago had "really gone to the dogs," but no, Daley had rolled out the welcome mat, Duncan narrated, with a soothing voice, because Chicago is "a gracious place" with Daley's "Irish face smiling at us even from the top of the telephone in the hotel" (fig. 8). National Guardsmen were at Soldier Field but had not been called up: "It's almost like a picnic ground." Daley was "man of dreams; . . . he has friends among all the ethnic groups, . . . and they vote for him en masse. . . . He's a modest man." The voice-over is soft and pleasant, like an ad luring housewives to try a new, gentle soap. It's also disturbing, in part because it sounds like how Daley describes himself (what modest man describes himself

FIGURE 8.   NBC's photographer David Douglas Duncan says that Chicago is "a gracious place" with Daley's "Irish face smiling at us even from the top of the telephone in the hotel." David Douglas Duncan Papers and Photography Collection, © David Douglas Duncan, 1968, courtesy of Harry Ransom Center.

as modest?) and because the modulation of Duncan's voice is similar to Daley's, too. Daley spoke in only two registers: blustery and apoplectic or soft and humble, explaining how he was just doing his best, with the help of his Creator.

It's still early in the night, and yet TV viewers have heard so much about Daley's self-promotion and heavy-handed security that Duncan's piece feels a bit off. Duncan's Daley doesn't sound like the "modest" man who earlier in the night had arranged a surprise bagpipe parade in his own honor on the convention floor. It's unclear what Duncan is up to until the last photo, which begins as a close-up of the fangs of a snarling attack dog and pulls back to show the Chicago policemen handling it (fig. 9). Duncan concludes, "There are sure a lot of big dogs around

FIGURE 9.   David Douglas Duncan's photo features for NBC reinforced the doom-and-gloom
tone that all three networks had set for Monday's coverage. He concludes his first photomontage
on a chilling note: "There are sure a lot of big dogs around here." David Douglas Duncan Papers
and Photography Collection, © David Douglas Duncan, 1968, courtesy of Harry Ransom Center.

here." The terrifying shot is held for a few extra beats, accompanied by
an uncomfortable silence. It is suddenly clear that the town really has
"gone to the dogs" and that Duncan was having one over on us, setting us up for this finale. An accomplished combat photographer knew
a police state when he saw one, and he had conveyed this to viewers
with a two-and-a-half-minute film that could have held its own at an
avant-garde film festival. It was a bold, experimental approach to news
coverage, and it also ably reinforced the doom-and-gloom tone that all
three networks had set for day one coverage.

R-E-S-P-E-C-T for Mississippi?

At last, the convention was ready to get underway, opening grandly
with Aretha Franklin's soulful rendition of "The Star-Spangled Banner." Franklin had performed at benefits for Dr. King's Southern Chris-

tian Leadership Conference (SCLC) in late 1967. Just four months before Chicago, she had also sung at King's funeral. At just twenty-six years old, Franklin had had a smash hit with "Respect" in 1967, for which she received a Grammy. She was a huge star, and Democratic organizers must have thought that kicking off the convention with a tremendously popular African American would appeal to both white liberals and Blacks across the board. Given her association with the slain leader—her brother Cecil told her biographer that "Aretha was Dr. King's favorite singer"[9]—Franklin's presence would not only implicitly memorialize him but also serve as a pat on the back to the party of LBJ, which had shepherded the Civil Rights Act of 1964 and the Voting Rights Act of 1965 through Congress. This was all wishful thinking, on multiple counts.

It is hard for a viewer fifty years later to judge Franklin's performance objectively. One instinctively jumps forward to a later symbolically and politically charged moment, her performance of "My Country 'Tis of Thee" at President Obama's inauguration in 2009. The latter performance was stronger, more tightly rehearsed and produced. Of the 1968 performance, her producer Jerry Wexler said, "I cringed when I watched it. . . . The orchestra was woefully out of tune. Aretha did the best she could, but it was not her greatest moment."[10] This assessment was fair; she did lose track of the lyrics briefly.

But the Queen of Soul's rendition arguably ranks with the Jimi Hendrix Woodstock version of 1969, and also the José Feliciano World Series performance of 1968, as "scandalous" performances (and, crucially, *nationally mediated events*) that were stunningly, subversively patriotic. The Franklin soul version, Hendrix rock version, and Feliciano folk arrangements of the National Anthem were "anti-American" only to listeners disdainful of soul, rock, and folk music, listeners who couldn't understand that these genres could be appropriate for expressing love of (or at least hope for) one's country. What many saw as the correct or conventional version of the National Anthem was, to put a fine point on it, the white version.

Cronkite told correspondent Harry Reasoner at the beginning of the next day's coverage that CBS had received "quite a few telephone

calls and wires . . . complaining about Aretha Franklin's presentation."
Viewers, he explained neutrally, felt that her "stylized rendition didn't
do the National Anthem justice." This was quite an understatement.
A letter to Cronkite from Florida written on the third day of the convention was among the more restrained: "May I be one of many who
will voice their disgust over the way Aretha Franklin sang the National Anthem?"[11] A viewer from Tennessee observed that Franklin
had talent, but that "the Anthem required dignity" that she was obviously lacking.[12] From a married couple in Georgia came this telegram:
"Heard tonight worse rendition of National Anthem ever. What for
encore? After soul version? Suggest Beach Boys, Vanilla Fudge, or Tiny
Tim."[13] Although there was a visceral reaction against Black performance style in these telegrams, complaints were basically framed as
a "taste" issue.

Others took a more overtly ideological line. A telegram sent to
Cronkite from New Orleans at 1:00 in the morning boldly claimed:
"As the hour of decision draws near on the Vietnam peace-at-any-price
movement now being discussed at the National Democratic Convention, it is rumored that a message of encouragement and promise of
reward from Ho Chi Minh to the proponents of the movement is on
its way, receipt of which to be acclaimed by another inspired rendition
of the Star Spangled Banner."[14] Bringing together the themes of patriotism, taste, and racial disgust, a telegram from a retired US Army major
from Texas pulled out all the stops:

> Rendition by Aretha Franklin of the National Anthem at your con-
> vention was and is reprehensible and intolerable to every American,
> there is only one orchestration of the National Anthem—it is not
> jazz—nor is it syncopated—it is not oogie woogie—nor is it any of
> the noise called music with names that are successors to those men-
> tioned above. She sang the Anthem in a manner which was insulting
> and revolting to my patriotism and to that of all the servicemen who
> have served and/or died, in the service of their country. . . . Public
> worldwide and national apology by your convention is the least that
> should be expected.[15]

At a time when telegrams were sent to communicate urgent messages (an elopement, a child in the hospital), these missives indicated a high level of commitment to registering a complaint.

Whereas Cronkite merely stated that there had been criticisms, Reasoner expressed a point of view, giving a cheerful, white-bread response, "Gee, I thought it was *fine*. I know you wouldn't want to sing it that way every time. It's a song that I don't suppose is anyone's delight musically. It's important because of what it is. And to hear it sung with some soul, I found very nice." As if to emphasize that this soulful moment was indeed fleeting, the DNC orchestra at this exact moment belted out a Lawrence Welk–style version of "Bells Are Ringing."

Reasoner was the only one to speak up for Franklin's rendition. In his book on the election, Teddy White went so far as to describe the performance as "a syncopated rock version that sounded more like a yodel than the national anthem."[16] If the Dems opened with Franklin in part to show that they were the party of civil rights, they had sort of succeeded. The backlash itself revealed a resistance to the progressive changes that many in the party wished to celebrate. It was hardly a coincidence, of course, that many complaints came from southern viewers. It's safe to assume that many southern delegates at the convention itself were also appalled. But of course, conflicts with southern delegates at a national Democratic convention were not unique to 1968.

In fact, the choice of Franklin should be seen not only as a nod toward the legislative accomplishments since the last convention but also, specifically, as a nod toward the delegate crisis of 1964, which was also not merely an important moment but also an important *televisual* moment. Franklin's presence on opening day in 1968 sought to signal that 1964's problems were in the past.[17] But the 1964 crisis continued to reverberate; indeed, the event provides crucial context for understanding the delegate challenges that arose in Chicago. Four years earlier, the Mississippi Freedom Democratic Party (MFDP) had arrived at the Atlantic City convention to protest Black disenfranchisement. Registering to vote remained an uphill battle for Blacks throughout the South, but in Mississippi the situation was particularly dire. In 1964, 23 percent of voting-age Blacks were registered to vote in Alabama. In Tennessee, 69.4 percent were registered, the highest percentage among the southern states. Mississippi was at rock bottom, with 6.7 percent. By 1968, Tennessee had gone up to 71.7 percent and Alabama to 51.6 percent. Amazingly, and due in no small part to the Voting Rights Act of 1965, Mississippi had gone up to 59.8 percent.[18] The increase was stunning, but it hadn't significantly affected the racial demographics of the delegates sent to Chicago.

In both 1964 and 1968, challenging Mississippi groups had presented themselves to the Democrats' credentials committee the week before the convention and had asked to be seated instead of the "regular delegates." Conventions always included credentials challenges, where delegates fought over who should be seated and get votes. In 1964, for example, there had been concerns about the seating of southern delegates because many had already gone for Goldwater. Why seat "Democrats" who supported the GOP candidate? This was a concern again in 1968, with segregationist Gov. George Wallace running on a third-party ticket.

In 1964, the civil rights lawyer Joseph Rauh had represented the MFDP. He learned shortly before the committee was to meet to hear the alternate delegates that they had been scheduled in a small room, and he raised hell for one reason and one reason only: there had to be TV coverage of the MFDP making its case. Their hope for success hinged upon showing the nation what was happening and, in effect, shaming the committee into supporting their agenda. The camera crews and lighting setups for all three networks simply would not fit in the small room. Rauh got a bigger room. His presentation of the case was strong, but the key moment was the testimony of Fannie Lou Hamer, a Black voting rights activist who had been savagely beaten at the direction of Mississippi state troopers.

On live national television, Hamer told her story in detail and with great care. By the end, she was in tears, as were many in the room, and by virtue of this performance she became a hypercharged symbol of the Black struggle against injustice and brutality. Johnson was watching from the White House and called a press conference immediately in order to interrupt Hamer's nationally televised image. He did not want to seat the MFDP for fear of losing southern support in the general election. Of course, he lost the South to Goldwater anyway, but he did succeed in cutting off Hamer's live coverage. Johnson had, in effect, intended to use network news policies against Hamer. Back then, when the president told the networks to interrupt their programming for him, that was what they did, no questions asked. No one could have predicted the rise of personalized media feeds and platforms like Twitter, but we might here ponder how presidential access to Americans has changed. If you were listening to TV or radio fifty years ago, you'd hear what the president had to say, like it or not. In this way a mass-media environment theoretically exposed all to the same limited number of news sources.

Notwithstanding LBJ's disruption of the live feed, the cameras kept rolling, and excerpts of Hamer's testimony appeared later on the news, making her the face of the MFDP struggle. Both the credentials committee and the White House were flooded with phone calls and telegrams in support of seating the MDFP.[19] Without the cameras, there would have been much less public awareness of what had happened in that room. Visual coverage had been crucial.[20] Hamer spoke of both policy and personal suffering, demonstrating moral power to receptive TV viewers. Yet the outpouring of supportive public opinion was not enough. The MFDP had requested sixty-four seats and were offered two non-voting seats. When they suggested that perhaps Hamer could take one of the two seats, Humphrey chillingly responded, "The president has said that he will not let that illiterate woman speak on the floor of the Democratic convention."[21] When Hamer confronted Humphrey, the conversation ended with both in tears. It was probably a relief to both sides that there was no footage of that encounter. If it had been shown on TV, the MFDP might have looked weak, too emotional in its appeal. The soon-to-be vice president might also have been deemed a crybaby.

Johnson himself always thought Humphrey was too soft, too weepy, a perpetual weakling in the macho game of politics.[22] LBJ had nick-

named the fleshy organ between his legs "Jumbo," which is relevant
not because it was anomalous (he was not the first to find his manhood
so special that it deserved its own name) but because he shared this
information frequently, giving the clear implication that Jumbo proved
his power, that he was a man not to be trifled with.[23] This macho powerhouse wasn't going to waste a single second on an "illiterate woman"
who expertly moved grown men to tears. The notion that she was a *dis-
empowered* victim of racism was nonsense: on TV, she was a pure em-
bodiment of moral purpose, an unstoppable symbol. Johnson's victory
had lain not only in keeping the MFDP from being seated, which would
have alienated southern voters, but also in doing so preemptively,
without the issue coming to a nationally televised floor vote.

In 1968, alternative delegates again arrived, this time calling themselves the Loyal Democrats of Mississippi, a group that included Hamer
and other former MFDP members. As a 1968 CBS convention briefing
book noted, the "regular" Mississippi delegation had three Negroes in
it; in 1964, the state had been alerted that by 1968 they would have to
have a delegation that was "broadly representative" of the state, and
yet, the briefing book further noted, the population of the state was
42 percent Negro.[24] So the presence of three Negro delegates did not
cut it. In an about-face from 1964, the 1968 credentials committee
ruled to seat the Loyal Democrats in place of the regular Mississippi
delegates. But the decision was made before the convention started;
as in 1964, a potentially embarrassing televised crisis had been side-
stepped. If programming Aretha Franklin to open the convention was
a nod toward the civil rights movement, it was also a symbolic nod toward the MFDP, a choice designed to show, on national television, that
the problems of 1964 were in the past. They weren't.

The problems of 1948 were not even in the past. At that convention,
Strom Thurmond and other segregationist southern delegates had
stormed out and formed the States' Rights Democratic ("Dixiecrat")
Party.[25] The crisis of party loyalty, with many southern Democrats
unwilling to support the party's candidate (in favor of Thurmond in
1948, Goldwater in 1964, and Wallace in 1968) or to embrace (or even

tolerate) the Democrats as the party of civil rights, remained a vital issue in Chicago. The southern delegates were still pining for the old Democratic Party, the party of segregation.

If the defection of segregationists to the GOP had been ongoing for twenty years, 1968 was the next great tipping point. By 1972, many of the arch-segregationists would be either gone or hanging on by their fingernails. This is worth remembering when we look back on the Chicago DNC: it is remembered as the convention when the police beat thousands of people senseless in the street. But on day one, the *indoor* spectacle revealed by the networks was less one of overt violence than it was a procedural battle over maintaining white supremacy.

It was not surprising that the southern states had not done much better at integrating their delegations than they had in 1964. What was surprising was that this became a first-day issue in 1968. For the schedule had been clear: on Tuesday, the second day, there would be a floor vote on delegate challenges. The credentials committee had met with the challengers the week before and had heard testimony on both sides. In each case except Mississippi, the committee came out against the challengers. So voting on the committee's reports on Tuesday, as scheduled, boiled down to voting to seat or not seat the challengers. Voting ended up being by roll call, with each state called on one at a time to give its votes from a microphone on the floor. This was time-consuming, and votes would be taken for Texas, Georgia, North Carolina, and Alabama. At the last minute, this was all rescheduled for Monday night.

Those in favor of the challenging delegates—the idealists and the outsiders—were furious. Their official line was that they had not yet been able to prepare. The unofficial line—and a story that the networks pursued—was that many of these folks (the idealists in particular) needed the night away from the Amphitheatre because they were active in the draft Teddy Kennedy movement, or because they wanted to use the night to drum up more delegate support for McCarthy. Many strings had to be pulled on Monday night, and this could not be done by delegates stuck on the Amphitheatre floor voting all night. And remember: there was a severe phone shortage, so late-night politicking would be difficult even if a delegate could escape. Another crucial part of the story was less complicated to explain: the pro-establishment, pro-Humphrey/LBJ forces—the realists—did not want the votes to come while people were still watching television. Shooting down every challenging delegation would make the Democratic Party look bad. It was best, then, to do such things after prime time. That would be a win for the realists, a loss for the idealists and the outsiders.

The fact that Mississippi challengers already had been seated could be vaunted during prime time, and after that, if the delegates had to stay in the Amphitheatre voting all night, so be it. The next day, the networks could report that the challengers had been defeated, but most TV viewers would have missed the infighting. Whether or not this was LBJ's idea, it could not have displeased him. He was, after all, an intensely image-conscious president, constantly monitoring news coverage. Doris Kearns Goodwin has described him "hugging a transistor radio to his ear as he walked through the fields of his ranch or around the grounds of the White House . . . listening not for music but for news."[26] Robert Caro recounts how he practically climbed inside the White House ticker-tape machine, seizing wire stories before the machine could even disgorge them. He had three side-by-side TV monitors in his bedroom for watching news on all the networks at once.[27]

Vain even for a politician, Johnson was not simply following news. He was specifically following news of himself and tracing how his image was crafted by the media. This is a man who always had staff photographers on hand; official White House photographer Yoishi Okamoto took more than five hundred thousand photos of Johnson in office.[28] JFK's White House photographers, by contrast, had taken about thirty thousand images of him.[29] All of this is helpful to keep in mind when considering what a public relations crisis the MFDP had posed for LBJ, how keenly he must have felt it, and how anxious he must have been for the 1968 Mississippi challenge not to be central to convention coverage. Another televised embarrassment for the Democratic Party would also reflect poorly on him.[30]

Seating the Mississippi challengers in 1968 did not erase the memory of 1964, and it did not help the challenging delegates from Texas, North Carolina, Georgia, and Alabama. The 1968 convention had a record number of delegate challenges (fifteen disputes from thirteen states), with almost all centering on the inequitable selection of delegates. Many of the details were too politically and bureaucratically esoteric to be faithfully conveyed by the networks. It was also hard for reporters to clearly tell a story for TV viewers when they had only off-the-record sources informing them about the president's involvement and other backroom machinations; they were inclined not to make the president look bad, out of respect for the office, and they also wanted to report carefully about anything that might sound like rumor or innuendo. The anchormen and correspondents had every reason to suspect, for example, that the convention's executive director, John Criswell, had a direct line to LBJ, and that the president was manipulating events from afar, but they made only carefully circumscribed references to this sort of behind-the-scenes maneuvering. Ultimately, the newsmen framed the narrative about the delegate challenges that dominated the first day of convention coverage around the notion of two competing players: there were establishment and anti-establishment forces, hawks and doves, pro-Humphrey and pro-McCarthy forces.

In virtually every instance across four days, the establishment forces won: the seating of delegates, the approval of the platform, the choice of candidates. A key exception on the first day was the abolition of the unit rule, where the McCarthy/anti-establishment forces prevailed. The unit rule allowed state delegations to vote as a single entity, with all votes going to the majority. Georgia, for example, had 43 votes to cast at the convention. If 22 delegates voted for one candidate and 21 voted against him, then under the unit rule all votes would be cast for the candidate. This was a preferred strategy for southern states, as it strengthened their power as a bloc. It also shut out token minority voices: if a handful of African Americans delegates in the Texas or Alabama delegations voted against the white majority, they would easily be silenced by the unit rule. The outsider delegates understood this, as did politically engaged people of color watching at home, but it was probably too much for many casual TV viewers to sort out. The networks did try to explain the situation but generally erred by oversimplifying and not stressing that a vote against the unit rule was a vote against the suppression of minority voices.

The only challenging delegation that had an easy time of it was the Loyal Democrats of Mississippi. One might naively assume that if the credentials committee found the Mississippi challengers to have made a convincing case, a similar verdict would be found for the other southern challengers. This assumption is underpinned by a notion of legal process, an idea that the seating of the MFDP would be understood as a precedent, in the legal sense, and that each challenging delegation's case would be fairly tried by the credentials committee. But as the authors of a 1969 *Harvard Law Review* article concluded, "the Credentials Committee was overwhelmingly a political, not a judicial, forum."[31] Seating the MFDP was a good political decision for the Democrats. And so it happened. On the flipside, there was no political gain to be had, from the national party's perspective (the realists), by being fair to the disenfranchised Blacks and Mexican Americans of Texas. The Texas delegation was run by LBJ's old friend Governor Connolly, and defeating the challengers was a victory for both Connolly and Johnson.

Each challenge was a complicated story, but even this brief recounting of some of the variables should convey how confusing the delegate challenges would be to anyone but the most devoted of political junkies watching convention coverage at home. If the networks erred in their coverage of the opening hours of the convention, their mistakes resulted not so much from any "bias" but from their reluctance to unpack much of the esoterica of the event. Such reluctance was less a political decision than a decision not to risk boring or confusing viewers. White stuck his foot in it with his foolish comments about Franklin's "yodeling," but he was right about one thing: by the time Franklin opened the show it was "already obvious that this promised to be one of the most unusual conventions in American political history."[32] And yet, with the networks under-explaining the Mississippi challenge and the unit rule issue, it would be hard for home viewers to grasp on the first day what exactly was "unusual" at this particular convention beyond the obvious militarism outside in the streets. The news teams did better with the Georgia crisis on Monday night, because it offered a more straightforward narrative trajectory.

By skipping the Mississippi and Texas stories to focus more on Georgia, the networks lost an opportunity. The nightly evening news was a sort of "headline service" that could offer only a limited amount of information, but with hours of time to fill, conventions theoretically offered an opportunity to dig deeper, and the network's massive internal briefing books (with individual sections written by correspondents according to their specialties) showed that the newsmen were aware of the complicated back stories underpinning all of the delegate challenges and other procedural issues. The professional constraint to stick mostly to the story right under their noses at conventions spoke not to a disinterest in American political history but to a professionally ingrained idea of what television news was. Journalists were there to show and explain what was happening, in the moment, and to be as objective as possible in their analyses. From this perspective, the lack of context given the unit rule or the suppression of the Black or Mexican American vote in Mississippi or Texas was not negligence but an attempt to be "fair" to the states of Mississippi and Texas. As frustrating as journalism is in the twenty-first-century environment of politically slanted cable news and atomized social media feeds, it is instructive to remember that in the network era, "fairness" sometimes led to responsive rather than proactive reporting, and to the omission of information that viewers should have been provided. Being "fair," in other words, could mean leaving undisturbed the most powerful people and institutions.

The Georgia Challenge

Although hours were spent voting on delegate challenges on the first night, the challenge that received the most TV coverage came from

Georgia, led by Julian Bond. This case took center stage in large part because Joseph Rauh was a player again in 1968, now working for McCarthy and organizing the credentials fights. In his definitive biography of Governor Connally, James Reston explains that to Rauh, "Connally was only the most effective segregationist in their midst, not the most lurid. [Georgia Governor] Lester Maddox had the latter distinction, and thus, for strictly tactical reasons, the McCarthy forces focused their challenge on the Georgia rather than [on] the Texas delegation. With Georgia, they had Maddox as the villain and the debonair Julian Bond as the matinee idol, and this provided a far better focus for a challenge than [did] Connally as the villain, [Texas liberal] Ralph Yarborough as the hero, and Lyndon Johnson as the wirepuller in the wings."[33]

In other words, although Rauh would have liked to have won all of the credentials challenges, Georgia was the one to focus on because it had the most potential as a media story—and, more specifically, as a televisual story. Maddox was an easy villain. The segregationist fried-chicken restaurateur had defied the Civil Rights Act by chasing Blacks from his establishment with a pistol in one hand and an axe handle in the other. He was a rube and completely unqualified to be governor, a sort of George Wallace manqué. What Bond had going for him, in addition to political savvy, was a great backstory and terrific charisma. Charles Negaro, a pro-McCarthy lawyer who worked on the Georgia challenge, said that "this delegation was unique . . . because it had the greatest sort of public relations going in this guy, whom the news people love and who is just extremely sharp and articulate: it could really capture the hearts of America." He ecstatically added, "Bond was the Fannie Lou Hamer of 1968! He became a television idol overnight."[34]

This assessment was all exactly right, and at the same time needs unpacking. To begin with, Bond was the first Black politician elected to the Georgia House of Representatives since Reconstruction. Following his election in 1965, the Georgia legislature voted not to seat him. Their official complaint against Bond was that he had endorsed a Student Nonviolent Coordinating Committee (SNCC) statement opposing the war in Vietnam, and he had expressed support for draft resistors. Therefore, they reasoned, he could not hold an office in which he swore to uphold the Georgia State and US Constitutions. Bond had also been a cofounder of and communications director for SNCC, an organization that Georgia segregationists opposed, to say the least. Bottom line: the Georgia legislators didn't want to seat him because he was Black and, to them, a radical. As Bond later explained, "They threw me out and called a new election. I ran in that election. I won that election. They threw me out again. And then another election was set for November of that year. I ran three elections in that year and a half."[35] Bond was finally seated after his case went all the way to the Supreme Court, which unanimously ruled in his favor, arguing that the Georgia House of Representatives had violated Bond's free speech rights.

For white liberals outside of Georgia, Bond's story was both disturbing and reassuring. Disturbing because it showed the vicious tenaciousness of racism. Reassuring because it showed that you could work within the system to fix things. Bond had followed proper legal channels and been elected to public office. Whereas others called for revolution, he called for systemic reform—though of course many Georgians found that revolutionary. He was also young and handsome. He wore his hair short, was slim, and looked good in a suit. In 1964, he had even been a model for a Royal Crown Cola poster campaign targeting Black businesses.[36] Even arch-conservative William F. Buckley Jr., no friend of SNCC, saw Bond as a symbol of Black achievement and often made positive references to Bond along those lines on *Firing Line*.[37] When Negaro said that in Chicago Bond had "become a television hero overnight," he was not exaggerating.

The comparison to Hamer is on the surface strange. She was stocky, middle-aged, and uneducated. Bond was the son of a university president, had enrolled at Morehouse College, dropped out to fight Jim Crow, and in 1971 returned to complete his undergraduate degree. He spoke like a polished politician. These were very different types, but both played well on TV. From the political strategists' perspective, Bond was the perfect face to represent the Georgia challenging delegates. The networks cut to interviews with him repeatedly throughout the first night, asking him respectful questions, which is worth noting in particular, because Hamer was virtually ignored. NBC's John Chancellor interviewed her only briefly, on the topic of the seating of the Mississippi challengers. He said, "Mrs. Hamer, you're not a great sophisticated political observer, but then most people who are watching are not either. How has the Democratic Party changed? What brought this about in these four years?" She responded that much had not changed, insofar as the white Mississippi delegates had done the same thing they did in 1964. It was a sophisticated political observation, even though Chancellor had set her up as a simpleton.

Bond got the opposite treatment: he was treated like a real player. As the evening unfolded, the battle to seat his Georgia Loyal National Democrats was a drama that slowly accelerated, and then finally gained momentum. At 9:20 p.m., Bond complained to an NBC correspondent that he and his group had only been given gallery passes: "We have to sit up in what they used to call in Jim Crow theaters the Buzzard Roost. The regulars on the other hand are down there on the floor." An hour-and-a-half later, as delegates voted on a motion to defer voting on the challenging delegations until the next day, the Wisconsin delegates used their brief moment in the spotlight to announce that they were inviting Bond and his delegation to come sit with them. And then they voted for the deferral. A loud cheer went up for both the invitation to Bond and for the Wisconsin vote. This was a classic moment of the idealists displaying their resistance to the realists for home TV viewers—all in support of the outsiders. Chet Huntley jumped in to predict that the deferral would fail, meaning that "we are going to be here until a rather late hour."

By 11:00 Bond and his delegates had made it down from the Buzzard Roost onto the floor, but security had arrived to take them out. The crush of people was so extreme that CBS couldn't get a camera near Bond, but the mounted cameras with zoom lenses could spot his head moving through the crowd, and at one point his body pushed flat against the wall, like a man riding an amusement park Gravitron against his will. At this point Mississippi stepped up and offered seats.

David Brinkley slyly offered, "So, this is a question not really of legality or authenticity or voting power. It is simply a question of *chairs*, and who gets them." John Hart of CBS reported to Cronkite, "So what you have here, Walter, is really squatter's rights."

By 11:45, the decision had been made to split the Georgia vote, so both the regulars and challengers were seated, but with only half a vote per delegate. Then the question became not only about the availability of physical chairs, but also about whether the regulars would allow the challengers to use their microphone. By midnight the regular Georgia delegates had confirmed that they would not, in fact, share the microphone. The primal power battles of the entire convention were concentrated exactly here: power was concrete, not abstract—a battle for *things*, for phones, for transportation, for chairs, for microphones.

By 12:45 a.m., the Texas challengers had lost their case, and Huntley explained, "We're probably not even halfway through the action on the report of the credentials committee." So the best-case scenario was that the convention would adjourn around 5:00 a.m., according to NBC. As the clock neared 1 a.m., the convention geared up for a more radical vote on Georgia, to decide on whether or not to overturn the credentials committee recommendation by *not only seating* all the challengers *but also ejecting* the Georgia regulars, as had happened with Mississippi. At this point, unexpectedly, Huntley reported that the police had used mace and tear gas to clear Lincoln Park of hippies and Yippies, but no images were available to show what happened. Meanwhile, activity had gone dead on the floor while Pennsylvania and Louisiana votes were re-counted on a motion that had already been passed. "While we are waiting," Huntley griped, "The total hours of lost sleep involving about 8,500 people and the rest of us must be monumental."

NBC's Sander Vanocur interviewed Connally, who seemed happy to hear himself speak. Connally was a pro. He had lost on the unit rule but defeated the challenging Black and Mexican American Texas delegation. Now he could power through the rest of the night fueled by nothing but a Thermos of Folgers coffee and a few packs of Pall Mall cigarettes.[38] He seemed to have all the time in the world to answer questions. Just moments later Vanocur's colleague John Chancellor reported being rebuffed by Mayor Daley, who, in stark contrast to Governor Connally, refused to go on television.

Meanwhile over at CBS, Cronkite was reaffirming his old nickname: Iron Pants. He was in the chair, and he would report to the bitter end, with no gripes. Huntley and Brinkley could make jokes about lost sleep and the search for chairs, but Cronkite was nothing but business. Cronkite had anchored CBS coverage of the Republican and Democratic conventions for the first time, both in Chicago, back in 1952. He had also covered NASA's Gemini missions for days at a time. CBS News had been on for fifty-five hours straight after the Kennedy assassination, with Cronkite on air most of that time.[39] He sometimes seemed superhuman, though the Chicago anchor booth design did confirm he was mortal: CBS included a discrete chemical toilet in their blueprints.

Finally at 1:00 a.m., the persistence of the CBS team paid off with a small, breaking story from the floor. John Hart had managed to fight his way through the dense crowd and ask Mayor Daley how the convention was going. It was Daley's first appearance on camera since his official welcoming address five hours earlier. Hart's question was pretty softball, and it was not unreasonable to expect the Mayor of Chicago, who was also chair of the Illinois delegation, to share a few thoughts on how things were going at "his" convention (as he understood it) in "his" city. But Daley refused to make eye contact with Hart, hid behind thick glasses, and pretended to read some documents, offering the observation that the décor and carpeting in the convention hall were impressive, creating a "fine color scheme for color television." This bizarre response was meant to show righteous contempt for the news media but made Daley look like a poor sport, if not completely unhinged. Hart then pointedly asked the mayor what he thought about the criticisms of excessive security at the convention. Daley simply looked down at his papers and refused to speak. Hart concluded, "The mayor is obviously irritated with the criticism he has received." So much for the breaking story.

"We're Taking Casualties!" Day One Goes Down in Flames

Finally, at 1:30 in the morning, CBS and NBC had footage of the disturbance in the street that they had described earlier. It was bad. The protestors were running, and police were chasing and clubbing them. At one point, a shot is abruptly cut short, seemingly because a police officer has attacked the cameraman. A swish pan reveals a man wandering past the camera in a state of shock, with blood running down his face. This is CBS cameraman Del Hall, who was clubbed in the face by the police and ended up at the hospital getting stitches. Hall had worked in dangerous conditions before. He had been chased by Klansmen, and he had filmed the 1967 riots in Detroit, where he felt that police and National Guardsmen had his back.[40] To be targeted for physical attack by police was new to him in Chicago, he later said.

The sequence showing the wounded cameraman is short, but even so it reveals a chaotic situation. Hall had been struck with a billy club because he was filming, and he is generally considered the first member of the press corps to have been beaten by police at the convention. It's impossible to prove and seems unlikely. In the *Walker Report*, another cameraman (NBC's Jim Strickland, not identified in the report) tells how on the first night of the convention a policeman struck him in the mouth with a club, knocking out a tooth. As he tries to flee, he spots a man holding a CBS camera (apparently Hall), bleeding from the head. Police were running around screaming, "Get their fucking cameras!"[41] CBS correspondent Jack Laurence shouted, "We're taking casualties!" but his exclamation (not to mention the police f-bombs) did not reach the final cut shown on TV.[42] Laurence, who covered Vietnam for CBS from 1965 to 1970, was instinctively reverting to his combat mindset, giving some indication of the intensity of the situation.

On the one hand, CBS and NBC could not ignore that this was a genuine news story. Cronkite took extra care to note that CBS's man Hall was in good condition, adding that the report about the violence that they had just seen had been prepared by Laurence, but "was delayed by the communications workers strike" and by the fact that Daley had seen to it that there would be no live coverage outside the Amphitheatre. It was a point he had already made several times, but like a dog with a bone, he was not dropping it. Cronkite wanted to report this story, and all the other stories.

On the other hand, it was not a story that management was thrilled about. Laurence's report was previewed by only one producer, Russ Bensley, who had been seriously wounded just a few months earlier in Danang, following the Battle of Khe Sanh. Bensley did not hesitate to approve the footage for air. But the footage shot by Laurence's team made the police look bad, and this was implicitly frowned upon. As Laurence explained, "No one from the news division or corporate headquarters criticized me to my face about the story, but they took me off the air for at least the next twenty-four hours. I just could not get a camera crew or producer to work with me, although there were stories to be covered everywhere you looked."[43] NBC's Reuven Frank later said, "Up until the serious violence, it was our conscious policy to avoid covering too much of the activities of the demonstrators lest we fall into the trap of doing their advertising for them." Richard Salant of CBS also made a claim about avoiding sensationalism: "We do have a policy about live coverage of disorders and potential disorders. . . . We will not provide such coverage except in extraordinary circumstances."[44] These statements have the ring of public relations: the networks did frequently—if cautiously—cover disorders.

But they were aware that they were seen as manipulable, and they wanted to act responsibly (as they understood the word) in the name of the public service role that they saw themselves playing. The networks didn't want to be played by activists, and were inclined—in Chicago, at least—to under-report violence against them. But their own reporters and cameramen were patently not pandering for media coverage, and that is, in part, why they got it. The newsmen were there to record what happened, not to protest, not to be part of the story, and as far as they were concerned, being beaten meant they were forced into the story, unlike the protestors, who might imagine themselves as creat-

FIGURE 10. The vote is in, and Georgia "regular" delegates are delighted they have not been unseated by Julian Bond's challenging delegation. The image was one of defeat for African Americans and of triumph for white southern Democrats. Segregationists would nonetheless continue to abandon the party for the GOP, which had already become the party where those opposing civil rights felt more welcomed. United Press International, 1968.

ing a media event by virtue of their very presence. That said, the biggest attacks on the first day of the convention had taken place in the afternoon (in Grant Park), and then later in the evening, but were not shown on TV until almost 2:00 a.m. Chicago time, when viewer numbers were low.

Meanwhile, back at the Amphitheatre, the final votes were being taken about whether or not to completely displace the Georgia regulars with the challengers, instead of seating both and dividing the votes in half. It went slowly, but finally at 2:37 a.m. the decisive votes were counted: the Georgia delegates' votes would be split (fig. 10). Though not a resounding defeat for Bond's delegation, it was not the total victory that he and other liberal delegates had hoped for. The crowd went berserk and began a deafening chant, first of "NO! NO!" and then, even louder, "JULIAN BOND! JULIAN BOND!" CBS's Dan Rather man-

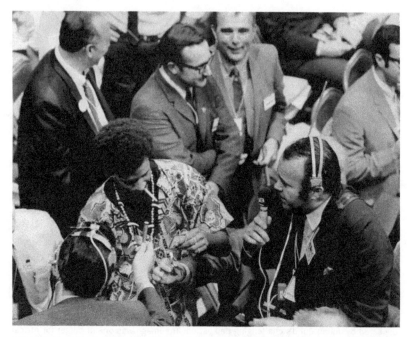

FIGURE 11.   New York delegate Eddie Anderson attempts to burn his credentials card, asking, "If the Democratic Party can't be democratic, I mean, what hope is there for democracy?" The card was not actually flammable, making this a symbolic act, and one that the networks quickly cut to late on the first night of the convention. Field Enterprises, Inc., 1968.

aged to get to Bond first, but just as they started to speak, the camera abruptly cut to a more dramatic image: a member of the New York delegation was attempting to burn his credentials, the identification card that all the delegates and journalists had to wear on the floor.

The young man was striking, tall, Black, with an Afro, wearing a dashiki and beads, cutting an altogether different figure from Julian Bond (fig. 11). CBS's Mike Wallace asked him who he was and what he was doing, as the crowd chanted around him with raised fists. His response is worth recounting at length:

I used to have a lot of faith in the democratic process. This just reaffirms to me the racist nature of this country. If the Democratic Party can't be democratic, I mean, what hope is there for democracy? My name is Eddie Anderson. I'm at UCLA. I'm a senior in philosophy. I decided to burn it as the overwhelming majority rejected the minority report [i.e., voted against seating only Bond's group]. This is my way of protesting. . . . The Democratic Party, they're still talking about "minority" people. They don't even realize that colored people are the majority in the world. From Texas, they kept talking about "our Negroes," as if they still *protect Negroes* in Texas. The whole rhetoric, the whole phraseology, I just can't take it. I might be back tomorrow.

So much exhaustion and frustration is bundled up here. And yet Eddie Anderson, who "just can't take it," still "might be back tomorrow." He's an outsider, but maybe he's also an idealist. He hasn't quite given up.

But the men who control the convention—Daley, the men on the dais, the realists—they have given up. The business is not done for the night, but it is impossible to seize control of the crowd. The convention is unexpectedly adjourned until 6:00 p.m. the next day. The exhausted delegates file out, to be loaded onto buses, as the network anchormen quickly summarize the events of the preceding seven hours. Home viewers had seen a few things on this first day. The idealists and the outsiders had made their cases and mostly lost—only the Mississippi challengers had been seated. They had won a small victory because millions of TV viewers had witnessed their struggles, but the networks had not dug into all the details, and many would have missed the political valence of the finer procedural points. The realists had lost control of the entire event, which viewers could not have failed to discern, even if they didn't make it to the bitter end of the broadcast day. The schedule for the next day promised to show the debate over the party platform. Could Tuesday's proceedings be any more difficult than Monday's credentials battles? The key issue up for debate was Vietnam.

Chapter Three Day Two

"We filibustered with Tweedledee and Tweedledum matters until the American people had gone to bed."

The first day of the convention had been scheduled to cover ground both procedural and inspirational. On the procedural front, the majority reports of the credentials and rules committees would be voted on. On the inspirational front, a keynote would set the tone for the week. After a closing benediction, the delegates would disperse for political strategizing and, no doubt, the sort of boozing and revelry that characterize most conventions, political or otherwise.

Of course, it didn't go that way. Everything fell apart at 2:45 in the morning when the vote went against Julian Bond's group controlling all the Georgia votes. There was no closing benediction. Delegates tried to stomp out angrily, only to have the drama deflated by the fact that they could only exit slowly, in single file, as they punched their credentials cards into the security boxes, creating a bottleneck for the more than five thousand delegates and alternates. They filed onto chartered buses and finally ended up back at their hotels, five miles away, at 3:45.

Tuesday seemed to offer a new beginning. The opening benediction was from Billy Graham, and then Anita Bryant followed with a lung-busting rendition of the National Anthem. Anyone who had been offended by Aretha Franklin's soul version the day before would be placated by this version, which was about as middle-of-the-road as it could get. Mayor Daley next suggested that Anita lead the room in singing "Happy Birthday" to the president, as large plastic candles suddenly rose mechanically from hidden recesses around the rostrum, transforming it into a giant synthetic birthday cake. Marilyn Monroe's sultry version for JFK had once left people gasping for air. This was the cold-shower version, a real eardrum pounder. Finally, as the icing on the plastic cake, Bryant closed with a song she claimed to be LBJ's favorite, "The Battle Hymn of the Republic," which she dedicated to our boys fighting in Vietnam.

It all made for a patriotic and rousing setup for the day. Cronkite noted that Bryant and Graham had also appeared at the RNC in Miami, and it's not unlikely that the DNC programmed them in Chicago to appeal to the more conservative delegates. This of course points to some of the political complexities of the time, with liberal Republicans to the left of some Democrats, and Dixiecrats to the right of some Republicans. In light of those complexities, it's not surprising the Chicago delegates were so contentious, and it's all the more remarkable that the GOP had been able to maintain tight control in Miami.

In theory, on Tuesday all the Democrats had to do was finish up the procedural stuff from the preceding day, and then the temporary chairman, Sen. Daniel K. Inouye, would step down, the permanent convention chairman, Carl Albert, would give a rousing speech, and the party could at last head into a spirited Vietnam debate. At this point, the convention would be past the logistical details, and delegates could roll up their sleeves and get to work finalizing a platform that night and choosing a presidential candidate the next day. This was why they were there, after all. This was what the heavy lifting of the convention was supposed to entail.

But this picture of "the heavy lifting of the convention" was not one that anyone who organized or participated in the Democratic convention in Chicago—much less the Republican convention in Miami—actually understood to be truly accurate. The image of a political convention is that it is a place where TV viewers at home can see democracy in action. A convention should reassure us that the two-party system is a fine system, that the devising of a party platform allows earnest men and women to disagree but ultimately forge compromises, and that the choice of candidate fairly expresses the will of the majority of the party, as represented by the delegates. This idealized understanding of what a convention does, that it performs a spectacle of democracy that may or may not include actual democratic elements, is a product of the network TV era. A cynical viewer would discern that the tidiness in Miami had been too good to be true. Any viewer could see that the democratic process was coming unglued in Chicago.

The parties had come to understand their conventions as public relations events, and yet the network news divisions did not like to think of themselves as servants to the Democrats and Republicans. The bald truth was that every four years the networks were covering an event largely organized by the parties for their cameras. And yet anchormen and floor correspondents asked probing questions, searched for breaking stories, and tried to cover conventions as *news*. These were not purely "pseudo-events," as Daniel Boorstin once put it—occasions staged specifically as publicity to gain news coverage.[1] The conventions really did conclude with the official choice of a candidate and the finalizing of a political platform; they weren't *just* theater, as they are today, when candidates have been decided via the primary process before the conventions. Back in 1968, the conventions were more than scripted events for preselected candidates, but as far as the parties (or at least the powerful players at the top, the realists) were concerned, they would *ideally* be mostly theater. The authors of one book on the 1968 campaign summarized it nicely: "The tendency in most post-electronic conventions has been to push controversy farther out of sight—i.e., deeper into the caucuses. Intraparty strife abhors the light. Thus, the convention that the nation views on its TV screens has, at least until the final balloting, precious little to do with the real action.... All the important struggles take place off-stage." They added that "Miami Beach fitted neatly into this pattern. The Democrats in Chicago, of course, were to provide a flagrant exception to the rule."[2]

The Republicans had played their political drama correctly to TV viewers, in other words, by showing their rigor and competence; ratings were not strong because it was boring, but that didn't hurt them in November. The Democrats had failed by airing their dirty laundry in public, but that didn't mean the event was a failure *as TV*, from the perspective of the vast majority of Americans who were not political operatives. On the contrary, notwithstanding the slower procedural bits, and the fact that the networks made some mistakes in how they told their stories, the sheer disaster of Chicago kept people in front of their TVs, regardless of party affiliation. To reiterate: the convention was the top-rated TV event of 1968; 50,500,000 households tuned in to watch the chaos.[3]

Even before the tear gas started to leak into the ventilation systems on Wednesday, the hotels were in chaos and couldn't keep up their regular laundry service for guests. By late Tuesday night a CBS floor reporter told Cronkite, "People are getting angry. The mustard smears are multiplying on the fronts of people's jackets." It seemed like every individual indignity—terrible hot dogs, spilled condiments, tepid coffee, poor transportation, hostile security guards, miserable Amphitheatre acoustics—could function as a synecdoche for the larger disaster of the convention, and, to add insult to injury, it was all being shown live on TV.

Tuesday took the nationally televised failure to a whole new level. On the surface, the problems appeared procedural. The Democrats just couldn't get all the voting finished up and move on to the actual business of the convention. That was one way that the networks told the story, as implicitly one of ineptitude. The other side to the TV narrative was that all of the slow, seemingly endless voting was deliberate stalling on the delegates' part, as they dredged up support for McCarthy or for a Kennedy draft. What sometimes looked like dead airtime at home was actually a frenzy of politicking behind the scenes by the idealists eager for an alternative to Humphrey, or at least to his Vietnam plank. Meanwhile, the outsiders, the people of color, were still waging credentials battles, which to them was a fight against white supremacy. The networks saw the ineptitude and stalled voting but were deaf to the importance of the white supremacy story. Black viewers at home were of course more likely to pick up on this underreported angle on both Monday and Tuesday.

One difference was clear, though. On Tuesday the police brutality in the streets was at a lower pitch than it had been the day before, and the action outside was barely reported by NBC and not at all reported by CBS. If you were a cranky Democratic operative trying to take a potshot at the media for the convention's problems, you couldn't blame the crises of day two on protestors outside, or on TV coverage of those protestors. On this day, Daley could feel that his efforts to eliminate live coverage outside of the Amphitheatre were paying off. The TV news blackout in the streets was almost total. The irony was that by trapping the networks inside the Amphitheatre on Tuesday, "Mr. Democrat" succeeded only in showing the party's abject failure to get its work done. There were a few notable moments of hostility on the floor, some of it physical, but Tuesday as shown on TV was mostly about waiting, voting, caucusing, and waiting some more. A lot was going on, but it didn't always look like much.

By looking critically at the approach the networks took to Tuesday night's coverage, one can see how the party failed to stage-manage its convention, and also how the news tried, with uneven success, to make sense of the chaos, the boredom, the stalling, and the shouting. Through it all, they strove to narrate the event in a way that would be engaging and informative for viewers, while also maintaining their professional notions of fairness, even when they provided analysis that made evaluative judgments. It was a tricky balancing act, made harder by the fact that several professional biases—internalized norms, if you will—shaped coverage in a way that limited stories.

There were three key professional norms of particular relevance on Tuesday night. First, the networks had a limited idea of what constituted a good convention story; they tended to look for telegenic heroes and villains and easy-to-tell dramas. Second, the networks were responsive to the dais and the official program, even as they did note the party's failure to maintain order and stick to their schedule; this tacit subservience to convention organizers often kept the networks from framing stories in ways that could have deepened context for viewers. For example, the Alabama delegate challenge could have been understood as a manifestation of the crisis of white supremacy but got more rhetorical traction as a procedural issue, which was how the convention organizers (the realists) understood it up on the rostrum—as a

"Tweedledee and Tweedledum" matter, as one delegate dismissively put it. Third, when in doubt, the networks reverted to horse-race reporting, a standard approach for covering election politics: who was running, who was ahead, who was behind? This scorekeeping prevented newsmen from pursuing other kinds of stories, especially those of importance to the outsiders. Perhaps the best way to make sense of the day is to break it down into a series of specific crises.

The Crisis of Staging for Television

Huntley opened Tuesday with a carefully scripted, somber assessment conveying NBC's setup of the tone for the day:

> Conventions can have, and indeed they do have, moods and a temperament. Delegates, even those who've been through it all many times, live out a convention in a state of emotional, physical, and psychological supercharge. They frequently may be detected actually *waiting* for their emotions to be aroused, and a good convention is frequently one that runs the gamut from laughter, through anger, to tears. Two weeks ago the mood of the Republicans in Miami Beach was something like that of a good natured, harmonious, and insouciant crowd at a well-heeled picnic. But this one is different. There are *angry* Democrats here, and the action is really just beginning. There are *disappointed* Democrats here. There are *aggressive* Democrats, *apprehensive* Democrats. In short, there are not many if any *completely happy* Democrats here. Chicago is not a fun city. And when the convention band strikes up "Happy Days Are Here Again" I would predict there's going to be no massive group singing from the audience. In view of the mood of this convention, if you try real hard you may understand the action of the Democratic National Committee when it heard, seconded, and adopted a motion to prohibit the use of ice in all the soft drinks to be served in this convention hall. No one was going to be permitted or tempted to hurl ice cubes at the Chairman, at newsmen, or other delegates.

Huntley's harsh words could not have been well received by top party operatives, or by the president, watching at his Texas ranch. Huntley did not describe a party in control of its televised image, and he was correct. There was no discernable "bias" here, liberal or otherwise. To fully understand what is going on here, it helps to start with the anchorman's background.

Huntley grew up on a sheep and cattle ranch in Cardwell, Montana, a relevant fact insofar as the growing conservative refrain after the convention and into the Nixon years (and beyond) was that the networks were packed with eastern establishment elites, which could not have been further from the truth. Like the legendary Edward R. Murrow (who hailed originally from Polecat Creek, North Carolina), Huntley did not come from a moneyed background or pursue an Ivy League education. Also like Murrow, he came to broadcasting via drama and radio, not from a newspaper career. This was unusual. Cronkite began his career as a war correspondent for the United Press International (UPI) wire service. Dan Rather started out at the Associated Press and later also worked for UPI, and then the *Houston Chronicle*. Both Rather and Cronkite had radio jobs, like Huntley, before they came to TV, but Huntley was a little different. He was a great anchorman but didn't have the investigative chops of many others in the TV news business, or significant experience in writing copy fast on deadline. During the regular *Huntley-Brinkley* broadcasts, Brinkley wrote and reported stories on the Washington beat, while Huntley read stories in New York City. He was smart, he was quick, and he had the looks and voice for TV, but he didn't have deep background in rooting out stories. When nothing seemed to be happening on the convention floor later on Tuesday night, Huntley did not push harder to pursue a story, such as the ongoing crisis for Black regular and challenging delegates.

Another helpful thing to know about Huntley is that when he came to NBC in 1955 "he was known as a fearless liberal" who, as a radio commentator, had "said nice things about the United Nations and criticized [Sen. Joseph] McCarthy."[4] He had survived right-wing accusations that he was a communist, and was hired by NBC for straight news work, not commentary. Viewers of the *Huntley–Brinkley Report* might have been aware that Huntley had a reputation as a liberal off-camera, but for the most part, there was little evidence of that on-screen. In fact, "liberal" and "conservative" are tricky descriptors for a man who started in radio in the 1930s and continued on TV until 1970. The meaning of these political labels changed very much over that period and, indeed, has changed a great deal since then. The GOP had a strong moderate wing in the 1950s and '60s, for example, yet by the time Ronald Reagan was elected in 1980, both political parties had shifted right, and Reagan became the "new normal" of conservatism. So when we say that Huntley had a reputation for "liberalism," we need to ask what that might have meant to TV viewers in 1968. For his own part, Huntley described himself on *The Dick Cavett Show* in 1970 as an "arch conservative" on economic issues, and yet, he added, "in terms of humanity, in terms of human beings, and the racial issue, I suppose I'm a screaming liberal." He added that he was concerned about environmental conservation, which he couldn't peg as a conservative or liberal issue.[5]

This brings us back to Huntley's introduction on Tuesday night. Notwithstanding later attacks on both NBC and CBS for "liberal bias" during the convention, Huntley's opening was a merciless takedown of the Democrats. And it was fair. His description of Democrats—as angry, aggressive, apprehensive, disappointed, and, above all, unhappy—did not show any kind of "bias" per se for or against the party. With so much TV news clearly politically slanted in the twenty-first century, it is useful to recall that in the network days, anchors and reporters not only did not slant the news toward their own political beliefs, they actively produced analysis that supported "the other side" when they thought that analysis was accurate. That Huntley personally leaned liberal was irrelevant when it came time to describe the Democratic Party's abject failures in Chicago.

If Huntley for one moment veered from objectivity in his kick-off analysis, it was only with a little closing joke. The anchorman chuckled and offered a naughty smile when he speculated that if armed with ice, some of the delegates would surely express their frustrations by pinging the network newsmen. Huntley was "somber, distant, and, in Brinkley's words, 'relentlessly serious,'"[6] so a discreet chuckle from him was the equivalent of a guffaw from Cronkite. A little smile was as "subjective" as he was going to get on the air. It was normally Brinkley who was known for his wisecracks. LBJ thought he was a real "smart ass."[7] If even Huntley was being a little bit of a smart ass on Tuesday night, things had truly gone awry for the Democratic machine.

The crisis in the opening moments of day two in Chicago, then, was not one of journalistic bias or insobriety, or even the wider challenge of liberals and conservatives battling to take control of the White House. Rather, the crisis was one implicit in Huntley's comments, a crisis specifically facing a number of key party players: the top hierarchy of the Democratic Party, in particular the DNC director, treasurer, and LBJ operative John Criswell; Richard Daley and LBJ, in many ways the puppet masters of the convention; and party operatives such as the chairmen of the credentials, rules, and platform committees. The crisis was one of thwarted intentions. The intention of the party machine was to stage a three-part show for TV. First, they would promote all that Presidents Kennedy and Johnson had accomplished since 1960. Second, they would make speeches denouncing Nixon and the Republicans, and indicating what a disaster it would be to have the GOP in the White House. Third, by virtue of all this, they would set the stage for the nomination of Hubert Humphrey, the candidate desired by the machine.

This was all standard operating procedure for televised political conventions: promote yourself, attack the other guy. Yet it was painfully clear that the party had failed to promote itself in any kind of positive way. Huntley could objectively point out that "the action" at the convention was "really just beginning," and yet already the assembled Democrats were angry, dispirited, and hopeless. As a public relations gambit, the thing was a failure before permanent chairman Carl Albert had even been handed the gavel. In striking contrast, Huntley had also noted the "good natured, harmonious, and insouciant crowd" in Miami. Richard Nixon was one of the least insouciant characters you could ever hope to meet in political life. But in terms of image, the analysis was spot on. It was a reversal of 1964 when, as reported in the *New Republic*, viewers had been "disquieted over what they'd seen on TV, . . . the chorus of boos that drowned out Governor Nelson Rockefeller's speech [and] the antagonism toward the press" from Goldwater supporters.[8] The Democrats had staged their show for TV much better that year. Clearly, the roles were reversed and amplified in 1968.

The demographics of the delegates had not significantly changed, though. Everyone knew that Republicans were more "well heeled" than Democrats, as Huntley put it, and the networks shared employment and income data of delegates (in brief, more lawyers in Miami, more teachers in Chicago) to illustrate the point. Miami TV coverage had opened with a profile of Nelson Rockefeller's wife, Happy, casually strolling past an Alexander Calder sculpture on the family's four-thousand-acre family compound. Brinkley commented on the magnificent beachfront hotels, adding gleefully "there's a hotel down there, Chet, that spends two thousand dollars a week for whipped cream!" A reception at the Americana Hotel featured "huge mounds of shrimp." The GOP didn't specifically want to portray themselves as the party of luxury, but this sort of breathless coverage was a win for them insofar as the convention did seem like a fun (if not altogether "insouciant") affair.

As for the idea that the convention was "harmonious," well, it certainly was, as portrayed on TV. Nixon cut his deal—the "Southern Strategy"—with South Carolina Sen. Strom Thurmond in private.[9] Nixon would go easy on enforcing civil rights legislation. He would put a southerner on the Supreme Court. And he would select a vice-presidential candidate that Thurmond and his cohort approved of. So whereas on TV Republican delegates opined that Nelson Rockefeller or John Lindsay might make a fine vice-presidential nominee, a wonderful way to keep moderate Republicans on board with Nixon, off-camera the deal had already been struck, and it was unthinkable that either of these men would be on the ticket.

Of course, the Democrats in Chicago also brokered deals far from the probing eye of the cameras. But it looked like they were fighting over everything out in the open on the convention floor. We should not conclude that the Democrats had failed on TV without adding one key note of clarification: it was the Democratic *establishment* forces (the realists) who had failed. Cronkite explained over and over again that the story of the convention was the story of the establishment forces versus the McCarthy forces (the idealists). In other words, the top party players were determined to both affirm the president's policies and nominate Humphrey. This "establishment" was not necessarily representative of the Democratic majority across America. Humphrey had not run in a single primary, and many pro-establishment delegates had been selected so long before the convention (up to two years in some cases) that it was difficult to see them as fairly representative of national Democratic support.

Supporters of McCarthy (and later of a Ted Kennedy draft) were advocating for an "open convention" in which genuine political debate could occur and Humphrey was not the preordained winner. They noted that the undemocratic selection of delegates had in some cases worked strongly against McCarthy delegates, while also disenfranchising African American voters. McCarthy supporter Allard Lowenstein, the brains behind the "Dump Johnson" movement, was also the man behind the "Coalition for an Open Convention," which had met in Chicago in June to pass a resolution opposing Humphrey.

By Tuesday night, the idealists had dug in their heels by derailing the schedule. The floor vote about the Alabama issue, which we will turn to shortly, was technically lost by vote count around 8:00. Yet the New York delegates had left the floor to caucus on Alabama, and it was impossible to officially finalize the voting until they returned an hour-and-a-half later. They might have really been caucusing about Alabama, but it was more likely that they were deliberately stalling the schedule, seizing time to strategize how to push back against the pro-Humphrey forces regarding the Vietnam platform debate scheduled for later that night, or strategizing for the candidate selection scheduled for the next day. If you were watching TV at home, it was hard to make sense of it all. Huntley and Brinkley didn't help much, but Cronkite gave viewers a story they could hang onto.

As a narrative strategy, the notion of two key players, the establishment (pro-Humphrey) forces and anti-establishment (pro-McCarthy) forces, was extremely useful for Cronkite. When endless procedural votes pulled TV viewers without PhDs in political science deep into the weeds, the anchorman could explain that voting yes on a certain item that seemed to have nothing to do with Humphrey was in reality "a vote for the establishment" and thus a sign of support for the would-be nominee. Likewise, when we say that the establishment forces lost control of the staging of their convention and the televised image of their party, we need to note the flipside of what was happening. The anti-establishment Democrats in support of McCarthy, of the challenging delegations, and of an immediate stop to the bombing in Vietnam were *absolutely winning* when it came to TV coverage, precisely because the cameras showed the endless delays and floor votes and shouting from both the floor and the rostrum.

Chairman Carl Albert finally took the stage for the first time shortly before 10:00 p.m. on Tuesday and gave a miserable speech. He opened by declaring, "this is an open convention, and we hope to keep it open until its business is finished." Everyone in the room knew this was untrue: Albert and his compatriots had no intention of allowing a dove platform to pass or for anyone besides Humphrey to be nominated. With the cards stacked against them, one of the most important tools the pro-peace, anti-Humphrey crowd had was the presence of the TV cameras. America *saw* the establishment Democrats working to suppress the democratic process at their own convention. Tuesday would offer multiple opportunities for TV to show what the anti-establishment delegates were fighting for. There would be the Alabama delegate crisis, security issues on the floor, the Kennedy draft crisis, and, for the networks in particular, the crisis of dead airtime.

Running through it all was the crisis of Black disenfranchisement. The networks declined to sink their teeth into that dilemma, but it is a story that can be reconstructed by digging into the images that the networks offered, reading between the lines, and providing some of the context that CBS and NBC neglected.

The Alabama Crisis

At a convention with numerous credentials challenges, Alabama presented a particularly complicated situation. The regular delegation sent to Chicago by the Alabama Democratic Party and chaired by Robert Vance was challenged by two groups: David Vann's Alabama Independent Democratic Delegate Party and Dr. John Cashin's National Democratic Party. The former group based its challenge on party loyalty alone and offered to replace any members of the regular delegation who would not take a loyalty oath pledging to support the national party's candidate.[10] The idea was that Vance's alternates could take over for any (probably pro–George Wallace) walkouts, and then Vann's people could step in as the new official alternates. As white racial progressives in Alabama, Vann and Vance were on the same page. Vann had been a key player in removing Bull Connor from power in 1962 and would be elected mayor of Birmingham in 1975.

The national party leaders justifiably assumed that the regular Alabama delegates who did not walk out in protest over the loyalty pledge might vote to nominate Humphrey, but they might still go home and work for Wallace. The oath the national party ultimately demanded was a mild compromise, demanding not loyalty to the national candidate but rather a specific commitment not to work for any candidate *other* than the one selected at the convention, a "non-dis-loyalty" oath, as CBS's Harry Reasoner put it. Alabama had gone for Goldwater in 1964, and there was no reason to believe it would swing any more liberal in 1968. Further, the Alabama Democratic Party was the ultimate arbiter of whether the national candidate would even appear on the state ballot. Following the Dixiecrat walkout of 1948, the States Rights Party candidate (Thurmond) appeared on ballots throughout the South, but the Democratic candidate, Harry Truman, had not even appeared on the Alabama ballot.[11] In 1968, the Democratic Party had no illusions about Humphrey capturing more votes than Wallace in Alabama, but the issue of attempting to maintain national party control remained on the table. What if the people of Alabama were not even allowed the option of voting for Humphrey? That scenario seemed likely. Like Truman in 1948, LBJ had not been an option on the Alabama ballot in 1964. Humphrey ultimately appeared on the ballot as the candidate of the Vann and Cashin challenging groups, not as the candidate of the national party.[12] In sum, one key aspect of the Alabama credentials challenge was its status as an institutional crisis for the party machine.[13] The networks dropped the ball on this story, perhaps seeing it as too complicated for viewers.

There was also the issue of bias—not for or against the Democratic Party, but the bias of professional norms dictating how to tell a good story to the widest possible audience. Georgia had been covered the day before. That story was fairly straightforward and, unlike Alabama's, featured a strong hero, the handsome Julian Bond, and a strong villain, Lester Maddox, who looked like "a three-month-old infant who is mean and bald and wears eyeglasses."[14] Bond was an elected Georgia state representative, but Cashin was an upstart activist who had never held elected office. The networks frequently referred to Cashin as "the Alabama dentist," not inaccurate but a disservice to the man who had almost single-handedly created the National Democratic Party of Alabama, a powerful effort to get Black candidates into office who would otherwise never have been allowed onto the consistently white supremacist ticket of the Alabama Democratic Party. Consider that the icon of the state party, shown in every voting booth from Reconstruction until 1966, was a rooster with a banner over its head reading "White Supremacy."[15] Illiteracy rates were so high in Alabama that Cashin's party had to come up with a new icon so that Black voters who might not be able to read the names on ballots could be instructed to "Vote the Eagle Party"; Julian Bond, Coretta Scott King, and Ralph Abernathy made an urgent appeal for "the Eagle Party" on Black radio stations.[16]

In Chicago, the Cashin-led delegate challenge was clearly more radical than the Vann challenge. Cashin's group charged that the Alabama regulars had not only a party loyalty problem but also a white supremacy problem. This never blossomed into a fully told story by the networks, who quickly shifted from the details of the challenge to the problem of the time lost during the voting over Alabama and the surge for drafting Ted Kennedy. Cashin was a story for Black viewers; the networks went for the story they understood as having wider appeal. Notably, though, the CBS correspondents' briefing book told an interesting story about how Vance claimed "Cashin will drive the party right back into the hands of the segregationists," and how he was "tired of the convention singling out Alabama as it did in 1964." The briefing book also noted that one of Cashin's would-be delegates argued that "the trouble with both Vance and Vann is that they have not done anything to change the internal party structure in Alabama, which is still Wallace-controlled."[17] There was plenty of good story material here to tap into, and the fact that it's in the briefing book indicates the newsmen were aware of it, but the story of the Cashin challenge simply didn't have the straightforward Manichean drama—and perhaps the mass appeal—of Bond vs. Maddox.

The networks didn't even report on Alabama delegate Eugene "Bull" Connor. At the convention, Connor nominated Daley for vice president and cast his presidential vote for football coach Paul "Bear" Bryant, a symbolic gesture to show Wallace support and to reject the national party's official stance on civil rights. (Although Bryant himself was a moderate on race by southern standards, "his fans made his all-white teams a symbol of white supremacy."[18]) One can safely assume that Connor was one of the many "law and order" types who approved of Daley's heavy-handed security; he had even written an amiable letter to the mayor in June inquiring if his Alabama gun permit would be recognized in Chicago, as he intended to bring his pistol to the convention.[19] Connor wasn't a strong political player at the convention, and yet the presence in Chicago of the man who had turned firehoses and attack dogs on Blacks at the peak of the civil rights movement could have been effectively used by the networks to narrate the Cashin group's challenge to the regular Alabama delegation.

One can take such counterfactuals only so far. We can ask how the networks could have better covered the racial crises at the Chicago convention, but the problem was that they barely saw the importance of that story. Surely Black TV viewers were plugged into this submerged crisis, which sometimes came closer to the surface, but in their desire to reach the *mass* audience as they understood it, the networks let drop material that seemed to them most relevant to "special interest groups."

Interlude: The Crisis of Chloe Breeze

So how might TV viewers have found meaning in stories of Black disenfranchisement that were implied but never fully developed? How might one cobble together the fragments on offer to make sense of the submerged racial crises at the convention on Tuesday? Here is one version of that assemblage, framed by a story that the networks touched on only lightly: the crisis of Black Minnesota delegate Chloe Breeze, who appeared just twice, bookending one hour of CBS coverage. Breeze's story allows a glimpse into the role that Black political power—and also disempowerment and rage—played at the convention. Just two minutes before Breeze's first appearance, a speech is delivered by one of the two Black women who spoke from the dais in Chicago.

At 7:16 p.m., Fannie Lou Hamer ascended to the stage to speak in support of the Cashin delegate challenge. Neither CBS nor NBC showed many speeches in their entirety throughout the entire four days of the convention. Viewers were able to watch Inouye's keynote, most of Chairman Albert's speech, and, finally, the speeches of the nominees, and that was about it. At other times, the networks popped in and out of speeches in progress. Indeed, NBC showed only a fragment from the end of Hamer's speech. To its credit, though, CBS showed the speech in its entirety, either recognizing the importance of sharing this voice with the nation or possibly (a less generous interpretation) recognizing that she was a rousing speaker and would make for good TV.

Hamer appeared in a plain dress with a slightly bulky zipper, without a trace of lipstick, her hair swept elegantly upward. She roared her speech, even though she had a microphone. Hamer was used to addressing crowds without a mic, and she had the lungs for it. Also, she knew that the acoustics were miserable and that most delegates could not clearly hear speeches from the rostrum. Many delegates walked around with small transistor radios to follow the action in which they were supposedly participating. If anyone heard any speech from the dais that night without the aid of a portable radio, though, it would be this one, belted out in full force. Here is that passionate two-minute speech:

> Mr. Chairman, Governor Hughes, I'm here speaking for the National Democratic Party from Alabama. 1964 Fannie Lou Hamer was on the outside trying to get in. We know the long pattern of discrimination, not only in Mississippi but also in the state of Alabama. We also know that Governor Wallace is running today for president of the United States, and he's only pledged as a Democrat in the state of Alabama. It is time for us to wake up America. We always talk about a minority. But we don't even say minority when you carry our sons to fight in Vietnam. [Crowd cheers.] I support Dr. Cashin from Alabama. Because it's time for us to stop pretending that we are loyal but act in a manner that we are. And if we are the Democratic Party of this country, we should stop just giving a tokenism, and seat so many this year, and four years later seat for another delegation. It's time tonight to seat the delegation with the National Democratic Party from Alabama, and that would be Dr. Cashin and his delegation, that represents all the people, not just the few. Representing not only the whites but the Blacks as well. Thank you.

Following the speech, Cronkite briefly explains the role Hamer had played at the 1964 convention before saying, "Mike Wallace is with several of the Negro delegates, disturbed by this Alabama challenge. Let's go to him now."

Wallace is with Cleo Breeze, a Minnesota delegate and Humphrey supporter who is considering walking out with the four other Black members of her delegation if the vote goes against seating Cashin's group. Minnesota is Humphrey's home state, and it would be humiliating for his own delegates to walk out on him. Further, Humphrey had been a key advocate for the civil rights plank at the 1948 convention, when the Dixiecrats had walked out. Truman won anyway, and, as Rick Perlstein explains it, "Democrats were on their way to becoming the party of civil rights. Hubert Humphrey catalyzed that change." Further, as a US senator in 1964, "he was instrumental in passing the landmark Civil Rights Act." Yet that same year, at Johnson's request, and as a sort of audition for the VP slot, he had sold out the MFDP in Atlantic City.[20] And now he was not supporting the Cashin challenge.

So Wallace cuts to the chase and asks, if Breeze walks out, wouldn't that be "a considerable embarrassment to the vice president?" Breeze responds, "I'm very sorry . . . my first concern is for *Black people*." At this point Cronkite intercepts via Wallace's earpiece, asking him to ask Breeze if this had to do with the Negro caucus that met today and if Negro walkouts from other states are likely. So Wallace begins, "Your Negro caucus met today—" but Breeze interrupts with "the *Black* caucus, not the *Negro* caucus, the Black caucus." Wallace smiles and apparently submits: "The Black caucus met today. How many? About three hundred of you?" Breeze responds, "It was beautiful. Maybe three hundred, three hundred and fifty." Wallace then asks, "Now is it conceivable that a good many Negro delegates from various states are going to walk out if indeed the voting continues this way?" and Breeze responds, "It, it could be, but I don't know. I'm just right now, I'm just familiar with Minnesota, the Black delegates of Minnesota." Wallace passes off to Cronkite, and Breeze moves away, head down. What a demoralizing moment for her. Wallace could have learned about the Black caucus meeting, but he doesn't work to get a good interview, even reverting to "Negro" after having said "Black" once. It's particularly disappointing considering how few women are interviewed during the entire four days. If you remove the puff-piece interviews with the candidate's wives, you could count the remainder on one hand.

Next comes CBS's only interview with Dr. Cashin. The questioner is Hal Walker, CBS's first Black correspondent. Walker had won a local Emmy for anchoring *A Dialogue with Whitey*, an hour-long documentary aired on CBS's Washington, DC, affiliate, WTOP, about the riots following King's death.[21] He opens by observing that the Black caucus has endorsed Rev. Channing Phillips as presidential nominee and asks Cashin if he endorses the idea. Cashin is caught off guard and responds, "I did not know that they had released this to the press, but if it has been released, yes indeed I do. I feel that it is quite important for Black people to see their leaders are trying to go for the very best at the very top."

Walker is off to a good start here, having found some still-off-the-record information about the Phillips nomination and having gotten his subject to open up. The Phillips movement was a symbolic one, but it was important. Though a completely forgotten political figure today, he was the first African American placed in nomination for the presidency by the Democratic Party (fig. 12). *Jet* magazine described the nomination as "a unique method of protest but actually an act of frustration."[22] It would have been ideal at this point for Walker to have asked Cashin about his Alabama delegate challenge, but Cronkite interrupts with a breaking story on the floor, and we never return to Cashin. The Walker interview was taped earlier, and CBS could have cut back to it at any point later, but they let it go.

Next, instead, follows one of the most famous moments of the Chicago convention. Chaos is rising among the regular Georgia delegates, some of whom are walking out in protest over sharing votes with the Bond delegation. They have tried to bring the Georgia standard with them, but the banner has been retrieved and returned to the Georgia section. This was a moment of white rage. One of the first CBS interviews on Tuesday, a few hours earlier, had been with a Georgia delegate who said he would not sit next to anyone who advocated burning draft cards or "doing away with one or the other of the races," adding that Julian Bond's objective was to "make every twenty-year-old Negro woman marry a white man." This was a rare, overtly racist comment

FIGURE 12. Rev. Channing Phillips was the first African American nominated for president by the Democratic Party. This fact was referenced by the networks, yet he received hardly any on-camera interview time. Floor reporters under-covered the convention's racial crises, focusing instead on horse-race narratives and on the possibility of Teddy Kennedy being drafted as a candidate. Associated Press, 1968.

at the convention, as most delegates censored themselves for national TV. When departing Georgia delegates tried to take their banner with them, it was to make the point that Bond's delegation did not represent Georgia because a mixed-race delegation was an abomination.

So the standard was returned, but the delegates again started to push their way out, as Dan Rather pulled himself into the crushing current of people and tried to ask questions. Suddenly he was on the floor, punched in the gut. Here's the follow-up that ensued with Cronkite, once Rather was able to get to his feet.

RATHER: This is the kind of thing that's been happening outside the hall, but this is the first time we've had it happen inside the hall. . . . I'm sorry to be out of breath, but somebody belted me in the stomach during all of that. . . . Security people, as you can see, put me on the deck. I didn't do very well.

CRONKITE: I think we've got a bunch of thugs here, Dan. If I may be permitted to say so.

RATHER: Mind you Walter, I'm alright. It's all in a day's work.

CRONKITE: Well, I saw that performance, and it didn't look very good from here, I'll tell you that. Thank you Dan for staying in there, pitching despite every handicap that they can possibly put our way from free flow of information at this Democratic National Convention.

Cronkite has lost his cool for a moment, and he's not comfortable with that. He changes the subject and says that temporary chairman Inouye is about to call for the hearing of the majority reports on the Alabama challenge.

The camera briefly shows Alabama chairman Robert Vance at the podium explaining that "the rules governing the [Alabama delegate] primary were the least restrictive in modern history." Neither NBC nor CBS reported what had actually happened with delegate selection in Alabama. In brief, Vance had managed to arrive with three Black delegates (two regulars and one alternate) because he made sure that they were the only candidates to choose from on their ballots. The only way

Alabama Blacks could find meager representation at the DNC was with a liberal white helpmate who in effect fixed the ballot for them. It was a start but hardly an auspicious one for the disenfranchised Blacks of the state.

CBS now cuts back to the anchor booth. Having allowed Rather a moment to catch his breath, Cronkite says, "Dan, when freedom of the press is trampled, nobody is going to defend it but we who work in the press. I think that's part of our job. I lost my temper a moment ago when I saw you roughed up down there. But I'd like to know something about this, a little more." He asks if the people around Rather had been Secret Service, sergeants-at-arms, or perhaps paid guards? Rather explains that none were in uniform, and all had refused to identify themselves. Two men were dragging a Georgia delegate out, with a third serving as a "blocking back." The blocking back told Rather, "Get the hell out of here," and Rather said, "Well, who are you sir?" He responded by pushing Rather and telling him again to get out. When Rather asked the delegate why he was being ejected, the blocking back punched him in the stomach. Rather added that he might have also taken a blow to the back. Cronkite noted, "Dan, quite clearly these people are employed by this convention," and Rather agreed.

The floor was packed with four kinds of security forces: plainclothes policemen, Andy Frain employees (a private agency providing uniformed sergeants-at-arms, some of them gum-chomping, teenybopper girls), uniformed ushers with authority to clear the aisles, and Secret Service agents. The Secret Service men wore sunglasses and earpieces. Hovering immediately over the shoulders of newsmen doing interviews, they looked like G-men straight out of Central Casting. Few of the security people wore uniforms or name badges, and it was hard to get a straight count, but one of them told CBS correspondent Ike Pappas that there was one security person for every three people in the hall. Add to this the metal boxes that attendees had to use to punch into and out of the Amphitheatre, and the fact that there were six different categories of color-coded passes, a different one for each day. Further, there was a shortage of punch-box machines for the delegates, and sep-

FIGURE 13. Dan Rather, moments before he is punched in the gut by one of Daley's "thugs," questioned why a Georgia delegate was being ejected from the hall. Cronkite decried the action, but viewer mail was mixed, with some celebrating the security forces for taking Rather down a notch. The widespread support for Daley against Rather has been largely forgotten. United Press International, 1968.

arate machines were designated for the use of gallery guests, service people, and so on. Plus, there were entry guards doing bag inspection, and all of this happened under the eye of closed-circuit security cameras. You can see why nerves were so frayed by the time Rather was belted (fig. 13).

A handful of celebrity delegate interviews are telling here. Actor Paul Newman said, "All the security makes me very nervous." Cartoonist Jules Feiffer said, "I think I'm probably too depressed to draw anything. I feel as if I'm in 'Prague West.'" Football player Rosey Grier said, "I thought that we were all here for the people, . . . and I feel very hurt, because of all the protection that we're having, . . . it's too much protection, too much keeping people out." That last comment is perhaps most revealing of how heavy-handed security was. Grier had been a bodyguard for Robert F. Kennedy. When RFK was assassinated in June, Grier had been among those who wrestled Sirhan Sirhan to the ground and disarmed him. And then he kept the mob from attacking the assassin. It was understandable that at both the RNC and DNC conventions there was a constant undercurrent of anxiety about possible assassination attempts. In his account of the conventions, Norman Mailer observed politicians flinching in tight crowds, obviously on edge in the wake of RFK's death. But if even a bodyguard for Bobby Kennedy thought that Amphitheatre security was too oppressive, it was too oppressive (fig. 14).

This is useful background for understanding what it must have felt like for everyone, including Rather, to be swept up in the security around that Georgia delegate. And it helps us understand his comment that this is the sort of activity we'd seen outside (Chicago's finest removing their identification badges and beating people, not just *including* but *especially* journalists), but that this was the first instance indoors. Everyone in the Amphitheatre, delegates and newsmen alike, knew that a sucker punch from an anonymous security man was not out of the question if you were standing in the wrong place at the wrong time. From this perspective, Rather getting slugged was news because it might mean that the dam was breaking and that the convention security forces were getting more physical. Mercifully, although Mike Wallace was socked on Wednesday, floor violence remained contained to small incidents. From Cronkite's perspective, though, attempts to suppress the free flow of information in Chicago were intensifying. He continued to report as much, framing the physical attacks as assaults on free speech. Later, a mix of viewer letters would come in, some bemoaning and some celebrating the violence against Rather and Wallace.

Rather, meanwhile, stuck to his "it's all in a day's work" line and tried not to overplay what had happened. Cronkite's producer Sandy Socolow later claimed that Rather actually threw the first punch,[23] though the scrum is so tight it's impossible to see where the blows come from. CBS's footage just shows Rather going down. It's the same in NBC's, shot from one of their overhead cameras: there's a wave of men in suits, and then Rather is sucked under, as if by an undertow. Ultimately, the important thing is not who struck the first blow but that blows were

FIGURE 14. Rosey Grier and Shirley MacLaine were among the celebrity delegates who complained about excessive security. "It's too much protection, too much keeping people out," Grier said. He had been one of Robert Kennedy's bodyguards the night of his assassination, and this gave added weight to his criticisms in Chicago. Associated Press, 1968.

struck because tempers were flaring, because the white Georgia delegation was furious, the security forces were furious, and Rather dared
to ask questions.

If, as I have argued, the second day of the Chicago convention was as
much about the battle for Black empowerment and enfranchisement as
it was about pro-Humphrey forces struggling against pro-McCarthy (or
Kennedy) forces, it allows us a different way to think about this famous
scuffle. It's instructive, in other words, to put the Rather episode and
all the security issues surrounding that climactic moment of violence
back in the context of the broadcast flow of this hour, framed by Chloe
Breeze. For fifty years, the Rather incident and Cronkite's "thug" reaction have been one of a handful of moments from inside the convention
hall that have found historical traction, and Cronkite's interpretation
of the assault as an attack on free speech has stuck as the correct explanation for what was going on. But when you consider that the whole
reason Rather was punched was because he was trying to talk to a white
man making a scene because a Black man had gained some power in
the Democratic Party, and when you consider that the whites in Humphrey's home state delegation were loath to go out on a limb for the
Cashin challenge or even the more modest Vann challenge, and that
Humphrey was mute on the whole affair, tacitly not offering support,
it becomes clear that white supremacy was central—not tangential—
to the convention. This was the complicated puzzle that TV viewers
concerned about civil rights would have been trying to piece together
from the footage shown by the network news that night.

The centrality of white supremacy continued after the Rather story.
The governor of Tennessee was walking out in disgust in response to
the credentials battles, a ridiculous move, considering that the challenge to his white delegation had been defeated, but he was still furious
about Monday night's Georgia compromise. On the dais, civil rights
lawyer Arthur Shores of Alabama, one of the Black delegates from
Vance's group, was speaking out both for the majority report (that is, for
not seating Cashin's group) and for the loyalty oath, a blow to the Wallace supporters in his own delegation. Viewers saw but a fragment of
his speech, and Cronkite did not provide background on Shores, but his

speech brought nuance to the story of the Cashin challenge for viewers who already knew his history: Shores's home had been firebombed in 1963,[24] and he had argued the *Lucy v. Adams* case for desegregating the University of Alabama before the US Supreme Court.

Disconcertingly, next follows a comic shtick sequence of Roger Mudd acting straight man for Art Buchwald as he irons shirts and cracks jokes about the Chicago laundry strike. (There was no actual strike, but it was true that there was no laundry service, in no small part due to the fact that the bus strike hit hotel workers hard.) The Alabama speeches conclude during the feeble comedy routine, and voting on the challenging delegates starts, as we make our way back to Chloe Breeze. Dan Rather is with Breeze now, along with another Black Minnesota delegate, Bill Smith. Their walkout threat had been in anticipation of what might happen with the Cashin vote. Now things have moved to the next level; the Minnesota delegates have split their vote on Cashin. Breeze says, "We're walking out because we feel that we have two presidential candidates [Humphrey and McCarthy] from the Minnesota delegation, [and] the Minnesota delegation should support what is in the best interest of Black people." She is at the end of her rope, expressing unadulterated anger and frustration. Rather speaks to Warren Stennis, the white chairman of the delegation, who did vote for the Cashin group and encouraged others to do the same. He's not walking out and says, "I think this is the only way we can make progress," by staying and not giving up on the political process. Breeze shakes her head and says, "We have been waiting for two hundred years. How long do we have to wait? I don't feel we have to wait any longer. The time is now. We don't want tokenism."

Rather responds that most in the delegation are for Humphrey and asks, "Mrs. Breeze, you're for Humphrey?" Breeze is speechless. What on earth does this have to do with two hundred years of disenfranchisement? Rather is looking for some interview meat and doesn't even realize that he just got it from her. An unnamed Minnesota Black delegate offers a response to Rather: "We do not intend to participate in this convention and be violated. . . . As Black people, . . . we intend to uphold our

responsibility to people, like representatives that challenge are depen-
dent upon all across this country, not only in the South but in certain
areas of the North where Black people are not represented. *We will not
participate in this type of thing.* And if the Democratic Party is going to
be viable, . . . [it] is going to have to face up to this issue full heartedly."

Rather now sees that he's got an interview line to pursue, if he once
again brings things back to Humphrey: "But Vice President Humphrey
has a long history of doing what he can for civil rights." His respondent
will not take this bait, this relentless return to the establishment's preferred candidate: "We are not buying history. We are buying *now*. We
are buying what are you going to do *now*. You know, a lot of people have
had good histories. You see, but people get old, they get tired. Maybe
this is what's the matter with the vice president. Maybe it's not. But the
point of it is we're not buying history. We're interested in dealing with
the issues right now, and the people who have the moral fortitude, and
the courage, and the presence of mind to deal with it right here and
now." And with this, the Black delegates from Minnesota walk out. CBS
cuts to Wallace interviewing a Humphrey aide about Teddy Kennedy's
prospects, and we are back to the horse race.

Perhaps it's not surprising that CBS was more interested in covering its reporter getting punched, and in circling back to the nomination
story, than in covering the Democrats' first Black presidential candidate
and the Minnesota Black delegate walkout, but what this one-hour segment framed by the Minnesota crisis illustrates is really quite powerful.
For one thing, it reveals that there was significantly more Black radicalism at play inside the convention than in the streets. On the one hand,
Black Democratic delegates seemed by their very presence to be suggesting hope for working within the system. They were not making calls
for Black nationalism or suggesting that Blacks should take up arms,
in the vein of Black Power militants. By virtue of the Black delegates
even being there, Vanocur, Rather, Chancellor, and all the rest assumed
they must have had some faith in attempting reform from within.

Black print journalists reported things differently. Interviewed by
Jet magazine, Chicago Black militant Calvin Lockridge (who did not

attend the convention) surmised that "the Democratic Convention is whitey's thing."[25] In a similar vein, a terrific 1969 film about the street violence in Chicago and the relationship between the antiwar movement and the Black Power movement was called *American Revolution II: Battle of Chicago*, with the telling alternate title "A Few Honkies Get Their Head Beat."[26] Russ Meeks, another politically active local who did not participate in or protest the convention, told *Jet*, "Black people have to look to blackness for the solution to their problems.... The convention has no intention of addressing itself to Black needs."[27] This, in fact, seems to be the position that Chloe Breeze was coming around to by Tuesday night.

Some Black delegates were accommodationists, such as the handful of token Black delegates hand-picked by Lester Maddox. More politically outspoken Black delegates, though, had to consider the efficacy of their presence and whether they were resisting or playing the game by the white majority's rules. McCarthy supporter Gail McHenry, a nineteen-year-old Black alternate delegate from Kentucky, told *Jet*, "Some of my more militant friends think I've sold out."[28] Profiled in *Ebony*, McHenry said she had come to the convention in order "to work within the established political structure and learn certain things so that I'll be ready when a Black party is organized."[29] Concerns about Black political and economic disempowerment among the three hundred and fifty Black delegates and alternates (seventy-two of whom were women) were real at the convention,[30] but you'd know little about that from watching network coverage, even though almost the entire first two days of the convention were taken up with Black delegate challenges. The strong reporting on Black issues came from a more niche source: Black newspapers and magazines. Indeed, a viewer trying to piece together the white supremacy narrative at the DNC would have profited from turning to that alternative reporting, which connected many of the dots that TV journalists did not see.

Before the convention, there was speculation in the mainstream media that there would be Black riots in Chicago. On the surface, this presumption did not seem far-fetched, given the racial conflict and urban upheaval the country had seen over the course of the 1960s. What the presumption ignored, however, was the demographics of the protestors. Black Power advocates were not swarming to Chicago to protest the Democratic Party, which would have been seen by most of them as beyond repair. Black comedian and activist Dick Gregory did attempt a march on Thursday night, and Black Panther Bobby Seale delivered a speech on Tuesday afternoon, for which he was later accused of inciting a riot. Those are separate, complicated stories of Black resistance in Chicago, but they were outliers. Another outlier was SCLC's Ralph Abernathy, who arrived in both Miami and Chicago with a mule train caravan to demonstrate for the Poor People's Campaign. The vast majority of Chicago's Black activists saw convention protest as a white project. Many left town because they reasonably presumed that if they stayed, Daley's police would have arrested them as a preventive measure—"rounding up the usual suspects," as it were. Black people were virtually always the ones who got killed by police in riots, not white people. That was what had happened at the Republican convention.

No matter how much the networks insisted that the big story on Tuesday was the surge for Kennedy, the other story was about civil rights and Black empowerment. Although it wasn't narrated and parsed out for viewers by Cronkite or Huntley or Brinkley, and although the floor correspondents did not aggressively pursue the story, it was still one that we can *see* in the footage. Chloe Breeze got only a few minutes of airtime, but she and her fellow Minnesota Black delegates offered an articulation of Black anger and frustration that viewers could not find anywhere else on NBC or CBS during four days of Chicago coverage.

A few weeks later, *Jet*'s Washington Bureau Chief Simeon Booker reported that Blacks struck out time and time again at the convention, and the mood was one of "disillusionment and disenchantment." One delegate said, "How can I go back to my ghetto and urge my people to vote Democratic. I can't even go safely to my hotel tonight to sleep."[31] The Democratic mayor of Chicago had made his contempt for Blacks clear long before the convention began, and the party had made it clear they took Black votes for granted, or, as one Black delegate put it, "the power boys believed that Blacks would vote for any Democrat over Richard Nixon."[32]

The Ted Kennedy Crisis . . . and the Crisis of Dead Airtime

An unwritten rule in convention coverage dictates that when in doubt, revert to a horse-race narrative. Which candidate is ahead or behind, by how much, and how can he or she catch up? If the networks didn't dive into the Cashin story, it was partly because the horse-race approach was their default setting. And so, the hours spent waiting for the Alabama vote to finish up became about Ted Kennedy's prospects, and the networks concluded that what was really happening was not a Road to Damascus moment regarding white supremacy in Alabama but instead an attempt to hold up convention proceedings to pursue behind-the-scenes maneuvering to bring delegates over to Kennedy.

Although the Kennedy story was late breaking, the idea that delegate challenges would help Humphrey's opponents had preceded the convention. In a letter he sent to Eisenhower at Walter Reade Hospital, dated the last day of the GOP convention, Cronkite wrote, "The Democrats seem to be brewing another of their convention donnybrooks. It is quite clear that the McCarthy people have laid in state conventions the groundwork for a rather massive credentials committee fight. They will take it to the convention floor with the hope of creating an issue around which their candidate might rally some late support."[33] By Tuesday evening, this assessment had changed only to the extent that the "donnybrooks" around credentials now seemed to be more about Kennedy's prospects than McCarthy's. As far as CBS and NBC were concerned, all roads led to speculation about Kennedy. And when that road dead-ended in interviews, as it often did, there emerged the crisis of how to fill dead airtime.

A CBS internal memo from late 1967 outlined a possible article to be written by (or ghostwritten for) Walter Cronkite on the topic "How to Watch a Convention."[34] The section on "What to watch when there's no contest" frankly acknowledged that issues like procedural reforms were "traditional inducers of sleep at conventions," adding that "outside demonstrations . . . on the civil rights issue and delegate seating at both conventions in '64, got enormous coverage at Atlantic City in particular, where nothing else was going on much of the time." Apparently the article was never written. Still, it's telling as a private acknowledgment of the challenge of reporting procedural issues. You had to find *something* to cover when things got snoozy.

Bill Leonard, vice president of CBS News, said in advance of the 1968 convention, "You can't just point the camera at the convention. Hell, nobody would watch after a while. Even the delegates don't pay attention to most of what goes on. They have to be chained to their seats. We have to try to report what's really going on."[35] By late night on Tuesday, the networks had found little besides the Kennedy story to report as "really going on," and that story was moving slowly, with correspondents pulling at threads that only sporadically led anywhere. Kennedy had been wishy-washy, alternately saying that he would not run, or that maybe he would accept a "genuine" draft. His brother had been assassinated earlier in the summer, and he was still in a haze. The crazy thing was, the networks were grasping at this story as if it were their only narrative option, when delegates were on the floor fighting with each other about Vietnam and other pressing issues, and the city outside was packed with protestors with stories to tell. Of course, it wasn't really crazy, just conservative in the sense that the networks didn't want to be accused of doing "advocacy reporting" by getting too adventurous in the stories they pursued. That's ironic, obviously, given the accusations of liberal bias that flew around later.

The networks did not dive into the Vietnam story because that debate hadn't officially started. In this way, they were being responsive to the dais. And they weren't seeking stories outside, out of anxiety about giving protestors free publicity and because it was too hard to do without access to live TV cameras. In fact, the biggest street story on Tuesday was that pastors were holding a religious service in Lincoln Park at 11 p.m. CBS didn't mention it, and NBC barely mentioned it, not because it wasn't of possible viewer interest—there was potential for a violent eruption from the police, who hadn't held back so far from striking nuns and clergymen. A key disincentive to covering this story was the technical hurdle of not shooting live. If you filmed events in the park at 11:00 on 16mm cameras, finishing at midnight, you couldn't reasonably expect to develop the film in a mobile van, edit it into a story, motorcycle it back to the Amphitheatre, and get it on the air in a timely manner. Things *usually* got boring at conventions, but there was also usually the option of popping over to the hotels to interview campaign workers and candidates, or finding local color to cover. When things turned boring in 1948, NBC had whipped up a local story on ladies' hats. Trapped inside the Chicago Amphitheatre, the networks' usual time fillers were closed off to them.

NBC had two tactics to handle the crisis of having nothing to show. First, they leaned into it, as Huntley and Brinkley chatted about how frustrating it all was. They even resorted to weak banter about the seating arrangements. New Hampshire had the worst position, and Huntley joked that their long lens could barely find them. Brinkley cracked himself up by observing, "Someone remarked here earlier today that if this convention had been rigged by the Humphrey forces, then they certainly made a mistake in putting the California and New York delegations, those two great big ones, together. They said that an infection had spread from the California delegation to New York." It was funny only to him, because the point was that these were the two delegations that kept holding things up, as if they were in cahoots to stall in order to dig up more votes for McCarthy.

The thing is, that was probably true. The real story here, to provide clarity to viewers, should have been that the Humphrey-Johnson camp had deliberately given California, New York, and New Hampshire (where McCarthy had done exceptionally well in the primary) bad seating. Good seating meant being close to the dais, where you could see and hear convention business clearly, and where you also could get the attention of the chairman when you wanted to make a motion. Technically, any delegate could pass a note or call the dais from one of the floor phones, but the farther away you were, the easier it was for the dais to ignore you. Pro-McCarthy states were patently ignored more often than were pro-Humphrey states. These flailing jokes about seating could have been a real story, but Huntley and Brinkley avoided attacking convention organizers, out of a sense of fair play. They could "objectively" observe that things were going badly—that the convention was *dragging*—but they didn't lean into the *why* of it all, which could have been seen as biased. It was a classic example of how the professional norms of "fairness" in the network era could actually impede the quality of reporting. So Huntley and Brinkley waited.

Shortly after 9:00, Brinkley said, "They're still just filling time here, listening to the music and milling around in the aisle, socializing. . . . The reason for the delay—it's been close to an hour now—is that New York retired to *caucus*." He clenched onto this word like it made his teeth hurt, adding that New York was "poll[ing] its delegation on the question of seating the regular delegation from Alabama. The issue is *settled*. New York's vote, however it goes, cannot affect it, because it is settled." If the vote against the Cashin delegation was *settled*, as Huntley and Brinkley kept confirming, the losing vote count having been hit over an hour ago, why couldn't the convention move on? Brinkley explained: "The answer is that . . . nothing can be done during a roll call [vote] except the roll call. At a convention, I don't know, eight years ago I guess, the parliamentarian was Representative Clarence Kenyon of Missouri who was the world's expert in that field, and somebody wanted to interrupt a roll call for something, and his ruling was that not even an earthquake can interrupt a roll call."

Two hours later, chairman Albert conjured up an "earthquake" when he announced from the podium that "nothing but a point of order can interrupt a roll call. . . . And it would be a bad precedent not to follow that rule. However, to expedite the business, we can suspend the rules by unanimous consent request. And the chair requests unanimous consent that we postpone the consideration of this roll call. . . . Is there objection?" At this, people shouted objections and whistled, and Albert responded, "The chair hears no objection." Then there was a screaming uproar, and he said, "The chair cannot interpret that kind of sound. The chair hears no objection, and so it is ordered." The crowd positively exploded, as voting on a separate issue proceeded.

It was the first new thing that had happened in hours, and Huntley and Brinkley did not seize on it, but this blatant disregard for procedure, and, indeed, for the democratic process, had lit a fire under Kennedy supporters on the floor, who began waving improvised signs reading "Be led by Ted," "Draft Kennedy," and, somewhat deliriously, "Magic Markers for Kennedy." The NBC floor correspondents got back to asking anyone who would talk to them if Kennedy would accept a draft. A narrative thread had been grasped, and NBC could move forward again.

The other strategy NBC took to fill dead airtime on Tuesday night was cutting away to a long segment on Czechoslovakia, from the New York studio, with correspondent Bob Abernathy. Huntley led into the segment, saying, "Events in Czechoslovakia have not escaped the attention of this convention by any means. The situation arises in the speeches that the candidates have been making before various delegations, and certainly it appears in the Democratic platform, which will be voted on before this night is over, we believe." The connections made here were simultaneously tenuous and accurate: tenuous in that this is the first we've heard from the booth about the situation in Prague all night, and this segment appears pre-recorded, a piece set aside for insertion whenever Huntley and Brinkley needed a break; accurate insofar as "events in Czechoslovakia" actually were relevant to the convention and would indeed be used as a reference point for both hawks and doves in the Vietnam platform debate later.

Soviet tanks had rolled into Prague on August 21, just a few days before the convention began. McCarthy initially described the invasion as "not a major crisis," not seeing how it could affect his stance on Vietnam.[36] Those supporting the LBJ-Humphrey plank, on the other hand, used the invasion as proof that the United States must be ever-vigilant against communist aggression. Meanwhile, protestors in the streets of Chicago made a much more primal connection: the armored vehicles, the armed soldiers, the barbed wire, everything shown in the streets of Prague looked and felt like what was happening in Chicago, except that people were being beaten but not killed in Chicago. That difference was important, but the anxiety was genuine that National Guardsmen and Chicago police *might* start firing live rounds. People started referring to the city as "Czechago."[37] Huntley and Brinkley had not dug into that ten-minute cutaway piece on Prague, but the connections to the convention would have made for a good story, perhaps explicitly framed as an "analysis" or "commentary" so that the discussion could be more far-reaching than a straight-up reported news story could be.[38] This was risky business, though. NBC was not going to make the connection that Chicago felt like Prague at the risk of being perceived as making an unfair attack on the city, or even as veering into "advocacy reporting"— the worst professional insult you could hurl at a network reporter at the time. That sort of reporting from a subjective viewpoint was Hunter S. Thompson or Norman Mailer territory, not network news territory.

CBS pursued tactics different from NBC's to tackle the procedurally induced slow-down on Tuesday. First, there was Cronkite's math. He often cut to running vote counts, patiently reminding viewers what a "yes" or "no" vote meant in terms of support for McCarthy or Humphrey. It was a return to horse-race politics, and an ongoing gauge of the relative strength of the establishment and anti-establishment forces. As Huntley and Brinkley devolved into banter about the futility of fighting parliamentary procedure, Cronkite kept counting, counting, counting.

The other option CBS pursued during the crisis of dead airtime on Tuesday night was to cut away from Iron Pants up in the booth to two other reporting hubs, one on the dais and one on the studio floor. CBS's man on the dais was Harry Reasoner, who had a "light touch" with the news.[39] He anchored the *CBS Sunday News* and delivered regular radio commentaries featuring a mix of stories. One day he might talk about a looming strike, whereas his next spot might be on, say, how irritating it was that women took so long to get their hair and makeup together before heading out for a dinner party.[40] Reasoner had a reputation as a solid writer and a heavy drinker. He was also known for his "wry wit and low-key unflappable delivery."[41] Cronkite was not lacking in wit, but he was also a hard-news guy known for doing his homework. Reasoner was known for *not* doing his homework. In fact, he had so underperformed during 1966 election coverage that he was "frozen out altogether from election night in 1968."[42]

Reasoner was planted up on the dais all night watching speakers pontificate and secretary Dorothy Bush record votes with a pencil on a cardboard diagram. He had a monitor and a telephone at his side, and CBS producers were probably checking in with him to see if he had any scuttlebutt from the rostrum, where organizers and politicians were shuffling about and might let drop some crumbs of information, but Cronkite had no motivation to give Reasoner a second more of airtime than he had to. When he *finally* cut to Reasoner on Tuesday night, it showed how slow things had really gotten. Cronkite asks about the delay, noting that "it must be driving the management of the convention there at the podium a little bit batty." Reasoner responds: "I think they're reasonably uncomfortable about it, Walter, [because] . . . they can't stop this kind of thing. One gentleman in a high place said that the New York delegation is . . . obviously stalling. . . . He finally sent a man with a walkie-talkie to see if he could find them. I don't know how you lose one hundred and ninety delegates. But somewhere in the Amphitheatre these are lost. Possibly they're being detained by security men somewhere."

This last comment was probably an overstatement (the delegates had not fled off-site), but the security guard quip was not an overreach. Earlier that night poor Allard Lowenstein, a New York delegate, had almost been arrested for trying to bring a copy of the *New York Times* onto the floor. Newspapers weren't technically allowed for fear the TV cameras would show people reading them instead of listening to speeches—which they did. If Lowenstein was hassled by Daley's security, it didn't strain credulity to assume he had been red-flagged because he was the man behind the Dump Johnson campaign. In any case, Reasoner had little to report on the schedule, adding simply that Anita Bryant was scheduled to sing again later but would probably be canceled.

Cronkite added, "Andy Rooney asked me to ask you if she's as pretty up there at the podium as she is a hundred and fifty feet away here in our anchor booth." Reasoner confirms, "She looks very nice up here." It's a cringe-y moment, and Reasoner's only appearance all night.

The other CBS cutaway space was the floor studio, another place to go to fill time. Eric Sevareid was down there talking with Teddy White. For some viewers, this might have been the highlight of the evening, but Cronkite wasn't too keen on Sevareid's analysis. It's not that he thought it was poor-quality work, but that Cronkite was devoted to hard news stories. With twenty-two minutes in each *CBS Evening News* broadcast, Cronkite hated losing two-and-a-half minutes of the "news hole" to Sevareid.[43] For its part, CBS News saw Sevareid as part of what made them distinct from NBC. Producer Sandy Socolow said, "They had Brinkley, we had Sevareid," and, while Brinkley was "a very good smart aleck," Sevareid offered something deeper.[44] Good for the ratings? Yes. But on the *CBS Evening News* he did tightly scripted commentary taped before broadcast. As his biographer put it, it was a "daily, isolated chore," and he was "not really part of the team putting together the news 'package.'"[45] Cronkite worked from New York and Sevareid from Washington, DC; they weren't accustomed to actually working together. Further, Sevareid suffered from terrible stage fright and was not a strong ad-libber, so he was a poor fit for convention coverage. Thus, Sevareid was exiled to the floor studio, a sterile, soundproofed room with a news desk and a giant, TV-shaped window facing onto the floor, where one saw not the speakers up on stage but rather a crush of indistinguishable delegates.

Cronkite cut to Sevareid three times on Tuesday. His solo, ad-libbed commentary on the possibility of a peace plank was weak, but his commentary on the credentials battles was scripted, and thus tight, offering solid insights on the fact that the GOP had little interest in courting "the Negro vote," while Democrats had troubles precisely because they courted that vote without consistently delivering. He closed in the classic Sevareid style: "If the establishment here is heavy-handed, as its opponents charge, the dissenters appear very fierce and very uncompromising. A good illustration of the weapons of the weak, by the way. They can always threaten to quit and walk out. I think that's the principle of fighting in karate. You just fall away from the other fellow's strength and hope he falls on his face." Cronkite had no use for this kind of rhetoric—Sevareid even pronounced "karate" pompously as "kah-rah-tay"—but this was the sort of stuff that enamored Sevareid fans.

Cronkite's later cutaway for a conversation between Sevareid and White was another ill-fated, ad-libbed exchange, in which White test-drove ideas for his forthcoming book, and Sevareid floundered even when he made thin comments he had clearly been fed by White before they went on-air. A short excerpt conveys the flavor of the exchange:

SEVAREID: Why do you think the whole McCarthy phalanx here has been sagging so much?

WHITE: Any candidacy reflects the personality of its leader. Gene McCarthy is the most enigmatic man I have ever met in American public life. I think he's interested in religion, poetry, and baseball, in that order, and is probably the greatest historian who has ever run for office in the USA. I don't think he really has that itch and that desire to push other people around, to get his hands on the throttles and the levers. I confess I can't understand it, but I think his campaign reflects a great many lieutenants and captains who don't understand him either. . . . There is a courage in Gene McCarthy. Courage, wit, irony, poetry. And historically, of course, he made opposition to the Vietnam War respectable. He brought it into the arena of public debate, forced the resignation of a president of the USA . . .

SEVAREID: There's a lot of talk about alienation these days among a great many of his followers. But there's an alienation between him [unintelligible], and I would think that a majority of these very practical politicians out on this floor, wouldn't you? I don't think they *dig* him really.

WHITE: They don't. They don't at all. I mean, he's much closer to Robert Lowell than he is to Dick Daley. His home lies on the poetic side of the fence. "Alienation" I think is a word that's so much overused, don't you Eric? We're all alienated.

SEVAREID: I'm tired of it. And I'm tired of "the establishment" and a few other things.

WHITE: I'm tired of the "youth revolt," and of all sorts of things, with all Americans, and all of us living in a country that faces problems that it hasn't faced for a hundred years.

Having taken ten minutes to establish that neither Kennedy nor McCarthy has sufficient lust for power to be president—White's macho line on politics, later reiterated in his book along with words like "vitality" and "vigor," which gave his analysis the patina of a Geritol ad—and that both he and White are grumpy, middle-aged men who cannot convincingly use the hippie word "dig," Sevareid closes acidly with, "Well, Walter, that's all the *instant wisdom* available from down here in the *basement* now." Cronkite chuckles and retorts, "Down in the basement! You're four feet from all the action!" To which Sevareid says, "You noticed our prison gray, I hope."

The tone wasn't quite snippy enough for viewers to get what was happening here, but Sevareid was poking at Cronkite. First, the small, soundproofed, sterile floor room felt more like a diving bell than a studio that was part of "the action." Second, "prison gray" referred not only to the atmosphere but also literally to the color scheme; this was CBS's first convention shot in color, and they were showing off their colorful design strategies everywhere, except in that cramped floor studio. Third, "instant analysis" was a shallow concept, as far as Sevareid was concerned, and he had proved it (though not on purpose) by not doing it well. As for Cronkite, he may have chuckled, but, really, he didn't care too much about what was going on down there. It was CBS's Siberia at this convention. It was even where that silly Roger Mudd–Art Buchwald laundry segment had been shot.

As the procedural voting continued, Cronkite filled time by cutting to Mudd several times in that basement prison; Mudd offered a very different kind of performance than Sevareid had. He was not a commentator but a correspondent, a reporter who was good at thinking on his feet and who offered trenchant analysis without all of Sevareid's verbal curlicues. Cronkite cut to Mudd to summarize and succinctly compare the Republican and Democratic platform planks. The work was solid, and obviously scripted, but Mudd's improvised comments were also revealing:

MUDD: Walter, just being next to the stockyards has created one massive problem. There's a fly problem. [Cronkite offers a hearty laugh from the booth.] And if you've ever tried to get off some heavy thoughts and had a fly alight on the end of your nose, you'll know what the problem is.

CRONKITE: I'm just always just wondering whether [the] camera's focused on the fly or on me when this happens. There're no flies on the speakers up there [on the dais], though, Roger. I don't know whether you know it or not, but the makeup is specially prepared for the speakers, and they are being made up, most of them, by the convention management . . . and they've got a special spray to keep the flies off of the speakers.

MUDD: Well, we all have our little spray cans down here [in the floor studio]. I just hope it doesn't get mixed up with the mace.

This was off-the-cuff banter from newsmen wondering if they were about to pull an all-nighter, as Tuesday night slipped into Wednesday morning. They had waited six hours for the Vietnam debate to start, and the stench of the stockyards and the attendant flies was a little detail that revealed how sour everything felt at this point. It was depressing to learn that CBS workers down in the basement needed bug spray and that speakers up on the dais had fly-repellent makeup. A casual aside about mace made things even worse, because neither CBS nor NBC had mentioned tear gas or mace all day, but here was a sudden reminder that the protestors were still outside doing their thing, and the police were still using chemical weapons on them.

The Vietnam Crisis . . . and the Prime-Time Crisis

Finally, shortly before 1:00 a.m., chairman Hale Boggs of the platform committee began to read platform excerpts, and it seemed like the debate on Vietnam would begin around 1:30 a.m. and continue until three or four o'clock. The disgusted delegates began to get rowdy. Rep. Don Edwards of California told NBC's Edwin Newman that "obviously, what the people who are running this convention are doing is to make sure that this very substantive debate on Vietnam comes after the prime television time." A Wisconsin delegate told Ike Pappas of CBS, "We think the television audience ought to have a chance to see the debate. And we think the audience ought to have a chance to see it not at 3:00 in the morning." Disgusted by the notion that the "establishment" (realist) forces running the convention were trying to hide the Vietnam vote, the furious and exhausted idealist delegates, led by Wisconsin, began chanting "Adjourn!" and "Let's go home!"

Chairman Albert had been pretending not to see notes sent from Wisconsin all night, and the delegates fumed that their floor telephone hadn't worked for two days, so they couldn't reach the rostrum that way. Finally, Albert allowed their microphone to be turned on, and Wisconsin motioned to adjourn. Albert responded curtly, "The motion to adjourn is not a recognizable motion." Booing went up from the floor, and Wisconsin delegates started to walk out. Albert screamed for order, his voice cracking. He desperately recognized Daley, and Daley called for order, claiming erroneously that all the hollering was coming from the *visitors' gallery* in the balcony, as if no one could see that most of those people had given up and left hours ago. Brinkley astutely noted that Daley's comments confirmed he was the one really in charge. Albert continued to screech for order.

And then finally Albert succumbed to the inevitable. Daley was shown on camera drawing a menacing slash across his own throat with his finger, signaling the day must end (fig. 15). Following that gruesome gesture, Albert recognized Daley, and the mayor grabbed his microphone and officially adjourned the proceedings. Reasoner had earlier told Cronkite, "We're talking again about another late night. Tonight the benediction is [on the official schedule as] 'time?' just with a question mark, scheduled by a Greek Orthodox representative. We trust they won't forget him as they did the benediction last night." Well, they did indeed forget him. As people slowly filed out, the correspondents

FIGURE 15. Daley brings the convention to a close on Tuesday by repeatedly making a slashing gesture to his throat. This becomes one of the iconic images of the convention, shorthand for his heavy-handed "law and order" approach to policing the event. Associated Press, 1968.

interviewed delegates who confirmed the importance of having the Vietnam debate aired in prime time. Sen. Albert Gore Sr. told Newman, "We filibustered with Tweedledee and Tweedledum matters until the American people had gone to bed, here at this late hour. So that those of us who have serious doubts about the Vietnam war policy and a platform that promises more of the same thing could not be heard. We shall be heard. We'll be heard tomorrow." The credentials struggles had not been "Tweedledee and Tweedledum matters," as Chloe Breeze, Fannie Lou Hamer, John Cashin, and Channing Phillips could confirm. The outsiders understood that procedural issues were political issues. Yet Gore's summation did reflect the way the inside story on procedural issues had been underreported throughout the night.

There was nothing left for newsmen to do but debrief on the failed day. NBC cut to Newman, Chancellor, McGee, and Vanocur gathered together in the now-abandoned Delaware section. The consensus was that Kennedy still might be in play and that the delegates were horribly bitter. Vanocur gave his reading of the delegates' mood: "It's symptomatic of something. The other day, remember we drove in, and we went back to that place where it says 'privileged parking,' and we saw the sign 'cattle, sheep, and pigs.' And these people tonight gave evidence that they feel, especially the Wisconsin crowd talking about Mayor Daley, feel like they've been pushed around like animals. . . . I got there when it started, and it just *blew up*. And they just wouldn't be turned back. And that is symptomatic of something that they're mad about, . . . the conditions under which this convention is being run. . . . They say they don't have any phones, they can't get phone numbers of other delegations. They were bitter about John Criswell, the man who is running this with President Johnson. They're just *bitter people*." There is general agreement on this point.

From the booth, Brinkley asks about having the Vietnam fight during prime time. McGee responds, "I think it'll help them more to have it in full view of the public than to have it in the middle of the night when nobody could see it, because no matter how damaging it might be in front of the whole country, it's a lot more damaging to have the suspicion around that you put it on at the midnight hours and later so that the public can't hear." They all agree that the LBJ-Humphrey Vietnam plank will win, but that the opposition will have at least a minor victory if Americans can see and hear the debate in prime time; the journalists understand the goals of the idealists. Chancellor astutely adds that the floor situation is so terrible that *only* the television audience will bear witness to the debate, because no one on-site can even hear what is going on. Delegates throughout the night had resorted to asking newsmen what they were voting on (i.e., what a "yes" or "no" vote was actually for), because the newsmen had radio headsets that kept them better informed than delegates. After some more kvetching about the crisis of delegates feeling herded like sheep, Chancellor says, "Well, we've all come out for convention reform," cracking everyone up. The

Chapter Four Day Three

"You do what's right, you don't have to give a
worry about the television medium."

August 28, 1968, was theoretically a good day for Hubert Horatio Humphrey. At 11:45 p.m., he won enough delegate votes to be nominated for President of the United States. CBS correspondent Martin Agronsky reported, "He jumped to his feet and turned around, spread his arms real wide, smiled at everyone and did . . . a little dance. Then just at that moment, his wife's picture came up on the television screen, and he immediately ran over to the screen, leaned down, and kissed Muriel Humphrey on the television, turned around and smiled at everyone, and leaned down and kissed her again . . . [and then] shouted at the room, 'I feel like really jumping!'"

Yet just two hours earlier, both NBC and CBS had reported that tear gas had seeped into Humphrey's twenty-ninth-floor suite at the Conrad Hilton Hotel. Sneezing and choking, with itchy skin, he had taken a shower, hoping for relief. At that same time down on the fifteenth floor, McCarthy headquarters had been converted into a makeshift hospital ward. Volunteers had torn up sheets to wrap around bleeding heads. McCarthy's thirteen-year-old daughter Margaret was put to work rolling bandages. Cronkite reported that "twelve young demonstrators were treated there for wounds received in the battle. They acted as their own security guards, sealed off the end of the corridor; . . . none of them seriously injured, but a few may require hospitalization." That was an iffy proposition, though, since, as one witness in Chicago reported, some "city hospitals were telling demonstrators not to bring their wounded to the regular hospital emergency rooms because cops were waiting at the door to jam the wounded into paddy wagons. The cops stormed into improvised hospitals—such as the Church Federation on Michigan Avenue—and jerked transfusion needles out of arms and, broken bones or no broken bones, crammed the wounded into vans."[1]

It was a bad day for those demonstrators, and anyone else in the streets of downtown Chicago. There was even a run on helmets. Police had started cracking skulls a few days before the convention started, and if you didn't have headgear by Wednesday you were probably out of luck. Chicago police had their signature powder-blue helmets. Protestors wore motorcycle helmets, sports helmets, whatever they could get their hands on. The Yippie-poet-musician Ed Sanders went to Marshall Field's department store to browse football helmets, hoping to find one with a face guard.[2]

In the middle of this mess, it's hard to imagine anyone dancing a jig and planting a kiss on a TV set, but that's exactly what happened. Shortly after the decisive delegate votes from Pennsylvania were cast that night, President Johnson called Humphrey to congratulate him, and the newly minted candidate chatted with Lady Bird as well. Nixon called, too, to offer niceties. Nixon was not a man whom one could easily describe as gleeful, but it must have been hard for him to suppress his excitement. A man nominated in the midst of such chaos could not possibly beat him, he accurately presumed: Nixon's "law and order" rhetoric resonated, and voters would remember the shiny orderliness of the Miami convention just a few weeks earlier. Lest TV viewers forget, the network anchors, floor correspondents, and commentators periodically injected Miami as a refrain throughout their Chicago coverage, noting in particular how strongly the chaos at the Amphitheatre contrasted with the perfectly stage-managed show in Florida.

We've already seen how poorly Monday and Tuesday went, as the Democrats floundered through their credentials battles. The crises accelerated on Wednesday, culminating around 8:00 p.m. (and aired on TV one hour later) with the "Battle of Michigan Avenue," when for seventeen minutes the police beat and arrested protestors and others in front of the Conrad Hilton Hotel. The network cameras recorded the action as protestors famously chanted, "The whole world is watching!" and "Sieg Heil!" It's a story that's been told a thousand times, ossified into a narrative that is accurate, but also inadequate. The police *did* go ballistic, and Americans rightly look back on that moment as a low point in our history, but what is less often remembered is that many Americans sided with the police and that a narrative of "liberal media bias" accelerated during and after Chicago. Nixon nurtured that narrative as a candidate and exploited it as president. Before Chicago, "liberal bias" in network news was a concern most strongly felt by southern segregationists, right-wing organizations like the John Birch Society, and conservative pundits like William F. Buckley. Of course, some were already frustrated by all the "ugly news" of the late 1960s, like that New York City airline pilot who wrote to Cronkite, but the most widely held perception was that the networks aggressively strove for balance and fairness.

The controversial televised images from Wednesday night have since become iconic, repeated in almost every subsequent documentary about Vietnam, Nixon, and the 1960s. More than just shorthand for the 1968 convention, they have come to be seen as more or less the only important thing to remember about those four days in Chicago. What if we approached the story differently, though, taking a closer look at how the TV networks news covered that entire day, not just the explosion of violence at its climax? A complicated picture thereby emerges, in which television journalists tried mightily to maintain their professional norms of fairness, though by the end of the day this became increasingly difficult; as the clear truth of police violence came into focus, the notion of showing "the other side" for balance became less and less tenable. A deep dive into TV coverage of August 28 complicates the dominant line that emerged right after the convention, that the networks had been terribly one-sided.

The hippies, Yippies, and other demonstrators, many contended, had played the newsmen like a fiddle, getting free publicity for their cause and, ultimately, getting what they deserved from the police. As conservative columnist and pundit Robert Novak later frigidly observed, "The demonstrators came looking for trouble and got what they wanted."[3] This comment exemplifies the loathing that the establishment had for the anti-establishment forces in Chicago: Angry anti-Vietnam activists in the streets *deserved* to be beaten. It didn't matter if you were young or old, male or female, wearing a cleric's collar or a nun's habit, clean-shaven or wild and wooly—you were *asking for it* by virtue of being there. It's true that some demonstrators insulted the police and hurled makeshift projectiles at them. They even hastily erected barricades—piles of park benches and trashcans that served little practical purpose, cobbled together out of sheer desperation. The police and National Guard had billy clubs, mace, bayonets, hand-grenade launchers, sanitation trucks equipped with tear-gas dispensers, and jeeps with barbed-wire sheep catchers on the front.

One haunting image is telling: NBC seized a few seconds of footage of a young man prostrate in the gutter, being tended by medics Wednesday night. The medics—volunteers in white coats with homemade crosses of red tape on their backs—leaned over the limp man and opened his mouth to make sure he was not choking. It's a quick image, taken from atop an NBC news van as the camera pans left to right. NBC offers no commentary and asks no questions about what we are seeing. We don't know who the young man is, though we know that he survived because somehow, against all odds, no one was killed during these four days. The question is, if this man lying in the gutter like a sack of potatoes *had* said something filthy to the "pigs" just moments before, or thrown a bag of pee at them, or shouted "Dump the Hump!," did they have the right—indeed, the *mandate*—to beat him senseless?

By Novak's logic, absolutely. And by the policeman's logic, absolutely. As one officer explained forty years later, "We were ordered to prevent these people from controlling the streets and we were gonna use force to stop them, but we went to work on them when they crossed the line and they did that a lot. Some longhair told me that he'd like to fuck my daughter up the ass, and I snapped. I grabbed him by the back of the neck and shoved my stick into his mouth. A couple of his teeth came out, half broken, and he was gurgling at me, making his sick, mewing noise, and someone grabbed me from behind, and I almost took a swing at him, but it was one of my own guys but he looked scared and confused—a rookie. I let the creep in my hands roll into the gutter and shoved the cherry officer ahead of me on to deal with the next pile of spitting and swearing scum."[4] It's notable that the disturbed rookie is denigrated by the more seasoned officer and feminized as a "cherry" officer, a virgin. A real man knocks out teeth when a longhair says something nasty. This is a particularly strong example of the "asking for it" logic that the law-and-order crowd referenced in the days following Chicago and on into election season.

Predictably, the networks never showed the profanity coming from both cops and activists. But they also didn't show the most gruesome violence. The cops loathed the press and targeted them, but the press didn't retaliate by showing protestors gurgling and spitting out busted teeth. On the contrary, in their Wednesday night coverage, the networks hung on to their professional norms of "balance" and "fairness" for as long as they could and tried *not* to vilify the police or the mayor. The tipping point came late in the day when they finally realized—or at least demonstrated by their reporting—that accurate and objective coverage did not always have to depend on "balance." There was no more reason for the networks to show why the violence in Chicago was "deserved" than there would have been for them to have defended Bull Connor's use of attack dogs in Birmingham.

Fifty years later, conservative charges of liberal media bias have taken deep root, yet the "protestors were asking for it" side of the Chicago narrative has largely faded away. The *Walker Report*'s determination that what viewers saw on TV was a "police riot" has stuck as the dominant reading of the event. There's a general consensus that these historical pictures mean what they obviously mean, which is a hamfisted but also sobering way to put it, because in the post-network era of social media, cable news, deepfakes, and authoritarian cries of "fake news," it is harder to understand a news image as "obviously" true or untrue. Put differently, fifty years ago irate TV viewers argued that the news media had *selectively* represented Chicago, but today some people peg news as "fake" if they don't like it. It's one thing to say that TV news has shown the wrong image or an image with insufficient context but quite another to contend that what you see is phony and that it never happened.

These are points to look at more closely in examining the fallout from the 1968 DNC, but one must start first by examining how that selective representation happened, how the networks made their choices. In other words, the people who cried "bias!" back in 1968 mostly got it wrong, but the point is not just to show that the police violence was both real and excessive but also that a complicated process of newsgathering went on throughout the third day of the convention. The coverage that unfolded throughout the day climaxed on Michigan Avenue that night, but it could have gone otherwise, and the story could have been told differently. The networks could have downplayed the violence, just as they had downplayed the rioting in Miami that had left three locals dead; that downplaying was not intended to benefit the GOP, but it did. Instead, this time they did the right thing, which ultimately worked to the disadvantage of the Democratic Party.

Fairness and Public Service

Revisiting the convention coverage of August 28 in its entirety, considering not just the violence on Michigan Avenue but also returning it to the context of a long day of convention reporting, provides an opportunity to think through how notions of balance and fairness functioned in the network news era. People tend to look back on this era as a golden age, and that tendency is not altogether wrong, but it can also be overly romantic. In striving for fairness, the network news always risked the possibility of amplifying perspectives that should not have been amplified, or of simply letting people off the hook. In the Trump years many criticized major print and electronic outlets for a similar kind of "bothsidesism," which created an atmosphere in which, say, neo-Nazi Richard Spencer or Klansman David Duke were seen as deserving airtime to defend their positions following the 2017 violence in Charlottesville. In the network era, TV journalists were less likely to "balance" debates by including extremist voices. The idea was to convey mainstream liberal and conservative stances, not extremist opinions on either side.

The network news teams were profoundly aware of their public service obligations, not so much at a procedural level (the executives bore most of the load when it came to license renewal details or FCC mandates) but at a professional level. On the one hand, the news turned a tremendous profit. It was not a "loss leader," as many assume. Further, the evening news was the lead-in to evening programming, and research showed that viewers often stuck with one network for much of the evening. Keep in mind that there were only three networks, ABC was the news underdog, and most people did not own a remote control.[5] Viewers without remotes were more likely to stay in the chair and watch one channel throughout prime time. So CBS–NBC news competition was *fierce*. When you realize that Huntley–Brinkley fans were more likely to stay tuned to, say, *Bonanza*, whereas Cronkite fans were more likely to stay tuned to, say, *Gunsmoke*, the picture comes into tight focus: a popular national newscast enabled higher ad rates across the board. Yet the teams creating the news were deliberately kept out of discussions about such things. As producer Sandy Socolow tells it, "When I joined CBS in '56, you would have been fired for talking about the ratings."[6]

The objective on the ground was fair and accurate reporting, and the news staff deliberated about exactly what that meant, especially when covering civil rights. Should bigots be interviewed to be "fair"? The answer was usually "no." But how far could one go in the other direction? Newsman Howard K. Smith did "blunt and aggressive commentaries" on controversial issues for CBS and was fired when he raised a stink about being censored; he had intended to end a 1961 *CBS Reports* documentary on violence in Birmingham with a quotation from Edmund Burke: "The only thing necessary for the triumph of evil is for good men to do nothing." CBS was already concerned that the episode would offend southern affiliates, and this seemed to go too far.[7] White southerners were displeased with the report even without the "offending" line, but the internal censorship does point to the fact that the network had an ideal of fairness that it tried to maintain. With civil rights coverage, it generally took a moral high ground that offended conservatives and pleased liberals, but that wasn't the objective, per se. The *fact* was that Birmingham police deliberately allowed thugs to beat the Freedom Riders; Smith observed it and reported it, yet at the same time, "the first three-quarters of the resulting news program seemed to be a primer on the Fairness Doctrine in action."[8] For CBS, Smith's commentary was the tipping point that pushed the report from observation to punditry, and yet the final quarter of the film centered on the Black perspective on the Birmingham situation, and CBS was fine with that. Bothsidesism had both its place and its limits.

Ultimately, to understand the protests of "bias" that emerged following the coverage of the third day of the Democratic convention, one must understand how "public service" was understood in the network era. What were the assumptions about the networks' public service duties as they headed into reporting those four difficult days in Chicago? Broadcasting textbooks tend to focus narrowly on policy and regulatory issues to understand the issue of public service. This can lead to narrow definitions of what public service means. From a pro-regulation perspective, for example, performing public service would mean conforming to the Fairness Doctrine and other rules, such as those governing the amount of time that broadcasters provide for political candidates. From a deregulatory perspective, the marketplace is the arbiter of public service; if a broadcaster serves the public adequately, ratings will be high, whereas if such service is inadequate, ratings will suffer, advertising rates will fall, and broadcasters will naturally go out of business. In other words, public service is often understood in a way one might describe as almost mechanical, with liberals and conservatives disagreeing about what the best mechanism is to make the machine that is "public service" function. What this leaves out is an element of public service that is less tangible and more difficult to pin down: the affective dimension.

What does it mean for "the public" (an imagined entity on some level) to *trust* a news broadcaster? This goes beyond the notion that a consumer trusts that information is *factual*—the obvious baseline for trust in the network era. If newscasters realized they had gotten a fact wrong, they were likely to issue a correction. If a viewer disputed a fact, he or she might send a letter or telegram. This is a mechanical notion of trust, as a sort of checklist. *Emotional* trust, on the other hand, was strongly linked to the reliability of the anchorman and his (almost always "his") correspondents. This was specific to the network era, decades before characters like Tucker Carlson or Sean Hannity emerged—news commentators who inspire trust more among a specific following than across a general, mass audience. Cynically, one might say that serving the public by providing newscasters who were appealing and seemed honest was a sort of public relations maneuver. It was, but it was also more. NBC news watchers found Huntley and Brinkley likeable and trustworthy. CBS news watchers felt the same way about Cronkite. Dedicated fans came to TV coverage in Chicago assuming that their news needs would be taken care of by many of the same men who had carried them through four days of uninterrupted coverage following the assassination of John F. Kennedy.

Letters from Cronkite's archive in the 1960s illustrate this succinctly. On the second day of the convention, a mother sends a photo of her toddler watching the coverage. At Christmas, strangers send the anchorman cards. A six-year-old girl from Buffalo sends a photo of her kitten, whom she has named "Cronkite." An entire convent of nuns signs a letter to Cronkite, lamenting that the local station has altered its schedule, and now they have to watch Huntley and Brinkley instead of Cronkite in order to make it to their evening prayer service on time. So many of these missives explicitly or implicitly point to the confidence and trust that the sender has in the anchorman; they should not be dismissed as frivolous fan mail, though some have a gushing quality that might seem far from the seriousness of the nightly news. One particular type of letter, however, points most deeply to the idea that the network news *serves* the public: the request letters to CBS from the mothers and widows of men who served in Vietnam.

Specifically, the women requested footage of their sons and husbands. A 1966 letter from Ohio reads: "This is the same stationary I used to write to my son in Vietnam. On the Walter Cronkite Show [*sic*], Monday August 29, you showed a film of the battle where he was killed.

A dog tag was read. It was my boy's! Please may I have a picture, I will pay any price for he already paid the greatest price. Please contact me." The letter was signed "Tommy's Mother."9 There are hundreds of such letters in the 1960s, and Cronkite wrote back over and over again, only occasionally passing the letters off to his assistant. The queries were sent to the research department to locate the footage, and then the network would mail the grieving mother or widow a kinescope (16mm footage) and a transcript of the segment. This was done free of charge. Sometimes it took a bit of work, as the letter writer might not have included the proper date for the episode or might have misremembered exactly what she saw. Follow-up letters ensued, and the footage was most often found.

This all happened organically. CBS never publicized the fact that they sent free footage to relatives of Vietnam vets; the requests simply came, and they were answered. That people turned to the network for help pointed not to the fact that they saw the evening news as charitable but rather that they understood the news as performing a public service by covering the war, and that therefore a request for footage of a loved one was perfectly reasonable. This is an example first of affective trust. The letters are raw in their grief, their authors obviously willing to share their pain with a man who is technically a stranger but who feels like a trusted friend or teacher by virtue of appearing in their living rooms every night. Second, it's an example of what one might call "civic trust." The requests for materials point to confidence that Cronkite and his network exist to serve the national community.

This attitude began to shift after Chicago, and into the Nixon years, but going into Chicago many viewers *did* feel this sense of trust. There were always outliers—people complaining to Cronkite that the nightly news devoted too much or not enough time to Martin Luther King or George Wallace, or just showed too many depressing stories, for example—but the predominant notion was that news provided public service. This background is crucial to understanding how truly dramatic the widespread criticism of network coverage in Chicago was—criticism that was initially spurred by Wednesday's coverage, from roughly 9:00 p.m. to 1:00 a.m.

Day Three Opens with a Whimper, Not a Bang

By the third day of a political convention, the participants will be tired, hoarse from cheering or booing, and maybe hungover. Wednesday was extreme, though. On NBC, Huntley opened at 11:30 a.m. with, "Good Morning. This is the Democratic National Convention in Chicago's International livestock Amphitheatre." Livestock? That wasn't the name of the convention hall, but he was tired and let it slip that the place reeked of the abattoir. Huntley continued, "It feels as though it were about one-and-a-half hours ago that we signed off from here. However, . . . [both anchors chuckling, Brinkley interjects that it feels like half an hour] actually, it was about nine. These Democrats, many of them angry and tired and quarrelsome, left here about two o'clock this morning. A few hours sleep have probably worked some restorative benefits. Also restored their inclination to fight." Huntley added that the movement to draft Teddy Kennedy was "absolutely dead" and that "with some editorial license" it was safe to say that Vice President Humphrey now "appears to be virtually unstoppable." Governor Maddox of Georgia had withdrawn from the presidential race and abandoned his delegation, saying that he wouldn't associate with "beatniks" and "criminal elements," referring to Julian Bond and his compatriots. Now, at last, the delegates were ready to debate the Vietnam plank, about twenty-four hours late, and then to move on to nominations. Even as he states the obvious, that Humphrey will take the nomination, Huntley labels the statement as one made with "some editorial license" so as to appear as nonpartisan as possible.

Cronkite covered the same bases on CBS (Maddox and Kennedy are out, onward to today's schedule), but also included a detailed opening monologue that brilliantly brought the whole scene to life:

> Turning this vast hall around with all of its facilities is a little bit like turning the Queen Mary around for a return trip to Europe in just ten hours. This whole convention hall has to be refueled and stocked with all of those small necessities that make it go. Delegates would have to allow at least an hour to get downtown [about five miles]

and back. That's two hours out of the ten. They had all of their conferences deciding where they were going today with both the platform and with the candidates. . . . So it didn't leave very much time for a night's sleep. . . . I'm sure that very few of them had more than three or four hours sleep, and that's not going to do any good for their nerves here today in what is likely to be a very nerve-wracking session. The turnaround is tough on all the maintenance people out here. When we arrived this morning, a couple of hours ago, the hall was still strewn with the debris of last night's carnival of politics. And an army of cleanup men were trying to make it look presentable again for this day's session. They seem to have succeeded. And incidentally, the hall here is quite a good-looking decoration job. They've done wonders with it. Reminds me of Jimmy Durante. There was an old nightclub here in Chicago. He used to come out, he'd open his act there, he'd say "Chez Paris, Chez Paris, what a beautiful name for a warehouse." Downstairs, the man at the cigarette machine was even complaining this morning that he hadn't had time to replenish his stock. . . . Breakfast was not easy for the delegates to this convention. The room service was over an hour at most hotels this morning in the early hours, and everybody tried to get breakfast at the same moment to get out to this hall. Those of us who would like a cup of coffee had to forgo that this morning. Chicago police, many of whom have been on duty for as many as seventeen hours, got some relief from that call-up of the National Guard in Grant Park overnight. But they're back, I suppose you could say, bright and early this morning. All of us here at CBS News wish Mayor Daley a very good morning, and we're all ready for the day's events.

This is classic Cronkite on several levels. First, he's drawn the scene with typical empathy for the little guy, the service staff trying to clean up and restock. He's also conveyed how exhausted everyone is, with the painful detail that coffee and cigarettes aren't even an option, the default breakfast of champions for TV newsmen and ink-stained wretches in 1968. That's not a necessary news detail, just one to set the tone. CBS was trying a little harder here than NBC to be fair to the DNC and not drive home the "party in shambles" narrative. Cronkite has used the Jimmy Durante line for color, but it's a bit of a head scratcher until you realize that, of course, the line makes sense only if the Schnoz said "whorehouse," not warehouse. It's an off-color joke cleaned up for broadcast.

Finally, Cronkite has included three details one might consider extraneous without extra context. First, the fact that the hall is a "good-looking decoration job" echoes Daley's bizarre, brief interview with John Hart on Monday, when the mayor refused to comment on how the convention was going but instead remarked upon the lovely color scheme. Second, the lightly friendly support for the Chicago police working overtime, with only some relief from the National Guard, was another nod to Daley, a nod that painfully deleted all the beatings, macing, and teargassing that had been going on all week but had been reported only minimally. And third, the cheery good morning to Daley was also an over-the-top attempt at fairness, as if to balance out Cronkite's repeated complaints that the phone workers strike had nixed live TV coverage outside the Amphitheatre and also his comment about "thugs" punching Dan Rather the day before, when Cronkite had lost his temper on the air, a professional blunder. Just one day after the "thug" comment, Cronkite is struggling to compensate.[10]

This setup was a sort of condensed version of the coverage Cronkite would do for most of the day, an often inelegant dance between reporting the grim realities in front of him, which escalated far beyond the coffee-and-cigarette crisis, and bending over backward to show he didn't have it in for Daley or the City of Chicago. Just half an hour later, Cronkite direly reported,

> The almost unbelievable restrictions, about which the delegates are complaining as well as the news media, to control this convention from beginning to end and not let anybody up, newsmen or delegates, has now extended this morning to new controls on our floor cameras and our floor reporters. . . . All floor interviews now today

must be conducted on blue carpet areas. They will not be permitted
on red carpet areas. The aisles must be kept clear. . . . The blue carpet areas are the areas in which the delegates are seated. . . . In other
words, you can't stand in the aisles to conduct an interview. By the
same token, the delegates are instructed they can't wander up and
down the aisles. They must stay in their seats or go directly to an exit
or an entrance. Incredible, really, for a supposedly democratic, small
d, procedure.

This news tidbit was not revisited, and it was immediately apparent
that the rule had not stuck at all, as interviews were being conducted
every which place, and the aisles were never cleared of people. Moments after his forced, cheerful good morning to the mayor, Cronkite
was already finding it challenging to stay upbeat because of Daley's assault on the professional norms of working journalists. He stops grasping for "balancing" statements about Daley only at 9:00 p.m., when he
sees video of what is happening in downtown Chicago. But that gets us
ahead of our story.

The point is that Cronkite is trying to distance himself from the previous day. It's a *new* day. The Vietnam debate will take place, Humphrey
will be nominated, and everything will theoretically get back on track.
Meanwhile, as the clock ticks toward noon, when the convention is
supposed to start up again, Huntley and Brinkley take a moment not
to distance themselves from Tuesday but instead to revisit it. Brinkley
says, "We have tape of all this confusion and anger and shouting, and
here it is. This is the way it went." As the tape rolls from the previous
night, Huntley provides a few voice-over explanations of whom we are
seeing and what is happening, noting that Daley suggests in the final
moments that the observation galleries should be cleared of loud protestors and that "the delegates, many of them, don't like this, feeling
that Mayor Daley has been clearing too many parks, streets, parking
lots, and other areas in Chicago all week." Brinkley archly adds, "What
right does Daley have to clear the galleries? It's not his convention."
It's worth adding that the night before, viewers saw Daley menacingly

slice his throat with his finger no less than four times to indicate "cut!"—
that is, shut down the convention. Also, Daley had flat out lied that the
protest was coming from the galleries, which were mostly empty. It was
the protesting delegates who had made it impossible to go on the night
before, and Daley knew it, but it made the Democratic Party look bad,
so he made up an alternative story.

The night before, disaffected delegates had called for a resumption
on Wednesday at 4:00 p.m. specifically so that TV viewers could watch
the Vietnam debate. The convention organizers had instead scheduled
a noon start time specifically to keep that debate from happening during
prime time—the same reason they had wanted the debate on Tuesday
at 1:00 a.m. Newspapers and magazines provided extensive coverage
of the convention, but those stories came out after the fact. It is impossible to overstate how important *live viewing* by a mass broadcast audience was to the whole affair. The pro-Humphrey forces did not want
Americans to see the Vietnam debate; the pro-McCarthy forces did.

This may be hard to understand fifty years later, when the post-
network audience experiences few televisual events live and collectively, outside of major sporting events and elections, but consider
one twenty-first-century example: the marathon debate on articles of
presidential impeachment held by the House Judiciary Committee on
December 12, 2019. The Republicans deliberately slowed proceedings
all day, demanding procedural roll call votes over and over again; the
final vote for or against impeachment had been scheduled to come at
5:00 p.m. The idea on the Republican side was to delay until TV viewers
had given up for the day. At 11:15 p.m. it was finally time to vote, and
Democratic Chairman Jerry Nadler declared it had been a long day and
that everyone should "search their consciences before we cast our final
votes." He then gaveled out, adjourning until 10:00 the next morning,
and blindsiding President Trump's supporters, who correctly assessed
that Democrats did it to "get better television coverage."[11] If the Democrats had allowed the vote, of course, the GOP would have said they
pushed through the vote in the dead of night. That's exactly what Daley, DNC Chairman Carl Albert, Lyndon Johnson, and Platform Com-

mittee Chairman Hale Boggs had all been hoping for in Chicago, and they had been foiled.

Reconvening at noon on Wednesday was not as good as 4:00, but it was better than voting on Vietnam at 3:00 or 4:00 in the morning. That said, in light of the conditions Cronkite had reported—deadly slow transportation, exhaustion, no breakfast, and, on the political side, the need for delegations to caucus before Chairman Carl Albert gaveled in the new day of proceedings—it didn't look like things would get underway at noon. Cronkite noted that there were supposed to be 5,611 people in attendance, but eyeballing it from up in the booth, it looked like a scant 1,000 had arrived. Overhead shots revealed the Illinois delegate area as completely empty. In fact, Daley and his delegates were caucusing and began to trickle in only at 2:00 p.m. But Carl Albert was determined to start on time as a matter of principle.

So at noon, the great African American gospel singer Mahalia Jackson sang the National Anthem before a handful of delegates. Jackson had closed out the Democratic convention in Chicago in 1956, and she was famous in particular for singing right before Rev. King's "I Have a Dream" speech in 1963. Like Aretha Franklin, she had performed at King's funeral. Arguably, no singer was more strongly associated with the civil rights movement. Jackson was a less controversial choice than Franklin, though, because she usually stuck to religious music. Ralph Ellison wrote in 1958 that Jackson saw the blues and jazz as "profane forms and a temptation to be resisted."[12] Jackson was a Chicagoan who was fond of her city, but when she bought a house in a white neighborhood she received bomb threats, and her windows were shot out. Whites moved away, and it became a Black neighborhood.[13] This white flight was exactly the sort of thing that Daley's city planning strategies worked hard against.

The convention organizers were taking no chances at further angering southern delegates or TV viewers. Jackson was not on the dais but was shunted off to the side, performing in front of the orchestra.[14] It's a full-throated performance that surprisingly fails to hit a few low notes; the arrangement is standard. NBC cuts to a shot of two flags waving outside the Amphitheatre, the camera slowly pulling back to show the expanse of the convention center, but stopping when the first ring of barbed wire appears in the lower left corner. Then NBC cuts inside to show a flag waving there, with the completely empty guest gallery as background. It's meant as a straight-up display of respect for the anthem, but the flag is fluttering wildly. Indoors. There has to be a wind machine making this happen. Between the awkward misplacement of Jackson, the glimpse of barbed wire, the obvious artifice of the rippling flag, and the low delegate count, day three does not seem to be getting off to a strong start.

The Vietnam Debate, at Last

Following the anthem, the networks wait for more delegates to arrive so things can get underway. NBC correspondent Sander Vanocur takes the opportunity to interview Donald Peterson, chairman of the Wisconsin delegation. Peterson was a McCarthy supporter and a dyed-in-the-wool Democrat, a self-described "child of the Depression." As a kid, he recalled, he had run down the street hollering, "We want Roosevelt! Phooey on Hoover!"[15] Peterson was the one who had called for adjournment the night before, and he would call for it again today. In fact, by the end of Wednesday Peterson emerged as a sort of hero who stood up for decency and democracy without grandstanding, or shouting, or sounding like a self-serving politician. Speaking with Vanocur, Peterson rejects Daley's tactics on the floor as "demagogic" and bemoans the policing of Wisconsin alternate delegates, who are being harassed about their credentials. He complains that the security guards are "not part of this convention. They're not running this convention. This is not a Gestapo country. This is *our* delegation, not theirs." It was the first time the word "Gestapo" was used in network convention coverage, but it would not be the last.

Brinkley follows up by declaring boldly, "I would like to cast one private, nonpartisan unofficial vote for something for Donald Peterson. I thought he was just great. He talked extemporaneously and eloquently for simple fairness and decency and the vast capacity of the American people, including the delegates, to resent mulishness, pigheadedness, stupidity, and pushing people around as if they were a band of *sheep*, which is pretty much what has happened here. That's the much-discussed electronic credentials machine at the front door [a camera cuts to the card reader]. It's quite complicated, rather slow, and it has caused considerable problems with delegates and alternates coming in and going out." Huntley adds, "Then after you get through the machine you step over to a table if you're carrying any sort of a case, purse, valise, whatever. You must open it and let it be searched," to which Brinkley sadly responds, "I must say, I couldn't argue too much with that. You know, we have had a few people murdered in this country, and there are a lot of nuts around, and if they want to open briefcases and so on. . . . It might have been nice if they'd had a little more security in Los Angeles." Brinkley is visibly moved by his recollection of the RFK assassination.

NBC's anchormen have done a lot here in just a little time. They've praised a delegate but made it clear that their respect for him is about personality and character, not politics, so as to maintain their professional neutrality. They've done some hard analysis of the technical crisis with the credential reading machines—analysis that would have chagrined Daley's security people. And they've realistically noted the need for some kind of safety measures in a year of street protests, violence, and assassinations. Those who later wrote off the networks as "biased" or "liberal" in Chicago were clearly not giving weight to moments like this. The coverage was too sympathetic to Peterson to please Daley, too sympathetic to the need for floor security to please the delegates, and too critical of the mechanics of the convention to please the Democratic bosses. It's not the intention of the anchormen, but the only player besides Peterson that comes out looking good here, in absentia, is the GOP.

It's not that no one in Miami had been opposed to Nixon's nomination. It's just that dissension never made it to the floor. In Chicago, Daley would have liked to have conveyed the same phony picture of unity, and so he made a pig-headed decision: he instructed security to keep delegates from bringing in any kind of signs or fliers that were not pro-Humphrey. The official rule to justify this was the prohibition against floor demonstrations, showy displays of support for candidates that included not only banner waving but also marching bands, jugglers, perhaps even a donkey or two—or baby elephants at a Republican convention. By ruling those out, the organizers had given security guards carte blanche to keep delegates from carrying paper materials, signs, flags, and so on into the Amphitheatre. They weren't even allowed to bring in newspapers, because it would look bad to see people reading on TV during speeches.

The reality was that *all* pro-Humphrey and pro-majority-Vietnam plank materials were allowed on the floor. If you were wearing a Humphrey button or hat, you were likely to be allowed to bring in as many newspapers as you wanted. During particularly dull speeches, the networks pointedly cut to delegates reading newspapers, which confirmed that the "rules" were applied only selectively. On Wednesday CBS even cut to a delegate reading a newspaper with the headline "CBS Protests Beating of Newsman," a reference to Rather's mistreatment. If Daley hadn't made a rule that angered many, who then complained in network interviews, there would have been less motivation to show people reading the papers. The harassment became the story. So Peterson's complaints about security excesses ended up being a preview of coming attractions as the afternoon devoted to Vietnam moved forward.

Finally at 1:00, the hall was filling up, and the Vietnam debate was ready to get under way. Speakers alternated between support for the majority plank (LBJ's policy, which he foisted on Humphrey) and the minority plank, which called for an immediate halt to the bombing in Southeast Asia. Each speaker had two minutes. No one really expected to hear any new arguments—a demoralizing thought. What was the point of debating? From the perspective of minority-plank supporters (the idealists), there were two goals, one for those on-site and one for TV viewers. The point of shutting down the proceedings the day before had been to show the debate when Americans were awake to watch it.

Ostensibly, this was to show democracy in action, a real debate about Vietnam. But the arguments were retreads that would not be new to many viewers. What the pro-minority-plank delegates wanted people to see on their TVs was less the logical arguments than the emotional responses in the Amphitheatre, people cheering and booing, to show that the Democratic Party could not as a whole stand behind LBJ's platform. The fact that pro-McCarthy and pro-peace paraphernalia had to be smuggled into the hall further revealed that the party machine and the bosses were contemptuous of the will of the delegates—and by extension the will of the people. The idealists prayed this display would advance their cause.

Recall also that the challenging delegations that had been shot down from Texas, North Carolina, Alabama, and other states were full of pro-peace McCarthy delegates. If Mississippi was ultimately the only southern state to go strongly for the pro-peace plank on Wednesday, it was because it was the only state where the challengers had fully displaced the "regulars." This all played out as a televisual spectacle, not because the networks were biased toward the pro-peace delegates, but because the networks turned on their cameras, asked a lot of questions, and showed what they saw. You'd have to bend over backward to miss the establishment's heavy-handed censorship of pro-peace and pro-McCarthy demonstration materials. At one point, Rather reports to Cronkite, "This cart is a serve-yourself Humphrey demonstration supply depot" full of streamers and commercially printed material. The stuff was literally brought into the hall on dolly carts. This, at least as much as an actual debate on Vietnam, was what the idealists wanted American TV viewers to witness.

On top of that, they wanted Americans to see the live vote, which was ultimately roughly fifteen hundred for the majority plank and a thousand for the minority. That did not point to a neck-and-neck competition for votes, but with 40 percent of the delegates against the official platform, it did illustrate the pro-peace delegates' claim that a vote for the majority plank was, in effect, a vote for Nixon. The Democrats simply could not win in November with such spectacular division displayed on national television.

In addition to providing this TV spectacle, a major reason the idealists had wanted to defer the Vietnam debate to Wednesday was to give them more time to beat the bushes for votes. This was tactically key, insofar as few expected to win, but the more numbers they got, the more likely it was (they hoped) that Humphrey might see the need to distance himself from Johnson's policy. One heard repeatedly in network interviews that if the "minority plank could become the majority plank"—if the official platform supported a stop to the bombing—the delegates would do for Humphrey what he had done for Harry S. Truman back in 1948, when he had powered through a civil rights platform that forced Truman's hand on the issue. Humphrey could likewise in 1968 be forced to support an end to the bombing, pro-peace delegates imagined. Numerous delegates were emphatic that they were pro-Humphrey *and* pro-minority plank. This was huge, revealing that some in the "establishment" would actually vote against LBJ's Vietnam policy. There was a televisual element here of showing home viewers that you could be pro-Humphrey and anti-LBJ, but a lot of what was going on here was work behind the scenes, off-camera.

Normally, such delegate politicking was done with the assistance of convention floor phones. Each delegation had a closed-circuit phone (for use only inside the convention hall) mounted on a metal rod. Daley had ensured that lists of phone numbers were not distributed to states that were strong McCarthy supporters, an obvious ploy to prevent organization against Humphrey and the majority Vietnam plank. Many delegations were not even informed of *their own* phone numbers. The California delegation had smuggled a phone number list in for distribution, which had not been easy, with security keeping an eye out for anyone with stacks of mimeographs. Again, convention organizers had defeated oppositional delegates through material means, by denying them the means of communication. It was hard to imagine that newsmen did not feel camaraderie with these delegates, as they too struggled with Daley's refusal to provide adequate numbers of floor passes, with his mule-headed rules about what color carpets could be stood upon, with his efforts to prevent live street coverage, and so on. Daley's authoritarian impulses backfired, even though he seemed to have succeeded with many of his material restrictions. (Actress Shirley Mac-Laine carried a portable TV, and security insisted on cracking it open to check for weapons, but she finally got it on the convention floor. And it still worked!) The mayor and convention organizers' efforts to censor failed precisely because they were so *obvious* that they could not be ignored by the news media.

Amazingly, at key moments on Wednesday, delegates from California and other pro-McCarthy states held up eighteen-by-twenty-four-inch "Stop the War" signs. NBC's Chancellor offered an explanation: "This is the first major antiwar demonstration here on the floor. . . . They were told they couldn't bring in regular signs, so they have printed on pieces of newspaper this 'Stop the War' emblem, which was printed hastily overnight and was smuggled into the hall. And this is an indication of . . . the intense feelings people have brought to this debate on the minority and majority planks on Vietnam. *These* delegates are not apathetic, and they're proving it in the literature they have smuggled in here" (fig. 16). Most of these "Stop the War" signs had multiple fold lines, indicating that they had been folded up and wedged into pockets, shirts, and pants. Some of the ladies' hats were large 1960s concoctions that could have hidden a folded-up newspaper page. There were even some low-tech signs that had been handcrafted on women's scarves, which were worn into the convention unnoticed by Daley's men and then later unfurled at climactic moments on national TV. In forbidding free speech at the convention, Daley had provoked these crafty, low-tech workarounds. His censorship efforts had fired people up.

The minority, pro-peace plank did finally lose, following three hours of mostly dull speechifying by dozens of speakers on both sides. Only five speeches stood out. First, in just one minute, Pierre Salinger gave a rousing oration against the majority plank, arguing that RFK would have felt the same way. The crowd was ecstatic, and David Brinkley said, "That's the first display of real enthusiasm since this debate started." The smuggled signs were whipped out, as NBC cut to people chanting "We want peace" and "Stop the war." A cluster of middle-aged ladies in cat's-eye glasses held up flimsy, poorly made signs that read simply "minority plank."

FIGURE 16. Amphitheatre security forces admitted people with pro-Humphrey and pro-Daley signs and banners, but tried to keep out McCarthy materials. McCarthy delegates responded by smuggling folded-up "Stop the War" signs into the Amphitheatre, hastily made overnight on newsprint. The homemade imagery spotlighted the underdog status of the pro-peace delegates. Associated Press, 1968.

A second unique speech was made by Kentucky senator Georgia Davis, speaking for the majority plank. Davis was the first woman and the first Black person to be elected to the Kentucky state legislature. She had been a personal and political intimate of Martin Luther King, and it was hard to believe she'd be speaking on the pro-war side. And, in fact, she did not. Rather, she made a tight argument against the white liberal notion conveyed in the minority plank that "but for Vietnam," we'd be able to fix up our cities and win the war on poverty. She argued instead that if the United States went back to the tax rates that prevailed before LBJ's 1964 tax cut, we would have the financial resources to solve the urban crisis. The crowd response was less than tepid; she had won no friends on either side of the debate by pointing out that it was the urban poor who were most harmed by the president's "guns and butter" approach. As a teacher might surmise, she hadn't done the assignment. Yet it was a radical argument, made by a Black woman (the only one besides Fannie Lou Hamer to appear on the dais), and aired in its entirety by the networks, in the course of an afternoon that brought mostly platitudes from the rostrum.

The third notable speech was by Senator Wayne Morse of Oregon, for the minority. Morse was one of two senators who had voted against the Gulf of Tonkin resolution, Cronkite explained. (He shares background on almost every speaker, and also little tidbits of convention history, a nice touch catering to the nerd demographic that set him apart from Huntley–Brinkley.) Morse delivered a history lesson on American policy, slamming Nixon for a speech he had made in 1954 about Vietnam, deflecting blame for Vietnam from LBJ, and ending with a shout-out to the repressed of Czechoslovakia. New 16mm filmed reports were still rolling in, and this story was on everyone's mind, including, of course, the young protestors facing off against the military in "Czechago." Notably, several hawks speaking for the majority plank argued that we had to continue in Vietnam to fight communism: look what happened in Czechoslovakia, after all. It was clear by Wednesday that the invasion of Prague could be used to prop up both pro-Vietnam and anti-Vietnam voices. All Morse did was call out Russia for sending tanks into Prague, but the crowd went wild, chanting "Stop the war!" again and holding up their earnest homemade posters.

One of the most disturbing speeches of the entire convention was delivered by Representative Wayne Hayes of Ohio, speaking for the majority plank. He was in favor of continuing the war LBJ's way, and that was standard stuff. But his attack on the Chicago demonstrators was really remarkable. "There's a minority among us represented over in Grant Park," he said, linking the "minority" plank to the depraved kids in the streets, "and let me say to that, the police department, Mayor Daley, must all be related to Job. They've shown that much patience." At this, the crowd erupts with clapping, booing, and a cacophony of noisemaking horns. NBC cuts to Governor Connally, LBJ's accomplice and vice-presidential aspirant, applauding and smiling. We see a delighted Ohio delegation, and then thumbs-down gestures in the Virginia section. The California delegation starts up a "Stop the war" chant, and the smuggled newspaper signs appear again. Hayes continues, describing "a minority, a minority of a minority, who would substitute anarchism for ambition. They'd like to substitute beards for brains. License for liberty. They want pot instead of patriotism. They like sideburns instead of solutions. They want slogans instead of social reforms. And they would substitute riots for reason."

As alliterative prose goes, there's nothing special here. You might encounter similar sentiments in a PTA newsletter, a John Birch Society pamphlet, or the editorial page of a small-town newspaper. In the context of the convention, though, this little speech stands out. It's almost 3:00 p.m. on the third day, and although the TV networks have been downplaying the street violence, the delegates have seen it for themselves and have read critical accounts in Chicago newspapers, such as the *Sun-Times* and the *Daily News*. They've also read pro-Daley, pro-police accounts in the *Tribune*. The idea of "Job-like" patience from the Chicago police was ludicrous, unless you thought that not murdering the protestors showed tremendous forbearance. That's how the police felt about it. Hayes's lines about sideburns and pot tapped into the establishment culture's collective revulsion for hippies. A Connecticut delegate, playwright Arthur Miller, told NBC's Newman at the end of the day that the Hayes speech had been a terrible low point. As he described it, Hayes "attacked the people, the young people, the people with hair, the people who didn't march in step, the people who were on protest marches, and so on. And then suddenly an electricity went through this place, and I saw the whole mob standing up and banging their hands together. And there's where the violence was to me. It seemed to me suddenly that they hated the young. . . . There is a certain kind of aged bitterness up on that platform among the leadership. A sneering refusal to look at these kids and say, 'These are our children.'" The author of *The Crucible* knew a thing or two about the electric charge of mob violence.

Finally Hale Boggs, worthy of singling out as the fifth speaker of interest, closes off the debate by saying, "I think that all of you must agree, and I am certain that the American people must agree, that we have debated here fully, openly, without bias this issue before this convention. I have reserved only a minute or two for myself." He then takes seven minutes to advance a hawk argument. It's the longest speech of the Vietnam debate. Boggs piously notes, "I profoundly wish from the depth of my heart, with every ounce of conviction that I may have, that I could agree with my friend Ted Sorenson from New York when he said that there's nothing in the minority [peace plank] that would not endanger our troops or that would not support our negotiators in Paris. I beg to take exception." His arms stretch wide as some of the crowd cheers. Boggs insists that they've had a full debate, that he has good friends on the other side of the aisle, and that civility and bipartisanship will triumph . . . just as soon as his side wins. He had opened by emphasizing that everyone in the Amphitheatre, as well as American TV viewers, had witnessed a wonderful and unfettered display of democracy in action. The night before he had determined that no one would see this wonderful display. But now he has made the best of it.

The voting followed a few moments later. As the rolling count showed the establishment forces winning, Cronkite pointed out that the numbers of delegates who came through for the minority plank proved that there really were Humphrey supporters who wanted a softer line on Vietnam. Still, by the time the vote concluded at 4:00, there was no doubt that the loss on Vietnam was a loss for McCarthy and the idealists. Wisconsin's Don Peterson explained twenty-five years later, "We did have some degree of success at least in bringing the antiwar sentiment in front of the American people. It didn't pass, but I think nevertheless we won outside of the arena."[16] It's not totally clear what "winning" means here; American opinion against the war had already started turning, months ahead of the convention, in the wake of the Tet Offensive. Any element of victory here lay less in changing people's opinions than in showing a deliberative process on live TV, to a mass audience. The objective had been more to sway Humphrey than to defeat him, although ultimately the push for the minority plank coupled with the chaos in the streets demonstrated to many viewers that a vote for Nixon was a vote for normalcy or some mundane idea of stability—if not a vote for the loaded idea of "law and order." The idealists wanted their resistance *seen*, assuming it would impact TV viewers in their favor. But their assumption was wrong.

Supporters of the minority plank had smuggled in black armbands to wear, to mourn the defeat of the plank. Interviewed by the networks, they despaired that the party had just given the election to Nixon, and they were correct. The convention recessed, with the evening schedule to begin at 6:30 p.m. The official nomination would happen then, and the Humphrey forces were confident of success. Daley left in a fleet of limousines. He was able to eat dinner. The mayor had strong-armed virtually all the restaurants near the Amphitheatre to "take a vacation," and most of the delegates did not have the means to get downtown and back in less than two hours, so they waited in line on-site for cold hot dogs. A resourceful few had arrived with chocolate bars in their pockets.

Interlude: An Afternoon of Tear Gas

In some respects, day three of the convention had gone well for the networks thus far. The newsmen had focused on looking for different through-line narratives to power through two days when the official convention schedule had been stymied. By Wednesday, though, everything was back on schedule for the Vietnam debate and the nomination.

Behind the scenes, journalists constantly faced problems caused by Daley's heavy-handed censorship efforts, and they struggled to keep themselves out of the story throughout the first part of Wednesday. The security man who had punched Dan Rather on Tuesday was correctly understood as expressing the policies of Daley's police force, and the demonstrators were getting their licks from Daley's men.[17] Delegates were increasingly attacking Daley's security protocols as the day wore on, and the networks reported their complaints. But still, the networks evenhandedly refrained from criticizing Daley. For example, even when there was clear evidence that Humphrey posters were being widely disseminated on the floor, Cronkite noted that he did spot some McCarthy and McGovern signs. CBS didn't even comment on the "Stop the War" signs smuggled in on newsprint.

As the day wore on, though, one could not be a responsible journalist if one did *not* report on Daley's excesses. A little after 4:00, NBC cut to videotape shot in Grant Park, where protestors had a permit to stage a rally. The segment has been taken from a distance, atop an NBC van. In fact, it's an unedited, single shot because editing video was difficult and time-consuming at the time. First we see a long view of the park, packed with people, as reporter Jack Perkins explains the scene in voice-over:

> The police had said they would not clear the demonstrators out of this rally. They said they would protect it and let them have it here. But the demonstrators then began throwing paper, tomatoes, [and] stones at the officers. Tried to kick in one of their police cars. And so the police responded with tear gas and then by moving back the line of demonstrators from the corner of the park. And the speaker on the platform [is] trying to keep some degree of order. [A megaphone voice says, "Sit down, sit down, sit down."] It is fairly tense here, and one factor that must be considered is that whenever . . . the police appear, they are automatically referred to as "pigs." [That] is the automatic term by these demonstrators for a police officer. This does not tend to ease tensions. [Camera tilts down to man holding a 35mm camera, bloody face and shirt; a handkerchief covers another man's eyes and nose, but his bloody chin protrudes at the bottom.] There have been a few injuries as the police moved the demonstrators back. [Camera tilts back up to show the crowd.] These demonstrators have just been making their plans as to what they will do this afternoon, and they have decided they will try to march on the Amphitheatre. *They will go ahead with it despite police determination to stop them short.* They will leave this park at about 4:00 [this videotape airs at 4:25] and try to get as far as they can. The police have said they will not let them get beyond the borders of the park. Demonstrators are convinced that many of them will be arrested, and they are prepared for it. [Camera

tilts back down to crowd, revealing a man with nose gushing blood.]
Others who are not arrested they say will try to work in groups of two
or three down the streets and sidewalks to the Amphitheatre and assemble there and try to demonstrate that way. Those are their plans,
and the plans of the police are to stop them.

These are the first shots of bloodied heads and faces that have been
nationally televised since late Monday night, when viewers saw CBS
cameraman Del Hall in the street, dazed, blood flowing freely from
a head wound. The Perkins narration here leans toward showing the
violence as merited. Protestors called police "pigs," kicked cars, and
planned to march to the Amphitheatre without a permit. The last point
made this scene suddenly directly relevant to convention coverage. The
convention center was surrounded by barbed wire, and police snipers
were positioned on nearby buildings. If protestors could make the five
miles on foot, things could get pretty ugly there. NBC cuts back to the
Amphitheatre following the Perkins report, and Brinkley says, "That
was a report by way of videotape. As we have said before, we do not
have the ability to cover these things live because of the strike of the
telephone workers. Since that was taped, the demonstrators have begun leaving the park. Order has been restored. Here in the convention
hall, we are awaiting the votes of two states." The segment had run all
of three minutes.

What was most important was that the images had been shown. The
voice-over sounded like the spot reports that had been sporadically
coming in throughout the convention: protestors threatened to break
the law (by marching without a permit or sleeping in the parks after
the 11:00 p.m. curfew), or actually took action (calling police names,
attacking them or their cars), and police defused those threats with tear
gas. What was different here was *seeing* the actual scene. Many of the
injured young men are wearing suits and ties; nobody looks like a ste-
reotypical "radical." Later on Wednesday, NBC reporter Douglas Kiker
shows additional footage from the same Grant Park scene, again ver-
bally emphasizing that police are striving to restore order, but the final

two images show a medic wiping blood off of a protestor's head and a demonstrator lying like a crumpled bag of garbage beneath a stack of benches, as another demonstrator tries to dismantle the pile-up.

A few hours later, action in the streets merited even more coverage. NBC reported that protestors had made their move toward the Amphitheatre, but it had been suppressed. Video footage from downtown, shot around 7:00, had been transported to the Amphitheatre for airing by 8:00 p.m. The footage runs seven minutes and is composed of fifteen shots—impressive editing for a segment obviously produced in haste, under great pressure. We never actually see the reporter on the scene, Aline Saarinen; we only hear her in voice-over. That had been true of the Grant Park coverage by Jack Perkins and Douglas Kiker, but this is different. First, Perkins and Kiker had a line on the story, and they told it neatly. Perkins later credited his reporting skills to David Brinkley, who taught him, "Say less, mean more. If a story is dramatic, you don't have to tell it dramatically. Be simple. Direct. None of this, 'the nation suffered a great tragedy' nonsense."[18]

Saarinen's coverage could not have been accused of being overly dramatic; she said very little. Saarinen was one of three female national TV reporters at the convention. On Tuesday, Marya McLaughlin of CBS got minimal airtime, and Nancy Dickerson of NBC snagged a few choice interviews later in the day on Wednesday, but was also given precious little airtime. Poor Saarinen was not shown once on camera and offered only a few descriptions of what we were seeing—bird's-eye shots from far away of protestors being pushed out of Grant Park alternating with closer shots of people on Michigan Avenue walking (not yet running) away from tear gas. Saarinen might seem an odd choice for Chicago street reporting. She had worked as a TV art critic, and she hosted a show called *For Women Only* that took on political issues such as the generation gap and abortion, but the title seemed obviously designed to undercut Saarinen's seriousness. (When Barbara Walters took over the show a few years later, it was pointedly renamed *Not for Women Only*.[19]) Saarinen's "camera style was informal to the point of hominess."[20] Reuven Frank, who produced NBC's Chicago coverage, described Saarinen as "an attractive woman of great presence and solid news background. I used to think she could have been the first woman anchor in American network news," but she died in 1972.[21] If Frank had chosen Saarinen for Chicago to test her mettle, what she actually endured was less of a "test" than a trial by fire.

Saarinen's seven-minute, interview-less feature (videotaped Wednesday afternoon but shown after the recess) is mostly shots of people walking with handkerchiefs, and the voice-over and editing is minimal enough that we might call it a sort of unintentional cinema vérité. The result is more affective than explanatory. Saarinen's sparse voice-over conveys both the disorientation and the terror of the scene:

> Both sides of Michigan Avenue are filled with people marching south. The marchers need to be on the Grant Park side; . . . police are obviously alert. [She's coughing now.] What's happening? Tear gas is now coming back in this direction. There's lots of it. We're coughing. . . . We haven't any masks. People are sneezing and fleeing into the [Hilton] hotel lobby. . . . A lot of people were out, just as observers, and are now finding that it's not too pleasant to observe this kind of activity. The marchers are still going on the other side of the street. Perfectly orderly, although everybody's coming by with handkerchiefs and with his nose covered, and I must say my own eyes are beginning to sting rather badly. People are covering their faces [stifling a gag]. It's extremely unpleasant. Uh. The police seem to be taking it better than most people. It's burning your lungs as well as your eyes. I don't know what you do about it [laughs uncomfortably]. I don't have a hand-kerchief. [Unidentified male voice: "Hold your nose."] In spite of the powerful gas, the kids are still marching. It's my first experience of this gas, and I don't like it. [Unidentified man with Saarinen says in muffled voice, "Holy Christ it's burning. . . . Cover your face, . . . and just breath through your mouth"; Saarinen mumbles and coughs.] The kids are still marching, everyone, looks like a . . . whole gathering of people with terrible colds. Everyone sneezing, holding his nose, and of course his eyes are smarting.

All Saarinen has explained is that people have been teargassed. Strangely poignant is the fact that even as her eyes and lungs are on fire, she tenaciously clings to correct grammar, saying of "everyone" that "his eyes are smarting."

Back at the Amphitheatre, David Brinkley states the obvious: Saarinen was gassed in the course of making this report. He adds that she is okay. Anchormen have been making almost casual asides about police using tear gas for three days. What this segment does is transformative by virtue of laying bare the obvious: tear gas hurts like hell. TV viewers have been hearing repeatedly that protestors have defied the police, but that police have "restored order." Only after viewing the Perkins, Kiker, and Saarinen segments is it clear what these words mean. You restore order by burning people's eyes and lungs, by tossing them beneath park benches, by breaking their heads and their cameras.

Nominations and Gallery Packing

The convention resumed the business of nominating the president around 6:30 p.m. NBC again kicks off with Wisconsin delegate Don Peterson, who dejectedly tells Vanocur,

> The Hubert Humphrey of 1968 is no longer the Hubert Humphrey of 1948. I can remember the first time I saw Hubert Humphrey, he was mayor of Minneapolis, standing in a Minneapolis auditorium. I think it was the auto show. . . . Humphrey was off in the corner kind of lonely, and he had a threadbare coat on, a little gaunt, and a little hungrier. . . . I can remember him very vividly coming out to help Senator McGovern in 1962 and how forcefully and well he spoke at that time, when he was the . . . majority whip in the Senate. And he was wonderful. Bring him on the small street corners and in the schools, or anyplace you took him, it was almost like a populist uprising. His subservience to the president seems to have changed him in my mind and in the mind of a lot of other people.

NBC cuts back to the booth, and Huntley remarks, "Donald Peterson of Wisconsin. Articulate, soft-spoken, doesn't get too excited. Regardless of the substance of his remarks, he carries himself well." Brinkley responds, "Yeah, I find him extremely impressive. Without necessarily agreeing with what he says and not . . . offering any view on it, what I like is that he says what he thinks, and he doesn't worry about what anybody else thinks about him." That was all well and good, but the more important point to drive home to viewers was about Humphrey. Was the old civil rights champion a fundamentally different man now? How had the president forced Humphrey's subservience on Vietnam policy? Would the vice president have preferred the peace plank? One could pursue these lines of inquiry without being "unfair" to Humphrey. Instead, Huntley and Brinkley praised Peterson without "offering any view" on his ideas, sacrificing a tougher approach to Humphrey. Later that night, however, Brinkley briefly noted the irony of southern delegations that used to hate Humphrey now being "among his warmest friends" and liberals being "among his warmest enemies."

Meanwhile, NBC's Chancellor was down on the floor pushing Senator Paul Douglas of Illinois to acknowledge that a thousand delegates voting against LBJ's policy on Vietnam indicated an "undercurrent of discontent" in the convention. Douglas responded, "I'm proud of my party that we gave full opportunity for discussion and full opportunity for people to express this point of view, and we won by one-and-a-half to one." Like Hale Boggs, he was emphasizing the performance of democracy that afternoon. NBC, too, was performing its idea of fairness by on the one hand pushing Douglas a bit but, on the other hand, letting Peterson's assessment of Humphrey just sort of drift away. Around the same time, when a story emerged that LBJ was controlling the whole convention from afar, Cronkite ventured, "Of course, there's nothing wrong with all of that, . . . there's nothing illegal about it. It's perfectly good party politics." This was a classic example of the limits of network-era "fairness," with a journalist bending over backward not to offend the president.

CBS also includes Roger Mudd's commentary on the "fairness" of all we have seen, making a full-throated defense of the establishment:

> I've heard dark talk about the retribution and the punitive action and the retaliation, but for the life of me I haven't been able to find any evidence of it. From the first day of the platform hearings in Washington, those hearings were conducted from my observation in the fairest manner that I've seen any group of disparate men collect together and operate on an emotional issue. Full time was given to anybody, to any dissenter, and I think that all members of the platform committee appreciated chairman Boggs's position and the way he conducted those hearings, and out here in Chicago for the last three days, we've had a full debate on Vietnam. Equal time was given to both sides, pro and con alternated. They all agreed to the limits of the debate. They knew that it couldn't go on endlessly. It was a fair vote. Everybody had their chance to speak. And the liberal side, that is the McCarthy-McGovern side, the liberal side on the war lost in a very clean vote. I think there probably is a tendency . . . among some of the delegates here to equate the heavy security with the desires and the mentality of the Democratic Party and the men who are running the convention. And it just occurred to me that we're seeing here a certain illiberality among the liberals on the convention floor. It's one thing to be advocating participatory democracy, but it's another not to be willing to accept . . . a losing vote.

Mudd here sets aside the censoring of floor materials, the control of floor phones, and the failed efforts to keep the Vietnam debate far from prime time. This analysis, which included criticism of the liberal delegates as sore losers, did not come from the anchor booth. Mudd was still stationed in the floor studio with Sevareid, and his analysis, like Sevareid's, was clearly *bracketed off* as analysis. Their literal distance from the anchor booth underscored their material as separate from Cronkite's straight-up reporting. Their work was understood as *accurate* but also as going beyond fact-gathering—a distinction that seems a million miles away in today's era of left-wing and right-wing cable news opinion.[22]

Nominations would be starting soon, and everyone assumed those speeches would take up the rest of the night. Following a long, deadly dull tribute to Adlai Stephenson by Paul Newman, Ralph Bellamy, and Dore Schary—so poorly amplified that the Hollywood men finally stopped pausing for their laugh lines—Humphrey would be nominated by Ed Muskie, the nomination would be seconded, and next up would be nominations for McCarthy and McGovern. Business as usual, after a harrowing afternoon, it seemed.

Yet an alternative story was building steam. The defeat of the minority plank had signaled that Humphrey was unstoppable, and although he had not yet won the nomination, Daley and his men were moving forward as if he had. The guest gallery was strangely empty at 6:45, and a Connecticut delegate complained to Sander Vanocur that this had to do with "the desire *somewhere* to control the demonstration in the galleries." Guest passes were suddenly extremely hard to come by. Vanocur noted that all this conspiratorial talk "sounds like a Kafka novel." The distribution of Humphrey signs was accelerating, though, and by 7:30 Chancellor reported that the gallery was rapidly filling with people holding up Humphrey posters: "It's the politics of the image here on the floor, and the image is now Humphrey." CBS floor correspondents were hot on the story and pushed it harder: Daley was packing the galleries for Humphrey. So much happened at the convention that it is hard to be sure looking back fifty years later what made an impact—outside of the Battle of Michigan Avenue footage—and what was more ephemeral, but there are clues, moments that viewers singled out as impactful in letters and telegrams to the network, and this was one such moment. One viewer from North Dakota wrote specifically to thank CBS for their "fair coverage" of "Daley's claque in the balcony."[23]

Although NBC had been out of the gate first with the Grant Park tear-gas segments, the rest of the night belonged to CBS. After three days of bending over backward to be "fair" to Daley, Cronkite was hitting a wall. At this moment, reporter Robert Pierpont called in from Texas to report on LBJ, and concluded by asking Cronkite how Rather was doing after being punched on Tuesday. The anchor responded, "I think he's alright. Dick Daley's a fine fellow, but when his strong hand is turned agin' you, as the press has felt it was on this occasion, he's a tough adversary."

Cronkite then reports a story that NBC totally missed, repeatedly emphasizing words that pinpoint his frustrations. "The story I [have] to report [is] that one of those *amazing*, almost unbelievable coincidences that have marked this whole convention in the restrictions on the press here, little things here and there that just so *amazingly* seem to come together to force the press into a mold that the convention managers wanted us to fit into here, well *another* one now. It turns out that . . . now that the threat of a revolt against the [LBJ-Humphrey] administration here at this convention has successfully been put down [because the majority Vietnam plank has won], and the nominee will be named to-night, well *at this moment* we learn that the telephone strike which has prevented us from covering the headquarters of the dissident candidates, as well as that of Vice President Humphrey, McCarthy, McGovern, and the others, and the demonstrations downtown, all of that, that [IBEW] telephone strike has been settled. It was settled apparently about an hour after the vote here this afternoon on the platform. An *amazing*, really quite amazing coincidence." Cronkite adds that in a few days, the membership will vote to end the strike "and consequentially [to end] the total news blackout. Of course, it won't matter then."

There wasn't quite a "total news blackout," but it sometimes felt that way to the networks. This development was not a big scoop, insofar as it would not change convention coverage because of the timing, and no one outside of Chicago cared much about the telephone crisis. In a sense, then, it was like when Cronkite had reported on the new rule about carpet colors and interviews: a bit esoteric to TV viewers who were not working journalists. Yet it took little reframing to see that the breaking strike story was part of a bigger narrative, that of Daley seeking to impose "law and order" on the Chicago convention, which

meant not only hammering the protestors but also hammering the journalists. No one had found any direct evidence that Daley had conspired
to extend the phone strike, but the settlement at precisely this moment,
when the Humphrey nomination was guaranteed, could not have felt
coincidental to Cronkite or any of the other journalists. And who the
hell had been cutting the electrical cables to their news trucks down
at the Hilton, just when the IBEW happened to be on strike? Cronkite
didn't dare ask this last question on the air, though Brinkley mentioned
the mysterious cable-cutting incidents later on Wednesday night, in a
flash of pique.

This moment, in which Cronkite leaned into his "amazing coincidence" rhetoric, was a turning point for CBS coverage, which continued to be *fair and accurate* for the rest of the night, but which loosened
its tight grip on the notion of "balance." No one from the Daley administration and none of the police were acceding to interviews, and at a
certain point it was untenable to show "both sides" or to assert that
police were just "restoring order." It took four years for American journalists to figure out that their "bothsidesism" was boosting the voices
of authoritarianism in the Trump administration. It took CBS News less
than three days to reach a similar conclusion in Chicago.

The next key moment for CBS came as the story about packing the
visitor galleries grew. For days, pro-McCarthy delegates had struggled
to get passes for their guests. On Wednesday, the security forces turned
almost everyone away, and the galleries were strangely depleted by afternoon. And then they started to fill up again. Cronkite asked his floor
correspondent Joe Benti what was going on. There were not supposed
to be any floor demonstrations tonight, Cronkite reminded viewers,
and yet it looked like all these new people in the balconies were holding
Humphrey signs. Benti reported the situation at some length:

> Well Walter, it's kind of a riddle that you can figure out the answer to.
> It's not a hard one. . . . It looks as though they emptied out some hiring
> halls and gave everyone a standard packet of pro-Humphrey mate-
> rial, flags and the like, Humphrey buttons, Humphrey campaign slo-

gans, and they're all waiting out there. . . . Many of them are wearing radio and television entry badges, and I've never seen any of them before, and they're all carrying Humphrey stickers and slogans. . . . I saw a man with a CBS identification and a Eurovision badge and carrying a great big Humphrey banner, and I don't even know how he got the CBS credentials. I've never seen him before. It's difficult to walk over to these people to try and find out how they got them, because they don't want to answer. I asked a man outside why they were here, and they said they came to demonstrate for Humphrey. . . . The conclusion to this riddle that I set up at the beginning is these galleries have been *packed*. And they've been packed in favor of Hubert Humphrey. . . . I've been told that there are [expired] credentials here from the past two days of this convention. . . . I wouldn't doubt that there are credentials that are out of date.

This report came in a little before 8:00 p.m. Two hours later, the galleries were even more crowded, and Cronkite followed up with Benti, who explained, "Our eyes tell us that over on the far wall there are many people who probably come from around this amphitheater and from the city of Chicago." "Our eyes tell us" is a strange way to open a report, pointing to the outrageousness of the situation. Up on the dais officials kept insisting that there be no demonstrations or disorder, especially insisting on this point when McCarthy delegates booed, cheered, or sang. And yet, all you had to do was *look* at the balconies to see the rules being flaunted, with the blessing of Daley and his Amphitheatre security guards. Benti continued,

They're telephone operators, for example. They're people from the AFL-CIO. They're people who apparently went to the mayor's office and were given credentials. There're others who picked up credentials in unknown places. Some who got them at the telephone company . . . there are many people here who have deprived others of places to sit. People in the press for example, the magazines . . . are finding that they cannot get into any of the entrances because seats have been taken by other people who also have "press credentials" and probably have never seen the inside of a radio or television station or a newspaper office. . . . When you get up here and you look at some of the credentials, . . . you find that these people are in here with what are called "service credentials." And those are credentials given out to people who work in the cafeteria, . . . in and around the convention hall but not in the hall itself. . . . And as I noted before, it looked to me, Walter, as if many of these people had just come out of a hiring hall. They looked like they were ready to go to work, hard work. And they each had what appeared to be a package of demonstration material, a bigger-than-life-size picture of the vice president, a flag, a noisemaker, and some other paraphernalia which would help the demonstration have more enthusiasm.

A clear picture was emerging. Not only did Daley's people select (or possibly hire, as Benti speculated) these local workers to come to the Amphitheatre, they also gave them credentials that should not have allowed them access to the galleries. Each kind of pass (delegate, press, service, etc.) lasted one day only and allowed access to very specific places. So all this did not add up. Or rather, it added up to Daley putting people to work to cheer for Humphrey. And let's double down on one painful detail here: Benti pointedly reported twice the presence of Chicago *telephone company workers*, knowing what it would convey to Cronkite and his other coworkers. By "the most *amazing* coincidence" the telephone workers had just agreed to a new contract that would end the strike right after the convention, and just a few hours later the gallery was packed with telephone workers with phony credentials. The shameless corruption was too much. The icing on the cake was that people had also been let into the gallery with expired *press* passes. CBS employee Joe Benti was pressing people for information about what exactly they did as employees of CBS, and they obviously had no idea.

In retrospect, historians have accurately concluded that one of Daley's biggest mistakes during the convention had been allowing his police force to physically target journalists in the streets. To put it mildly, that was not a smart tactic if he was looking for sympathetic coverage. The tactic misfired immediately in the print media, as photographers and newspapermen, both local and national, told the truth about what they were seeing. Only the *Chicago Tribune* was a persistent booster for the mayor. And yet this assessment fails to account for how tenaciously the *television* newsmen clung to a sense of objectivity and neutrality, under-reporting the street violence until late on Wednesday. What made them shift gears? A key moment for Cronkite was that "amazing" coincidence of the strike resolution. A second key moment was the packing of the galleries. There were two more key moments: the attack on CBS correspondent Mike Wallace, and the arrival of violent footage from the Battle of Michigan Avenue and from a grenade-launcher incident from Wednesday afternoon. First, the Wallace incident.

Mike Wallace Is Mauled

At 8:17 p.m., Cronkite reported that things had gotten "unruly" downtown and that tear gas was "being rather liberally used" and had even seeped up into Humphrey's suite in the Hilton. NBC reported this as well. No one had footage showing the breaking news on Michigan Avenue yet because of the IBEW strike. So details were deferred.

At 8:20, Mike Wallace interrupts his own interview with New York delegate William VandenHeuvel, telling Cronkite, "There seems to be some kind of battle going on over there" across the convention floor. Wallace makes his way to the hot spot, while Cronkite reports that he sees security "carrying a man out bodily by the legs and the arms." There's a lot of shouting and shoving, he adds, but the aisle is blocked, so the man can't be carried out. CBS cuts to the scrum, a crush of people so dense that no one could even raise or lower a fist to swing a punch; the threat of being crushed or trampled was real.

Security is trying to remove a New York delegate who won't show his identification. Meanwhile, his fellow delegates confirm his identity and that he is a McCarthy supporter, which can hardly be surprising at this point to viewers who have been paying close attention—Humphrey delegates are not being targeted by security. Wallace reports, his voice shaky and breathless from the pressure of the surrounding bodies, "Now comes the strong arm. The Chicago police are coming in. They're coming in hard. They are trying to open the aisle. They have billy clubs out." And then he's gone from the image, as if he has fallen into a sinkhole. Cronkite says, "Whoa, Mike has just been shoved down on the floor there." Rather interjects, "This is by far the roughest scene of the convention so far." The overhead camera searches for Wallace, but all we see is a dozen powder-blue police helmets. Moments later, the camera has not located Wallace, but one can hear his voice reporting that "a whole line of cops and Andy Frain [private security] ushers gave me the bum's rush and kept me from following out. They used the word 'please' but there was no possibility of getting through." Wallace is quite out of breath again. "I'm being pushed back now. And they're trying to obviously cool things down."

A concerned Cronkite says, "Yes, Mike, I saw you shoved down by those fellows. It was a duplication of the Dan Rather scene last night, except I guess they didn't use their fists. But they sure gave you a rough shove." Wallace is now visible, his credentials dangling off of his headgear above his right ear like Christmas tree ornaments, and two cables hanging down the front of his face. He says somewhat unconvincingly, "I'm fine." AP photographers get a shot of him being "escorted" out of the hall by security (figs. 17–18). Cronkite summarizes, "About the worst thing you can say here to these people here is that you're from the press, apparently. They don't recognize *that* as any sort of a pass." Cronkite and his compatriots expected hostility from cops when they were covering civil rights in Alabama or Mississippi, but were shocked to receive the same treatment in Chicago, at an official Democratic Party event. The notion that journalists were the enemy of "law and order" was spreading beyond the South and cracked right open in Chicago.

There were no images of what happened after Wallace was dragged out by security, but both CBS and NBC reported on it. NBC had virtually ignored the Rather episode the day before. The Wallace incident was a bigger crisis from the network perspective, though, even though

FIGURE 17.   Mike Wallace is "mauled" in the crowd, as Cronkite describes it. It is the violence against Rather that has since come to symbolize Daley's attack on freedom of the press, whereas the Wallace incident has been largely forgotten, perhaps because Cronkite did not lose his cool as he had when Rather was struck. Associated Press, 1968.

it has received very little historical traction compared to the Rather incident. Two hours later Cronkite followed up, recounting that, earlier, "Wallace was pushed and shoved, he was *mauled*," and that "during the course of the crush, police commander Paul McLaughlin of the Chicago police told Wallace and other members of the press to clear the . . . area. . . . After an exchange of increasingly heated words, Commander McLaughlin, mistaking a Wallace gesture apparently for a physical threat, struck Wallace in the jaw. The men were quickly separated. Wallace was put under arrest. After questioning at the Amphitheatre, the police command post, at which Mayor Daley and several senior police officers and CBS News President Richard S. Salant were present, Mr. Wallace and Inspector McLaughlin shook hands and agreed to forget this incident." Cronkite was probably burning inside, but he had lost his cool the day before, and he would not allow himself to do so again.

FIGURE 18.   Mike Wallace is hauled out of the hall by security, his headgear (a fancy new kind of transmitter CBS premiered at the convention) knocked off, and his credentials dangling. The crush in the crowd moments before had been spontaneous, but his arrest pointed to how quick Daley's men were to blame journalists for altercations. Associated Press, 1968.

On NBC, even more incredulity was expressed. Chancellor emphasized that this was the first time in his years of attending conventions that armed police had come on the floor and removed someone over a credentials dispute. David Brinkley cut in to add "first time in the United States, John," and indeed, he and Huntley would revisit the notion that what we were seeing both on the floor and in the streets was not what you would expect in America, implying that this was the stuff of authoritarian regimes. Reporting the Wallace story, Brinkley said, "Well, the news media has taken another casualty. . . . Mike Wallace of CBS was . . . detained by Chicago police in a command post trailer on the second floor of the Amphitheatre after the disturbance on the floor of the convention. There is a report that Wallace was struck by a security guard. Chicago's Mayor Richard Daley was called to the trailer shortly after nine p.m. to meet with police, Wallace, and CBS News executives who had also been called there. Reporters were barred from the trailer by a ring of seven plainclothesmen and fourteen uniformed policemen. Twenty minutes later, Wallace was freed." This was similar to Cronkite's telling of the story, except Brinkley pointedly included the detail of reporters being kept away. Wallace ended up being OK, but Daley's men had escalated violence and the threat of violence over and over again—sending police on the floor with batons out, hitting a reporter, arresting the reporter, keeping other reporters away—and all in response to a minor infraction, a delegate who would not show a credentials card, but who had been clearly identified by the chairman of his delegation.

By targeting Wallace specifically, Daley's men had angered the entire TV press corps and made them assume, not unreasonably, that the mayor's objective was to censor. Their response was in no way a form of petty revenge; they did not turn on Daley because he had done all that he could to make their jobs harder. But he had made it impossible to continue the "balanced" approach of ping-ponging between pro and con opinions on every issue. The TV networks would not support any particular candidate or political position, but as the chaotic evening advanced, they would increasingly report violence as violence, not as the police "restoring order." The time for euphemisms had passed. Brinkley signaled this turn when he tartly reported, shortly following the Wallace incident, "We're told the Chicago police are under orders that if they come into the hall to arrest delegates or otherwise perform their duties they're not to wear helmets. Presumably because it doesn't look very good." The tone was snarky, but the analysis was accurate. There was no need to find a balancing comment from the Chicago police. And they wouldn't have given one anyway.

The Battle of Michigan Avenue

The story of things turning violent in front of the Hilton a little after 8:00 had made it to the Amphitheatre immediately, because a reporter downtown could still contact the Amphitheatre if he or she could find a functioning pay phone. Police were keeping some working phones clear for their own use by hanging "out of order" signs on them, a ploy some of the more clever journalists figured out. Plus, the wire services were still working, and teletypes were rolling into the press rooms at the Amphitheatre. So the story that even Humphrey had gotten a noseful of gas went on air immediately. Brinkley also reported that McCarthy's wife could not come to the Amphitheatre because the Secret Service had decided it was "not safe for her to leave the hotel because of all this rough stuff outside." The anchormen reported right away on the impact on the bigwigs, the candidates and their wives, but there was no big story yet about the street demonstrators. The pictures changed everything.

Around 9:00, the motorcycle couriers made it to the Amphitheatre. Cronkite reported, "We've just received a video tape of one of the encounters between police and anti-Vietnam protestors outside the Hilton Hotel that we reported earlier." The network then cut to overhead images, presumably shot from atop the CBS news trucks. NBC used a range of narrators but showed similar overhead imagery, meaning viewers could see a wide shot of police beating protestors with nightsticks, but not much in the way of faces, and no interviews. Cronkite explained in voice-over,

> These are demonstrators quite clearly, as you can see, as I'm seeing for the first time, being loaded into police vans outside of the Hilton hotel. Many were arrested and many injured, dozens injured according to the reports from our correspondents down there. This was at the

height of the demonstrations. The National Guard was called about this time. They advanced into the lobbies of the hotels into which the demonstrators had gotten, with bayonets fixed and with tear-gas masks on. [The images are all in the streets.] This was recorded a little over an hour ago. It is this news blackout, you know, that keeps us from showing these . . . scenes to you live. There seems to be a minister in trouble with the police [the shot shows a man wearing a clerical collar], manhandling him [the minister] pretty severely. [The crowd starts chanting "The whole world is watching."] Since this picture, the scene grew even more wild [camera pans right, revealing chaos, as police run while dragging men and women across the pavement] down at this Michigan and Balbo corner in Chicago. . . . [A cop chases a man with his nightstick flying, but he gets away.] That cop certainly had his eye on a target . . . thousands of the demonstrators . . . they were organized by several groups. Some of them are Yippies, which are politically involved hippies. Others are members of the National Mobilization for Peace.[24] . . . [I'll] remind you that this was recorded about an hour or so ago. We are told that there is a comparative calm at this area now, that guardsmen have since these scenes cleared the lobbies of the hotel. . . . These are the masses of the police roaming up and down Michigan Avenue, chasing down individual demonstrators it would appear, those they consider to be creating difficulties and trouble. . . . There's a young lady, seems to be quite well dressed. [She is crying. This is the first image where we can clearly see facial expressions.] We have almost an hour of such tape as this. . . . The demonstrators shouting "*Sieg Heil*," the cry of the Hitler Jugend and Hitler supporters in Germany during the Nazi regime.

This footage has interrupted official speeches at the convention, and CBS now cuts back to Julian Bond speaking for McCarthy from the dais at the Amphitheatre. The initial scenes on Michigan Avenue rolled for just five gruesome minutes, but at 9:44 Cronkite returns to reporting the crisis downtown, noting that "As there is this display of enthusiasm for Vice President Humphrey over here in the hall, there has been a display of naked violence in the streets of downtown Chicago." CBS producer Phil Scheffler has reported to Cronkite that "the violence seemed to be unprovoked by the demonstrators; . . . police just charged the demonstrators, swinging at the crowd indiscriminately." CBS shows the chaos, but only for two minutes. The reason for abruptly cutting back to the Amphitheatre is clear: Dan Rather has managed to reach Daley. The mayor has been surrounded by a double row of security men all night, and he has refused interviews since the convention began. Rather's access to him now is huge. It is the harrowing street footage of "naked violence" that has dominated our cultural memory of Chicago, but the exchange that ensues with Daley is the single most important moment of the convention from the perspective of understanding the news media, its coverage of the event, its standards for analysis and fairness, and, as if we needed any more evidence of it, Daley's authoritarianism.

Rather opens with, "Mayor Daley, Walter Cronkite is reporting that downtown there is considerable turmoil around the Hilton Hotel. Have you received a report?" Daley responds, "The situation is well in hand. There was demonstrations by people who were violating the law and coming into hotels, contrary to the hotel management and were creating acts of violence. The police report in the last five minutes [that] the situation is well in hand." Rather asks, "Did the hotel people complain, Mayor?" Daley responds, "Everyone has complained. The guests complained about people being there all night, until three or four in the morning. And tonight they were told they couldn't do it, and the police took the proper action to have them comply with the law." Rather pushes on: "Well Mayor, so far as you know, the police did not respond with undue violence down there?" Daley says, "They never do. Our police department is the greatest police department in the United States. And the men in there are all family men, and decent men, and they don't respond with any undue violence."

In light of Daley's shoot-to-kill and shoot-to-maim comments back in April, this notion of no "undue violence" is a tough pill to swallow. The mayor has already made it clear that he favors violence, so if anything is up for debate here, it would be the definition of "undue." Rather follows up on his baseline question: "Mayor, anywhere around the hall this evening or downtown, do you have any report of the police responding with undue force?" Daley again gives his "Our police are the finest men in America" line, but in the middle of this response, CBS makes a key editorial judgment. They cut to a videotaped image marked "OUTSIDE HILTON HOTEL" showing the National Guardsmen, thereby bluntly making the point that Daley can say that "the situation is well in hand," but we know otherwise because the pictures prove it. Note that CBS does not cut to footage of Chicago police beating protestors, which would be an even more blunt retort to Daley. A viewer who had been following TV coverage closely would understand that after the local police made their large-scale attack, the Guard was brought in to relieve them. By using the images of the National Guard, CBS confirms that the situation downtown has turned violent, without going out of their way to attack Daley's "family men."

At this point, Rather pointedly switches gears: "Mayor, do you think the news media have treated you fairly in this matter of the whole convention being here?" Daley says, "I don't worry about being treated fairly or squarely [laughing]. All I know is you do what's right, you don't have to give a worry about the television medium [laughing], or any other medium." This exchange is again aired over images of the National Guard, and while that picture is held, Rather says, "Mayor, you seem to be in a good mood." Daley is jubilant: "I am, we're going to nominate the next president." Rather asks if Humphrey will carry Illinois, and Daley says he will. The image cuts back to the Amphitheatre, Daley slurs a bit through a short exchange about who the VP might be, and then Rather again swoops in with, "What about these reports that downtown is strictly an armed camp? For a businessman coming into Chicago tomorrow, should he cancel his reservations?" Daley responds, "Totally *propaganda* by you and your station and a lot of eastern interests that never wanted this convention in Chicago and a lot of other people who are trying to hurt the fair name of this great city."

CBS now *again* cuts to footage of the National Guard outside the Hilton, as Rather says, "Are the National Guardsmen operating, mayor? We've had a report to that effect. My job is to confirm whether some of these things are true or not." And here's how the interview finally closes out:

DALEY: Why don't you go and see them?

RATHER: Well, they're on the streets right now, mayor.

DALEY: Well what are you asking me the question when you know yourself?

RATHER: Well, I haven't been downtown and I thought that you have communications downtown, I thought perhaps you'd know.

DALEY: Oh, go ahead. [CBS cameras finally cut back to the Amphitheatre here.]

RATHER: Thank you, mayor. Walter, Mayor Daley is in a good mood, but in the Daley style, as you can see.

Daley smiles and applauds a speech on the dais, as a large security man cuts between him and Rather, officially ending the interview. Cronkite immediately confirms what Daley will not: "The National Guard *is* downtown, and the latest report . . . you saw, videotape [was] recorded about . . . forty-five minutes ago, I'm informed, that's what it takes us thanks to the communications strike which Mayor Daley was unable to settle so that we could cover downtown Chicago during this convention."

It is almost 10:00 p.m. on the third of four convention days, and the police have been beating and gassing protestors all week. They've even slashed tires of cars with McCarthy bumper stickers. Now, finally, the networks have given the story some oxygen. In interviewing Daley, CBS has allowed him the opportunity to give his side of the story, and he's made very clear what his feelings are: the police have done a fine job, and the media have offered nothing but "propaganda." Yet CBS avoided what we today pejoratively label "bothsidesism" by cutting to footage that affirms the truth. The video has clearly provided evidence that downtown Chicago is indeed "strictly an armed camp."

News of Violence Filters into the Amphitheatre

The acoustics at the Amphitheatre were bad, and many delegates held transistor radios to their ears to follow the action. A lucky few had portable television sets. The most resourceful attendees managed to get their hands on network news teletypes for live updates on news both outside and inside the Amphitheatre. So delegates did not learn about the crisis on Michigan Avenue all at once. It's hard to discern the exact timeline, but the anchormen got the news right when it happened at 8:15, and they aired footage when they received it at 9:00. There was no acknowledgment from the platform, as the nominating and seconding speeches droned on.

Carl Albert, chairman of the convention, certainly had no self-interest in alerting the delegates that protestors were being beaten just a few miles away. In his autobiography he writes, "Thousands of antiwar protestors, ill barbered, ill clothed, and ill tempered, descended on the city, determined to close the proceedings in the name of peace. . . . When they met Mayor Richard Daley's policemen in the city's parks, . . . riots resulted. All of that the television cameras picked up, and most of the nation saw it. We in the convention hall were among the few who did not." He bemoans the difficulty of transacting "orderly business" in these circumstances and adds that if it all seemed "confusing to a politically inexperienced television viewer, I can only say that it looked and sounded awfully confusing to the presiding officer up there on the rostrum. Confusing, yes, but I got the job done. The job was not to entertain a television audience; it was to see that every view was heard in an orderly fashion. It was."

Having patted himself on the back for his fine management of the Vietnam debate on Wednesday, Albert adds that the next day at 9:00 p.m., prime television time, Americans saw Humphrey give his acceptance speech, "not some riot." He contrasts this with the next convention in 1972, when nominee George McGovern, whom Albert claims was selected by a "hand-picked, stacked convention," gave his acceptance speech at 3:00 a.m., when only insomniacs were watching. He adds, correctly, that few remembered that three rioters had been killed at the GOP's convention, but that in Chicago the Democrats had had "an open convention" and "no one was killed."[25] Here, then, was his assessment of what made the convention a success: no one was killed, and the candidate gave his speech during prime time. This was Carl Albert, in a nutshell.

Daley was in frequent contact with both his men in the street and his men up on the platform. That meant that Albert might not have seen the riots on TV, but he had certainly been informed of the situation. Nonetheless, he made sure that business plowed forward, even as the throng on the floor began to panic, desperate for more details. Senator Abraham Ribicoff of Connecticut was the first to acknowledge from the podium that there was a crisis. At 10:00 p.m., Ribicoff made his nominating speech for Senator George McGovern of South Dakota. McGovern was barely a presence at the convention. He had entered the race only two weeks before Chicago and was obviously in the running purely as a symbolic gesture to oppose Johnson, Humphrey, and the war. He merits barely a page in Teddy White's *The Making of the President 1968*. In theory, a nominating speech for him would offer a moment to speak out for peace in Vietnam, and then the convention would move on. But Ribicoff opens by toying with going off script: "Mr. Chairman, I have a speech here. As I look at the confusion in this hall, and watch on television the turmoil and violence that is competing with this great convention for the attention of the American people, there is something else in my heart tonight and not the speech that I had prepared to give. I'm here to nominate George McGovern just for that reason." At this point, having raised expectations, he goes back on script, praising McGovern on Vietnam, hunger, infant mortality rates, and housing. It seems pretty boilerplate. Perhaps he has lost his nerve. And then he *does* improvise with a line that has become a touchstone in political history and TV history, a line repeated in documentary after documentary: "And with George McGovern as president of the United States, we wouldn't have to have Gestapo tactics in the streets of Chicago! With George McGovern, we wouldn't have a National Guard."

The crowd cheers, and Daley stands and shouts directly at Ribicoff, "Fuck you, you Jew son of a bitch, you lousy motherfucker, go home!" The forceful exclamation was shown on live TV, but this was the one time all night when Daley did not use his microphone, and home viewers could hear nothing. His words were later deciphered by professional lip readers. Friends around him insisted that Daley called Ribicoff not a "fucker," but a "faker." Enemies suggested he had called him not a "Jew" but a "kike." The CBS newsman who was closest simply reported that Daley had gone bright red with anger. The men seated around Daley in the Illinois delegation were grinning and laughing, as they generally did all night. These grins were one of the most gruesome sights in the convention hall. When Frank Mankiewicz seconded the McGovern nomination a few minutes later, he said his man was the candidate not of "night sticks and tear gas and the mindless brutality we have seen on our television screens tonight and on this convention floor," and again the men around Daley smiled and laughed. Francis Lorenz, a Daley man who had been Cook County Treasurer and director of the Illinois Department of Public Works and Buildings, was seated directly in front of Daley and visible in almost every shot of the mayor. He ghoulishly grinned harder with each attack on his boss's Gestapo tactics. It's a strong reminder that the enablers of authoritarianism are not just the men with the nightsticks but also the pencil pushers.

There's a reasonable chance that Ribicoff and Mankiewicz had actually seen the televised images of police brutality on a portable TV. But whether or not they had, they referred to television, because they were fully aware that their audience was not five thousand people in a Chicago convention hall but millions and millions of people in living rooms across America. Referencing an event many Americans had seen on TV, Ribicoff himself became a TV event.

Looking right at Daley, Ribicoff continued, "How hard it is to accept the truth," and then returned to his prepared text. On NBC, Brinkley explained what we had seen and then added some new information:

Senator Abraham Ribicoff of Connecticut, putting Senator McGovern in nomination, standing about fifteen feet in front of Mayor

Daley, looking him squarely in the eye, and talking about Gestapo tactics in the streets of Chicago. NBC's reporters on the floor tell us [that] in general, delegates on the floor are in their seats. Nevertheless, the aisles in the convention are crowded, and we don't quite know with whom. We do know that wherever our reporters go on the floor, they are followed by unidentified, faceless men who attempt to listen to everything they say. Some of them wearing Humphrey badges, some of them wearing badges saying the Textile Workers Union of America, others aren't wearing any identification at all. We don't know who they are, but we do know they are following our reporters around the floor trying to eavesdrop and to see what they say when they converse privately with the NBC control room. As I say, the aisles were clogged with those people, and we don't know who they are. They're *not* delegates.

This is a breaking point moment for Brinkley; the "Gestapo" comment has pushed him to report on strong-arm tactics endured by news people in the Amphitheatre. Like most network-era professional journalists, Brinkley wanted to report the story, not be the story, but it was hard to remain a neutral observer when Daley's men loomed everywhere like Stasi henchmen.

Around 11:00 p.m., NBC's Frank McGee interviewed a young worker for McCarthy named Bob Fitzpatrick, who explained that a proposal was floating around to adjourn the convention in light of the crisis and to reconvene in a week or two at another location. McGee explained that Fitzpatrick had a teletype in hand that had been sent to the Amphitheatre "from a girl named Anne down at the McCarthy headquarters downtown. Copies have been made, and they're using it in their effort [to call for adjournment]. Now tell me first of all, who is Anne, and then read the telegram." Fitzpatrick responds that "Anne is one of our telex operators, . . . and this is what she witnessed: 'The front of the Hilton is bloody. People are being brought in here to first aid station which is across the hall from us. And they have gashes, gaps, and God it can't be described. They are being pounded on. It is the most unsightliest mess I have ever seen. Please pass this information on. . . . Tell everyone . . . the newsmen are getting it much worse than the demonstrators, because they [the police] don't want to publish or show this scene. You would never believe your eyes. Our staff is almost in hysteria. It is too much. I just don't believe that I see all of this. God, please help.'" Mike Sass, a delegate from Seattle, cuts in, "I took a copy of the telegram over there to the Minnesota [Humphrey] delegation. A gentleman there told me it was a cheap trick. . . . He hasn't been watching the TV, and some of us have." McGee is dubious: "Now look, this is clearly a hysterical telegram. Do you really believe it's all that bad?" Fitzpatrick does believe it is that bad: "The Senator himself just visited the floor, the fifteenth floor, where these wounded people are, and was apparently terribly horrified, and our people have been witnessing it on the monitors [portable TVs], and when we received this fifteen minutes ago and in full confirmation, we decided to hold a caucus. And we're going to ask for adjournment." There's a good chance that McGee himself hasn't seen the footage, as he's been working the floor and receiving audio reports via his headgear—hence his response that this all sounds "hysterical." Was it really "all that bad"? Yes, if you saw the footage.

NBC cuts to Newman with Larry O'Brien, Humphrey's floor manager, and asks him if the convention is getting out of hand, with the surging movement to adjourn. O'Brien sugarcoats it, says the convention has been conducted "extremely well," compliments Carl Albert, and adds, "Law and order must prevail in this nation. And it will prevail. And it would be deplorable if a national convention of a great party in this democracy was interrupted in any way by violators of the law, outside or inside the convention hall." This was technically a "balancing" perspective, NBC's attempt to continue the ping-pong between two points of view on how the convention was going. It was one thing to say that the protestors outside were "violators of the law"; they had announced plans to march without a permit, and someone like O'Brien might understand that as a threat to law and order. Inside the convention hall, though, the notion that delegates were somehow "violating" the law by trying to adjourn the convention was tenuous. At best you could say they were violating Robert's Rules of Order. Twenty-five states actually sent telegrams to Carl Albert on the podium on Wednesday stating, "Humphrey has the delegates but not the people." This was a sad testimonial to the fact that half of the delegations had tried to reach the podium with their floor phones, were ignored, and finally found pay phones and called Western Union to get a message to a man less than a hundred yards away from them.

As news of the street violence continued to permeate the floor, the inappropriateness of ignoring the crisis and moving forward to nominate the president had become unbearable to a substantial number of delegates. An alphabetical roll call was being made of every state, allowing them to make nominations. It was largely procedural, and most states passed, but it was a *technologically* strategic moment. The men on the dais controlled when microphones would be turned on and off, and they had to be turned on as the roll call moved from state to state. When Colorado was reached, they should have just said "Colorado passes," since they had no one to nominate. Instead, chairman Bob Maytag asked, "Is there any rule under which Mayor Daley can be compelled to suspend the police state terror perpetrated this minute on kids in front of the Conrad Hilton?" With his typical bureaucratic sangfroid, Carl Albert informs Maytag that he can only answer the roll call and moves on to the next state.

Most states continue to pass, but then someone else speaks up: "New Hampshire is deeply concerned about the situation in downtown Chicago. New Hampshire calls upon the chair to recess the convention until such time as the situation can be clarified for the delegates assembled." The room explodes with applause and whistling, and the official response from the podium is "New Jersey." Moments later we arrive at Wisconsin, where the star of the previous night's shutdown, Don Peterson, says, "Mr. Chairman, most delegates to this convention do not know that thousands of young people are being beaten in the streets of Chicago, and for that reason, and that reason alone, I request the suspension of the rules for the purpose of adjournment for two weeks at six p.m. to relocate the convention in another city of the choosing of the Democratic National Committee and the presidential candidates." Carl Albert responds in his usual manner: "Wisconsin is not recognized for that purpose." Booing ensues once again, as Peterson says, "We want to relocate this convention to another city—" His microphone is cut off, and the vote moves on to Wyoming.

Peterson did not go on to a high-profile political career, and few today would recognize him as an important figure from 1968, and yet for decades, this shot of Peterson insisting the convention be shut down and relocated has reappeared in documentaries as a key moment of the convention, along with footage of Michigan Avenue and the big Ribicoff "Gestapo" moment. In other words, the man has been forgotten, but the moment has become part of the iconography of Chicago. The immediate silencing of Peterson was not because he was a stand-alone hero but because the chairman and others on the dais had made a practice of stifling voices of dissent throughout the convention. Peterson was particularly articulate, but he was no more heroic than anyone else in that room who stood up to Albert, Boggs, Daley, DNC Chairman Bailey, and, by extension, Humphrey and President Johnson himself.

Day Three Closes with a Bang, Not a Whimper

The evening events at the Amphitheatre had been, on the one hand, chaotic and frenzied, as alienated delegates pondered whether they should walk out when Humphrey was nominated, whether they should meet after the convention closed for the day to strategize about forming a fourth party (George Wallace was already a third-party candidate), whether they should organize a vigil with candles in Chicago, and, ultimately, whether they should—or could—force the whole thing to adjourn.

On the other hand, the evening events had gone exactly as planned so far as the pencil pushers were concerned. The proper speeches were made, and Humphrey was nominated. Just after midnight, Carl Albert declared his victory, and the band struck up "Happy Days Are Here Again." Maybe some Humphrey delegates actually believed that sentiment. The other delegates were too tired and frustrated to comment on the irony. To make matters worse, an Illinois delegate moved that the vote for Humphrey be declared unanimous, a standard motion at conventions, Huntley noted. Albert brought the motion to a voice vote, delegates responded by booing, and he declares that all have unanimously agreed that Humphrey is their man. Humphrey had already won by regular vote, and this didn't change anything, but it was a bracing slap in the face to many in attendance, and surely boggling to home viewers. Huntley adds simply, "We've all seen motions like this carry. By what process of logic I've never been able to figure out." Cronkite was more brusque: "The chairman of this convention hammered though the unanimous motion." There was a closing benediction, and delegates began to file out slowly to the buses. The band absurdly played them out to "Everything's Coming up Roses."

At last, CBS and NBC were ready to close out their coverage. Standard operating procedure would have been to take a half-hour or so to review what had happened and to set up the schedule for the next day. This usually included some analysis from both networks, and on CBS some special commentary from Sevareid. But this had hardly been a standard day. The two networks approached the end of the day a bit differently, and ultimately it was CBS that went farther out on a limb to critique the day's violence.

NBC's closing began with Huntley reporting that Daley had been furious—*seething*, even—with DNC Chairman Bailey for giving some tickets for balcony seats behind the rostrum to McCarthy supporters. Huntley subtly stifled a laugh here, since the story of Daley's security men harassing McCarthy supporters and packing the balconies with Humphrey boosters was well known. Next up are a few interviews with sad delegates, one of whom assesses that tonight the Democratic Party "completely lost its soul." We then see a fragment of a speech that had been interrupted earlier to show the "disturbances" downtown.

At 12:30 a.m., NBC cuts to correspondent Nancy Dickerson, who has procured an interview with Walter Mondale, the co-chair of the Humphrey campaign. It's the network's first interview with Mondale, and a bit of a coup. Dickerson had been the first network female reporter to cover a convention, back in 1960 when she was with CBS. In typical fashion, the networks highlighted their newest technology at that convention, and Dickerson had posed with the "transi-talkie," a "miniature" unit for sending audio that correspondents had to cart about. This was considered inappropriate enough for a woman that a well-meaning friend had designed a ridiculous hat to house Dickerson's transi-talkie, but she had instead lugged the unit around in her hands like everyone else.[26] This had always been Dickerson's problem—people saw her as a fashionable girl reporter, and she wanted to be taken seriously. At the same time, her route to success was bound up in being not only fashionable but also sociable; she made many of her interview connections via fancy cocktail parties, and many did not take her seriously precisely because of this. Roger Mudd once said she was "known more for her social skills than her reporting skills."[27] To add insult to injury, a lot of people incorrectly and unfairly presumed she was having an affair with LBJ.

With Johnson on his way out, the assumption was that Dickerson's glory days might also be coming to an end, at the ripe old age of forty-one. This background is relevant, because regardless of the quality of her martinis or canapés when off duty, she was very good at procuring interviews and should have been viewed by NBC as a true asset throughout the convention. She had had very little time earlier in the evening, when she snagged an interview with Abraham Ribicoff, who conveyed McGovern's concern about the "blood on the streets." NBC blew it by not allowing Dickerson to dig deeper with him. She probably could have nailed an interview with Mondale earlier in the night, before Humphrey's victory. But instead here she is after midnight, pushing a story that had been recurring but never fully teased out: "Who ran this convention?" she asks. Mondale replies, "We didn't run it," meaning the Humphrey campaign. Dickerson goes to the heart of the matter: "What about President Johnson? He's been a sort of mystery figure so far at this convention. Was he behind a lot of these arrangements?" Mondale says he has no knowledge of that and that his team won "in a convention which was as fair as any's ever been." Dickerson's not buying it and starts to push, when she is forced to cut to Newman, her interview scuttled. NBC was experiencing some technical problems that made it hard for them to stick with any interview for too long. Huntley hinted that it might be sabotage: "Cables have been cut on a couple of occasions since we all came to Chicago." It turned out to be just a regular technical glitch, but that offered little solace to Dickerson.

Huntley and Brinkley close out the day by replaying excerpts of Aline Saarinen's teargassing footage and also the later, bloodier footage in front of the Hilton. Brinkley offers this introduction: "NBC's reporters and camera crews in Grant Park have turned in a performance that certainly is above and beyond the call. They've had their heads smashed. They've been sprayed with tear gas. Their cameras grabbed and destroyed. That, plus the difficulties we expected, difficulties in live coverage caused by the telephone strike, has made this one of the most difficult assignments they've ever had. But in spite of all that, and more, they have done their job anyway, and they got the news on the air anyway. And from all of us here, all of us, our respect and our thanks." This is a dramatic moment, because Huntley and Brinkley have minimized their frustration with the phone strike (more successfully than Cronkite, who circled back to it over and over again), but they are finally fed up. The cut to tape, however, represents a return to measured objectivity. Here are the events that took place, tout court.

After the replay, Huntley says, "Well, I should think, David, what we've seen requires no comment. It's just unpleasant." Squirming a little, Brinkley replies, "I have nothing further to say about it." Huntley says, "I think that's a goodnight," and David says, "Alright, goodnight." It's a pointed break from their trademark "Goodnight Chet, Goodnight David" sign-off, which would feel very business-as-usual and therefore ridiculous in light of the violent footage they have just shared.

Cronkite takes this not-business-as-usual attitude much further. First, he phones Martin Agronsky over at Humphrey headquarters in the Hilton. Cronkite asks about the mood in the Humphrey suite, suggesting that it must be tinged by the events in the streets. Agronsky tells him that Humphrey "paid very little attention to what was going on outside" and saw it all as "programmed" by the protestors and not representing how rest of the country felt. "The demonstrations were pretty much ignored, Walter."

Cronkite finishes with Agronsky and warns viewers that he now has a "rather graphic piece of footage" from the Michigan Avenue demonstrations. By way of introduction, he says, "We reported earlier that part of the McCarthy headquarters at the Hilton had been turned into a makeshift hospital for many of the young people injured in the clashes outside the hotel." He has just received the film from there. Unlike video, the 16mm film stock had to be developed. This material had been shot from 9:00 to 10:00 p.m., developed, edited, and raced to Cronkite, and it was finally airing at almost 12:30 in the morning. (Network news footage was still being flown in from the Soviet invasion of Prague a few days before, and was considered "breaking," which speaks to a slower understanding of the pace of news dissemination that can be hard to fathom by a generation of media users weaned on social media.)

The four-minute segment features four interviews with people who were attacked by police on Wednesday night. David Schoumacher opens with a man with a bandaged head in the improvised first-aid area of McCarthy headquarters. He and his girlfriend had been sitting in the Hilton lobby, when police had burst in shouting, "Get them the hell out of here!" and tried to shove them through a glass door; both escaped by diving and crawling out through the revolving lobby door (fig. 19). The interview continues:

SCHOUMACHER: Let me get this straight. You weren't out in the streets. You weren't on Michigan and Balbo.

MAN: We were sitting in the lobby of this hotel.

SCHOUMACHER: And what were you doing?

WOMAN: Just sitting.

SCHOUMACHER: Not demonstrating.

MAN: They were releasing tear-gas canisters outside. So we wanted to escape the gas.

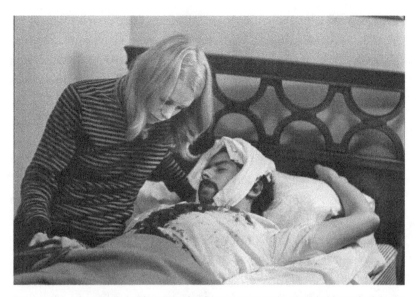

FIGURE 19.   The wounded of the Battle of Michigan Avenue are bandaged with torn bed sheets in the McCarthy hotel suite. David Douglas Duncan Papers and Photography Collection, © David Douglas Duncan, 1968, courtesy of Harry Ransom Center.

CBS cuts to another interview with a wounded man who explains, "I was standing, talking to a mixed group of demonstrators and delegates, out in front of the hotel. We were up against the wall of the hotel, and the police charged. All the people who were standing there were forced back into the windows of the hotel, and they started to break, and I got cut." Schoumacher asks, "Was there any provocation that you could see for the police attack on the group that you were with?" The response is, "Well, there was absolutely none. What happened was they waded into the middle group of demonstrators, and they got done mopping them up, so they just switched. Came after the next group of people that they saw standing there. We fell through the window of the [Haymarket] bar, into the inside, and we're standing there when . . . a squad of police came in and started clubbing everybody, screaming, 'We have to clear this area.'"

Another young man in the improvised hospital ward, also wearing a head bandage, tells Schoumacher, "All of a sudden police charged, . . . and they started swinging, and I fell with several guys and about ten girls. And I tried to cover several girls and myself and just laid there on the street, face down. And I was pulled off and clubbed, and then I was dragged towards the paddy wagon and clubbed again and started to be pushed toward the paddy wagon, when I felt faint, . . . and the only reason I was saved is because a Negro policeman stepped in. I saw many, many people get clubbed, for no reason at all. They were just swinging their clubs. Just a bunch of idiots."

What these interviews do smartly is twofold. First, they dive into what we saw earlier, footage showing police violence that appears to be indiscriminate. For most of three days, the networks favored the mayor's own narrative, that these troublemakers were breaking the law, and the police were just getting the situation "in hand," as Daley put it. You might wonder where the interviews with the police are. Shouldn't CBS be looking for a response from the other side? Such "balance" was impossible, since police consistently responded to journalists with violence or threats of violence. No police complained later that they weren't interviewed. They just claimed the media were "out to get them."

Second, the CBS interviews in McCarthy headquarters allow us for the first time to hear from the victims, making them not generic "protestors" or "hippies," as they had been referred to by newsmen all week but, instead, people. By the end of the day, the networks were even calling them "kids," and for this they were roundly attacked by Daley and others. NBC includes no similar material—their footage is all shot from overhead and from a distance, which conveys the brutality, but in a less personal manner. CBS humanizes the story by showing us faces.

In fact, this was the second time that night that CBS had been able to give a more intimate view of the street violence than NBC. A little before 11:00 p.m., Cronkite reported that things had quieted down at the Hilton, but new footage of earlier events had now reached the Amphitheatre. Like the earlier video, the film showed the Battle of Michigan Avenue, yet it looked quite different. This new segment was shot for WBBM, CBS's Chicago affiliate, by men with 16mm cameras on their shoulders, not by men on top of network trucks; the cameras on the trucks could tilt and pan and zoom in and out, but they didn't convey the immediacy that comes from footage shot with a handheld camera.

Overhead shooting was standard operating procedure in dangerous situations. As Dan Rather explained in his 1977 memoir, TV reporters covering civil rights in the South had a dictum: "Get high and shoot bloody." That is, you'd look for "where the heads were being knocked" to get "the most memorable film," but not from close-up if you could avoid it: "If it appeared there was going to be violence, climb as high as you could."[28] The idea was not just to get the best footage but also to stay safe. Sometimes this meant a trade-off in terms of the impact of the image, for there was an indisputable "You are there" feeling that came from the shaky footage produced by a small camera in the hands of an operator chasing down an image—or being chased away from one. Shakiness conveyed not only presence but also authenticity.[29] The ideal for network news remained a steady image, which was understood as baseline professionalism. But, of course, battlefield footage was normalized as an exception, and the scene at the Hilton was nothing if not a battlefield.

To be clear, the networks *did* have reporters and cameramen in the streets throughout the convention; these mobile crews were using portable 16mm, and getting their fair share of knocks. They all had extra-sensitive film stock to shoot in low-level lighting, and also portable handheld lights. The lighting was tricky, though, because it drew attention from the police, who would shatter the bulbs. But the initial Wednesday-night footage shot outside the Hilton did not come from these journalists but from the network trucks, which had massive lights that policemen's billy clubs couldn't reach. If the 16mm operators in the streets were like combat units in the thick of things, the giant trucks and lights felt more like a Hollywood movie set. You *knew* you were on camera here. Hence the "whole world is watching!" chant.

The whole world got a chance to look differently, more up close, with the WBBM handheld footage. Cronkite narrated over the images: "Demonstrators [are] being hustled, that's the kindest word for it, into the police wagons. These are Yippies and peace demonstrators . . . [who] sought permission to camp out in the public parks and were denied that permission [and] have been demonstrating ever since. The demonstrations have grown increasingly violent." The segment next cuts to bystanders, a middle-aged man in a business suit, with a woman in pearls. The man says, "I've never seen anything as horrible in my whole life." Cronkite observes, "The interesting thing about this is that, almost universally, the bystanders have been horror-stricken apparently by this action of the police. . . . We've had a lot of telephone calls and complaints from people who saw scenes and wanted to report some of them, *people of substance in the community.* Some [of the callers were] delegates to this convention who were downtown." Cronkite next reminds viewers that tear gas had crept up into Humphrey's suite on the twenty-ninth floor and adds that the vice president "made a statement that he was dismayed by the outbreak," but, Humphrey added, "These dissenters do not represent the people of Chicago. They've been brought in from all over the country. We knew this was going to happen. It was all programmed."

Cronkite then reiterates Daley's claim to Rather that there were demonstrators in the hotel lobbies and that it was the hotels that had called the police for help. The reality is that there had not been much protesting per se in the lobbies, aside from the setting off of stink bombs by demonstrators; people did flee to hotel lobbies, though, in an effort to escape tear gas. The WBBM segment ends, CBS cuts back to the anchor booth, and Cronkite reminds us of Rosey Grier's earlier statement. When asked about the notion of law-abiding citizens calling the police for help against protestors, he had replied that this was a bit like saying the people of Czechoslovakia called for help and received Russian tanks.

Cronkite is tapping into journalistic standards of fairness: he shows the footage, he describes it and provides some objective context (demonstrators were denied permits, etc.), he includes one comment from the proverbial man in the street (the middle-aged businessman), one from a politician (Humphrey), one from an official (Daley), and one from a delegate (Grier). But he has also included some key material that conveys his analysis of the situation. Bystanders are horrified. Even "people of substance in the community" are calling CBS to report the violence. This part is striking because, of course, white, middle-class professionals would normally call the *police* to report concerns about violence, but that's not an option when the police are the perpetrators. Cronkite retains his composure, but he is obviously struck by the horror conveyed by bystanders and "people of substance" on the scene. That newsmen were gassed and beaten by the police in the street—and struck and arrested on the floor of the convention—was understood by him as an assault on free speech. Yet the job of journalists was to be in the middle of all of this. As Rather had stoically put it after he was punched, "It's all in a day's work." When delegates themselves— accountants in Brooks Brothers shirts, librarians with prim leatherette handbags—who wandered onto Michigan Avenue found themselves flying ass-over-teakettle through plate-glass windows, though, things had gone too far. Given Cronkite's concern for both the free expression of ideas and for the plight of the proverbial little guy, there is no doubt that if *only* bearded and side-burned protestors had been beaten by police, the newsman would have been sympathetic to them, but his sense of middle-class propriety had been bludgeoned by the new WBBM footage. It was the straw that broke the camel's back.

"You saw the whole episode from the beginning to the end."

As the Amphitheatre emptied out, Cronkite could have called it a day. But he had just received more new film at 12:30 a.m. The material had been shot earlier, during the teargassing of Grant Park that NBC had largely covered with distanced, high-angle shots. Cronkite's new material, however, was at street level, like the WBBM footage, and it had been shot by CBS's own national crew.

Cronkite begins his setup as follows: "We just received a piece of film that perhaps describes most symbolically the situation in the city tonight." That's already strange. Who needs a "symbolic" picture of these events we have already seen quite literally? For Cronkite, this is one of those little-story-revealing-the-big-story moments. He sets the scene for the four minutes of footage he is about to air. "A woman driving through the downtown area at dusk stopped to pick up two of the demonstrators near the Hilton Hotel, shortly after the first tear gas was used by police. Then as she attempted to drive away, she was literally trapped between bayonets and rifle-toting National Guardsmen and the demonstrators. Cameraman Dick Perez filmed the scene. It seems to us that these pictures speak for themselves. Indeed, no further narration."

It is very unusual to mention the name of a cameraman on-air, and it seems likely that two things are happening here. First, the usual way to cut to a segment would be by naming the reporter on the scene, but there is no reporter on-site in this footage, and no voice-over has been added. So Cronkite is, in part, mentioning the cameraman because there is no one else on the ground to tag as the person bringing viewers the story. The second thing happening here is a bit more speculative, but given how moved Cronkite is by the ferocity of the images, I believe he is tagging Perez because he thinks he is damn brave for pulling it off.

Four shots follow. First, there is a quick establishing shot of the scene in the street near the park, showing a man in a suit in the foreground, National Guardsmen in the background, and tear gas and protestors between them. An unidentified man says, "That's gas, . . . oh, gas is being used again!" as the camera pans right to reveal medics carrying someone away. The second image is the heart of the scene. A medium-distanced shot shows a white, middle-aged woman in a two-door sedan. She's in a cardigan, her hair in an up-do, looking very middle-class. She's got a protestor in the front seat with her, and three or four wedged in the back, wiping their faces because they've been gassed. She doesn't know them. She's found herself accidentally driving through a battle zone, and she has instinctively swept up a handful of the wounded. As her car starts to move forward, a line of guardsmen, all wearing gas masks and holding rifles and bayonets, signal that she cannot pass and must turn around. "I just want to get them out of here," she protests.

A guardsman removes the person from her front seat and tries to get everyone else out of the back. One young woman with a peace sign gets out, but the others do not. Now a National Guardsman points a grenade launcher through the open window of the car, a few inches from the woman's head. Cronkite has said there would be no voice-over, but here he does interject that this is an M79 grenade launcher—helpful to know, since it looks like a sawed-off shotgun. Needless to say, it's not the sort of weapon you want to fire about six inches from your target, but if you want to intimidate a housewife who is in way over her head, it's very effective. The woman now says, "You want 'em out of here..." She is trying to use logic: you don't want them, and I'm taking them away. She's confused. The kids have been accused of no crime, and she's been accused of no crime. Why can't she just drive away with them?

A medic is looking in the backseat, because the people in there are suffering from exposure to tear gas. The girl who a few moments before got out of the front seat is now screaming into the back seat, "Get out of there." Another protestor screams at the driver, "Roll up the window and go!" Now a guardsman points his bayonet at the tires of the car. He doesn't strike, but the threat is clear. Another protestor shouts, "Roll up your window, lady, do something beautiful!" Now she's getting it from all sides. What is the right thing to do? The camera zooms in on the masked guardsmen and then the bayonet, and then cameraman Perez swishes left and right, showing the tires, visually building the story. Someone screams, "Do it officer! Show the world!" The handheld camera conveys the growing chaos. And then, quite brilliantly, there is a cut on a swish pan, and we are on a third shot, slightly farther away from the car. A protestor with a bullhorn shouts, "Don't antagonize them!" More gas is released, and the car windows are now rolled up for sure. A man in a suit and tie who has been gassed rushes past the camera, but Perez stands firm. A final short shot shows the car backing up and starting to turn around, away from the guardsmen. End of scene.

Cronkite concludes, "Well, ultimately the woman was permitted, as you saw, to turn the car around, drive away from the area. You saw the whole episode from the beginning to the end. We do not know who the young people were nor who the woman in the car was. We do not know whether the young people were wanted for anything by these particular National Guardsmen. We saw the episode at any rate." Cronkite's angle is clear: the scene speaks for itself.

That's not exactly right; the images are not as patently obvious as Cronkite implies. He depends upon a viewer with inherent sympathy for the well-meaning, white, middle-class woman who appears to have accidentally fallen into a difficult situation. Similarly, he had depended upon the idea—and he was probably right—that many of his viewers would be moved by the WBBM footage of the well-to-do woman with pearls, aghast in the street. They will be moved by the notion that "people of substance in the community" are phoning CBS to report criminal behavior in downtown Chicago. Many viewers will be aghast when they see a minister being manhandled by cops on Michigan Avenue. For most of the convention, Cronkite, like Huntley and Brinkley, has reported on hippies, Yippies, and the Mobe only as a source of trouble, as people "threatening" to march without a permit, as people creating "disorder," which is then restored to "order" by police. He's not completely unsympathetic, but he also knows that the protestors came to protest, they knew there were risks, and they knew about Daley's shoot-to-kill and shoot-to-maim comments from April. Cronkite wasn't taking a right-wing, "they were asking for it" line, but he wasn't being naive about it either: no protestor came to Chicago presuming that everything would go smoothly. In climaxing the day's coverage by showing the beaten in McCarthy headquarters, CBS gave a face to what had been pictured or described mostly as a horde of protestors up to that point. And then, in closing out the day with the lady in the car, Cronkite had shown viewers an image he considered obvious and transparent: the do-gooder was caught up in a scene that was beyond her ken, she was threatened by extreme violence, and she survived, but was it just dumb luck?

Cronkite had made an editorial choice to show these images to make the point that the violence in Chicago was out of hand, and that it was the police and the National Guard who were to blame, not those who had been beaten. This was not a situation that required the view from the other side, a balancing perspective, or a tip of the hat to Chicago's hard-working police—the platitudes he had included in his opening comments thirteen hours earlier. This was, to his mind, simply accurate reporting.

CBS Sums Up "a Shaking Day"

After a commercial break, Cronkite was finally ready to close out the coverage. He tried to get his correspondents going about who the vice-presidential pick would be, but they kept circling back to the street violence. John Hart opined, "I was reminded in watching him [Daley] seated behind a phalanx of security men tonight of similar, perhaps less bloody scenes in other cities in the South while covering the news there. And I also recall the words of some of those sheriffs who told us, 'Well, if you newsmen would go away, and if you outside agitators would go away, we wouldn't have any trouble.' Mayor Daley gave the same feeling. And the same sense in his statements here. I think that one immediate result of this convention, the effect of it, whether or not it is deserved, . . . would be to replace George Wallace with Dick Daley as the symbol of repression by the white power structure." Hart was on to something: if the widespread reaction among TV viewers of the convention had been liberal, this is how it might have gone. Instead, the conservative "law and order" response dominated, and the villain was not Daley and the white power structure but the "liberal" who had "misrepresented" the mayor and his police force.

Joe Benti responds:

The one other thing that we have to be looking at here is, what happens to these Black people who are at this convention, and these intense, angry—I won't call them "radicals," but they're really left. And they're left out now as a result of what happened here tonight, and they're very intense about it, and they're talking about either a fourth party or direct action. The Blacks are talking about *nothing* in this convention that was here for them. I'm not talking about the kind of Blacks that were brought in in Mississippi [the challenging delegates]. They have other problems. I'm talking about the urban Blacks. The people who live in the ghettos and sense the problems and the frustrations that come with all of these riots. These people are very militant, and they don't feel they have any place with Hubert Humphrey or the Democratic Party after tonight.

The dam has burst for these journalists, who are extrapolating from what they've seen tonight to the broader implosion of America on all fronts. That's 1968 in a nutshell.

Cronkite makes some cursory comments about the VP pick again, and then cuts to Mudd and Sevareid for analysis, down in the lower studio. The exchange that follows is blistering.

SEVAREID: This is the most disgraceful night in the history of American political conventions. And I don't mean what happened in this hall but what happened in downtown Chicago. . . . The mayor of this city wanted order. He was going to demonstrate that it could be held in his city of which he's so proud. . . . He has got the opposite of everything he intended to have. I'm sure it's true that the hardcore of the organizers of the protests downtown, the marchers and demonstrators, . . . wanted to produce what was produced in terms of police reaction. But why the police handed it to them is something I don't understand. Do you, Roger?

MUDD: No . . .

SEVAREID: Well, I have personally never seen such cold ferocity by policemen on young men and women. Whatever they've done, they haven't done much more than try to demonstrate. Why it is necessary in order to put a boy or girl into a paddy wagon to beat them over the heads and kidneys and what not is beyond me. I've never been so shaken by anything in a long time. The problem now here is not to heal the wounds of this party, the political problem. That can't be done for some time. The problem is to put some first aid Band-Aids on this party and its warring

factions. That has to begin tomorrow. The nominee has only two immediate weapons for that, two tools. One is his [acceptance] speech, . . . and
the other his vice presidential choice. . . . I'm sorry to sound angry about
some of this, but it's been a shaking day.

MUDD: . . . Nixon just can't wait to get out on the hustings and say, How
can you trust the Democratic Party in office for four more years? They
can't even run a convention. . . . The angry people at this convention
you know, Eric, chose on the floor to link the political management of
this convention with what was going on downtown. I don't think really
that was fair to Vice President Humphrey. . . . During the worst kind of
rioting downtown, the anti-Humphrey people were circulating on the
floor of the convention wire copy stories, an obvious attempt to buttress
the argument that we must recess tonight or must adjourn tonight. . . .
If any man is a goat of this convention, it would be Richard Daley, now
the arch-enemy of his party, and he symbolizes, it seems to me, to the
practitioners of the new politics [the liberal "my way or no way" Mc-
Carthy crowd, i.e., the idealists] all that's wrong with the old politics. I
can't imagine one man doing more damage to a great party in a shorter
time than Richard Daley, and I'm sure the hierarchy of the Democratic
Party is kicking itself, the collective seat of its pants, for ever agreeing
to come here.

SEVAREID: Well, we know the place that is paved with good intentions,
and his were good no doubt.

This exchange was "analysis"—an opportunity to work through ideas
outside the boundaries of straight reporting that dominated on the
floor—but it also had an atypical emotional resonance.

As Sevareid's biographer Raymond Schroth explains it, analysis
was a specific genre, separate from editorial or commentary. Given
how common politically biased news delivery is in the post-network
era, this might be hard to grasp now, but Schroth explains that "an editorial proposes a line of action; an analysis selects a news item from
the disparate events of the day, dissects it into its parts, and puts it in
a broader perspective; a commentary gives the journalist's personal

opinion."[30] Sevareid's remit was analysis, and it's likely he thought the notion that he had just witnessed "the most disgraceful night in the history of American political conventions" was an impersonal and accurate observation. That said, he was personally, visibly shaken by the "disparate events of the day." Although his image at CBS was that of a sophisticated elder gent, he had been one of Murrow's Boys in World War II, and had even parachuted out of an airplane that went down over Burma, where he awaited rescue for two weeks. (He and the other survivors never found the body of the copilot, but they did find Sevareid's typewriter, melted.)[31] He wasn't a tough guy, but he was perhaps a bit tougher than his erudition might have led his fans to believe, and he had been disturbed enough by Wednesday's events to indicate in his own circumlocutory way that Daley could go to hell.

Mudd was a different sort. A hard reporter who worked in CBS's Washington bureau, he had made his name reporting every single day of the epic Senate filibuster against the Civil Rights Act of 1964. When the bill finally passed on June 19, Mudd dramatically recounted later, "the clock read 12 weeks, 67 days, 607 hours, and 4 minutes."[32] Four long days in Chicago was not exactly a marathon for Mudd, and stuck in the lower studio doing some comic bits with Art Buchwald and more serious analysis with Sevareid he was, by his own admission, "out of the loop." Mudd had been the most moderate voice in that studio outpost for three days, and the most critical of the McCarthy supporters. By late Wednesday, Mudd continued his critical analysis of the anti-Humphrey delegates, but he also pointed to Daley as a complete disaster for the party. Even Mudd had reached his limit.

So too had Cronkite, who closed out the day with some frustrated comments about the licks his own people had taken, which he elevated into a statement about the importance of a free press to the existence of true democracy. "I think that we are all wrung out, emotionally undoubtedly as well as physically from all of this. And with those poor kids who took such a lacing down there tonight, still nursing their bruises and some of them hospitalized, we don't know how many of them in jail, it may be a poor time to bring up our own little woes, but I'd like to just add one more note that the newsmen are still being roughed up in Chicago. There were some down there tonight. We had a report of one who was beaten to the floor in the lobby of the Hilton Hotel. One of our people, Paul Sirroco, an associate producer of our evening news program, tried to aid the man, said he was a press man, clearly identified as such, the police wouldn't even let him call an ambulance for him. If this sort of thing continues, it makes us in our anger want to just turn off our cameras and pack up our microphones and our typewriters and get the devil out of this town and leave the Democrats to their agony."

Following these tough words, Cronkite shifted gears. "But of course that's quite impossible. That's just what they want, the people who try to manage the news, is to drive us away from the sources of news. We don't intend to let that happen. We'll take our risks, and we'll be there wherever news is being made. We'll differentiate between those who are injured, wounded in the line of duty simply because they're there, where wounds and injuries are part of the job, . . . and the newsmen who are wantonly attacked *because* they are trying to gather the news for an informed public, by which a democracy must, and will, continue to function." This was a very lucid and energetic defense of freedom of the press, especially considering that the anchorman had been on TV for thirteen hours straight by this point.

After a quick summary of the day and the agenda for Thursday, Cronkite signs off just after 1:00 a.m. The convention will start up again at 7:00 p.m. the next day, with ceremonial speeches, the nomination of the vice president, and a memorial tribute for Bobby Kennedy. It seemed like the worst might be over, and, indeed, the street violence had peaked on Wednesday night on Michigan Avenue. Still, the Chicago police were not down for the count, and neither was Richard Daley.

Chapter Five   Day Four

"Maybe this is a kiss-and-make-up session, but it's not really intended quite that way, Mayor Daley."

Preface: Three Men Face Their Final Day in Chicago

Imagine Norman Mailer, David Douglas Duncan, and Donald Peterson leaving their Chicago hotels on the morning of August 29. An icon of the New Journalism, a renowned freelance war photographer on assignment for NBC, and the chairman of the all-McCarthy Wisconsin delegation—all three had endured a three-day maelstrom of crises, each in his own way. Each was entangled in the convention not only as an individual with strong political opinions but also as a player in this complicated and controversial media event. Each no doubt was ready to go home, but one day of work remained. How to face Thursday?

Mailer was in town to write the second half of *Miami and the Siege of Chicago*. In Florida, he had observed the "muted tragedy of the WASP" delegates, each caught up "in life's harness."[1] He had called out the phoniness of Nixon and had mocked the opulence of the Rockefeller reception, a gilded attempt to seduce delegates with goulash, hams, aspic, and ladyfingers. There was a lip-smacking fervor in Mailer's account that could compete only with Hunter S. Thompson's climactic description of the District Attorney's Conference on Narcotics and Dangerous Drugs at the end of *Fear and Loathing in Las Vegas*. ("These poor bastards didn't know mescaline from macaroni."[2]) Mailer had been in the thick of things in Miami. He had even snuck into a Ronald Reagan reception posing as a plainclothes security man. In Chicago, he had given some rousing speeches but had so far missed out on big convention-hall crises, like the credentials battles and the possibility of a Ted Kennedy draft. He would attempt to lead a delegate march on Thursday but couldn't pull together enough participants. He had somehow managed to miss getting beaten or arrested on Wednesday night, instead watching the riot from the window of his nineteenth-floor room at the Hilton.

In 1967, Mailer had marched on the Pentagon and was arrested and ended up in a holding pen with Noam Chomsky, who gave him the cold shoulder. He wrote it all up brilliantly in *Armies of the Night*. But in Chicago, Mailer seemed to be shooting blanks, making arch observations but not really *participating*. Every scene in *Miami and the Siege of Chicago* that described events at the Amphitheatre itself had also been shown on TV. He certainly appears to have written one of the most memorable accounts of the Chicago convention without actually having attended the event itself. Even Allen Ginsberg—who spent most of the week leading chants in the parks and earnestly suggesting police strip naked and join in—could be spotted on CBS one night shooting double gyan mudra yoga hand gestures from the gallery, and William S. Burroughs, with press credentials from *Esquire*, had popped in on Wednesday night to boo Humphrey during the roll-call vote for his nomination. Mailer assessed that "the greatest excitement in the Amphitheatre was often a reflection of the war without."[3] And so he was without.

As he left the Hilton on Thursday morning, Mailer's thoughts surely did not turn to the official schedule. His challenge was to find some interesting action in the streets. First, though, he had to make it through the lobby. The Hilton had been fouled by mace and stink bombs, the former coming from police, the latter from protestors; the scent of sulfur dioxide, the "rotten egg gas," had wafted into the lobby. The police had discharged so much tear gas on Wednesday night that people desperately scuttled into the lobby, where they involuntarily wept and emptied their stomachs. On Thursday morning the air was still heavy with the stench of vomit. Pity the bellhops and front-desk workers enduring this miasma. It wasn't a scene that a weak man could navigate under the influence of a heavy hangover.

Luckily, Mailer had talent in that direction. In fact, he stopped on his way out for a beer with journalist Murray Kempton and poet Robert Lowell in the Haymarket Room. This was a marvel in itself—the previous night, the barroom's picture window had been shattered by the pressure of police pushing protestors up against it, and then the police had climbed through the empty window frame and beaten patrons, nightsticks thrashing in all directions. That the Haymarket was open for breakfast pints a few hours later is both impressive and nauseating. Eventually, Mailer—having failed to convince Kempton to persuade the New York delegates to march to the Amphitheatre—made it out the door and onward to pursue the day's adventures.[4]

Duncan was also in the business of interpretive journalism, and he had a final photomontage to produce with NBC's crew.[5] In July, Duncan had struck a deal with Reuven Frank, for prime-time "photo essays of the air," with his own voice-over narration offering live "captions," as Duncan—a still photographer, not a TV producer—called them.[6] Frank needed Duncan more than the reverse. Duncan was considered the preeminent photographer of the Korean War, but had also taken hundreds of photos of Pablo Picasso. He brought extra class to NBC's convention coverage. The idea was that the segments would run each night before the opening gavel. At the start of Monday evening, viewers had seen the riveting photomontage that had climaxed with the snarling dog.

Duncan had been working twenty-hour days in both Miami and Chicago. It was impossible to shoot all the photos, develop and edit them, and then air a segment during a single day. Each montage thus drew mostly on photos from the preceding day. "The whole project was suicidal," he said.[7] The last segment, to air Thursday night, would draw on photos shot on Wednesday. Duncan had been traveling from the Amphitheatre to downtown during the Michigan Avenue showdown on Wednesday night, so that street action could not be his focus. Even lacking those key photos, he must have struggled madly to sort out exactly what he wanted to create from the chaos on Wednesday, and ultimately his montage for Thursday did not air until after midnight—not setting the tone for the broadcast day as intended but marking the end, a grim postscript to a grim convention. Given his grinding work days and this final grueling assignment, his thoughts on Thursday morning as he left his hotel were probably on little more than acquiring coffee and cigarettes to fuel the final leg of the marathon.

Don Peterson had fallen asleep thinking about strategy and woke up thinking about strategy. As chairman of the Wisconsin delegation, he had moved to shut down the convention the night before and to reconvene later, in a safer town. His throat was raw from shouting on the floor and chairing endless caucus meetings. As McCarthy's man in Wisconsin, he was bitterly disappointed by the defeat of both the minority (dove) Vietnam plank and of the senator himself on Wednesday. It was hard to know how to push back now; he wasn't a slick political operative. In his book on the 1968 election, Teddy White paints Peterson as a bit of a rube. White first met him at a December 1967 meeting of Concerned Democrats in Chicago that had been organized by Allard Lowenstein, for whom White had little goodwill.[8] Peterson was a sales manager for a dairy products company in Eau Claire, an earnest political amateur with a business card promoting thin-crust pizza.[9] White had sympathy for Peterson, but he also undersold him.

Peterson and his delegates caucused and came up with a plan for Thursday. They would not be transported to the Amphitheatre on buses "like sheep"; that trip was feeling more like going to the slaughterhouse every day. Instead, Peterson and a cadre would walk there. The Conrad Hilton, where Humphrey and McCarthy were staying, was five miles from the Amphitheatre, but the Wisconsin delegates were at the Bismarck, six miles away. It was a long trip to make on foot on just a few hours of sleep, and given the room-service crisis in all the hotels, it would have been hard to secure a forty-cent pot of coffee from the Bismarck kitchen, much less thirty-five cents worth of dry toast. Fueled mostly be adrenaline, then, Peterson and his delegates began their trek, hoping that people might join them along the way, but it was not a *march*, Peterson emphasized. It was a *walk*. Marchers had been denied all permits by Daley. This would be a test. Could walkers—delegates with credentials, and also others, as the crowd grew—be allowed to make their way to the convention center?

Early in NBC's coverage that night, Frank McGee interviewed Peterson, and he surmised that a couple of thousand "clergy and citizens" had joined his walk. There were no signs or singing. Peterson was suggesting that this was not a militant action, that this was not about hippies and Yippies and the Mobe. Peterson was obviously already aware of the fallout from Wednesday night's TV coverage: the media were under attack for showing the police violence, the protestors were seen by many TV viewers as "militants" and "terrorists," and many saw Mayor Daley as a hero. That was a narrative that would gain momentum throughout Thursday and build to a frenzy in the days and months following the convention. Peterson did not believe that the protestors beaten in front of the Hilton had in any way "deserved it," but he did want to offer up a sort of counter-image to the media, a peaceful and dignified "walk." At Sixteenth Street, still almost four miles from the Amphitheatre, the police stopped Peterson's crowd and said they were marching, not walking, and that only people with delegate badges could proceed to the convention hall. Worried that the situation might escalate to violence, Peterson encouraged the crowd to disperse. It was a rare moment in which bloodshed was avoided. McGee followed up a bit coyly by asking if the delegates had continued the fifty-block walk, and Peterson confessed that they had found a ride.

Peterson had not struck a terribly powerful blow for freedom of assembly, but he had made an effort, before attempting more direct action at the convention hall. There, he and other McCarthy delegates would seek out a protest candidate for the vice-presidential nomination. Really, the biggest decision Peterson had made that day was not to make the peaceful protest walk but to go to the convention at all. Was the right move to skip the event altogether, as some frustrated McCarthy delegates did? To him, no. Peterson remained an idealist, with hopes for the party and faith in the system.[10] He left the Bismarck Hotel on Thursday with all of this on his shoulders.

Daley and Cronkite Kiss and Make Up

Network coverage on Thursday night seemed to pick up where Wednesday had left off: the galleries were packed with Daley boosters. But it was quickly apparent that the situation had been dramatically amplified. As Daley boasted to LBJ on the phone that night, he had brought five thousand boosters to fill the balcony seats and told convention organizers who wanted room for others "to hell with you."[11] Now, the galleries were positively overflowing with professionally printed signs reading "We love Mayor Daley." In fact, before the delegates arrived, NBC's camera showed that these signs had been placed in each seat of the Illinois delegation.

The entry credentials used by these local boosters were made of paper, not like the official cards given to the regular delegates, NBC's Edwin Newman explained. The high-tech cards had been manufactured by Card Key Systems of Burbank, California. These cards had to be punched through electronic entryway machines, flanked by sometimes-menacing security men, and this had irked delegates all week (fig. 20). Now a flood of guests was being let in via side doors—locked tight until today, Huntley noted—by flashing pieces of paper distributed by their local precinct captains. Brinkley informed viewers that "the thousands of posters saying 'We Love Mayor Daley' were printed this afternoon at the request of a representative from the Chicago Democratic Organization, [by] a printing plant in the stockyards area near the Amphitheatre, Progress Printing Company." The anchorman added, "There's a print shop here in the hall, and they charge six dollars for signs, unless it is for Mayor Daley, in which case it is free. And somebody went and asked for a sign saying 'Chicago is Prague' (Czechoslovakia), and they refused to print it."

Aside from the obvious censorship and just plain meanness of the Amphitheatre print shop, the situation was galling because Daley's team—Frank Sullivan, the Public Relations Director for the Chicago Police Department—had held a press conference earlier that day maintaining that the "revolutionaries" and "communists" in the street had had "the cooperation of the news media."[12] It was typical for the Daley administration to blame the media for making people act out, but that was usually an accusation they made against *local* journalists, and it must have been vexing for the national networks, who were so keenly

FIGURE 20. The credentials machine policed traffic into and out of the convention hall, frustrating delegates. The chairman of the New Hampshire delegation was arrested shortly after discerning that the devices responded to any magnetized card, indicating the whole system was a sham. Press images of the machines were circulated to convey the technological sophistication of Daley's system, but instead revealed that system's oppressiveness. United Press International, 1968.

aware that demonstrators wanted to manipulate them and were making careful judgments in an attempt to avoid that manipulation in Chicago. Sullivan reiterated Daley's complaint that protestors' main objective was the creation of television spectacles, and yet here was Daley doing exactly the same thing, attempting to micromanage a televisual event. The network cameras were drawn to the pro-Daley signs all night, and now what "the whole world" was watching was a stage-managed surge of pro-Daley excitement. In reporting on Daley's actions, the networks were amplifying them, a problematic scenario that might feel familiar fifty years later to Americans who tracked the media's reactive coverage of the Trump administration. How does one report on authoritarian spectacle without boosting it?

The mayor's motivation was to demonstrate his power. The TV cameras had shown downtown out of control, and now Daley would force them to show the opposite, an exhibition controlled tightly by him. The most discouraging thing of all, arguably, was how meaningless the display was beyond that symbolic value. Demonstrations for Humphrey or McCarthy had direct relevance to the business of the convention, but Daley was not a nominee or even a would-be nominee. At several key moments of anti-establishment upheaval throughout this final night, the gallery crowd broke into deafening chants of "We want Daley!" But for what? It was like going to a George Foreman–Muhammad Ali fight and cheering for Don King all night.

The convention was scheduled to start at 7:00 p.m. but had been nudged to 7:15, so the network coverage of pro-Daley sentiment kicked off the day before the singing of the National Anthem formally set it in motion. But first something extraordinary happened. Daley, who had mostly been snubbing the press for days, had consented to an interview with Walter Cronkite.[13] What followed was a low point of Cronkite's entire professional life: an astonishingly terrible interview with the mayor. Cronkite was not known as a strong interviewer, but he underperformed above all expectations.

The anchorman led with this introduction: "Maybe this is a kiss-and-make-up session, but it's not really intended quite that way, Mayor Daley.

I think we've always been friends, from a distance at any rate. . . . I can tell you this Mayor Daley, that you have a lot of supporters around the country as well as here in Chicago in your own bailiwick. We've had hundreds of telegrams, a lot of telephone calls supporting your position and how things have gone here in Chicago. And the Louisiana delegation today passed a resolution supporting you. George Wallace praised in a news conference the 'restraint' of the Chicago police, as he put it. How do you view it now, sir, after these three days?" Cronkite wobbled his way throughout much of the interview, saying nonsense things, such as implying that he and Daley were friends, and then acknowledging that CBS had received negative feedback on their coverage, the latter move predictable for an anchorman whose professional standards demanded a high level of transparency. Yet he did slip in the line from George Wallace, a comment obviously intended to show that Daley's police had acted inappropriately. If George Wallace gave your police force's assault tactics a thumbs-up, you were doing a very poor job.

Ignoring the Wallace comment, Daley responds with a bit of phony civility: "Well, first let me say that you're a constant visitor in the Daley home every evening." (Cronkite: "Well, thank you sir.") "And we've gotten to respect you for what you say and what you do. Of course as I always said, people can disagree and can differ without any hatred or jealousies. . . . But I'd like to read this statement if you wouldn't mind." Daley then launched into prepared comments about "terrorist" plans to disrupt the convention and "paralyze" the city. He emphasized that the proof that protestors had planned everything that happened was that "they came here equipped with caustics, with helmets, and with their own brigade of medics. They had maps locating the hotels and routes of buses for the guidance of terrorists from out of town."

Bringing helmets and medics didn't mean that the protestors all *wanted* to be beaten but, rather, that they *expected* they would be. In April, the Chicago police had beaten six thousand local peace protestors at a march in broad daylight, and this was a march for which a permit had been granted. *Chicago Daily News* columnist Mike Royko reported that those protestors did not taunt the police. They were not hippies.

They were, in fact, "predominantly white, all ages, middle and upper middle class. They were orderly, relaxed, and cheerful." And yet they were maced, dragged, beaten, and arrested. Police Superintendent James Conlisk had been on-site and approved of his men's actions.[14] That event may well have primed the expectations of convention protestors, and it undercut statements Daley made about demonstrators' malice aforethought. Further, Daley's line about caustics was basically made up. The *Walker Report* found that a rumor had floated around that protestors were planning to blind police with oven cleaner, and in response stores cleared oven cleaner off their shelves, which led city officials to see the empty shelves and declare they had been right and that protestors had bought up all the oven cleaner. The fact that not a single person was blinded during the convention should have been enough to confirm that oven cleaner spray had never actually been weaponized.

Having monopolized the "interview" with this scripted monologue for four minutes, Daley continues off script with a rant specifically directed at the networks, claiming that the electrical strike was not his fault and that the networks had not been allowed to park their trucks where they needed to because they never asked him for better parking. That notion is fabricated from whole cloth, but Cronkite's pushback is modest. Cronkite even concedes that maybe all the networks' requests had somehow ended up on the desk of "an underling." Daley counters, "Why wouldn't you send me a letter and say that you have made this request and nothing has happened? *I said, we want full coverage.*" This last statement is perhaps most galling, given how hard the mayor had worked to stymie coverage. Indeed, a CBS internal memo on "difficulties encountered" as the network headed into the convention, specifically cited "Mayor Daley's repeated statements that this would be a great convention 'with or without television.'"[15] He was on record making such comments. Politicians often lie. That's the game. But they also dissimulate, a fancy way of saying that they tend to lie with finesse. Daley was the kind of man who would look at a blue sky and say it was green, with God as his witness. Cronkite's ingratiating response to the notion that Daley was not involved in impeding TV news coverage only makes things worse: "That's the problem, Mayor Daley, with having your face out there, as the headman. You get the blame as well as all of the credit."

Continuing to steamroll Cronkite, Daley asks why the networks didn't show any injured police lying in the street. Further, "Did anyone show the picture of the confrontation with the deputy superintendent telling them you *can* march if you march on the sidewalk? . . . No one has carried that on this television [network] or any other television [network]. . . . Here's the police saying to them you have no permit, you're unlawfully marching, but we will let you march on the . . . sidewalk if you'll follow instructions. Did you show any pictures of anyone sitting in the streets of Michigan Avenue, blocking the traffic? No pictures of that were shown." This is nonsense: the few times when police said marching on the sidewalk was acceptable, they lobbed tear gas anyway. In a way, Daley's odd suggestion that the networks should have shown the protestors sitting in the streets said more about him than anything else: the misdemeanor of blocking traffic was a criminal act, in his mind, and one which, if pictured, would disgust TV viewers. Sadly, given the level of hostility that conservative middle Americans felt toward young anti-war protestors, that was probably true.

Throughout this interview, Daley repeatedly cuts off Cronkite mid-question. The anchorman does attempt to set the record straight a few times, but Daley tramples him. When Cronkite pushes back on the beating of newsmen, Daley says that they often did not identify themselves (untrue) and that some of the reporters were hippies themselves. Here Cronkite scores what one could fairly say was his only win: "But the fact that some of these newsmen might have been hippies, and that might be true, they might represent these underground newspapers, that's still part of the free press in this country, even if it's underground newspapers."

Daley has no strong response and so switches the topic to the profanity of the protestors, complaining that they used "the foulest language that you wouldn't hear in a brothel house" and asking, "Did you see some of them what they have on their foreheads?" presumably referring to Abbie Hoffman, who had written "FUCK" across his brow. Cronkite is tongue-tied and tries a new angle, awkwardly asking about Daley's throat-slashing gesture the night before: "We don't manufacture the scene, we've just got the camera there, but the other night when Wisconsin was calling for the microphone and suggesting a recess or something, you gave a big cut signal." Daley bizarrely responds that Cronkite does the same thing when he wants his cameras to cut. Realizing this line is not gaining traction, the mayor adds that he was just *suggesting* that a recess be called, as *anyone* could have done. Cronkite attempts to push back: "Did they react to your suggestion?" Daley: "Not necessarily. Not all the time. Sometimes they're like my children. They listen to me sometimes and again they don't." Fact check: Daley made the cut suggestion over and over again, and the dais was directly responsive, a point that Cronkite has failed to make clear to viewers. This is starting to feel like a "Who's on first?" routine.

Cronkite again attempts to shift gears, asking, "Mayor, why when you knew that you were going to need police and protection and so forth, and the mood of the country today, and this isn't [just] Chicago, . . . this is the mood of the country today, . . . why would any mayor want to have a convention in his city when he knew that this was likely to happen?" It wasn't hardball, but it was an attempt at a question with some teeth. Daley jujitsued the query:

Because, Walter, it's about time someone would have some courage in our country. Sure, the easiest thing, and people talked to me the same way you did: "Dick, you're bringing on a lot of trouble for yourself. Why don't you just pass it up?" But if we all think of that, I think there's too much of that. Why is there the lack of cooperation by the citizens with the police? Why is this question about not being involved? We're fortunate in Chicago. Our kids get involved. *They go to the aid of a girl that's or something.* [*sic*] And I love them and admire them for what they're doing. *In many cities that doesn't happen. They walk away.* They see a fellow knocked to the ground, and nothing happens. I hope to God it never happens in our city. I hope men have enough guts and enough red blood to go and help someone that's in trouble. We saw, you saw a Negro go to the aid of a newspaper photographer and flatten a couple of people and threw his body over him to protect him when he was being assaulted by six or eight. It's something about Chicago that has that spirit. This is . . . what prompted me to urge the convention to be held. Furthermore, Chicago's a great convention city. No [other] city has the hotels and locations, no city has the accommodations.

There's a lot to unpack here, amid the expressive knots, but the gist is that Daley is taking the question as an opportunity to explain why Chicago was the best possible choice ("a great convention city"), a city of loving and compassionate red-blooded fighters, where even Negroes help people out. There was also here an indirect attack on New York and, by extension, Mayor John Lindsay, a man whom Daley held in low regard as someone who did not control his city with an iron fist. In 1964, a woman had been raped and murdered in Queens. The assault was prolonged, and reportedly no one came to her assistance.[16] The case came to symbolize the crisis of urban America, but also, specifically, the crisis of New York City. Further, the criminal had escaped from prison in March 1968, so the story had been reanimated. Daley had only to say, "Our kids . . . go to the aid of a girl," and any 1968 viewer could grasp the subtext. Further, a more esoteric political point, but one of which Cronkite was well aware, was that Chicago avoided strikes, unlike New York (which had suffered a garbage strike in February), because Daley had the unions in his back pocket, which again begs the question of why there just happened to be an electrical workers strike during the DNC that crippled the network news.[17] In any case, Daley's response to Cronkite here was truly masterful: Chicago is not a city of police brutality but rather a good city of concerned—and gutsy—citizens. Cronkite was at a loss for a response.

Daley closes out with an Oscar-worthy performance, saying that he had evidence of assassination plots, and that's why security had to be heavy. The Secret Service had in actuality investigated these threats, hardly unexpected at a major political event in 1968, and they were not judged credible, though the Service was obviously on high alert. Daley would recycle this material later in his own film defending his actions after the convention, another bit of irony: CBS let Daley use the video he needed to attack CBS as unfair to him.

Cronkite closes out with his biggest blunder of the entire convention, telling Daley, "I don't envy the mayor of any big city in the United States today. Mr. Mayor, I want to say this too before we leave here, that in the days *just before the unhappiness began*, we were commenting, several of us driving back to the hotel one night, on the politeness and the genuine friendliness of the Chicago police department. We were saying it with a feeling of great . . . friendliness toward them. I think that we all feel it's unfortunate that it's happened. I don't know that you and I have come to a complete meeting of minds on just exactly how these matters should be handled perhaps." Daley responds, "We never will," as Cronkite offers a final uncomfortable laugh; Daley adds, "But that shouldn't be any reason why we can't be friends." Cronkite agrees, they shake hands, and the interview ends.

From the twenty-first-century vantage point of politically polarized cable news and divisive social media, nostalgia for the ideals of fairness and civility that were more common in the network news era is reasonable: there is good reason to long for those high ideals. But Cronkite's closer was "civility" at its absolute worst, demonstrating how a dedication to "fairness" can backfire. These two were not friends and never would be, and the phony cordiality served only to make Daley look strong and Cronkite weak, which was exactly Daley's intention. The milquetoast reference to police violence perpetrated on pro-peace demonstrators as "unhappiness" was jaw-dropping, and the "great friendliness" that CBS newsmen felt toward Daley's police force is weak sauce coming from America's most trusted anchorman. Certainly, CBS employees did not arrive in Chicago filled with simmering hostility toward the police: they were professionals there to do a job, did not expect to be beaten, and had some appreciation for the need for security. And yet all were aware of Daley's shoot-to-kill and shoot-to-maim comments, and also would have been aware of the police attack on local peace demonstrators in April. Cronkite seemed to be seeking the very kiss-and-make-up session that he had rejected as his opener.

Cronkite's strategy going into the interview had been to "outfox the mayor by asking him simple questions and giving him plenty of room to hang himself with his own words."[18] At least that was his excuse according to his biographer Douglas Brinkley. It was not a far-fetched tactic, given Daley's tendency to make off-the-cuff malapropisms and lose his temper, but it didn't account for how to manage an interview subject prone to lying. Cronkite wasn't going to call the mayor a liar out of a sense of propriety, and, further, he did not like that he had lost his own temper on Tuesday and referred to Daley's men as "thugs." It was genuinely weak interview skills coupled with the very notions of propriety, fairness, and balance that are so often lacking today that prevented Cronkite from making strong counter-arguments. He sacrificed defense of the truth to be polite. This sort of sacrifice was unusual for Cronkite, and the point is not so much that he did a poor job; rather, it is to highlight that there were real fault lines in the heroic notion of network-era fairness, fault lines that cracked open a bit wider in Chicago. Today, an emotional TV reporter might be less likely to hide those feelings. And if he or she were dedicated to facts rather than misinformation, pushing aside certain notions of civility—and rejecting bothsidesism—could lead to better reporting with an emphasis on facts over an impoverished notion of "balance" that means including falsehoods.

Years later, Reuven Frank offered a sharp appraisal of what had gone wrong in the infamous interview: "CBS gave Daley a platform all his own, to attack with no one defending, to make unchallenged, unrebutted excuses for four days of what, when they happened in other countries, we called human rights violations."[19] David Brinkley gave his own appraisal not of the interview but of Daley's loud Thursday attacks on the networks, modeling how a journalist might better respond. He reports that Daley had been complaining, as he has every right to do, that he was dissatisfied with television's reporting, coverage of the riot in the streets last night, and he said it showed only the violence and did not show other aspects of it. Well, without attempting to engage in any debate with the mayor, that is not the function of a reporter. . . . The mayor said the television networks did not show all of what happened, [but that was] *because of limitations put on the networks' cameras* by the mayor and his police department. They were not allowed to move around or to operate *anywhere* in the streets of Chicago. What we had on the air last night . . . was made from the windows of the Hilton Hotel, and whatever happened within range of the windows of the Hilton Hotel was what we had on the air. It was impossible to get anywhere else. And so it was impossible to get anything else. The tape we put on was *unedited*, nothing was cut out of it. It was exactly as it was made, continuously, from the Hilton Hotel.[20]

It's hard to say if Brinkley could have gotten a word in edgewise if he had interviewed Daley, but this was arguably the toughest takedown of Daley's censorious impulses by any reporter during the convention. It was "fair" because it was accurate; no phony "balance" was needed.

Of particular concern to Cronkite heading into the interview with Daley were the negative phone calls and telegrams that had been flooding CBS since the airing of violent scenes the previous evening. He had followed his usual professional norms and had been attacked for it. This must have undercut his composure when he faced Daley. The heavy negative skew in viewer responses troubled Cronkite because he knew that his team's reporting had been accurate: the police *had* overreacted and been excessively violent. Every report he had received from CBS employees working in the streets confirmed this, and he would double down on this on air whenever he had the opportunity during Thursday night's coverage.

The Johnson-Stanton Connection

Shortly after Daley's appearance, President Johnson phoned CBS president Frank Stanton. Stanton asks right away, "Did you see us with Mayor Daley?" in a futile attempt to soothe the president, whom Stanton rightly assumes is not calling to compliment the network. LBJ responds by attacking CBS coverage for seven minutes straight, and particularly Cronkite, for "very unfair, personalized reporting." He asserts that the anchorman and his correspondents have "political motives," and even gets conspiratorial, noting that CBS hasn't "hired Bobby's secretary yet, but you've got some of the same crowd and . . . you have evil influences working." Although the notion that RFK forces have somehow infiltrated the CBS news operation is patently nutty, the comment is the only clue as to what exactly the president believes is motivating Cronkite, et al. Johnson thinks they are undercutting the party either out of fidelity to Robert Kennedy, who might well have been nominated if not for his assassination, or out of fidelity to Ted Kennedy, who seemed like a contender to be drafted for the presidency throughout Tuesday, and who some thought might still be drafted for the vice-presidential slot.

LBJ loathed the Kennedys, and the feeling was mutual. Johnson had been seen by Jack Kennedy's team as useful on the presidential ticket for attracting southern votes but had been disdainfully referred to by staffers as "Rufus Cornpone." The conflict was in no small part one of taste and style, a toxic clash between New England reserve and Texas energy. Johnson's feud with Robert Kennedy in particular went back decades.[21] As Arthur Schlesinger concisely surmised, "No affection contaminated the relationship between the Vice President and the Attorney General. It was a pure case of mutual dislike."[22]

The very fact that the Kennedys were an undercurrent at the convention (and a frequent interview topic for floor correspondents on Tuesday) was galling to the president, and to add insult to injury, Johnson was aware that a half-hour Bobby Kennedy tribute film was coming up on the schedule in just a few minutes. Johnson continues, "I hang my head in shame at y'all's performance, both NBC and CBS, and particularly Cronkite for his bitterness and his failure to be fair and objective." He adds one accurate point about the Cronkite interview: "Daley just made a perfect ass of him." (A week later, still fuming, he would tell the editor of *Broadcasting* magazine that "Daley just burnt Cronkite's britches."[23])

Next, the president picks up on Daley's line that the networks didn't show the police being injured by protestors, and then he attacks CBS for giving 90 percent—a hyperbolic figure—of their interviews to New York and California, complaining that he had not seen "one interview from Arkansas. I've not seen one interview from Idaho. I've not seen one interview from Wyoming. . . . I've just seen this pure, damn propaganda of the Kennedy machine. And *you've* seen it." Stanton manages to squeeze in here, "I have, and I raised hell about it." Johnson concedes only that CBS had been fair to Governor Connally of Texas. CBS wasn't avoiding particular states because of their passion for "the Kennedy machine." There really weren't any breaking stories from Wyoming, Idaho, or Arkansas. Most of the news came from states with a large number of delegates. And there was also the credentials crisis among southern states, especially Georgia, an undeniable news story that deserved reporting and had nothing to do with the Kennedy family.

Making an unhinged and incoherent assertion that Brinkley and Cronkite had been "used for political purposes," the president suggests the two anchormen "had a few cocktails, a few miniskirts, been out and seen the [Kennedy] sailboat and had a little political thing [done] to them." To fix things, he demands, CBS should interview governors at the convention who have thus far been ignored. From here, Johnson proceeds to make threats, both veiled and overt. He's just giving his friend Stanton a heads-up, he claims, asserting that this Chicago coverage is just the sort of thing that will get the networks "run completely out of power," and adding, "Now, all of this is going to be looked into, Frank, and all of us are going to have to explain this. And the only test I would use is objectivity, and if these reporters got to get their personal society politics in this thing, I'd damn sure tell them it's dangerous business, and they're playing with fire; . . . you just can't keep punching a guy in the nose without getting something back." Stanton offers a feeble "Thank you very much," and the call abruptly ends. This was all bluster: Johnson had no real plan for an FCC attack on the networks. He was throwing the threat of regulation around as a scare tactic.[24] It was the Nixon administration that would end up punching the networks in the nose over and over again.

There are three key takeaways from this phone call, beyond noting the Kennedy feud and Johnson's trademark bad temper. First, the president was good friends with Stanton, a frequent White House visitor. Daily presidential activity logs often included casual entries like, "Shortly after ending his conversation with Senator Russell, President Johnson headed to the pool with [Jack] Valenti, [Walter] Jenkins, [Pierre] Salinger, and CBS president Frank Stanton."[25] David Halberstam describes a remarkable, somewhat atypical relationship: "He treated Stanton with a respect and deference he showed to very few men—perhaps Clark Clifford, perhaps Abe Fortas. . . . Johnson displayed kindness toward Stanton, a respect for his professional abilities, . . . that he displayed to very few others. 'You always come through, Frank, and I am grateful for it,' he wrote in a note to Stanton in 1964, and those were very rare words for Lyndon Johnson, he liked to keep most people off balance and in his heart felt that no one really came through for him."[26] This phone call on the last day of the convention was not the only time Johnson had discussed CBS coverage with the network's president, but it stands out for its intensity, channeled against a friend who usually received softer treatment. The call points to his especially heightened anger and also, to a lesser extent, to Johnson's privileging of Daley's claim that that coverage had not shown the violence of protestors against police. His complaint about ignored midwestern states was not a Daley complaint; it might on the surface sound like a general concern about overall fairness, but was more likely a complaint about ignoring states that were not pro-Kennedy.

Second, if one can get beyond the issue of the Kennedys and some kind of wild conspiracy involving cocktails and metonymic miniskirts, it is striking to the contemporary ear *not* to hear some accusation about "liberal media bias" in Johnson's diatribe. That's a specific wording that would not take root until the Nixon years, growing throughout the Reagan years thanks to right-wing think tanks and watchdog groups like Accuracy in Media. We do not even hear that the specific problem is that Cronkite is "too liberal." Since the rise of television, no president has been universally pleased with his coverage, but throughout much of the network era, there was reluctance among presidents to paint all journalists with a wide brush as expressing a universally liberal or conservative worldview. Instead, a more common response, before Nixon's rise, was to attack journalists for a lack of professionalism, for not being "objective," or for being too liberal or too conservative on certain issues.

There are two angles to presidential concerns about the media: the situational and the ideological. Presidents expect some amount of deference to the office and willingness among the press to respect the president and convey his messages to the public (a sort of stenographic imperative, which chafes journalists) by virtue of the situation: the president has told them what's what. And then there is the ideological angle, whereby presidents would prefer journalists to agree with their politics and to report accordingly. During the network era, the latter notion was inherently distasteful to most journalists, and yet they did often toe the line. A sort of Cold War consensus, for example, positioned the media to report on Vietnam without questioning presidential motives for many years.

TV journalists, for their part, often stated that pure "objectivity" was impossible, but that they would strive for "fairness" at all costs. In a 1964 phone call with aide Walter Jenkins, Johnson expressed his frustration with Cronkite by asserting, "he's really a Republican."[27] Cronkite was nothing of the sort. He was privately a Democrat and professionally as fair and neutral as he could be. The point is not so much that the president was wrong to gripe that CBS and NBC were in cahoots with the Kennedys or that Cronkite must be a Republican but that at this moment, an oppositional relationship between politicians and television had not petrified into the stark liberal politician vs. right-wing media or conservative politician vs. left-wing media type of structuring narrative that developed later.[28] When the networks reported things the way he liked, Johnson understood them as apolitical carriers of information. When they did not, he called them names and griped to Stanton, among others. As threatening as all that punching in the nose stuff sounded, and as wrong-headed as Johnson's (and Daley's) criticisms of Chicago convention coverage were, the president did not see the media as "the enemy of the people," the sort of language that the Nixon administration was very comfortable with and which the Trump administration would refine into a twisted sort of art form.

Third, the call did result in some blowback, with consequences for the content of CBS coverage on Thursday night, although we may never unearth the details of exactly how it all played out behind the scenes. For context, one must understand that CBS News employees were aware of the Stanton-Johnson relationship, and it made them "very uneasy. . . . They knew that Stanton was in constant touch with Johnson, and they were sure that in his own mind Stanton had his priorities straight, that he was helping a friend who happened to be president, helping CBS in Washington, and alleviating the sting of some of its correspondents [when they displeased the president]. But they did not like it."[29] The discomfort was real, but did it affect coverage? Douglas Brinkley contends that Cronkite did not intentionally go easy on Johnson, but that from 1963 to 1967 "the *Evening News*, except for a few tough Vietnam stories, rarely drew blood against the administration."[30]

In fact, neither CBS nor NBC had particularly drawn blood against Kennedy or Eisenhower before him, though it was only in 1963 that broadcasts increased from fifteen minutes to half an hour, allowing a little room to go beyond the headlines. Even given a full half-hour (twenty-two minutes of actual news time), Cronkite himself was not prone to offering analysis. That was what Reasoner and Sevareid did. As Sandy Socolow summarized, "Cronkite, if he had his way, he would have filled the whole broadcast with hard news: events that happened today, speeches that were made today, or anticipating something that was going to happen tomorrow."[31] In a 1970 interview Cronkite observed that "trying to capsulate everything to get it into that half hour, we can only give a lick and a promise to the *explanation* of why it happened and to the other side in each case." The half-hour evening news was "a headline forum," he concluded.[32]

This is all relevant because if we ask, "Did Stanton's relationship with President Johnson directly affect news content?" we must understand the news's status as *mostly* though not exclusively a "headline forum." When stories were explored in more depth, or with commentary, that often meant full documentary coverage on *CBS Reports*, not via the regular evening news broadcast.[33] Cronkite narrated a long-running and now mostly forgotten documentary series called *The Twentieth Century* (1957–1966), but this offered more historical lessons than political analysis or investigation. There was also an opportunity for more extensive investigation via CBS's innovation, *60 Minutes*, which premiered a month after Chicago. All of which is to say, the "headline format" dominated, and Stanton's interactions with Johnson and any passing of feedback to CBS News was a concern, sometimes a headache, but not a daily or even frequent *crisis* because of the often neutral nature of TV reporting and the fact that Stanton did not have the Machiavellian impulses of, say, Roger Ailes. He was dedicated to the dominant standards of professional journalism of the time.

That said, sometimes Stanton *did* give the newsmen a shove, and it seems likely that this occurred after the difficult phone call with Johnson on Thursday at 7:12 p.m., because about an hour later, CBS did its very first interview with a delegate from Wyoming, a state that LBJ had singled out as one he had not heard from. Joe Benti asked Sen. Gale McGee about the qualifications of Maine senator Edmund Muskie, who had just been nominated for vice president. McGee touted the senator as having "earned his spurs by doing his homework . . . without razzle dazzle. . . . He has a very wry sense of humor. He enjoys a good pun and invents a great many of them. In other words, he believes that it's all worth going through, and living, and enjoying." This was pretty square stuff evoking Dale Carnegie—or even the popular TV priest Bishop Fulton Sheen, who believed "life is worth living!"

Immediately after this interview, Cronkite quoted Sen. Joseph Montoya of New Mexico, again just the type from whom Johnson was saying he wanted to hear more. Asked about the Maine senator, Montoya "commended Muskie highly but said he's completely unknown in the Southwest and wasn't going to help the Humphrey ticket very much there." On the one hand, this was what Johnson had demanded, more coverage from those middle states. On the other hand, it was exactly what CBS—like NBC—had been doing every single day, ping-ponging between pro and con views on *everything*, like clockwork. Cronkite had apparently responded to a request from Stanton—whether relayed directly to him or via an intermediary—to reach out to more conservative states and had done so, while also maintaining his professionalism. Much later that night, he would apparently respond to the concerns expressed by Daley (and by extension Stanton and/or the president) regarding the showing of "provocation" of police brutality by the protestors. That would prove much more problematic.[34]

Robert Kennedy Remembered

But all that was a few hours away. The convention formally opened shortly after the Daley interview. CBS skipped the National Anthem. NBC viewers did hear it, which was unlucky for them. After three days of impressive renditions of this notoriously difficult song, the final day featured Mrs. Warren Hearnes, the wife of the governor of Missouri. She was not up to the task. Given that Thursday felt like some kind of massive hangover from three truly hellish days, a wobbly, sporadically out-of-tune rendition of the "Star-Spangled Banner" was an appropriately deflating way to start the final proceedings.

This was intended to be a pro-forma day dedicated to nominating Muskie and then listening to his and Humphrey's speeches. Before that happened, though, the convention would screen a half-hour tribute film, *Robert Kennedy Remembered*. Kennedy's widow Ethel and brother Teddy had planned to travel to the convention to introduce the picture, but had canceled owing to their own grief and, obviously, security concerns. Flanked by Ethel and her children, Teddy ended up making a pre-recorded introduction. Bobby had introduced the memorial film for his brother Jack at the last convention, which increased the pathos of this moment four years later. Indeed, that 1964 introduction was included in this remembrance film, as was footage from the Robert Drew films *Primary* (1960), *Crisis* (1963), and *Faces of November* (1964).

The film's director, Charles Guggenheim, had done his earliest political commercials for Adlai Stevenson in 1956. He produced a biographical film and TV spots for RFK's New York senatorial campaign in 1964, as well as 120 television ads and 6 half-hour films for his presidential campaign.[35] Guggenheim obviously worked well under pressure; he knew his subject well, and he had a sizable amount of footage upon which to draw for *Robert Kennedy Remembered*.

The film was narrated in hypnotic baritone by Sir Richard Burton. Guggenheim opens with the image of a Black woman in sunglasses, her fist raised, clutching a bouquet of flowers as RFK's funeral train passes. The documentary includes excerpts from speeches in which Kennedy addresses the crisis of Black and poor men bearing an unequal burden in fighting the Vietnam War. It includes his support of César Chávez's movement for Chicano farm workers, showing the senator with Chávez on the day he broke his fast. The opening includes a rather maudlin tune—an instrumental version of "To Dream the Impossible Dream," the theme from *Man of La Mancha*—but later compensates during a campaign montage with "If I Had a Hammer," Pete Seeger's song, as interpreted by Peter, Paul, and Mary. Guggenheim later won an Academy Award for the film, which was simultaneously a comprehensive homage, a celebration of the anti-establishment, liberal faction of the Democratic Party, and, no doubt about it, a heavy-handed tearjerker.

When the lights came up, delegates were hugging and weeping and applauding. Gradually, from somewhere, people began to sing the refrain of "Battle Hymn of the Republic," and soon the whole room vibrated with song. The network cameras cut around the vast room, showing a homemade banner hanging from the gallery, reading "Bobby We'll Seek Your Newer World," and Massachusetts delegates holding up "Bobby We Miss You" scrawled across a queen-sized bedsheet, presumably swiped from a hotel. California delegates held up United Farm Worker "Huelga" signs. It was quite a moment.

Then it became more than a moment. It just kept going. At the eight-minute mark, Carl Albert began to pound his gavel, starting with a benign "This has been a great tribute for a great American," and when that failed to quiet the room, following up with "Will the convention please come to order?" Albert quickly becomes flustered, imploring, "Will the sergeant at arms please clear the aisles?" Albert was a small man with a naturally high-pitched voice; his nickname was "the Little Giant." The glacial blasts of air-conditioning on the dais were meant to counteract the intensity of the TV lights, but they gave him a cold almost immediately, which developed into laryngitis. With each shout from the rostrum, Albert's screech seems to intensify. In the NBC booth, Huntley says, "What started out as a very genuine, emotional tribute is now being transformed into a kind of show of defiance against the chairman, the podium, and the executives of the convention." The network anchors try to discern which delegations are leading the unending tribute, but they can't sort it out, although they do note around ten minutes into the singing that Texas and Illinois—under the control of LBJ's men Connolly and Mayor Daley—are the only delegations that have stopped applauding. CBS attempts to get a few delegate interviews. Through her tears, Shirley MacLaine manages a few words to Mike Wallace. She's attending the convention with Rosey Grier, and he puts a comforting arm around her. Wallace gets even fewer words from Rafer Johnson, another man who had served in RFK's security detail—and, like Grier, a famous athlete. One wonders if CBS correspondents will target Paul Newman next, since they seem to be going for celebrity reactions.

Instead, Dan Rather gets the only really usable interview from this moment, with a minor California delegate, Harry Sublett, who says,

We're just losing democracy in this country as I knew it and as I think Robert Kennedy knew it. You yourself have been subjected to fascist-like treatment in this hall. And when I say that, I don't talk as an extremist but as a concerned American in the name of liberty. We beat young people because they want to express an opinion. And I'm not at all sure that this is too much different than the way that the Czechoslovakian young people were treated by the Russians. I would like to have seen the delegation [*sic*, convention] move to another city, as was suggested by the chairman from Wisconsin last night. And only for that reason have I submitted to this inquiry.

It's a tough closing line, pointing to the difficulty of speaking articulately at such an emotional moment. Mercifully, CBS at last gives up on interviews, as the cacophonous singing continues. One voice rises above the rest, and it turns out that Rather has stuck his microphone in front of folk singer Theodore Bikel.

CBS cuts to an attempted conversation between Cronkite and Reasoner up on the dais. Cronkite is fine in the booth, but Reasoner can barely hear from behind the podium. The anchorman asks what Albert and the organizers are going to do to stop the singing. Reasoner responds, "It looks to me, Walter, that the podium has no plans. I think they're causing it is what's happening. If chairman Albert had not gotten up rather precipitously and attempted to stop this tribute it would have been over by now.... This is now a contest between the delegates, who want to sing for a little while, and the chair. If this is a controlled convention with any intelligent planning, it's very well concealed." Cronkite responds, "Well, you know, Harry, there was a printed program, or the *mimeographed* program, because they haven't been revealing programs to us very far in advance. The mimeographed program came out earlier this evening, had this tribute to Senator Kennedy last on the program. Perhaps they did contemplate something like this but then thought better of placing it at that anticlimactic moment after the [Humphrey] acceptance speech."

Cronkite's emphasis on the word *mimeographed* is more important than it might seem. It's telling that the DNC organizers had given up on using a preprinted program and switched to distributing mimeographs; a mimeograph machine is hand-cranked and uses stencils, a technology that could be used at the last minute to put out revised schedules. It is even more telling that this last-minute schedule had been immediately broken, when the Kennedy tribute film was moved from last to first place. Reasoner tells Cronkite, "I saw that program and couldn't believe that [the film was scheduled at the end] either. It seemed to me elementary that if you are trying to focus the attention of the party and the country on Hubert Humphrey you don't end your last night with an extremely emotional tribute to Robert Kennedy. This is the time from the standpoint of the operators of the convention when it should have been, as early as possible. But to end it up with this argument between chair and the floor is surprising." Cronkite adds that there had been talk among some delegates of walking out after the film, and that's why screening it last had seemed like a good idea to some; a walkout at the end of the night would obviously have been defused of dramatic impact. Reasoner responds that some organizers on the platform are suggesting that the best way to stop the singing would be for Lou Breese and his fifty-piece orchestra to strike up the National Anthem.[36] It's not a good idea, but shows how desperate they are. The orchestra had run through "This Will Be the Start of Something Big," "A Lot of Livin' to Do," and "Happy Days Are Here Again" to drown out delegates insistently singing "We Shall Overcome" after the defeat of the peace plank the night before, and it hadn't made a dent in their revolt.[37]

Now, the whole place has been shaking with "Glory, glory hallelujah, . . . his truth is marching on!" for a full twenty minutes, when suddenly things change. NBC picks up on the fact that a plan is brewing a few minutes before CBS does. Throughout the convention, they've had a slight leg up on CBS by keeping a closer eye on Daley and noting when he has picked up his floor phone to talk to the dais or has left his seat, which generally meant entering the elevated stage from the door beneath it. In this case, he has done both. When Daley returns to his seat, there are two dramatic turns. First, Brinkley reports, "Mayor

Daley's troops have now been called into action on a signal from some-where, and . . . his claque in the gallery have come alive." Exactly on cue, Daley's five thousand guests with phony paper passes up in the balcony start chanting "We want Daley," in an attempt to drown out the singers. At the same moment, a Black man ascends to the dais, and Daley stands and applauds wildly. This speaker was not on the program.

The man is Chicago Alderman Ralph Metcalfe, and he has been sud-denly selected to give an unscheduled tribute to Martin Luther King. Of course the anti-establishment, pro-Kennedy forces will stop singing now to hear this tribute. It works. Unbeknownst to most in attendance, Metcalfe was one of the "silent six," the Black aldermen who were un-der the thumb of Daley's machine. At the Atlantic City convention in 1964, the six had followed Daley's orders and actually taken the lead in speaking in favor of the all-white Mississippi delegation, against Fannie Lou Hamer and the Mississippi Freedom Democratic Party.[38]

Metcalfe had also been on hand in 1966, when Daley handed King one of the greatest defeats of his political life. King had come to Chi-cago to fight for fair housing, and Daley bested him by nodding and smiling and having meetings and showing a willingness to fix things, while doing absolutely nothing. About the only win King secured was the fact that Daley did not simply deny there was a problem; in 1963 the mayor had absurdly declared, "There are no ghettoes in Chicago."[39] King found Chicago to be a tougher nut to crack than any city in the South. In Birmingham, white supremacy was maintained by prevent-ing the Black vote. In Chicago, white supremacy was maintained by controlling the Black vote, and it was in large part the Black aldermen who made that happen. In return, their constituents received patron-age jobs, and money was directed to Black communities. As Adam Cohen and Elizabeth Taylor explain, "Black leaders, and their armies of patronage workers, had a personal stake in the status quo, in a way that few Blacks in Selma or Birmingham did."[40] The silent six did not greet King with open arms and helped to seal his failure in Chicago. A white alderman who stood up to the Daley machine, Leon Despres, said "Metcalfe could hardly conceal his pleasure" when King left town after months of failure.[41] How monstrous it was for Daley to select Metcalfe to deliver a King tribute at the convention.

The meager, improvised speech ran less than three minutes, including a final memorial twenty seconds of silence, a blistering final ploy to calm the unruly delegates. Chairman Albert follows this by announcing the death of the daughter of the governor of Virginia, who had been struck by lightning—hardly relevant to convention business but another part of the plan to keep the delegates quiet. Cronkite offers one of his typical factoids here, informing viewers that Metcalfe is an alderman and also a former Olympic runner who had won his first silver medal in 1932 and his second against Jesse Owens, in 1936.[42] The convention moves on.

Metcalfe would later make good. Elected to the US House of Representatives in 1970, he opposed redlining, and he was a founding member of the Congressional Black Caucus in 1971.[43] In 1972 he began to break with Daley by protesting police brutality in Chicago's Black community (fig. 21). "It's never too late to be Black," he declared.[44] By the time he backed a candidate opposing Daley's reelection in 1975, the rupture was definitive. Metcalfe was not always Daley's man, but he was squarely under his thumb in 1968; Daley's use of him here was both ruthless and also standard operating procedure.

The convention rumbled onward with nominating speeches for Muskie. The only real story on that front was that the more radical delegations were still sorting out who their vice-presidential protest nominees might be.

The David Hoeh and Dick Gregory Crises Begin to Unfold

Early on Thursday evening, the networks reported that the chairman of the New Hampshire delegation had been arrested. Upon arrival at the hall, David Hoeh had noticed the suspicious number of Daley guests with their flimsy paper passes, and he was both disturbed and offended. Delegates were issued new color-coded credential cards each day and punched them into a high-tech box to gain entrance to the

FIGURE 21. Alderman Ralph Metcalfe was "Daley's man" for years, and he was cynically used at the convention to quiet protesting delegates with an improvised tribute to the recently slain Martin Luther King. By the early 1970s, he had broken with Daley, saying, "It's never too late to be Black." Here, he is pictured at a 1973 press conference on police brutality in Chicago. Field Enterprises, Inc., 1968.

hall. The light on the box would blink green if the information encoded in your card was correct (e.g., you weren't trying to use a Tuesday pass to get in on Wednesday or a service pass to get into a delegate area) but red if your card was rejected. Hoeh had an idea for a mad experiment: what if he punched his Dartmouth ID card into the machine instead? He did. The light blinked green. If *any* magnetized card worked in the machines, the whole thing was a hoax and delegates had been corralled like livestock for days by a phony system.

Rather than entering the hall when the light flashed, Hoeh called over some other delegates to demonstrate his trick. This drew attention to him. Soon convention security was involved, and then the Chicago police. A fracas ensued; Hoeh was cuffed and arrested. Huntley said that according to a witness, "Hoeh was grabbed by guards, hustled to the corner of a stairway, where a guard choked him and beat him. . . .

[He] was bleeding from his forehead when he was hauled away. Hoeh protested the arrest yelling, 'It's a phony convention!'" Huntley then quoted another witness, who said, "Hoeh did not slug a cop, as was claimed by the police." Huntley closed by noting that bail could not be posted for Hoeh until 11:00 p.m. The news slowly spread across the floor, enraging the McCarthy delegates. Hoeh was even considered as a protest vice-presidential candidate, which would have shined yet another light on Daley's security forces: Hoeh would be unable to accept his nomination from a jail cell. Roughing up the chairman of the New Hampshire delegation was already bad. Arresting him for exposing that the high-tech security system was at best flawed, at worst a complete fiction, was even worse. With Hoeh in jail and no further information in sight, the networks turned back to floor coverage. It was almost 8:30 p.m.

The secretary at the rostrum, Dorothy Bush, was going from state to state, and delegates were instructed to either nominate a VP candidate or pass. The California delegation looked like it might be planning a walkout. When called upon, their official response was, "California passes and will continue to pass until we are apprised of the reasons for the arrest of the chairman of the New Hampshire delegation." Bush offers a bureaucratic "Thank you" and moves on to the Canal Zone vote. A weary home viewer might note now that it's after 9:00 p.m., Muskie hasn't officially been nominated yet, and this vote is going alphabetically, so there's still a long slog ahead. California leaves the floor to caucus about the Hoeh situation.

Both networks now have some breaking news on action in the streets. Cronkite reports that

in a very peaceful, calm, orderly, unexcited peace march out from downtown that was to have passed near the Amphitheatre here on the way to his old Chicago neighborhood, Negro comedian Dick Gregory—and Negro activist Dick Gregory—[was] arrested by the police along with nine delegates to this convention who were carrying their credentials. There was nothing disorderly about the matter. They knew that they were going to run into a police and National Guard barrier. And apparently it was a very peaceful . . . antiwar demonstration. There were no harsh words apparently and no difficulty, but when they reached the barrier, the police said that those who crossed the barrier will be arrested, and Gregory and these nine delegates did cross and were arrested.

Reading this as a follow-up to the Daley interview, it seems that Cronkite is buckling down on two ideas: that the police did not use excessive force in this case, a notion that was implicitly a sop to Daley, and that the marchers themselves were peaceful, a notion that was an affront to Daley.

Left unsaid are two facts that would have helped viewers make better sense of the situation. First, this crowd included a number of Black marchers, which was unusual, because throughout the rest of the week the protest crowds were almost completely white. Second, Daley and the Chicago police had been very concerned that there might be Black rioting,[45] and their objective during the Gregory action had been to cut off the marchers before they entered Chicago's Black South Side. The rioting in Chicago after King's assassination earlier in the year had been devastating; eleven people had been killed, and miles of Black neighborhoods had been burned to the ground. Daley feared a reprisal, utterly failing to grasp that most Black citizens were not interested in putting their necks on the line to protest the Democratic National Convention.

This complicated story was not pursued by the network news before, during, or after the convention—demonstrating the fragility of the criticism that the networks loved to give "radicals" free publicity. The lack of engagement with this bigger story also resonates with the networks' lack of attention to Black disenfranchisement during the Alabama credentials crisis on Tuesday. In both cases, the networks either couldn't see Black issues as pressing to the mostly white, middle-class, mass audience that they served, or couldn't see the issues as relevant to the convention story, or both.

In 1969, an ambitious local production company called Film Group did release a brilliant, three-part documentary series entitled *American Revolution II*. Not only did these films feature more street-level protest footage than the networks had, they were also one of the few non-print media sources to consider the Black perspective on the DNC protests. Black Chicagoans interviewed expressed frustration at the media frenzy around the beating of whites by Chicago police, for police brutality in Black Chicago communities was an everyday reality. As one young woman put it, "So everybody gets uptight when a few honkies get their heads beat. What did they do when we was getting our heads beat?" It's hard to say definitively whether more Blacks might have joined Gregory's group, as Daley feared, if they had been allowed to cross Eighteenth Street, but the bottom line is that for many of Chicago's Black citizens, the convention—and the street protest of it— were understood as white events.[46]

Remaining mute on this issue, CBS left off around 9:00 with Cronkite announcing the basic peacefulness of the Dick Gregory street action. NBC noted that the crowd still remained an hour after Gregory's arrest, indicating that there might be more activity building there. NBC was correct, and both networks would circle back a few hours later with more reporting on the scene.

The Vice-Presidential Protest Nomination

The roll call for vice-presidential nominations has been trudging forward and is near completion. This should be pro-forma; everyone knows that Muskie is Humphrey's choice. But the resistant delegations have finally found a protest candidate. Wisconsin rises to offer a name, and Carl Albert allows it—legitimately, since the rules permit it, but no one would have been surprised if he had found a way to suppress the nomination. Albert just wants to push everything forward and get on with the Humphrey and Muskie acceptance speeches. He and Dorothy Bush stand tense at the podium.

Don Peterson is too hoarse to speak for Wisconsin today, so his vice chairman is at the microphone making an earnest but ineloquent speech:

> Mr. Chairman, we of Wisconsin, as Democrats who are interested not only in what the party is but in what the party is to become, if it will truly live up to the promise of the [Robert Kennedy] movie that we saw on that screen tonight. If it will truly live up to the inspirational promise that Senators McCarthy and McGovern have given to this convention and this country. If it will truly make the American dream a reality not only for affluent delegates but for the young people who march in the parks looking for quality in life. Mr. Chairman, I think that I am going to surprise some of the people here tonight, because there is a disease known as microphonitis. And I could talk on for half-an-hour about the man that we are going to put in nomination, but I think our positions are by this time eminently clear to this convention and to the American people. So I will say . . . simply and . . . sincerely . . . that we wish to offer in nomination the wave of the future. It may be a symbolic nomination tonight, but it may not be symbolic four years hence. We offer in nomination, with the greatest pleasure, the name of Julian Bond.

A cheer goes up as the network floor correspondents rush to interview Bond. Bond was twenty-eight years old, and still would not have reached the qualifying age of thirty-five by the next convention. In his interviews, Bond dodges the age issue; it's later apparent that the co-ordinated plan was for his name to remain in nomination for a while, and then for him to withdraw, citing his age, when it came time for Georgia to vote. Albert is shouting for order, though it's not really a chaotic scene compared to the fallout from the Bobby Kennedy film. Bush quickly moves on to Wyoming. Meanwhile, Allard Lowenstein is waiting at the Wisconsin mic. He has been selected by the resistant delegations to give the seconding speech for Bond. It's now clear that the Wisconsin vice chairman had pleaded "microphonitis" because the big speechifying was lined up for Lowenstein. Once this speech was completed, the protest would be accomplished, Bond would get some symbolic votes, and the idealists could feel that their work at the Amphitheatre was done. Though defeated, they would at least have made one last stand against the realist, establishment forces on the dais.

But that's not how it went. It's been seven minutes since Wisconsin made the nomination, and Lowenstein is still waiting to be recognized for his seconding speech. Albert now announces that the roll call for nominations has been completed, and therefore the request for a seconding speech has come too late. Of course, the roll call has only been completed because Albert had Bush move on to Wyoming as quickly as possible. The crowd erupts into booing, and Albert pounds away at the lectern with his gravel, screeching twice, "The chair is trying to be fair!" Cronkite asks Reasoner up on the podium what the heck is going on, as Lou Breese, absurdly, strikes up a blaring rendition of "God Bless America." The camera shows Daley and the entire Illinois delegation singing along. Reasoner says, "They're swamped. They just don't know what to do. And Chairman Albert is not distinguishing himself with his immediate reaction to these problems either. I suppose you could say it's a final act of desperation at a convention when you tell a band to play while you think. It's like a television director saying, 'Go to black.'"

Although the booing continues, Albert manages to push the schedule forward. Nominations have been completed, and now everyone will vote on the VP candidates, another pro-forma part of the evening. NBC's McGee reaches Lowenstein for comment, and he makes an impassioned plea:

> Well, I was about to second the nomination of a candidate for vice president of the United States, pursuant to the rules of this convention, and the chair at the podium cut off the Wisconsin microphone in order to prevent me from doing that. What mystifies me is, Why are they so afraid of allowing the convention to hear speeches on behalf of candidates? Presumably they have the votes to nominate senator Muskie. I would think it would serve their purposes better to allow

discussion under the rules, and then proceed to an orderly vote. But as you can see, that's not what they're prepared to do.

The idealists had been defeated by the realists insofar as Lowenstein did not get to make the speech. The fact that he got the NBC interview, on the other hand, could not be seen as a clear win or loss: the idealists wanted their message seen, but swaying home viewers was not enough: they wanted to sway Humphrey.

Lowenstein next separates himself from some of the protestors in the streets:

> We're not kooks, we're not leftists, we're not far out. We're Americans who won votes in our areas, and I won a primary against opposition on the issues that I've tried to support here. . . . *What is it* that makes it improper for us, following the rules of procedure, to exercise our rights as elected delegates? . . . The tragedy is that it's all so stupid, because obviously we could not have won the vote for Julian Bond. They would have had Senator Muskie. We have nothing to say against Senator Muskie. He is a man of ability and integrity. We believe the Democratic convention . . . should allow people free speech within the rules as opted by that convention. . . . We felt particularly on an evening when we've seen a movie about Senator Kennedy and all the things that Senator Kennedy stood for, to so many of us, that we ought to follow some procedure of democracy in this convention.[47]

This last line points to the residual pathos from the film screened two hours earlier. It's quite possible Albert feared that a Lowenstein speech would have brought that pathos forward again.

Meanwhile, as the voting for vice-presidential candidates advances, Brinkley reports that, lo and behold, "Mayor Daley has sent his car and two of his bodyguards to the precinct jail. David Hoeh, the chairman of the New Hampshire delegation, has been let out. The mayor's car is picking him up to bring him back to the hall." If it was embarrassing for

Daley—at least from a public relations standpoint, if not from a moral one—to beat and arrest a man for sticking a college ID card in a slot, it should have been equally embarrassing to drop the charges and dispatch a limo to escort him back to the Amphitheatre, underscoring the absurdity of the whole thing.

Both CBS and NBC secured interviews with Hoeh upon his return, and he told the story mostly as it had been reported by them earlier. The long cut across his forehead had been cleaned up but was still quite visible. He clarified that he had been "wrestled" and "twisted" and "pushed," but not beaten by police. Hoeh was disturbed that the police would not tell him with what he was being charged or give him their badge numbers as they seized him. He grabbed the badge off of one officer and threw it to a friend, which accelerated the scrum. By the end, not only was his forehead bleeding, but also his glasses had been knocked off and his watch broken. Hoeh was adamant that he had not *bitten* a police officer, as he had been accused. Bill Matney, one of NBC's few Black correspondents (and the first in their employ), snagged the Hoeh interview, in part because he was working on the periphery of the Amphitheatre, which had many top-notch reporters but was sort of the B-team staging area.[48] The star line-up was the reporters who were able to work the floor, and the discrepancy between the two groups was exacerbated by Daley's distributing so few floor passes to journalists.

Muskie, At Last, and the Gregory March Comes to a Head

As voting moves along for Muskie, Wisconsin includes one protest vote for New York delegate Paul O'Dwyer, which Bush mistakenly hears as "Paul 'Bear' Bryant," the Alabama football coach. She's never had this sort of hearing problem, and has to ask for several repetitions. One might reasonably guess that someone in charge has managed to get Wisconsin's microphone turned down, since this is their very last chance to access a hot mic at the convention, and Albert doesn't want any more trouble from them. Thunderous cheering and booing erupts a few minutes later when Alabama offers three-and-a-half votes for

Mayor Daley.[49] Rather interviews an Alabama delegate who confirms that he'll be supporting Wallace, contra the convention loyalty oath he took. As a deafening chant of "Down with Daley!" rises up to compete with Daley's cheering supporters both on the floor and up in the balcony, Albert pounds the podium, and the orchestra inexplicably strikes up "It's a Grand Old Flag" and then "Give My Regards to Broadway." The band finally stops, and Albert declares that Muskie is officially the candidate.

Muskie opens his speech at 10:00 p.m. with two jokes about his mother, the first garnering polite applause and chuckles, the second met with silence. He calls for "respect for the rule of law as a dispenser of justice as well as a maintainer of order." The not-so-subtle trick here is not to use Nixon's exact phrase "law and order" while saying essentially the same thing. Muskie speaks up for young people who want to change the world but decries their "exploitation by militants whose motives are suspect." This was another familiar stance: protest was good, violence was bad. The rest of the speech was filled with platitudes like "Freedom does not work unless we work at it." The speech had all the energy of a bar of Ivory soap, and it was delivered with excruciatingly slow enunciation. Of. Every. Word. In his chronicle of the 1972 presidential campaign, Hunter S. Thompson characterized ad spots for the "extremely slow-spoken" Muskie as giving the impression of a man "hooked on a bad Downer habit," adding that "the first time I heard a Muskie radio spot, . . . I thought it was a new Cheech & Chong record. It was the voice of a man who had done about twelve Reds on the way to the studio."[50] Muskie's seventeen-minute speech feels much longer.

CBS and NBC show the entire speech and then cut away for news and analysis. Brinkley says that they have contacted the Chicago police department to invite the officer who arrested Hoeh to give his side of the story. He then reports words of praise from Gov. Connolly regarding the police the previous night. Next, Huntley gives a more pressing update: "Downtown tonight, David, tear gas has been used to disperse about two thousand demonstrators at Eighteenth and Michigan. At least four vanloads of demonstrators were arrested, including Dr. John

Cashin of Alabama, who led one of the groups of Alabama dissidents, and the comedian Dick Gregory. Two National Guardsmen were injured during the incident." This builds on earlier reports on the Gregory march as peaceful; the crowd had not dispersed, and things had turned violent, though nothing like the night before on Michigan Avenue. On a separate note, Huntley assesses that Muskie did a "formidable job" of trying to unify a badly divided party with his speech, and that Humphrey will have to do even more heavy lifting on this front. NBC cuts to the rostrum for Humphrey's big speech. There's more to report on downtown, but they will not return to that until after this speech, the putative climax of the convention. This is a great illustration of how network news tried to balance out different points of view: we've heard from Hoeh, so now let's try to hear from the man who arrested him; a major Democratic player says the Chicago police are doing a great job, but we also see more poorly managed violence in the streets; the party is badly divided, but the candidates are working hard to unify their constituents. The segment perfectly ping-pongs perspectives.

Cronkite takes a different tack, jumping right to the streets: "Tonight there has been more violence in Chicago. A peaceful march of demonstrators, anti-Vietnam war demonstrators, was stopped at a roadblock. They were warned that they would be arrested if they crossed the roadblock, and to test it and to protest, they did cross and were peacefully arrested. But then according to CBS News personnel at the scene, some Black militants charged the line and triggered violence after some seventy-five marchers had been peacefully arrested. And National Guardsmen had to use rifle butts and tear gas apparently to try to break up that demonstration." CBS cuts to videotape, with correspondent Bert Quint offering his blow-by-blow voice-over commentary:

> This was an incident that was *provoked* . . . by a Negro militant leader who decided that the move toward the jail vans was too slow, a man who I've seen out here trying to cause trouble. He said, "Let's go, go." A few missiles were thrown by the crowd. They've pushed ahead. Now the guards, trying to cool it. They're moving, they've

got their gas masks on, rifles up, ready. This is the moment. Either the Guard will toss the gas or perhaps, just perhaps the fact that they have the gasmasks on and are moving forward, it may not be necessary to throw the gas. But the people, the protestors, are beginning to move back. They're trying to cool it, but it may be a little bit late. . . . They're sitting down now, so that if the Guard does throw the gas, they can say that it was against defenseless people. [Next shot shows gas and people running.] The Guard is moving in. There's some fighting. I see . . . several guardsmen, using their rifles as clubs, hitting the demonstrators. . . . They're pushing them back. . . . There goes more tear gas. There goes a wave of it. . . . The people are engulfed by the tear gas. The demonstration is over now at Michigan and Eighteenth Street. The Guard has dispersed it by firing gas.

Cronkite follows with, "This scene was an hour ago, and since then we understand that this demonstration has quieted down. It did not reach anything like the proportions of last night's demonstration involving Chicago police. And as you heard Bert Quint say, *this* demonstration was *provoked* . . . by a militant, clearly seen by the reporters present." Like NBC, CBS has to cut at this point to go to Humphrey's live speech.

CBS has scooped NBC with videotape of the confrontation. Clearly, NBC's crew and motorcycle couriers couldn't work fast enough to get the images to the Amphitheatre. But that is not the only way that CBS's coverage is different. Cronkite has drilled down on the notion that this confrontation was incited by protestors, and Quint has done the same, while also emphasizing that the source of trouble was a "Negro militant leader." It's impossible to say whether this is in response to criticisms channeled from LBJ to Stanton to the news booth, or whether it is because Cronkite is responding to the negative phone calls and telegrams from the night before, or whether he is still reeling from the Daley interview and trying to show extra fairness to the Chicago police, but it is clear that CBS News is set on this framing of the event as "provoked." The claim that it was specifically instigated by an unidentified "Negro militant" is particularly disturbing. Given the slim participation of

Blacks in the street demonstrations, it was troubling to single out one Black man saying "Let's go, go" as a provocateur. But now it is time for Humphrey's speech.

Humphrey Makes His Case; "Democratic Clambake" Ensues

Humphrey opens by condemning violence, follows with a moment of silence and then—against the counsel of his advisors—offers up the peace prayer of St. Francis of Assisi. He then moves into a tightly struc-tured, three-part speech outlining what America needs: peace in Viet-nam, peace and justice in our cities, and "unity in our country," this last point actually boiling down to a plea for solidarity within the party. He goes further than Muskie, declaring, "We do not want a police state. But we need a state of law and order." There, he's said it, the dreaded Nixon phrase, but Humphrey then switches to a more touchy-feely call for developing not just "outer space" but also "inner space here on earth." He has the good sense not to try too hard to speak to the "Now Generation," though, realizing that nothing makes a middle-aged man look older than trying to look younger.[51]

With everything going against him, Humphrey managed to hold the crowd. As both CBS and NBC commentators noted afterward, his most important line was that "the policies of tomorrow need not be limited by the policies of yesterday." He had managed not to repudi-ate the Johnson-Humphrey administration, while also indicating that the Humphrey-Muskie administration might do things differently. This was obviously a reference to Vietnam, though he remained hamstrung by the victory of the majority Vietnam plank. Humphrey moved toward his conclusion by asking for the support of McGovern and McCarthy. McGovern was in the crowd and got much applause. McCarthy had not shown up and had even made a speech to protestors in Grant Park that afternoon. Still, Cronkite noted that he had never seen a presidential candidate at a convention reach out to the defeated candidates in this way, and he emphasized that the speech "roused a great deal of enthu-siasm in the hall." Huntley remarked that it was one of the few times when Californians were applauding at the same time as delegates from Texas and Illinois.

As the culmination of a very difficult convention, Humphrey's speech succeeded against all odds . . . except that in an extraordinarily idiotic move, someone (Daley? Albert? Criswell?) had given the orchestra special instructions. When Humphrey paused for applause lines, standard practice in a presidential acceptance speech, the orchestra inserted an emphatic stinger, a few bars of "Happy Days Are Here Again." They did it over and over again, and several times played too many bars, as if to artificially extend the applause. Humphrey surely would have loved to have simply ordered them to stop, but such a move would have further undercut the gravitas he was reaching for. Later, in his closing commentary, Mike Wallace described these musical intrusions as "surreal" and "bizarre," adding, "Every time they played it, the delegates, a good many of them, got up and cheered, because they wanted so badly to believe it, and they knew that it wasn't so. . . . I don't envy Hubert Humphrey his chore, trying to put this party back together. . . . My hunch is that a good number of these McCarthy people are going to stay inside the party. They may not work for Hubert Humphrey. Richard Nixon can take some heart from what happened here tonight, what happened here this week." In other words, Humphrey had made a solid plea for unity, but it would be an uphill battle. The silly song had not single-handedly tanked Humphrey's chances in November, but it did underscore that happy days were *not* here again.

Outside, an electrical sign reading "OUR NEXT PRESIDENT" flashes to celebrate the nomination. All the networks show it. But the *N* and *T* immediately start flickering, and the newsmen tell it like it is: it looks like the DNC is flashing a sign for "our ex-president." On the heels of the "Happy Days" interjections, this *seems* to be the final possible failure of the convention planners to celebrate their man. But it isn't.

Back inside, Daley had come up to the platform and been booed, but TV viewers missed seeing that live because of the shots of the "ex-president" sign. The orchestra is now blaring again, switching from "Yankee Doodle" to a hyperactive rendition of "Everything's Coming

FIGURE 22. Humphrey and Muskie are finally nominated. Cronkite declares it a "Democratic clambake." This is the sort of triumphant convention image you'd expect to be used in a presidential campaign, but Humphrey's media played down the events in Chicago and used as little convention imagery as possible. Associated Press, 1968.

Up Roses" as Humphrey waves various governors and senators up to the platform for handshaking and photo ops. Cronkite says, "We've never seen a scene like this, never seen this sort of informality after a presidential acceptance." It's a "Democratic clambake" he exclaims repeatedly. Finally, Humphrey and friends leave for the private victory celebration next door at the Stockyard Inn. Albert passes the gavel back to Senator Inouye, who announces that there will now be a screening of a film on Humphrey. The film begins to roll as the delegates walk out (fig. 22).

The Convention Finally Comes to an End

Cronkite states the obvious: "The Humphrey film didn't attract much attention here in this hall. It was quite anticlimactic after the speech of the vice president and the presidential nominee, Hubert Humphrey, and the little Democratic clambake up on the rostrum, and the hall emptied during that film. The management of the convention, realizing that there was not going to be anyone left here to say goodnight to, cut the film short." Having opened with a rousing Academy Award–winning film narrated by Richard Burton, the day closes with this film narrated by Gregory Peck, cut short, and never seen again.

The next thing to do was to officially gavel out and close the day, but, Cronkite reported, "They found that three of the gavels that they had up on the rostrum already had been removed by either maintenance men or souvenir hunters, probably the latter, and they quickly had a benediction and said goodnight at ten minutes after twelve." The benediction constituted an official ending, but the mild-mannered looting continued: "Meanwhile, souvenir hunters have begun to strip the hall. They took all of the flags down that were hanging around the Very Important Persons box, the box that it was thought that President Johnson might at some point during this convention occupy, before he decided that he would not come to the convention. And now the hall is empty except for the news people pounding out their last stories."

Cronkite was referring to typewriter keys, but CBS and NBC had a few more on-screen stories to pound out as well. To start with, they had follow-ups on the stalled Dick Gregory march. NBC had finally obtained its own footage, showing the marchers being teargassed and attempting to flee. Then NBC moves to Grant Park, where many of those who had not been arrested at Eighteenth Street had gone. Although the brutality and arrests had not been as intense as the night before, there were thousands in the streets, many of them "well dressed," NBC correspondent Paul Duke notes in voice-over, his microphone pulled up beneath the wet handkerchief covering his nose, a futile attempt to protect himself from tear gas. The point of the sartorial comment is that this is not exclusively a crowd of Yippies and hippies—it's more the Mobe and clean-cut McCarthy supporters. NBC shows that there were more National Guardsmen than policemen on this night. The crowd is being pushed not only by the gas but also by the Guard's jeeps, their front ends covered with barbed wire (fig. 23). A dummy with a "Daley" sign on its back is being burned in effigy. A "Sieg heil" chant against the police rises up. Once you are in this sea of people, you can't

FIGURE 23.   There were thousands of demonstrators in the streets on Thursday night, and more National Guardsmen than policemen. The crowd was pushed not only by the gas but also by the Guard's jeeps, their front ends covered with barbed wire. David Douglas Duncan Papers and Photography Collection, © David Douglas Duncan, 1968, courtesy of Harry Ransom Center.

really get out. A young woman in a pretty frock escapes the crush of the crowd by crawling onto the hood of a car. It's all alarming, because police or National Guardsmen might start madly swinging at any moment, as they had moments earlier at Eighteenth Street.

But now back at Grant Park, they don't. Duke makes a very important point that had eluded CBS: "While Dick Gregory, who is a Negro nightclub entertainer, led a march tonight, or attempted to, there are no civil rights connotations or civil rights connections with the demonstrations tonight or as far as we know any other night in Chicago. These are principally antiwar demonstrations." A few minutes later reporter Jack Perkins adds over another roll of tape that he's hearing people singing "Down by the Riverside," "which hardly seems as menacing as the National Guardsmen with their rifles, and gasmasks, and jeeps, and barbed wire would suggest." This is NBC's final coverage of convention protestors.

CBS keeps going, now playing a longer version of its earlier tape of Quint reporting on the "Negro militant." It seems like another attempt to respond to Daley's (and Johnson's and Stanton's) complaint that the provocation of police had not been properly shown. This more complete version shows the unnamed provocateur, a young Black man with a white cap and matching jacket—certainly not looking very radical. His "provocation" lies in suggesting the crowd move forward to be arrested. The leaders of the march have been arrested, but "We're all leaders," he says through a handheld loudspeaker: "If they lock us up, they lock us up. . . . God'll give us the power to keep going. Let's go." It's hardly the plea for violence that Quint implies, although it is a provocation of sorts. He even calls out for no more "bullshit," the only moment of uncensored profanity aired by CBS during the entire convention.

Village Voice staff writer Paul Cowan explained the situation more precisely. The National Guard was deliberately arresting people very slowly, at minute-long intervals. There were thousands of marchers at Eighteenth and Michigan. Cowan assessed that the Guard's plan was "either to bore people so thoroughly that they dispersed or to annoy them so intensely that they provoked an incident." When the Black militant urged people to cross the street, "canister after canister of tear gas hit the ground." As the jeeps menacingly advanced, the marchers fled back to Grant Park, across the street from the Hilton, where they stayed up all night singing along with Phil Ochs, as well as Peter Yarrow and Mary Travers of Peter, Paul, and Mary. Throughout the night, delegates in the Hilton registered their acknowledgment and support of the protestors by flashing their lights on and off, with the crowd applauding in response. Guardsmen were all around but did not attack again. Cowan offered a strong assessment: a stalemate had led to escalation and then, finally, de-escalation.[52] Unlike CBS, NBC had carried this story through to the end, from the teargassing at Eighteenth street, to the Daley effigy in Grant Park, to "Down by the Riverside."

At this point, after midnight, Brinkley finally introduces David Douglas Duncan's photomontage segment. Duncan starts by narrowing in on activity the night before in McCarthy headquarters at the Hilton. This is where CBS had scooped NBC with its interviews with those who had been beaten by police and had landed in the makeshift first-aid ward on the fifteenth floor. Duncan offers a different take on the story. CBS had done interviews to assess the causes of the violence on Michigan Avenue. In short: the police were the perpetrators. CBS also showed the damage that had been done, the bandaged heads. But it was basically informational reporting, albeit accompanied by dramatic images. Duncan was up to something different, more *affective* reporting. It wasn't *news* at this point that the wounded had been tended by the McCarthy volunteers—the idealistic, white, middle-class college students who had gotten "Clean for Gene" by shaving, showering, and getting haircuts before doing their door-to-door canvassing.

What did it *feel* like to be a McCarthy kid on Wednesday night? Duncan showed a boy who was "blood from chin to waist." He showed some kids numbly watching television. He noted that Senator McCarthy's own doctor was there, pitching in.[53] His commentary was not strictly descriptive. He said that "the girls became mothers really" as he showed an image of a girl who sat silently stroking a boy's head. One of his most moving photos didn't show the wounded at all: as he described it, "Further down the corridor it looked as though a girl had been fitted for a trousseau. Not at all. Those are bed sheets being torn into bandages" (fig. 24). Here, Duncan echoed what others on the scene had noted, that many of the kids, panicked and not really trained for first aid, helped the only way they knew how, by tearing the sheets to bits. It was more bandages than anyone needed, but what else could be done? An additional photo later included in Duncan's book was ironic, showing the wounded watching delayed TV coverage of the Battle of Michigan Avenue, as they are being bandaged from that encounter (fig. 25). As his final NBC montage comes to an end, Duncan cuts to the streets, showing the jeeps reinforced with barbed wire and people marching through the streets with candles, singing "We Shall Overcome" and "Where Have All the Flowers Gone?" The photographer concludes, "I've never seen anything like this in my life."

Duncan is a weathered war photographer just back from Vietnam.

FIGURE 24. Following the Battle of Michigan Avenue, David Douglas Duncan took this photo of girls making bandages, poignantly describing the image as evoking a bride's trousseau. David Douglas Duncan Papers and Photography Collection, © David Douglas Duncan, 1968, courtesy of Harry Ransom Center.

He's obviously seen more violence and bloodshed than what transpired on Wednesday night. It was the militarism in collision with peaceful protests and disillusioned, formerly idealistic youth, coupled with the mix of the square kids and the hippie kids, and all of it happening in the streets of America that had shattered him. In the introduction to his 1968 book of Khe Sanh photos, *I Protest!*, Duncan declared flatly, "I'm no peacenik, Vietnik, pinkie, Commie, liberal, conservative, kook, hippie, hawk, or dove. I'm just a veteran combat photographer and foreign correspondent who cares intensely about my country."[54] The grand finale of his convention coverage reflected an emotional reac-

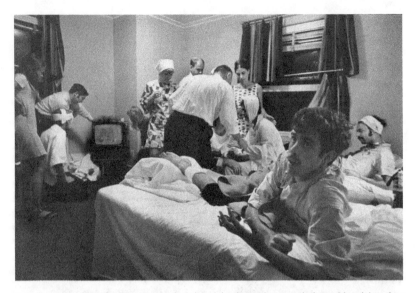

FIGURE 25.   An image from late Wednesday night shows the wounded watching delayed TV coverage of the Battle of Michigan Avenue, as they are being bandaged from that very encounter. David Douglas Duncan Papers and Photography Collection, © David Douglas Duncan, 1968, courtesy of Harry Ransom Center.

tion (shock) coupled with a sort of primal—not to mention masculine, paternalistic—patriotism that he understood as bigger than himself.

Following Duncan's poignant segment, NBC cuts back to hard reporting, and they've got an exclusive. The police officers who arrested David Hoeh have consented to an interview. For four days, the police have chafed at "unfair" TV coverage while also avoiding interviews. Now, however, two officers sit down with Bill Matney in NBC's barebones floor studio. Matney had been an NBC correspondent in Chicago since 1963. He had covered the urban uprisings of 1967, including Detroit, where rioting had gone on for a week and left forty-three dead. Looking out over the smoldering wreckage, the city's mayor had said, "It looks like Berlin in 1945."[55] In 1987, Matney was asked to talk about civil rights coverage after Detroit, and he basically said, no, wait, I have to start with Chicago, meaning the crushing enormity of King's failed efforts to open up housing in 1966.[56] Matney knew not only how Daley's machine operated but also how the police worked hand-in-hand with that machine, not to mention the reality of police brutality against people of color such as himself.

Seated between two white Chicago police officers at the tail end of a week of violence, protest, and chaos, Matney was in total control of the interview, asking careful and dispassionate questions like a lawyer adjudicating evidence. The officers express little concern about Hoeh's use of the college ID card. Instead, they emphasize that Hoeh was screaming and fighting: "He kept getting more violent all the time." What emerges is two conflicting stories, the earlier story of an arrested delegate who says the officers used undue force, would not identify themselves, and would not state why he was under arrest, and this one of two officers arresting a man who had flown into a blind rage when they tried to "straighten out" his argument with the usher at the pass gate. To put it bluntly, each side is contending that the other side flipped out. There were no cameras, and since the case was dropped, there was never witness testimony to confirm either story. Matney asks a list of precise questions about what happened, and the police are unable to recount two key moments in detail. Officer Long can't offer a clear story about how he was bitten—either his hand came up to Hoeh's mouth or, conversely, Hoeh's mouth was lowered to his hand. Also, asked how Hoeh's forehead was cut, Officer McCann offers, "He probably caused it himself by all the twisting and turning and fighting. There was no officer that struck him at *any* time." The notion that Hoeh had inflicted his own head gash was unconvincing, a disturbing and familiar police defense in brutality cases.

Matney closes out with two zingers. First, he raises the question of the credibility of the accused: "You realize that Mr. Hoeh is the chairman of the New Hampshire delegation, and he is also a candidate for Congress. You're saying that he's a liar?" Long answers, "I would say that a man in his position could have used a little more decorum." Long has stuck to his guns, while Matney has made the point that Hoeh is what one might call a man of position. Why would he fly into an unprovoked psychotic rage, bite a police officer, and cut a gash in his own forehead, in front of a large crowd of witnesses? Certainly, he might have panicked. Viewers can decide for themselves which explanation seems better. Then, Matney shifts gears completely to ask questions that the officers probably would not have agreed in advance to field.

MATNEY: Well, perhaps you can clear something else up. You men are rank-and-file policemen. You have intimate contact with rank-and-file policemen as a sergeant. What are your feelings about all this trouble that has been going on this week? All the charges that have been leveled against the police department, against Mayor Daley? You've been called Gestapo. You've been called fascist pigs. You've been called unprintable names. What's your personal reaction? How does this make you feel?

MCCANN: It doesn't make me feel very good, but these accusations are unfounded, completely. This is a perfect example. . . . Does it make me angry? It could make me angry, but I have self-restraint.

MATNEY: How do you feel about the antiwar demonstrators? The hippies and the Yippies. How do you feel about them? What's your personal reaction to the sort of demonstrations that have been going on here in the city?

MCCANN: I don't like them. I don't like them one bit. There's no reason for 'em. They accomplish nothing. Accomplish nothing.

The fact that the police did not like the protestors one bit, felt there was no reason for them to be there, and, above all, believed that they accomplished *nothing* was the one moment of truth heard from the police during the entire week of convention coverage. McCann and Long conveyed some awkward spin on police operations throughout the interview, but here they accurately conveyed how they felt about the whole thing.

NBC cuts back to the booth, where Brinkley offers a neutral assessment: "There was certainly a marked difference in the two descriptions of what happened wasn't there?" and Huntley agrees. Then Brinkley offers one of his classic chuckle lines: "A radio station in Charlottesville, Virginia, has been broadcasting the Democratic convention proceedings, and the sponsor of the program is the local Republican campaign committee. And the broadcasts are interrupted every once in a while for the Republican commercials, and their message is, 'If you don't like what you're hearing, vote Republican.' And after four days of the goings-on here, they may very well have picked up some votes." This must have provoked an inventive expletive from LBJ, who was watching the coverage in bed with Lady Bird at his Texas ranch.[57] At the same moment out in California, one imagines Richard Nixon raising a tumbler of scotch to Brinkley. He'd have plenty of time to publicly trash the networks later, but he could have felt only exuberance at this moment: even those so-and-so's at NBC were willing to admit that the Democratic convention had benefited the Republican Party.

At last, the networks close out with some conclusions from their commentators and correspondents. It's all about what you would expect—it's been a hard week, the debates and divisions on the floor were a microcosm of American divisions in 1968, and the Democratic Party now has an uphill battle to get their man in the White House. Both end with shout-outs to their teams. Brinkley advises viewers to stick through their very lengthy credits, adding that they really tried to list "*everyone*, down to the motorcycle couriers. Look at these people and remember them. Because they are the ones that did the work." CBS offers less comprehensive credits, but Cronkite, following an analysis of the campaign challenges facing Humphrey and Muskie ("a senator whose name . . . is about as well known as that of Spiro Agnew of Maryland"), closes out with a final note of support for his own crew: "And so for the hundreds of our devoted CBS staffers here, eight hundred of them it took to put us on the air, all of these you never see, have done such a valiant job behind the scenes and have taken just as much of the *pummeling* around here as those you've seen on camera, for my colleagues . . . I'd like to say goodnight from the 1968 conventions." The anchorman had started the day under attack for showing too much pummeling, and he had done poor damage control with a phony "kiss-and-make-up session." He closed out by hinting there had actually been much more violence than viewers could imagine.

David Douglas Duncan was hopefully asleep by now. Don Peterson was probably still riding the bus back to his hotel. Norman Mailer had gotten good and drunk, got himself busted and released by the police— twice—for being belligerent, and finally, around 3:00 a.m. or so, headed off with newspaperman Pete Hamill and NBC correspondent Douglas Kiker for drinks and whatnot at the Playboy mansion. The last day of the convention had dragged right on into early Friday morning, but it was finally over.

Coda

Around 4:30 a.m. on Friday, the National Guard stationed outside the Hilton reported to the Chicago police that empty beer cans and other objects had been thrown out of the window of room 1506A. That was part of the complex of rooms in the McCarthy suite. A guest staying on the nineteenth floor later said it looked like the projectiles came from the eighteenth floor. One later version said that ashtrays had been thrown, not beer cans. Another account was that herrings and sardines had been thrown. Teddy White said there was simply "no evidence whatsoever that the McCarthy students had been throwing anything."[58]

A McCarthy staffer in the lobby overheard four policemen discussing the situation. One officer explained the report from the guardsman, and another responded, "OK, give the order to drag them all in and give them a beating. Teach them a lesson." The police got passkeys from hotel management and headed upstairs. Some of the Clean for Gene kids were up late, drunk or playing cards. Some were asleep. Just the night before, they had shredded the bedding to make bandages; their physical and emotional fatigue must have been extreme by now. A number of the rooms in the suite did not face Michigan Avenue, a relevant point only if one foolishly assumed that the cops would only go after those who had allegedly thrown stuff from the windows. On the contrary, everyone was beaten. Imagine the shock of being sound asleep in a hotel and suddenly being dragged out of bed, called a "bitch," and beaten by a policeman with a nightstick.[59] Four of the kids went to the hospital with head injuries.

Senator McCarthy was asleep on a higher floor when his staff woke him up. He came downstairs, but the damage had already been done. "You can't just come up here and knock heads," he told the police, a meaningless protestation at this point.[60] A report from Daley's office later explained what they claimed really happened: "The police spoke softly and dealt gently; . . . nobody was shoved or prodded."[61] It was outrageous that the mayor thought he could get away with this made-up nonsense, but there had been no cameras. Daley had complained that protestors acted out only to get free publicity from the news media; if this were true, then the "whole world is watching" chant on Wednesday night was inculpatory. But the attack on the kids in McCarthy headquarters laid bare the fact that police were violent not only when "provoked" and on-camera. Absent the news media, the only record of the event was eyewitness reports, and four hospital records. Richard Goodwin, manager of McCarthy's New Hampshire campaign, had stopped by to say goodbye to the volunteers, and he saw most of what happened. Down in the lobby where the beaten volunteers were corralled by police, Goodwin instructed some of them to slip away and notify the networks. He then told the police that "television was coming." He thought the threat of being seen by the news might deescalate the crisis.

By now McCarthy was also in the lobby. He sent the kids into the elevators slowly, and the police did not follow.[62] Was it McCarthy's presence that deterred the police? Or was it Goodwin's threat? Daley's response to TV images of police brutality could often be boiled down to the pure gaslighting of telling people, "You are not seeing what you are seeing" or "They showed you this thing instead of the more important thing." So perhaps TV cameras in the Hilton lobby at 5:00 a.m. would not have made a difference in preventing more violence. Even so, apparently, the police were tired enough—or apathetic enough, just sick of the whole thing—that they took this opportunity not to be seen. They dispersed before any cameras arrived.

McCarthy put off his early morning flight, instead holding a press conference with his volunteers, where he told them he was waiting to depart to give them all more time to leave the city safely. He was

FIGURE 26. McCarthy holds a press conference on Friday and attempts to reassure his dejected volunteers. A majority of Americans reacted negatively to news coverage in Chicago and positively to the use of police force against "dirty hippies," yet most of those beaten on Michigan Avenue on Wednesday night and in the McCarthy hotel suite early Friday morning looked more like these young, clean-cut college kids. Field Enterprises, Inc., 1968.

concerned the police might return to arrest them. There was a photographic record of this gathering. One image showed a sad row of five young women, wearing the black armbands that McCarthy delegates had put on when the minority Vietnam peace plank was defeated (fig. 26). This was exactly the sort of image that one might mistakenly think would sway a national, white, middle-class audience to question the presumption that the Chicago police violence had been merited, provoked by a bunch of dirty hippies and communists whose behavior and appearance were repellent to so much of middlebrow America. Even the NBC and CBS anchormen and correspondents striving for neutrality had described the street protestors as "obnoxious," their language, "vile."

The networks had, conversely, described the McCarthy volunteers in much warmer and even romanticized terms. McCarthy himself had conceptualized his movement as a liberal campaign that would undermine the "radicalization of the peace movement" as embodied by New Leftists like Tom Hayden.[63] His well-groomed volunteers modeled how young people could "come back into the mainstream of American life," as one campaign ad put it, and bridge the generation gap.[64] David Brinkley had at one point recounted that McCarthy volunteers, mostly eighteen-to-twenty-year-olds, had taped up a sign reading "Sen. McCarthy is backed by the most improbable political machine in American history. It works for nothing. It runs on peanut butter sandwiches and soft drinks." This encapsulated the feeling that these were the idealistic political players, the wholesome kids. Brinkley thought it was wrong to beat people up for yelling obscenities at the police, or blocking traffic, or having long hair, but like many mainstream journalists he obviously had a sweet spot for the more clean-cut activists.

It had been a year of endlessly demoralizing events: assassinations, riots, police brutality, the Tet Offensive. All of that had been covered by network television, making white middle-class Americans frustrated and angry, but Chicago was the last straw. TV viewers across America attacked the coverage as wrong-headed and stood up for the police, rejecting protestors and even newsmen as "communists," while embracing the authoritarian Mayor Daley as a hero. If a political boss like Daley was a hero, if "Uncle Walter" was no longer "the most trusted man in America," and if even the Clean for Gene kids could be beaten indiscriminately by Chicago police, how much room could be left for idealism in American politics? Obviously, very little. As McCarthy's chartered plane finally left the city on Friday afternoon, the pilot announced on the PA system, "We are leaving Prague."[65]

Chapter Six   The Storm after the Storm

The fallout from the 1968 Democratic National Convention was immediate—delegates were demoralized, TV viewers were appalled regardless of their politics, and Mayor Daley was enraged that anyone dared question the integrity of his cops. But the aftershocks were also longer-lasting, coming to a head at the 1972 Democratic convention and beyond if you consider the post-convention, anti-network fallout as a sort of test run for the Nixon-Agnew assault on mass media "bias." In the intervening years, Humphrey and Nixon battled for the presidency, with Humphrey losing in large part because he could never spring back from the impact of Chicago; the Democratic Party made extensive procedural reforms with long-ranging consequences; an official government study, the *Walker Report*, found that the attacks on Michigan Avenue could most accurately be described as a "police riot"; Daley did his best to discredit the networks and, on a more primal level, to take revenge by creating a counter-narrative about the events of August 1968; and the TV networks came under extended attack from both the viewing public and a range of government officials for their "biased" coverage of police brutality.

Further, the DNC's procedural reforms, forged in reaction to Chicago, led to the decline of the brokered convention, in which candidates were decided on-site and often via multiple rounds of votes. Instead, candidates would be decided in advance via the primary process. TV coverage of primaries increased, while convention coverage waned. By 1988, the networks had settled on spot coverage and live broadcast of acceptance speeches. In effect, the parties had finally achieved the controlled event they had always wanted; it was boring, but at least there were no derailing surprises. Gavel-to-gavel coverage thereafter could be seen only on PBS and C-SPAN. Ultimately, it was the rise of cable and the fracturing of American TV viewers into niche demographics that were the final nails in the coffin for gavel-to-gavel coverage; given more than three viewing options, people went with scripted entertainment over live political coverage.

But before cable, the rise of the totally controlled convention was already underway. The ratings were perhaps the first tea leaves portending change. NBC won the overall ratings war against CBS in the conventions of 1960 through 1968. CBS had better numbers than NBC at the Republican convention in 1972, but the number-one network at the 1972 GOP convention was ABC, again running its truncated ninety-minute nightly coverage. ABC had always been a joke, the poor stepchild of news, but with this victory they demonstrated definitively that less was more. It was a preview of coming attractions, and all based on their idea in Chicago that they could offer viewers "unconventional convention" coverage.

Networks Under Attack

CBS and NBC news divisions were impacted right away by Chicago. Their reliability as public servants thrown into question, they were put on the defensive to an unprecedented degree. Politically, it was a tangled skein.

Let's start at the top. President Johnson, like Mayor Daley, felt that TV journalists had betrayed him in Chicago, but he remained hung up on the notion that the network newsmen were out to get him because they were pro-Kennedy. Further, he couldn't forgive them for amplifying the "credibility gap" regarding Vietnam ever since the *New York Herald Tribune* had coined the phrase in 1965.[1] The president's relationship with the networks—and the print media—had soured before Chicago, but things had not always been so dire. David Brinkley and his wife had been welcome for a weekend at Camp David a few years earlier, and LBJ had dined at the anchorman's house, but as public sentiment toward Vietnam went south, and the networks covered that discontent, Brinkley's phone had been tapped by Johnson. A few years later, Brinkley made Nixon's enemies list, too.[2] By late 1968, Frank Stanton was the only remaining man in the network news business whom Johnson could count as his friend. Realistically, Johnson was on his way out of office and had neither the time nor inclination to ignite a new vendetta against TV. Further, even if he didn't like the interview choices that correspondents had made on the convention floor, the incendiary images that had Daley and TV viewers all over America up in arms were not of the Amphitheatre crises but of Chicago police. LBJ was sensitive and paranoid, but probably understood these images as more Daley's problem than his own.

Further, he knew the notion that the media had deceived viewers about the nature of the violence on Wednesday night was not an open-and-shut case. Attorney General Ramsey Clark told him unequivocally on Thursday morning, the day after the Battle of Michigan Avenue, that hundreds of people had been viciously clubbed by the police; some were "troublemakers" and others "just happened to be standing there. There were kids that would give a Bronx cheer, and three or four policemen would lay on them and just beat the hell out of them, and not even arrest them. I think it was caused by law enforcement. Absolutely unnecessary." Johnson asked if anyone was seriously injured and then disingenuously shifted gears, asking, "Did you get incensed any at the subjectivity of the networks?" Clark responded that they were subjective, ignorant, and did not perform "professionally," although he gave no specifics. Still, the Chicago police were the ones in the wrong, and the Attorney General knew it.[3] It's possible LBJ disbelieved him, but Clark included details that others also observed, and it was all confirmed just a few months later by the *Walker Report.*

TV journalists had sought to cover events in Chicago as fairly as they could. What they witnessed was an excess of police violence against protestors in the street, and that is what they showed, though not much of it. The networks thought they were showing police "overreacting" (their squishy euphemism), but viewers disagreed, and they deluged the networks with complaints. Polls during and after the convention revealed overwhelming sentiment against the protestors and for the Chicago police.

Each day, nationwide viewing of the convention had dropped off after prime time, and most of the violence had been shown late at night. Yet daily convention footage was repurposed for capsule stories in the morning and nightly news in the days that followed, still photographs from each day had made the front pages of newspapers across the country, and more photos appeared in magazines, such that the story of Wednesday night's violence was inevitably amplified. Americans saw capsule stories from inside the Amphitheatre that they might have missed when they aired live. In particular, the clash in the streets on Wednesday night was so dramatic that even people outside of the 50.5 million households who had watched the convention would pick it up, whether or not they usually followed politics.

This presented a challenge for the networks. The Battle of Michigan Avenue remained a big story, which they couldn't ignore, but they didn't want to push it too hard either. As "bias" accusations surfaced, the old problem of TV journalists wanting to tell-the-story-not-be-the-story loomed large, and the networks didn't see a way out of being the subject of their own coverage. It was a story that snowballed quickly, though its dissemination seems almost quaint today. Without social media, without algorithms pushing material into people's feeds, without angry cable TV pundits blasting out their opinions, the story nonetheless, in today's parlance, went viral. Daley, too, boosted it with his own protestations of being victimized.

Reproduced widely at the time (and since) was the image of Daley holding his hand up to his mouth on Wednesday night and shouting at Ribicoff, "Fuck you, you Jew son of a bitch, you lousy motherfucker, go home!" (fig. 27). The lipreaders did not immediately deliver the exact words; regardless, the image was understood as Daley defending himself against an unfair attack. By contrast, CBS viewers who had missed late-night analysis by Eric Sevareid or Roger Mudd, the former offering a gently liberal interpretation of events, the latter a somewhat more conservative interpretation, would not get a chance to revisit those

FIGURE 27. Daley puts his hand to his mouth as he hurls obscenities at Sen. Abraham Ribicoff. Daley's people claimed he called Ribicoff a "faker," while lip readers later interpreted it as "fucker." The cropped version of Daley's face is the widely circulated one, but this wider shot conveys the crush of the crowd, the strange mix of angry and contemptuously smiling faces surrounding the mayor, and the ring of security standing in the aisle preventing press access to Daley. Associated Press, 1968.

carefully measured interpretations. It was the images recycled in news-papers, on TV, and, in the coming months and years, in documentaries and news specials that had the most staying power. And so, public opin-ion continued to run in favor of the forces of authority in Chicago.

A *New York Times* survey published on August 30 confirmed imme-diate antagonism toward the protestors. Two months later, a detailed survey by University of Michigan researchers found similar results, but with more nuance. The results of one query were particularly striking: "Did you happen to hear anything about what went on between the po-lice and the demonstrators in Chicago at the Democratic convention? If yes, do you think the police used too much force, the right amount of force, or not enough force with demonstrators?" The breakdown of responses was:

Did not hear about what went on 12%
Too much force 19%
Right amount of force 32%
Not enough force 25%
Don't know 12%

The striking revelations here were not only that 57 percent of those who had heard about the street violence were pro–Chicago police, and less than 20 percent were not, but that one-quarter thought the police had not been violent *enough*. Notably, 63 percent of Blacks (and 82 percent of Blacks with "at least some college," and 78 percent of Blacks under fifty) surveyed said that the police used too much force, statistics that gained little traction at the time.[4] The dominant media narrative was that "most Americans" disapproved of network coverage and approved of police actions in Chicago.

NBC News president Reuven Frank boldly defended his industry in *TV Guide*, then the publication with the largest circulation in America, reaching some 14 million households.[5] The guide first and foremost of-fered program listings, but it also included light articles and profiles of celebrities, and, on the heavier side, "prestige pieces" from contributors such as Margaret Mead, Arthur Schlesinger Jr., and John Updike.[6] As a serious essay, then, Frank's contribution was not anomalous. Frank argued that viewers were blaming the messenger for what they had seen in Chicago. Yet Frank did not take an angry or defensive tone. He noted at the outset a key point: the events of the convention itself were important and had been completely lost in the shuffle of angry viewer mail and a brief FCC inquiry spurred by citizen complaints.[7] He didn't attack Daley for preventing live coverage outside the Amphitheatre, or for his heavy-handed security, although he did point those things out. He also explained that NBC News had formulated a plan once it became clear how heavily the network's coverage would be stymied outside the Amphitheatre: if they could use video, they would; if not, they would use film; and if film wasn't possible, still photos with walkie-talkie audio from the streets would enable coverage.

The point was thus strongly made that Daley would not—indeed, *could not*—stifle free speech in Chicago; TV journalists would find a way to tell their stories. Frank had staked a claim for the dogged tenacity and professionalism of his team. Given that the street violence was underreported, Frank perhaps thumped his chest too much here. On the other hand, he didn't even mention that both print and TV journalists had been beaten in the streets, a point he could have emphasized for dramatic effect, but Frank was trying to keep the emotional temperature down; in effect, by omission, he had managed to tell-the-story-not-be-the-story, to sidestep the issue of violence against journalists. He did offer a few fact corrections, most importantly that, of the thirty-five hours of coverage provided by NBC, sixty-five minutes had shown street protest, of which only thirty minutes had been in prime time. In all, street demonstrations had constituted about 3 percent of NBC's convention coverage. He calculated that the other networks' coverage came closer to 5 percent. So the accusation that the networks had played into the hands of the Yippies by providing endless, positive, free publicity simply did not match up with reality.

Frank gently called out viewers for blaming TV for all that they didn't like, not only violence in the Chicago streets but also violence in Southeast Asia. But the most forceful part of the essay was its concluding paragraphs, where Frank took a strong anti-censorship stance:

> Let us postulate that there is a unanimously accepted social good which television journalism should set itself to achieve or promote. And the decision would be made by five Albert Schweitzers sitting around a table. Whoever put them there could, in time, . . . replace the five Albert Schweitzers with five Joseph Goebbelses, or five Joseph Stalins, or five George Lincoln Rockwells. You see, it's not the five Albert Schweitzers who are important, but the table. I say the table itself is evil. . . . If you tell a medium of journalism what to put in and what to leave out, even if you know in your own heart you are promoting the public welfare, even if most people agree with you, then you are changing journalism as it exists in America. Whatever you call it, censorship is censorship, and all censorship is aimed not at the transmitter but at the receiver.[8]

What was canny here was not getting pulled into the "When did you stop beating your wife?" nonsense of debating whether or not the network had shown "enough provocation" from the demonstrators or whether Frank and his coworkers had fairly evaluated the performance of Chicago police officers. He had already argued that his team had done its best, using their standard operating procedures, thereby ably standing up for his industry. And as he noted later in his memoir, this was just a warm-up for the tortuous self-defense moves that the network news divisions would be forced to undertake in the Nixon years.

Julian Goodman, president of NBC, sent a copy of Frank's *TV Guide* piece to Gen. David Sarnoff, the chairman of the board of RCA, which owned NBC. In fact, Goodman sent copies to all the members of the board. In his cover letter to Sarnoff, Goodman praised Frank's low-key approach, stating that "NBC has not participated in the public debate over the coverage of the Democratic convention in Chicago. . . . We have preferred to wait for the opportunity to make our points dispassionately in the best forums possible. One such opportunity has arisen, . . . and this week's *TV Guide* . . . has published an article on the subject written personally by NBC News President Reuven Frank. . . . I found it calm, persuasive and frequently eloquent, particularly in its closing paragraphs." Goodman made it clear that *TV Guide* was "the best forum" because of its wide circulation. A cynic might observe that Frank's article was intercut with ads for products not often associated with eloquent prose: Lysol, Preparation-H, and Inver House Rare Scotch Whisky ("soft as a kiss"). Regardless, Sarnoff was pleased and scribbled a short note of appreciation to Goodman. CBS president Frank Stanton likewise dashed off a note to Frank: "Your article in *TV Guide* is superb. All of us in the industry are in your debt."[9] The networks were rivals, except when they were collectively under attack. Like the quiz show scandals of the late 1950s or the later attacks by the Nixon administration, the Chicago fallout was a crucial moment for the Big Three to circle the wagons.[10]

CBS's viewer mail ran eleven to one against its coverage. The network news was not in the habit of publicizing their negative viewer mail, but now they sought transparency. Harry Reasoner noted the imbalance on the third episode of *60 Minutes* on October 8, 1968. He said the network had received 8,670 letters so far, and he read excerpts. A viewer from Urbana, Ohio, wrote, "I've never seen such a disgusting display of one-sided reporting in all of the years I've watched television." Another from Columbia, South Carolina, wrote, "your coverage . . . was slanted in favor of the hoodlums and beatniks and slurred the police trying to preserve order." Writing from New York City, an angry viewer inquired, "Our Lord whipped the money lenders out of the temple. Are you going to accuse Him of brutality?" From Plymouth, North Carolina, came this assessment: "You may think you have crucified the Mayor . . . of Chicago, but you have in fact crucified CBS." From South Bend, Indiana, a viewer wrote, "I sincerely hope you choke on the wine of your sour grapes during the Democratic convention." Reasoner read from three positive letters as well, two of which were, pointedly, from Chicago. One of these read, "As sad as it may seem, you have shown the real face of Chicago," and the other described the network's coverage as "the best and the most fair reporting job, . . . even when . . . [Mayor] Daley makes it pretty hard to do." It was bold for this new investigative program to include attacks on its own network's integrity. This was in keeping with CBS News's notion of itself as a public servant.

Predictably, angry complaint letters came in because Reasoner had read nine letters and three of those were positive, which didn't match the eleven-to-one ratio of con-to-pro letters. It was a niggling complaint, but it points to how strongly people didn't want to hear anything bad about Chicago police or good about CBS. *60 Minutes* followed up in a later episode, noting the new complaint letters and acknowledging the numbers had not matched the ratio of mail received. The back-and-forth could have gone on for months, but after this *60 Minutes* let it drop.

Daley Fights Back

We can never be sure how long the public outrage against TV news would have boiled if left to its own devices. After all, the crisis in Czechoslovakia continued, student demonstrators were massacred by the police of Mexico City in early October, the raising of Black Power fists by American athletes at the Olympic Games later that month drew international attention, and the war in Vietnam continued, with the Cold War as backdrop. There was no shortage of distracting events, not all of them strictly negative—both Apollo 7 and Apollo 8 launched before the end of the year. Plus, there were two candidates for the presidency, which was guaranteed to seize the political oxygen on TV. The Chicago debacle was too apocalyptic not to be guaranteed a place in the history books, but the temperature of public outrage might have cooled more quickly—and thereby damaged Humphrey's campaign less—if not for one person, Richard J. Daley, who in the weeks following the convention insistently amplified the idea that the networks had misrepresented events in Chicago.

Conventions typically provide momentum for newly minted candidates, but Humphrey limped out of the gate, and his messaging about the events of August was not consistent. During the convention itself he said, "We ought to quit pretending that Mayor Daley did something that was wrong."[11] In November, by contrast, he awkwardly told a rally of ten thousand in Chicago that "things happened in Chicago and at our convention that I'm not proud of and you're not proud of, . . . but if we quarrel over the past, we can lose the future. Blame is not important: self-examination is."[12] Daley was just a few feet away, smoke coming out of his ears. If the mayor was keen on "self-examination," only his priest had seen evidence of it. In his convention interview with Daley, Cronkite had asked him if he would have done *anything* differently, if he could do it again, and the answer was an unequivocal no.

The harm Daley did to the Humphrey campaign with his attacks on the networks was ironic. Daley was supposedly the great team player of the Democratic Party, eager to please the White House and to use his machine to keep his people in office at the local, state, and federal levels. If LBJ had told him just to shut up about the convention because it made Humphrey look bad, he would have snapped to attention and buttoned his lip. But Johnson did no such thing. Thus, Daley exacerbated and encouraged public distrust of the networks and demanded restitution: people had to know that he and his police had done a great job. Pride won out over party.

The odd thing was, as Daley told it and as polls confirmed, most Americans agreed with him that the police had acted appropriately. The mayor even bragged that he had received sixty thousand letters of support and only four thousand negative letters following the convention.[13] If public opinion was already with him, what difference had news coverage made, and why work so hard to prove that the networks had erred? The most obvious explanation was that this was a personal issue for him, and by extension an issue of Chicago pride, because he so strongly felt that the city was "his." A different sort of politician would have used the fallout and vilified the networks to bolster his national profile, perhaps aspiring for higher office, but Daley had no such ambitions.

Nonetheless, the convention and its fallout did raise his national profile, and one unexpected outcome was a list of pro-Daley correspondents from across the country. The mayor's staff hand-copied 6,913 names and addresses from Daley's post-convention fan mail onto spreadsheets.[14] Were there really just under seven rather than sixty thousand positive letters? It's impossible to know for sure. Telegrams came in without return addresses and so were not logged on the spreadsheets. Also, some letters came in with multiple signatures but just one return address on the envelope. Still, the master spreadsheet was useful, likely for Democratic fund-raising.

At the time, Daley focused his public statements more on the numbers than on the details of the correspondence. The specific content of the letters reveals a bracing picture of the "pro" side. In fact, Daley's convention mail resonates strongly with support letters sent four months earlier following his shoot-to-kill and shoot-to-maim comments after King's assassination. Many writers saw the convention as an extension of that earlier moment of crisis: both events illustrated the value of Daley's stance on maintaining "law and order." Daley claimed the letters he received about the shoot-to-kill-or-maim order ran fifteen to one in his favor. He didn't share the details of the letters. A particularly harsh one reads, "Hi Mayor Daley: If all the mayors looked at this jig problem like you do, it would stop right now. Only thing they should use machine guns. We are too good to them. Go ahead and bump them off."[15] Somewhat softer letters complimented him on his approach to handling the "hoodlums and the trash of society."[16] Others took a more civic-minded approach, suggesting that citizens who paid their taxes deserved protection from arsonists and looters. Letters came in from Chicago and across the country, on Holiday Inn postcards, on cute poodle notecards, and on official business letterhead, both typed and handwritten.

The geographic and tonal range of supportive mail following the convention in August was strikingly similar. Daley supporters understood that the protestors at the convention were mostly white, but they lumped them together with those who had risen up after King's assassination, seeing them all as lawless troublemakers who did not deserve kind treatment from the police. An attorney from North Carolina suggested that someone had funded the convention protestors, just like the "'Beatniks' [who] were paid fifteen dollars per day, food and lodging, and all the n*gger sex they wanted to . . . join the march from Selma to Montgomery." He advised Daley to investigate who had sponsored the convention rioters, although he already had an answer: the Jews. As corroborating evidence he pointed to Abraham Ribicoff and other "Zionist" Democratic delegates.[17] Another correspondent mailed the mayor a copy of a radio editorial by future senator Jesse Helms, celebrating the Chicago Police for their actions against "dirty, smelly hippies threatening to take over the city," attacking the news media for their "phony charges of 'police brutality,'" and suggesting that newsmen deserved to have their skulls cracked.[18] San Francisco State English professor S. I. Hayakawa—another future senator—offered a more high-toned response, suggesting that Daley get in touch with the author of *The Image: A Guide to Pseudo-Events in America*: "If you want a thorough study of how the networks and the cameramen and the commentators were conned into broadcasting to the world that dreadful image of Chicago and its police department, you can do no better than to call on Professor [Daniel J.] Boorstin" of the history department at the University of Chicago.[19] A US Air Force colonel wrote to the mayor, "Bravo! Bravo! Bravo! Your treatment of the Yippies, hippies, junkies, hoodlums, bums, and other scum during the recent convention was perfect. I noted with delight that the police devoted some richly deserved attention to the prime provocateurs—the press."[20] A ninety-two-year-old doctor from Irvington, New York, praised Daley for his fairness and courage, adding, "You have fearlessly upheld law and order and saved the City of Chicago from disaster in the presence of criticism and misrepresentation by press, radio, and television."[21] There were also cheerful greeting cards with prayer cards attached and fawning notes like "In a world gone mad, thank God there is you."[22] If not every letter was explicitly pro-police violence, many were, and even more singled out the mass media as the key source of the city's problems before, during, and after the convention. As for the four thousand (perhaps) negative letters, only a handful are in Daley's archive. It seems that he more often hung on to his positive mail.

Daley's first step following the convention was to demand an hour of prime time from all three networks to give his side of the story—and he made sure that this request was publicized. CBS responded that it had already given him a half-hour, prime time interview with Cronkite in Chicago. That had gone badly for CBS's anchorman but ultimately played in the network's favor; it could reasonably say that it had already rolled out the red carpet for Daley.

NBC had a different initial response to Daley's request: the network started with fact-checking, reviewing their coverage in laborious detail. (This was also an ongoing self-inspection in response to inquiries made to all three networks from both the House of Representatives and the FCC.) NBC could not find in its footage any attacks launched against Daley or the police. Further, while Daley had charged that the networks hadn't shown protestors "provoking" the police, for example by ripping down an American flag, NBC had shown the flag incident not once but three times.[23] Ultimately, both ABC and NBC invited the mayor to be on one of their interview programs. On NBC, that would have been *Meet the Press*, its long-running news panel discussion show. The network even offered to expand the running time of the show to an hour.

Daley flatly refused both networks, implying that this was some kind of a setup and that it was completely unfair to ask him *questions* about what had happened in Chicago. That makes no sense unless you consider that he was a terrible public speaker, easily falling into embarrassing malapropisms and gaffes. Soon after the convention, he had chastised reporters, telling them to get it straight: "The policeman isn't there to create disorder. The policeman is there to preserve disorder." When cornered on an issue, he glowered and turned bright red. Outside of a machine system like Chicago, a man so lacking in charisma would have struggled in politics. Daley had been mayor since 1955 and was popular with his white ethnic base and business interests; he didn't need to be charming. Further, what it meant to be "telegenic" was still a work-in-progress for politicians in the 1960s. (New York City's John Lindsay would not have needed a slogan that made him sound like a deodorant—"he is fresh and everyone else is tired"—to get elected in 1965 if the Tammany Hall machine had not fallen apart by then.) Daley's refusal of NBC's and ABC's offers was seen as a brilliant act of resistance by his fans. Three supporters sent him a homemade two-by-three-foot poster, decorated with drawings of shamrocks, a horseshoe, and a wishbone, and reading "GOOD LUCK DALEY. . . . We back you 100%. . . . Stay away from panel discussions."[24]

Finally, a broadcaster gave Daley airtime. The non–network affiliated, independent company Metromedia owned TV stations in Washington, Los Angeles, New York, San Francisco, and Kansas City. It would distribute a one-hour film commissioned by Daley's office.[25] Other independent stations also signed on to air it, most predictably WGN-TV, which was owned by the *Chicago Tribune*; the *Trib* had lauded Daley and the police throughout the convention, except for a brief complaint lodged about violence against its own reporters. By September 15, 1968, more than 130 stations were on board to carry the film, awkwardly titled *What Trees Do They Plant?*

For Daley this was a small triumph. *Trees* also aired on more than a thousand radio stations.[26] (There were more independent radio stations than TV stations, in large part because the medium was so much cheaper.) We have no exact numbers on how many heard or saw Daley's film, but by sidestepping the networks, he had found a way to saturate the country with his message on one day. He probably would have preferred to have aired *Trees* on the networks, but you might say that he won by losing, because huge numbers of Americans saw the film and also heard his complaints of being victimized and censored by the networks.

September 15 was a Sunday, when ad rates were low, which meant it was the day when stations sacrificed time to religious and informational shows in order to demonstrate to the FCC that they fulfilled public service requirements. In fact, *Trees* opens and closes with redundant title cards, the first one reading "The following program was furnished by the City of Chicago" and then a second one reading "presented as a public service by the city of Chicago." The film was thus framed as neutral rather than as the propaganda that it was, although, to be fair, it was not unheard-of for public service programming to take a strong point of view—polished up as "balanced" public service—in the late 1960s.[27] At 9:00 p.m., LBJ watched *What Trees Do They Plant?* in the Aspen Lodge at Camp David with Lady Bird, one of his daughters, and Mr. and Mrs. Arthur Krim of United Artists.[28]

Reuven Frank makes several shrewd observations about the program. First, much of the material in *Trees* was footage shot by the networks, supplied to Daley at his request. This was generous since Daley commissioned the film to get his revenge on the Big Three. In fact, Daley goes out of his way to thank the *local* Chicago CBS, NBC, and ABC stations at the end of *Trees*. This is an esoteric point, but to put it simply, the three networks had affiliates all over the country, which were local stations contractually tied to them; the networks also had "owned-and-operated" stations ("O&O's," in the lingo) that were directly under their control. In Chicago, the network stations were O&O's, so acknowledging the networks by giving their local call signs was disingenuous, but it subtly stoked the growing feeling among Americans that it was specifically *national* TV news that was untrustworthy. Before Chicago, that was an idea that had most often been promulgated in the Deep South, where local news was understood as a friend to segregationists and national news as their enemy.

As one would expect, *Trees* curates footage that mostly leaves out images of police beating protestors. Frank adds that much of the newly shot material in the film centers on police describing violence propagated by protestors and displaying seized weapons. Two details that stand out are the remains of a Molotov cocktail and a baseball bat with "Kill the Pigs" written on one side and "love" written on the other. The *Walker Report* also included a jar containing a black widow spider in its list of protestors' dirty tricks, though it seems like a hard item to weaponize.

Frank argues that the film "was a letdown. The [*New York*] *Times* said 'it showed no more provocation than network news had shown while the convention was going on.'"[29] Asserting that the networks got it wrong was different from proving it. The newsmen had catastrophically failed, Daley contended, by not showing protestors hurling profanities and projectiles at cops, but Daley himself didn't have any such footage, although his film did include a draft-card-burning session and self-defense training in the park. The city's director of Police Intelligence goes so far as to contend that the hippies and Yippies were learning "movements which are hardly defensive, one being how to kick to the groin. Now, I have never heard of a kick to the groin being a defensive tactic," a laughable assessment of a maneuver that most people would point to as the single *most* effective defensive tactic to use in a brawl. *Trees* was all sizzle and no steak, from Frank's perspective, but that was correct only if you understood it as a fact-finding venture. The film reinforced the idea that protestors had been violent and deserved to be beaten, implying that TV had gotten the story all wrong. Similar to the "Big Lie" about the 2020 presidential election being stolen, Daley's anti-protestor, pro-police, and network-bias narrative was hard to disprove because people who believed it were looking only for "facts" confirming what they already believed. No counterfacts could change their minds.

Frank closes his discussion of *Trees* in his memoir with two observations. First, he explains that "with the broadcast of the film, the Daley incident evanesced. The fuss had been about carrying it, and that had become moot." Having shown his side of things, Daley receded from national media coverage and mostly fell back into his old routines in Chicago, at least until the *Walker Report* was released in December. The mayor's personal momentum may have slowed, but the network-bias narrative he had fostered was slowly building up a life of its own, and here Frank's second observation is vital: a new era had begun of TV journalists and executives seizing every opportunity for writing editorials, attending panels, pleading, and "generally wrapping [themselves] in the First Amendment." He archly adds, "We did not know what good practice this would be for the years of Richard M. Nixon and Spiro T.

Agnew."[30] The fallout from Chicago had shown how easy it was to whip up mass opinion against network TV, with minimal evidence. *Trees* did not *prove* Daley's allegations, but it did reinforce and boost his false and misleading claims. Angry viewers not only believed he had socked it to the networks, they also changed the content of their complaint letters, adding bullet points from the film to their angry missives to Walter Cronkite, including Daley's shaky claim—from Cronkite's interview, as excerpted in *Trees*—that he had made Chicago a fortress in response to threats of assassination. Daley never explained that the FBI had investigated those threats and found none of them substantial. It was a clever move by Daley, if his goal was to frighten people and boost their support for law enforcement in a remarkable year of assassinations and upheaval. After the film was broadcast, editorials and letters to the editor continued to reference Daley's victimization and, as with the shift in letters to Cronkite, to include details that had only appeared in the film—further evidence that *Trees* had made an impact on public perceptions of network news.

A Closer Look at Daley's Counter-Media

What Trees Do They Plant? is not a particularly artful film, though impressive by virtue of being created in a mere three weeks by Henry Ushijima Productions, an educational and industrial film company that generally made more politically neutral material, with titles like *Farm Petroleum Safety* (1954) and *The Serve with Billie Jean King* (1972). *Trees* was likewise a work-for-hire project, and it may have pained Ushijima, who had been interned in the Manzanar internment camp during World War II and presumably had strong feelings about due process, civil rights, and propaganda.[31]

In a 1959 essay, Ushijima argues that a sponsored documentary "stands or falls on the truth of what it has to say. . . . This is not to imply, of course, that the sponsor is not entitled to a voice in the project. He's paying for it, he's the customer, and without him the film probably wouldn't be made. . . . But, in any event, sponsor rights do not include willful and deliberate falsification or distortion of facts."[32] Perhaps Ushijima felt comfortable making a film that would be helpful for Chicago's image. His company had been hired by the city in late 1963 or early 1964 to make *A New Look at Chicago* to boost Daley's projects.[33] *New Look* was one of the city's "motion picture reports," sporadic films made to promote Chicago, all broadcast locally and funded by taxpayers.

What Trees Do They Plant? was also locally funded. The Democratic Party of Cook County paid $24,500 toward the film, and the Chicago Democratic Host Committee paid $65,500—a startling reallocation of convention funds for post-convention activities.[34] *A New Look at Chicago* had been a shiny little film emphasizing the positive and, since the city was the customer, leaving out the negative. One might call it light propaganda or simply a seventeen-minute advertisement for Chicago. *Trees* might have been pitched to Ushijima as a similar kind of film, a production that would balance out network coverage of Chicago that the Daley administration found harmful to the city.

Ruth Ratney, who co-wrote the film, later said that *Trees* originally had been intended, from her perspective at least, to be truthful. And then Daley's people demanded changes. It is impossible to know for sure how much the film was changed because of pressure from Daley's office, but a close analysis of the film takes us beyond the general assessment that it was sheer Daley propaganda and, instead, into specifics of what the administration hoped to convey to viewers.

Parts of the film do willfully falsify facts, most patently when the voice-over declares that the police did not engage in violence until the battle in front of the Conrad Hilton on August 28. The film is most distorted, however, not in its direct misrepresentations but more subtly in what it assumes and in what it leaves out. First and foremost, *Trees* presumes a viewer who is repulsed by hippies and Yippies, hence a number of long sequences just showing protestors milling about, as if their very appearance was proof of ill intentions. This maneuver requires an awkward voice-over to finesse the fact that plenty of the people are wearing coats and ties, not love beads. *Trees* also presumes a viewer who is not particularly concerned about the rights of free speech or free assembly. Hence, there is a recurrent emphasis on the idea that the assembling of protestors was *illegal* because the city denied them virtually every permit for which they applied, and also an emphasis on offensive statements and chants from protestors. Saying and doing are conflated throughout the film, as if voicing support for "the enemy" in Vietnam was the same as taking up arms with him.

Further, the films' interpretations are debatable: two strong examples are the claim that police had to take aggressive action against protestors in front of the Hilton to "protect the hotel" (from what exactly?) and, especially, when the voice-over states that, following the convention vote against the dove plank, protestors' "contempt for the government of the United States is shown as the American flag is lowered to half-mast." Burning a flag might indicate contempt for the government; lowering a flag is an expression of grief. One lowers a flag to mourn, not to deride.

Above all, *Trees* minimizes interviews with protestors, except for canned news footage of Jerry Rubin, Tom Hayden, Rennie Davis, and Dave Dellinger, and one interview with an ineloquent college student. More often, the film leaves out the faces of protestors, so they appear as swarming masses of angry criminals, not concerned citizens. A notable exception is a beautiful, fleeting moment in crowded, teargassed Grant Park on Wednesday afternoon, when a demonstrator in a suit and tie holding a bandage to his head, walks straight toward the camera, smiles, and waves. (This happens to be Peter Bonerz, both part of the protest and on hand to participate in material that later appeared in Haskell Wexler's feature film *Medium Cool* [1969].[35]) It's worth adding that network news coverage of the convention similarly avoided direct engagement with demonstrators, outside of CBS's brilliant, late Tuesday and Wednesday night footage showing the crises as they played out on the faces in the streets, and also the interviews with the wounded in the improvised infirmary in McCarthy headquarters.

Notably, CBS and NBC had each shown about one hour of street action, spread out over four days, and mostly late at night. The networks focused their coverage on floor fights, not street fights. Daley's one-hour film, by contrast, focused exclusively on the protest and aired at variable times, according to the whims of each TV market. His attempt to set the record straight emphasized and amplified that protest. The networks showed bits and pieces of violence only sporadically, but Daley offered an entire hour of violent imagery, interviews with wounded cops, displays of weapons, and so on, all at once. Perhaps the Humphrey campaign took solace, at least, in the fact that the convention was largely irrelevant to the story told in *Trees*. You'd never know from watching it that the convention itself had been over-policed.

Trees closes out with a voice-over of a protestor on a megaphone declaring, "We're going back to create . . . two hundred, three hundred Chicago's in our local communities," over an image of rubble and broken glass in an auto dealership, followed by the narrator intoning, "The extremists will fail. Our cities were not built to become the targets of anarchy. The trees of liberty spring from the roots of our constitution and the Bill of Rights, from justice and compassion." Here, the film cuts to the Chicago skyline, with four trees in foreground, as the narrator ominously asks, "What trees do they plant?" Apparently this rhetorical question was "one of Daley's favorite swipes at reformers, who sat back and criticized while men like Daley were getting things done."[36] That's a helpful tidbit of information unlikely to be known to non-Chicago viewers, who would have found the title perplexing. For viewers versed in American history, the more meaningful phrase would have been the narrator's reference to the "trees of liberty," from the famous Thomas Jefferson line, "The tree of liberty must be refreshed from time to time with the blood of patriots and tyrants." It's a quotation that has been used by both left and right to bolster reformist and/or violent impulses as patriotic. Perhaps Ushijima's people snuck this reference past Daley's people, who just didn't get it, as a wink of support for the *protestors*, not the police. If Daley missed this subversive gesture, so did the viewers who wrote to Daley—and the networks—to praise the film as a corrective to TV coverage of the conventions.

Daley's team also produced a seventy-seven-page, bare-bones report attacking the demonstrators, entitled *The Strategy of Confrontation* and, shortly thereafter, *Crisis in Chicago*, a sixty-four-page magazine packed with photos and available for a dollar.[37] The latter closes ominously with the line, "Daley may have saved Chicago this time—but will your city be as fortunate?" *Crisis in Chicago* is notable on two counts. First, *Trees* had a heavy-handed voice-over forcing a negative interpretation of its images. The footage of *Trees* flew past the eyes of a viewer and was framed exclusively from Daley's perspective. One could, conversely, linger over the still images of *Crisis in Chicago*, and not necessarily read them as Daley's team intended. Did a single man grasping a lamp pole, screaming, facing off against several dozen helmeted National Guardsmen pointing bayonets, provoke hatred or fear, as intended by the editors of *Crisis in Chicago*, or, instead, empathy? A photo of a crowd of protestors in clown and death's-head makeup satirized the delegates. The protestors even thematically dressed by state: an Alabama sign was held by someone dressed as a Klansman, and an Illinois sign was held by someone in a large box done up with homemade dials and gauges and labeled "Mayor Daley's Political Machine." Did this come across as monstrous or, rather, as clever street theater? Did the nighttime images of jeeps encased in barbed wire celebrate the triumph of law and order, or, conversely, evoke the Soviet tanks rolling through Czechoslovakia? The film had worked hard to simply leave out images that made the police and National Guard look bad. The magazine arguably failed on this front.

The publication is also of interest for claiming to offer an official interpretation of events to the citizens of the city. Although Daley contended that the vast majority approved of his actions, a group of locals who disagreed were angered enough to produce a counter-publication, *Law & Disorder: The Chicago Convention and Its Aftermath*, which also sold for a dollar and was underwritten by *Playboy*, with proceeds going to the Illinois division of the ACLU. Hugh Hefner contributed a short description of walking a block from his house with cartoonist Jules Feiffer and columnist Max Lerner as the police turned shotguns on them at close range; one officer hit Hefner across the back, without explanation. Other contributors to the impressive, sixty-four-page publication included Arthur Miller, I. F. Stone, Murray Kempton, William Styron, and Studs Terkel. It's closely typeset with an emphasis on argument over image, although political cartoons and photos of police brutality are included.

Lew Koch, a journalist at the local NBC affiliate, not only contributed to *Law & Disorder* but also was a cofounder of *Chicago Journalism Review* in early 1969, a publication directly inspired by the media's coverage of the street action during the convention. The new journal's editors had observed, for example, that the *Tribune* had been a booster for Daley throughout the four-day debacle. Jack Mabley of *Chicago's American* (owned by the *Trib*) had become a sort of poster child for the way that even local newspapers that had initially provided honest coverage later second-guessed themselves. Mabley had reported how "a policeman went animal when a crippled man couldn't get away fast enough," but once the dust settled on the convention, he followed up by writing that "80 to 85 percent of the callers and letter writers [were] cheering for Daley and the cops: You can't help that gnawing feeling—can all these people be right and I be wrong?"[38] Mabley's paper had installed an undercover reporter with the Mobe during the convention—a pretty heavy summer job assignment for a college student—and Mabley had long taken a pro-cop stance in his columns. In one he even extolled the virtues of arming them with mace. That said, Mabley was a political moderate on some issues and had taken guff from right-wingers for attacking John Birch Society founder Robert Welch for his "dictatorial" organizational tactics and for revealing that Welch had described President Eisenhower as a "dedicated, conscious-agent of the Communist conspiracy."[39] Mabley was pro-Daley 90 percent of the time but also thought that Jerry Rubin had some interesting things to say and appreciated the "fresh satire" of *The Smothers Brothers*.[40]

Mabley had a cameo in *The Seasons Change*, a film made by the Mobe and the ACLU, created largely as a rebuttal to *Trees*. Only Mabley's negative comments about the police were included, to his chagrin, and he dismissed both Daley's and the Mobe's films as cheap propaganda.[41]

He's not wrong insofar as each takes a one-sided perspective and aims to persuade, but *Seasons* includes interviews from a broader range of people—Yippies, delegates, McCarthy volunteers—and it also grasps the fact that the problems of violence and protest in the streets were interconnected with the problems in the Amphitheatre. The film came out after Daley's film, in December, and made the rounds of college campuses, sometimes shown as a double feature with *Trees*, presumably for "balance." Ironically, *Trees* was the sort of "public service" film doomed never to be rebroadcast or to enjoy theatrical release, yet *Seasons* gave it a second life. Daley's film ultimately had more impact: its arguments were repeated verbatim in angry newspaper editorials and letters to the networks. Although the Mobe-ACLU film was unabashedly pro-demonstrators, it ultimately came to some of the same conclusions about Chicago police brutality as the official, "balanced" *Walker Report* did.

The Walker Report

Everyone knew it as "The *Walker Report*," but the official title of the government's investigation of Chicago was *Rights in Conflict*. The study was commissioned by the National Commission on the Causes and Prevention of Violence, and helmed by Daniel Walker, whom Max Frankel of the *New York Times* describes in his introduction to the report's paperback edition as "a prominent Chicago attorney and civic leader, the president of the prestigious but unofficial Chicago Crime Commission, . . . a distinguished citizens group that has devoted itself to fighting gangsterism and crime syndicates."[42] Walker was also general counsel for and vice president of the Montgomery Ward department store. He was an upright citizen, a populist when he entered politics a few years later, but not a radical. He was elected governor in 1972, "on the strength of his personality." His campaign gimmick was hiking across the state for 116 days, sporting a red bandana, and "sleeping in farmhouses along the way."[43]

The report was not conceived as a vendetta against Daley, but Walker *was* an outsider to the machine, and therefore the kind of man whom the mayor instinctively loathed: he assembled and managed a strong team to investigate the convention, but he was not a "team player." In a phone call to LBJ right after the report came out, a furious Daley described Walker as "one of these pseudo liberals that, you know, lives up in Kenilworth [a suburb, implying he's not a real Chicagoan], comes in and sheds his crocodile tears to the people in Chicago. He did a hell of a hatchet job.... He's a bad man."[44]

The report was produced quickly—in just two months—but not carelessly. As Frankel described it, "Walker built a study team of 90 full-time and 121 part-time interviewers and researchers. Many lawyers and trained investigators were lent to him, at no cost, by prestigious Chicago law firms and banks. Together they took 1,410 statements from eyewitnesses, reviewed 2,017 others provided by the Federal Bureau of Investigation, and studied 180 hours of motion picture films, more than 12,000 still photographs, and thousands of news accounts."[45] Walker's assistant director, Victor de Grazia, later praised his "fantastic organizing ability," adding that the "damn good lawyers" who worked on it "were not hippie lawyers.... The guy we sent to interview Abbie Hoffman was absolutely a classic Republican establishment, three-piece suit lawyer." Chuckling, he added, "and of course Hoffman charmed him."[46]

De Grazia also noted that they went into the undertaking as skeptics, and once evidence against police became overwhelming, Walker had de Grazia play a pro-police devil's-advocate role within the research group, to force everyone to work harder to confirm every account.[47] Walker also did extra fact-checking, confidentially calling in a reporter who had numerous contacts among rank-and-file policemen. The man had moved to the East Coast (more than twenty years later, Walker still kept his identity secret) but returned to Chicago and spent two weeks talking to policemen off the record, asking, as Walker put it, "Hey, what really happened out there?" Walker recounted later that "based on what he told me the policemen told him, it was even worse than I'd reported, so that gave me a sense of corroboration."[48] Still, Walker seemed to be bending over backward to find evidence that things were not as horrible as they seemed. It was responsible to confirm the stories he'd gathered, but his approach also smacks of what we now call "bothsidesism." As with the networks, Walker's sense of "fairness" meant diluting his story at several points and stepping back from making conclusions about systemic police brutality. That said, he did tell a gruesome story of violence in the streets. To state it tautologically: What people had seen on TV was really what they had seen on TV.

The report came under attack from both the left and the right, but the rigorous attempt at neutrality, the effort to just nail down the facts and not embellish them with interpretation or stylistic flair, was notable. Walker and his team didn't evaluate the quality of the media's coverage of events, although they did include details on police violence against journalists, and also material showing that the Yippies understood what they were doing as not just a political action but also as a media event. As Hoffman put it in his interview with the three-piece-suit lawyer, "We wanted to fuck up their image on TV. I fight through the jungle of TV, you see; . . . it's all in terms of disrupting the image, the image of a democratic society being run very peacefully and orderly, and everything is according to business."[49]

Walker's report offers evaluation but consists mostly of relentless recounting of events by witnesses. Though it read more like a series of depositions than a narrative account, *Rights in Conflict* was inherently readable to anyone who had a taste for the scandalous, not just because it pushed back against Daley's story, but also because the language was so filthy. As per the report's introduction, Walker's team had not censored the work because "extremely obscene language was a contributing factor to the violence." *Time* magazine archly concluded, "Since the report is otherwise couched largely in the turgid prose common to bureaucracy, the insertion of so many pungent Anglo-Saxon expletives relating to or synonymous with copulation creates a surrealistic effect."[50] That was an extremely polite way of describing a book replete with every linguistic backflip that could include an f-bomb; it doesn't convey the playfulness of Yippie uses of the word (one of their convention posters read "fuck nuns: laugh at professors: disobey your parents: burn your money . . .") or the sheer ugliness of a policeman saying to a "hippie-looking girl of 14 or 15, 'You better get your fucking dirty cunt out of here.'"[51]

The widely publicized conclusion was that the events in the Chicago streets during the convention constituted a "police riot." This notion was rejected by Daley's supporters, who saw his version of events as unfalsifiable: literally no evidence could prove that TV hadn't intentionally left out the "real story" that would have vindicated the mayor and the police. Less often noted is that the report did catalog various instances of protestor violence and cursing, the very "provocations" that Daley said the biased networks had ignored. In other words, the report supplied some of the "evidence" that Daley implied would be in *Trees* but that was mostly lacking. *Time* magazine observed, "The report confirms the earlier impression that the Chicago police force—in Mayor Daley's celebrated euphemism—'overreacted.' But it also stresses the provocations they suffered and records some examples of police restraint," as when a deputy superintendent of police on Wednesday night in front of the Hilton "had to pull berserk officers off battered and bruised demonstrators, shouting at them: 'Stop, damn it, stop! For Christ's sake, stop it!'"[52] Protestors *did* relentlessly taunt the police with lines like "Your mother sucks dirty cock!" and they did assemble makeshift weapons, even stripping ceramic wall tiles from public restrooms and hurling the sharp projectiles at the cops.

On the flip side, some protestors sought to de-escalate the violence. When NBC showed a major teargassing incident on Wednesday afternoon, they reported about Mobe leaders on bullhorns beseeching protestors, "Don't provoke them!" but that sort of coverage was a rarity. In a Pacifica radio segment, Allen Ginsberg in Lincoln Park, with Jean Genet at his side, suggested that Yippies should march together naked on Wednesday and that if police learned to chant "Om," perhaps peace could be maintained. On a more practical note, Ginsberg also offered the analysis that the network news never made: if people were simply allowed to sleep in the park, there would be no need to gas or beat them to drive them out. The mayor and Chicago police were *choosing* violence, not simply responding to provocation. In his *Esquire* article on the convention, Genet repeatedly emphasized the gentle qualities of the hippies he encountered.[53]

Many of the protestors anticipated being beaten for protesting the war, for trying to march to the Amphitheatre, for enjoying dope, for chanting with Ginsberg, for throwing a "Festival of Life" in Lincoln Park as a counterpoint to what they called the DNC's "Festival of Death," for inviting bands to the festival (they all bailed out except for MC5), for taunting police with profanities, and for throwing hard projectiles. Even those who deeply opposed violence *expected* to be beaten because they looked different, talked different, and smelled different. The police loathed them not just for what they did, but also for what they represented: revolt, left-wing politics, nonconformity. They hated them for being white, middle-class college kids who opposed the war and tapped into the revolutionary energy of the Black Power movement. As one Chicago cop explained years later, "When your country asks you to serve, you serve, and you don't ask questions. But these snot college kids said, 'Hell no,' and got the double *A*s [African Americans] to get all riled up, so we had both barrels of the shotgun pointed at us. They [Blacks] were already calling us 'motherfucking pigs,' but then the college kids began to copy them, calling us that and worse. . . . And since we were 'oppressing Blacks,' then we were suppressing them when we arrested them for antiwar demonstrations that got out of hand."[54]

Overall, the *Walker Report* chronicles bad activity on both sides, downplaying the peaceful activities of demonstrators but also laying bare overwhelming evidence of police brutality. Daley was actually right that the networks had left a lot out of their coverage: they omitted not only the nonviolent protestors but also graphic profanity from both cops and kids, as well as the fact that the police consistently struck harder than did the demonstrators.

Activists on the left decried the report for implying that, although police behavior was violent and inappropriate, it was not a matter of *policy* on Daley's part. The report did note that his shoot-to-kill-or-maim comments from April had primed the police to act as they did, but *Rights in Conflict* did not directly acknowledge that Daley tacitly approved of such behavior. The report also emphasized that it was a *minority* of police who had behaved sadistically. Ultimately, it was easy to interpret the more than three-hundred-page document as conveying a standard "few bad apples" criticism of the police—the notion that the problem was not systemic but rather that some cops happened to be criminals, as in any profession.

It was fair to criticize the report for that conclusion, but, at the same time, there was no paper trail or direct evidence or witness testimony that the police were acting as Daley intended. That said, experiences of locals could confirm how typical the behavior was. Black Chicagoans, for example, could attest to the pervasiveness of police brutality. What had happened to whites in August was business as usual for them. Furthermore, given the mortality rates for Blacks across the country during urban uprisings, in Watts, Detroit, and of course Chicago itself, the refrain that emerged from Daley's office and elsewhere after the convention, that "no one was killed," rang hollow. If no one was killed, it was fair to assume that at least one reason was that the vast majority of protestors were white. Several police officers interviewed years later suggested that the notion that they had been out of control was ridiculous, offering as counter-arguments statements like, "Some . . . would have killed those bastards had they the chance, but a guy doesn't want to lose his pension over something like that."[55] It's a terrifyingly banal argument against murder, and, even worse, one suspects that similar thoughts about retirement benefits were rare during the King riots in Chicago, which ended with nine Blacks dead, hundreds injured, and more than two thousand arrested.[56]

Police officers did not express such thoughts to Walker's team in 1968, and it should not be surprising that the "bad apples" notion undergirded the final report, although one does come away from it with the feeling that overly violent policing was common in Chicago.[57] Circling back to the issue of whether or not the police were operating by the book—of course, they were not. To cite the most obvious, com-

mon breach of the rules, it was a violation of policy for a Chicago police officer to strike someone on the head with a nightstick; this was
literally the most common assault tactic used during the convention.
Were they *ordered* to beat protestors by higher-ups? Not directly. It was
more of an implicit expectation. Clearly, Walker was not going to find
a paper trail or a string of interviewees confirming that Daley or his police superintendent wanted protestors beaten. On the other hand, the
cops later confirmed that their actions were expected, especially mass,
rough arrests.

In fact, they used a catch-and-release system. More than 1,000 arrests were made, judging from footage and photographs, but only 668
arrests were logged. "So much of what took place that week was an
act. . . . We carted them up, drove them out of the loop, and dropped
them off. . . . Who wanted to do the paperwork on these guys?" People
were roughly arrested but not beaten in custody, they explained later,
"*because it was a show—a sham for [Police Superintendent] Conlisk and
Daley* that we were not going to let this generation and the Negroes run
free in his city and embarrass *his* city."[58] In addition to pointing to a
conceptual grouping of the counterculture with Blacks, this testimony,
repeated by others, points to the notion that Daley and his administration *expected* police to harm protestors. As John Schultz argued in the
Chicago Reader, what happened "during the last week of August 1968
was not a police riot." Rather, the cause of the chaos "was a premedi-
tated disposition to subdue protest by whatever means necessary."[59]

Ironically, Daley and the police loathed the press, but there was
value in their reporting the street brutality during the convention, because rough policing was implicitly understood as a *show*, displaying
Daley's control over his town. None of this comes across in the *Walker
Report*, but it adds an important new twist to our understanding of the
issue of "media bias" during that week in August. Daley wanted to control media coverage at all cost. At the same time, he wanted his power
displayed and documented. He needed the police to perform that display, and the media to document that performance. He just wanted the
documentation to be exclusively from his point of view.

One unexpected twist in the story of the *Walker Report* was that James Harrison, who ran the Government Printing Office, declined to print the report because of all of the obscenities. This was more a symbolic gesture than anything else. Harrison was refusing to produce *sales* copies, but a Philadelphia company under GPO contract did print 3,000 official copies for government use.[60] Walker had refused the option of printing the report with dashes filling in the dirty parts—a solution that he felt would have diluted the report. As is often the case with GPO reports, commercial publishers stepped in, with Bantam producing at least 250,000 copies at a dollar each, and E. P. Dutton releasing a hardbound version.[61] Harrison did not make the report less accessible, but he did make it more desirable. A book full of violence and profanity, centered on controversial political events, and which the government didn't seem to want people to read was not going to linger on bookstore shelves.

Daley was not pleased. Publicly, he said that the widely circulated official summary of the book, which included the "police riot" line, was not very good. It was important to read the full report to see the big picture, he said. That was just spin. He had amplified his claims against the networks with *Trees* but was not keen on any other initiatives that stoked the embers of the convention.

The 1968 Campaigns in the Aftermath of Chicago

The night that Richard Nixon was nominated in Miami, *New York Times* TV reviewer Jack Gould confirmed a widely held view: "Wednesday night coverage of the Republican National Convention should qualify as cruel and inhuman punishment." Nixon's triumph that night was a foregone conclusion, and there was little left for the networks to do but say this over and over again and show a lot of speechifying from the dais. The problem was a lack of dramatic tension. Gould also made a different sort of political assessment: "For the young viewer or the disadvantaged citizen, the spectacle at Miami Beach cannot have been too reassuring—the spectacle of grown men and a grown medium behaving like cathode idiots amid the sacrifices of Vietnam or the uneasiness of the slums."[62] In an alternate universe in which the Democratic convention had gone off without a hitch, the stiff, scripted, and out-of-touch proceedings in Miami could have marred Nixon's campaign. Instead, by September, the televisual boredom in Miami not only seemed like a paragon of "law and order" to Nixon supporters but also appealed to a wider swath of moderate Republicans. It even appealed to some Democrats fed up with Johnson, the war, and the crisis in Chicago.

The Chicago convention had a huge viewership, but if any had missed finer details such as unit rule debates, credential crises, and so forth, TV critics like Gould helped them catch up. Newspaper coverage thereby made this extended, live event less ephemeral. Gould described how the excess security on the convention floor was shown on TV, he conveyed the dramatic impact of Aretha Franklin's National Anthem ("the generation gap was never so wide"), and he noted that some disturbances were shown outside. But until the explosion of violence on the third night, he focused more on the frustrations *inside* that kept delegates up late into the night ("To join in the procedures of government these days it is not enough to be twenty-one and registered; citizenship also entails being a night owl with a stash of Benzedrine").[63] He also offered good analyses of where the networks made mistakes, criticizing CBS's obsession with the Ted Kennedy "boomlet," a story he felt they more created than followed. Overall, it was clear from Gould's reviews that this was a better *show* than the one in Miami. Although the Democratic Party itself was in flagrant crisis, if the chaos outside had not erupted so strongly, Humphrey could have walked away spinning a reasonably convincing message: yes, we struggled and fought at the convention, but that's because we were engaging with real problems, unlike the Republicans. That's a lot of ifs and maybes. The violence outside did escalate, and the disorders the networks showed could be debated, but they could not reasonably be interpreted by anyone as helping the party or Humphrey.

Humphrey ultimately lost largely because of his association with LBJ. Indeed, as voting day neared, he was polling behind Nixon and finally crept closer only when he subtly distanced himself from Johnson's Vietnam policy, in a speech on September 30. It was too little, too late, and Nixon won by a razor-thin margin.[64] If the peace plank had won in Chicago, Humphrey might have felt free to turn away from LBJ sooner. Protesting delegates—the idealists—had hoped for exactly this. But the idealists lost, and then so did Humphrey.

Yet the image crisis coming out of Chicago was equally important to Humphrey's loss. Nixon deviously tapped into this by opening his campaign in Chicago. The Coke cans, broken glass, fliers, and blood had no sooner been cleared than Nixon was riding down the street creating a new mess with a ticker-tape parade, just one week after the convention (fig. 28). As a media ploy, this maneuver was a one-two punch. Nixon not only showed how he, unlike Humphrey, could totally control the streets of Chicago, but also, pointedly, he had returned for a triumphant photo-op in the very city where he had suffered his greatest media failure back in 1960, when he debated John F. Kennedy, and radio listeners reportedly believed he had done very well, but TV viewers did not.[65] His five-o'clock shadow had not stood a chance against Kennedy's movie-star looks. Nixon had started airing carefully stage-managed TV panel discussion shows in July 1968, and the very first one had been shot in the same Chicago studio where that fateful Kennedy debate had taken place.[66] Further, it was widely believed, though never ultimately verified, that Daley's machine had engaged in voter fraud that had cost Nixon Illinois eight years before. So Chicago was where Nixon's handlers—including his new TV man, Roger Ailes—would logically stage his triumphant emergence from the ashes of 1960.

Nixon's spots were created by Gene Jones, who had just made *A Face of War*, a tough Vietnam documentary that the *New York Times* described as "a sermon on human waste that draws the viewer into a void as objectively as any war movie ever made."[67] Half of the Marines in the film were killed or wounded. Crafted in the cinema vérité style, the film lacked interviews, context, and voice-over, and ultimately thereby conveyed sympathy for the soldiers and antipathy toward war, without directly expressing a political stance. Clearly, Jones was not an

FIGURE 28.   Richard Nixon opens his campaign in Chicago, soon after the convention, as a kick in the gut to Democrats. This image generally conveys Nixon's popularity, but the importance of the moment for his campaign was that he was greeted with ticker tape and cheers specifically in Daley's town. United Press International, 1968.

advertising man with experience in conventional persuasive media, but his work stoked *emotions*, which was what Nixon's crew was going for.

The campaign had initially approached David Douglas Duncan to do their TV spots. His work for NBC had been fairly neutral about the GOP convention and more critical of the Democratic convention. Joe Mc-

Ginnis wrote that Harry Treleaven, of Nixon's team, "wanted Duncan because he [Treleaven] had decided to make still photography the basis of Richard Nixon's sixty-second television commercial campaign. . . . He thought [photographs] were the perfect thing for Nixon because Nixon himself would not have to appear." Nixon would speak over the images, but his words would mainly serve as background Muzak to a positive visual impression of the candidate. Duncan was too busy but suggested Jones.[68]

Although McGinniss reasonably emphasizes the phoniness of the planned spots—and, indeed, of the whole campaign—it is equally relevant that the first choice for the job was someone who had documented the crisis in Chicago and that both choices were men whose specialty was gritty realism.[69] Jones made all his ads in the photomontage style with voice-over, which conveyed Nixon as a man in control not only in broad political terms but also in charge of his own image. When one of these spots started, you knew immediately that you were watching a Nixon ad. The voice-overs were standard stuff excerpted from speeches, but the image montages were gripping, dramatic, and often sensationalist. There was no light touch here.

The spots ranged from negative ads centered on Vietnam and the theme of "law and order" to ones intended to create warm feelings for Nixon, with titles like "Child's Face" and "Unity." Excerpts from Marshall McLuhan's *Understanding Media* were distributed to the staff; the New Nixon would tap into TV's inherently "cool" qualities as a medium, "a medium that rejects the sharp personality and favors the presentation of processes rather than of products."[70] Most important in terms of direct fallout from Chicago was a hit job entitled "Convention." The forty-nine-second ad includes twenty-seven still photos, seven of which are shots of Humphrey on the dais in Chicago, and several of which are processed to make his face appear menacing. In one, Humphrey's image appears to be shaking left and right, as if it were a moving image shot by a shaky hand, and this is immediately followed by a similarly shaking shot of troops in Vietnam, brutally linking Humphrey to the men's suffering in one deft aesthetic move. In the final shot, the candidate's head splits into three overlapping, phantasmago-ric images.

The first eight images are rapidly cut shots of the convention, and from there the ad moves back and forth between shots of violence and suffering—rural people stricken by poverty, buildings ablaze from a riot, the wounded and dying in Vietnam. The music alternates between celebratory, brass band, oompah music ("Hot Time in the Old Town Tonight") typical of a convention and electronically distorted music that would not be out of place in a horror film. The bleeding people in the streets seem to be convention demonstrators, while the images of the burning buildings, if they were of Chicago, probably came from the conflagrations following King's assassination. They could just as easily be from Detroit or any other city that had suffered massive upheaval in the late 1960s, but viewers attuned to recent events in Chicago would make the association with the chaos in April. Throughout, the cam-era zooms in and out or swishes left to right. Through the collision of images, street protest, arson, Vietnam, and poverty are all laid at the feet of the Democratic Party, the convention, and Humphrey himself. Worse, Humphrey is often smiling, as if to mock the suffering he has inflicted.

The Democratic National Committee was furious and sent protest telegrams to NBC. Nixon campaign manager John Mitchell indignantly defended the ad in public, but behind the scenes the campaign perhaps realized it had gone too far. Len Garment later said, "It was skillfully done but in terrible taste, particularly the scene showing Humphrey smiling after a scene of Vietnam carnage. It got on through bad judg-ment. . . . We yanked the ad and never put it on again. I said, 'Pull it as fast as you can.'"[71]

The spot aired during *Rowan and Martin's Laugh-In*, and some view-ers apparently thought it was part of the show; Kathleen Hall Jamieson describes *Laugh-In* as "irreverent and sometimes tasteless" and thus, by implication, similar to the ad.[72] I'd suggest that the ad teeters right on the edge of avant-garde satire, with rapid pacing and visual effects akin to those on the show, which "abounded in hallucinogenic flashes, zooms, breathtakingly quick cuts, and a barrage of psychedelic colors."[73] It was the moderating effect of Nixon's voice-over that made the other ads in this style legible as *campaign ads* rather than as short, satirical critiques of American political culture. Without any narrative voice-over and just a final title card crediting the Nixon-Agnew victory committee, it was hard even to grasp that this crazy ad was for Nixon, a man normally understood as abysmally square. The ad actually might have backfired if aired more widely, so the DNC's objections may have offered an easy way out for Nixon's team. What sort of viewer confusion might have ensued if "Convention" had aired during an episode of *The Smothers Brothers Comedy Hour*, less stylistically wild than *Laugh-In*, but even stronger in its political satire? Or, on the flip side, imagine the potential befuddlement for older viewers seeing the ad aired during the *Lawrence Welk Show*. The wild style outweighed the benefits of zapping Humphrey by mining the repercussions of the convention.[74]

TV viewers would not have been aware that the ad was entitled "Convention," and yet the startling opening images of angry delegates were instantly recognizable. Further, the distorted shots of Humphrey on the podium undercut literally the only moment of party harmony from August, when he held the attention of the floor and made impassioned arguments against violence and for unity. If you had missed the entire four-day spectacle, this little advertising spot recapped the worst moments, at least on an emotional level if not on a substantive one, while also recontextualizing and warping the best moments.

The fact that the ad was pulled did not diminish the impulse behind it. In fact, parts of it were recycled in other spots, again recontextualizing and amplifying images that might have otherwise been ephemeral. One widely aired ad was "The First Civil Right," a call for Nixon's trademark law and order that focused on images of bloodied protestors, police, burning buildings, crowds holding up pro-communist and pro-socialist signs, and rubble in the street. The first half of the spot includes images of bloodied protestors from "Convention." Another spot, "Failure," opens with shots from the Amphitheatre and a voice-over (not Nixon) intoning, "How can a party that can't unite itself unite the nation?" No specific politicians are identifiable, though there is a quick image of the folk singer Theodore Bikel shouting in protest. It was strategically canny to avoid recognizable politicians or celebrities, for the Nixon campaign hoped to seize Democrats disaffected by the events in Chicago, and why risk turning off fans of movie stars? Either the ad's producers did not recognize Bikel, or they thought that folk singers had enough popular association with hippies and Yippies and communists that he was a safe target. The spot next reuses several "Convention" street shots.

Of course, all the spots don't call out the convention. Upbeat ads showed Nixon pulling the country together, featuring smiling children and happy workers in feel-good montages that felt more like Coca-Cola ads than campaign spots. Overall, though, Nixon's TV ads weaponized the convention, and the withdrawal of "Convention" in no way tempered the salt that Nixon's media team continued to pour in Humphrey's wounds.

For his part, Humphrey did all that he could to distance himself from the events of August. He did not even campaign in Illinois until just a few days before the election. The day after Humphrey's loss, Daley told Johnson that he had "pleaded with him" to come sooner. Humphrey was reluctant to return to the city, as was his staff, who felt that "Illinois was already lost and that a renewed association with Mayor Daley could not possibly produce benefits."[75] This was a logical argument, but shocking when you consider how important Daley's support had been to previous Democratic candidates. When Humphrey finally spoke to a rally in Chicago, he swooped right in on the elephant in the room. As Daley told LBJ, "Christ, he comes out here Friday and . . . talks about the convention, and 'We're all sorry what happened in Chicago.' Well, we're not sorry. . . . Mistakes were made; that's one thing. But goddamn it, you don't be reminding an audience of twenty-five or thirty thousand knowledgeable Democrats that we regret what happened in the city."[76] And then the mayor bragged that, nonetheless, Chicago had gone for Humphrey, thanks to Daley's pushing not so much for the candidate's agenda as for the Johnson legacy.

It was impossible for Humphrey to erase the convention from his campaign media insofar as the acceptance speech is generally a golden moment for a candidate. Jamieson observes that broadcast spots of five minutes or less tend to "entice the unsuspecting viewer" whereas half-hour productions, like biographical campaign films and election eve programs "attract true believers."[77] The one exception is the half-hour nomination acceptance speech, because conventions draw voters from both parties, not only because people watch such programming, theoretically at least, out of a sense of civic duty but also because conventions preempted other programming during the network era; if you wanted to watch TV, the convention was the only game in town. A half-hour opportunity in prime time to actually pull in new voters, even the much-coveted "undecided voters," makes the convention speech a prized moment. Excerpts from that golden half-hour are typically included in TV spots.

This left Humphrey in a bind. He had made a very good speech in August, followed by the "Democratic clambake," as Cronkite had put it, when disparate players joined hands and rallied behind the newly minted nominee. It was a solid TV moment. And yet it would not do to remind voters too much of Chicago. The only option was to minimize an event that under better circumstances would have been maximized. And so, the one-minute spot "Every American" consisted merely of three shots of Humphrey at the dais in Chicago, with a fourth shot of delegates in a rare happy moment. Humphrey declared that "every American, Black or white, rich or poor, has the right in this land of ours to a safe and a decent neighborhood. . . . I put it very bluntly, rioting, burning, sniping, mugging, traffic in narcotics, and disregard for law are the advance guard of anarchy, and they must and they will be stopped." The spot here cuts to a long shot of the Amphitheatre, the audience whistling and cheering for words that would not be out of place in Nixon's mouth, then back to Humphrey: "The answer lies in reasoned effective action by state, local, and federal authorities. The answer does not lie in an attack on our courts, our laws, or our Attorney

General." A closing voice-over says, "Humphrey has the answers. Now let's give him the authority."

In his own convention acceptance speech, Nixon had proclaimed that "the first civil right of every American is to be free from domestic violence" and then suggested that the first step toward this would be replacing Attorney General Ramsey Clark. So Humphrey's only campaign ad directly referencing his own convention was, arguably, purely reactive to his opponent. On the flipside, Nixon's "The First Civil Right" spot, with its horrifying montage of bloodied protestors, suggested that Nixon, like the police in the ad, would take the offensive. The only way "Every American" indicated a policy distance from Nixon was Humphrey's reference to state, local, and *federal* authorities, a carefully guarded response to the ongoing cry of "states' rights" from the Deep South, a constituency that Nixon courted with his Southern Strategy. The bottom line was that Chicago was irredeemable as a source of campaign material for Humphrey, but it was a gold mine for Nixon, who could also recycle numerous clips from his own acceptance speech.

If Humphrey's campaign media left something to be desired, it was not for lack of production talent but rather for lack of a coherent and consistent vision. Humphrey's media were produced by Bob Squire, Tony Schwartz, Shelby Storck, and Charles Guggenheim, among others. Schwartz had been the creator of the famous "Daisy" ad from the Johnson campaign against Goldwater in 1964. Guggenheim had worked for the US Information Agency under JFK and had produced the RFK film that brought down the house in Chicago. Storck came out of industrial filmmaking.[78] Any one of these people might have been a reasonable choice for the campaign, but choosing all of them resulted in ads produced in a multitude of styles. Humphrey couldn't dig his image out of the trench from Chicago with TV spots that were thematically and stylistically all over the place, ranging from broadly insulting (a Schwartz spot featuring little more than grating, hysterical laughter as the image zooms back from a TV image reading "Spiro Agnew for Vice President?") to flailing and desperate (a single, medium shot of Frank

Sinatra saying that Humphrey "needs your help. He needs money . . . as soon as possible," with a mailing address for checks filling half the screen, both tacky and a waste of Sinatra's star power). After the media disaster in Chicago, this all read as desperation.

The 1972 Democratic Convention

So much happened on the floor of the Chicago Amphitheatre in 1968 that it was easy to lose track of the procedural ins and outs from the rostrum—the thank-you speeches, formulaic votes, and Robert's Rules of Order-type actions that appear in the DNC's six-hundred-and-forty page official transcript but created not even a ripple in TV news coverage and were thus left unseen by home viewers.

One such detail was the decision to create a Commission on Party Structure and Delegate Selection, which would revise the delegate-selection process, rework party structure, and increase grassroots participation. This eventually become known as the McGovern-Fraser Commission, after its directors, George McGovern and Minnesota Rep. Donald M. Fraser. The commission's consultant committee included Richard C. Wade, a famed urban historian who also had a cameo in *What Trees Do They Plant?* in which he decried both the radical left and the radical right and predicted that ultimately the winner in Chicago would be George Wallace and his followers, while the loser would be "the decent center of American politics." For McGovern-Fraser, Wade outlined two choices for delegate selection: the creation of national party guidelines or sticking with the current state-controlled system, which had enabled procedural chaos not only in Chicago,[79] but also going back to Truman's nomination in 1948, when pro-segregation southern states had walked out.[80] Obviously, national guidelines were in the cards. The Democrats were now the party of civil rights, and yet southern states could still arrive at conventions with all or mostly white delegations, and they had enough votes to create trouble for the national party.

McGovern-Fraser has long been seen as the force that democratized the party by increasing representation at conventions by women, people of color, and the young. Historian Jaime Sánchez has argued that the committee was not simply about ideological reform, as it is so often remembered, but even more importantly about institutional reform. The national party in effect saved itself from the states by creating uniform delegate-selection standards. In 1964 and 1968 the Democratic convention had been packed with southern delegates who were unwilling to support the nominee of their own party, going for Barry Goldwater and George Wallace, respectively, rather than LBJ and Humphrey. It had to be stopped.

McGovern-Fraser was also a key step to wiping out "boss-ism," and here's where the 1972 convention is particularly relevant to consider in relationship to 1968, if one is to understand both as highly charged media events. In the wake of McGovern-Fraser reforms, Teddy White observed correctly that "the impression this open convention made on America outside, in this new age of television, would be, politically, of as much weight in the campaign of 1972 as what anyone at the convention said or did."[81] The new rules seemed to indicate that in 1972 viewers would witness nothing like the Mississippi crisis of 1964 or the Georgia crisis of 1968. And yet, 1972 would also lay bare the fact that such crises of disenfranchisement were not confined to southern states. Daley—mayor of the most segregated city in America, a northern city—was the key operative in ensuring the Illinois delegation was filled by machine-approved, mostly white candidates.

Even if Georgia and Alabama had gotten the most airtime for delegate-selection conflicts in 1968, Illinois had been just as culpable. And in 1972, Daley—the party player, the kingmaker, "Mr. Democrat"—was shut out. Now, "Blacks, women, Spanish-speakers, and people between the ages of eighteen and thirty had to be represented as delegate candidates in proportion to their population in each congressional district. The new rules also required that delegate selection be done in public, with the time and place of the sessions publicized in advance."[82] Daley responded that the new rules simply were not valid under Illinois law, so his machine selected a slate of fifty-nine candidates, which Chicagoans could vote for or not, with no attention paid to the party's new diversity rules. Independent Chicago alderman William Singer, with Rev. Jesse Jackson, selected an alternative delegate slate confirmed via caucuses held throughout Chicago, with "informal, voice-vote elections, where voting was conducted over the heckling of machine representatives who had infiltrated the meetings. The Daley slate and the Singer-Jackson slate represented two extremes of the cultural chasm that had split the Democratic Party four years earlier."[83] Daley's slate won, capturing the vote of white ethnics and others who followed the lead of their precinct captains. There was a complicated legal fight, and ultimately the national party's Credentials Committee voted 71–61 to seat the alternative slate. Daley and his people complained that this violated the will of the nine hundred thousand Chicago voters who had gone for the machine's slate. Daley's narrative, suggesting that democracy had been defeated by quotas and radical leftists, gained plenty of traction in the national media.

The Jackson-Singer slate thereby seemed extremist, while the Daley slate appeared to be the product of fairness and moderation. Even Chicago's best anti-Daley newspaperman, Mike Royko, disapproved of how the Jackson slate had been selected, wisecracking that "anybody who would reform Chicago's Democratic Party by dropping the white ethnic would probably begin a diet by shooting himself in the stomach."[84] Daley was ultimately both loser and winner: loser because his own party shut him out, a grand humiliation that took him completely by surprise; winner because he played the indignant victim so well, as he had right after the 1968 convention. This newest victimization made his supporters in Chicago love him even more. He was ice-cold toward McGovern and took the "I told you so" line when he lost to Nixon in a landslide. Teddy White, a voice of liberal moderation back in 1964, by 1968 more of a centrist, and rather taken in by the "New Nixon" of that year,[85] was appalled by the ouster of Daley in 1972: "Whatever one's sympathies, how, now, could one avoid wondering what the political effect would be, on the television audience, of the sight of Black people jumping up and hugging each other with glee as Dick Daley was humiliated, or the sound of Spanish-speaking ladies jubilating over their triumph."[86] White's condescension is galling (and he wasn't really "wondering"), but he was on the mark about the effect that the televised proceedings would have on the Silent Majority of home viewers. All the McGovern-Fraser positive spin seemed to unravel at once with Daley's rejection.

Between the 1968 and 1972 conventions, the national party had worked carefully to present its reforms to the public in a positive light. In 1969, on NBC's *Meet the Press*, DNC chairman Senator Fred Harris argued that what Americans were witnessing was not "fracture" but "reinvention."[87] In 1970, McGovern wrote in *Harper's* that "amidst the madness in Chicago" few had noticed the vote for procedural reform, but now he and his compatriots were "in the process of invigorating our party with a massive injection of democracy. The day of the bosses is all but over."[88] And in June 1972, McGovern and Humphrey appeared on ABC's *Issues and Answers* to convey party unity, confirming they would support whoever the nominee was. The problem was, there were three other candidates, all of whom declined to make such a pledge in advance (fig. 29). The national party's public relations efforts were already faltering, with little more than a month before the convention.

By the time candidates and delegates assembled in Miami, the image of party unity was even more fragile. Democratization brought in a slew of new delegates—young people, feminists, Black activists (fig. 30). If the Singer-Jackson victory against Daley played out as a radical left-wing takeover of the Democratic Party on national TV, the late-night debates on the dais over feminism, Black empowerment, and gay rights were also a crisis for a party trying to defeat a conservative incumbent with high approval ratings. As one member of the Platform Committee put it, critiquing the newcomer delegates, "Their struggle is between the wild wing and the mild wing; what they're doing is selling out their true believers on things like pot, amnesty, and abortion. There won't be any riots in Miami because the people who rioted in Chicago are on the Platform Committee—they outnumber us by three or four to one."[89] Even Jerry Rubin and Abbie Hoffman had endorsed

FIGURE 29. Shirley Chisholm, pictured here at the 1972 Democratic convention, was the first Black woman elected to Congress and also the first to vie for the Democratic presidential nomination. Before the convention, she and other candidates declined to pledge support for the eventual nominee. Reform efforts intended to unify the party were wobbly before the convention even got underway. U.S. News & World Report Magazine Photograph Collection, 1972, courtesy of Library of Congress.

FIGURE 30.   The McGovern-Fraser committee's reforms led to an opening up of the delegation selection process in 1972, leading to more diversity on the floor and to imagery that many American TV viewers found too radical. Pictured here is McGovern supporter and welfare rights advocate Margaret Opie. Photo © Diana Mara Henry, 1972, www.dianamarahenry.com.

McGovern.[90] Ironically, the 1972 reforms, crafted in part as a response to 1968's televised crisis, had produced a new sort of crisis. Four years before, the idealists had fought for a more open convention, and now the convention *was* more open; the protestors and the outsiders had moved inside, seizing the attention of network cameras and creating a new set of problems by displaying enthusiasm for issues such as the Women's and Gay Liberation movements.

Three books by powerhouse authors of rather different political orientations chronicled the impact of the neophytes in 1972. Teddy White supported the cause of women's rights but saw the homosexual cause as "nonsense."[91] Norman Mailer felt pretty much the reverse on those two issues.[92] Hunter S. Thompson didn't even mention the gays and understood the feminist activists correctly as pawns in McGovern's tactical maneuvers. That is, the gonzo journalist was the one who just focused on the convoluted political game, producing what McGovern operative Frank Mankiewicz described twenty-four years later, with only a little exaggeration, as "the most accurate and least factual account of that campaign."[93] None of them could clearly explain some of the procedural crises, but Thompson nailed it when he said that *even the networks*, well versed in procedural minutiae, couldn't understand that McGovern needed to *lose* one of the credentials challenges in order to later *win* another one: "What an incredibly byzantine gig! Imagine trying to understand it on TV—not even Machiavelli could have handled *that*."[94] The one thing that all three had a handle on, though, was the fact that it was a disaster for McGovern and the party for home viewers to see these crises play out in prime time. What a blessing, from the perspective of the McGovern campaign, that the gay rights plank was only debated and ultimately rejected by delegates at 5:00 a.m.[95]

From the TV angle, McGovern's luck was the worst on the final day of the convention. Again, 1968 was a reference point. Even in Chicago, White observed, "with all the violence, bloodshed, and dissension, the party had pulled itself together well enough to let Hubert Humphrey speak to the nation when the nation was ready to listen" at 10:30 p.m. Chicago time—11:30 p.m. on the East Coast.[96] In 1972, by contrast, McGovern's acceptance speech began at 2:48 a.m. Eastern Time. It was a little before 6:00 p.m. in Guam, making that the only place where US citizens watched the speech at a reasonable hour. (Nixon of course was up late watching in San Clemente.[97]) A prime-time speech would have reached 17,400,000 homes, but the senator's ill-timed speech hit about 3,600,000. Today, interested viewers could seek out such a speech on C-SPAN or YouTube. In 1972, though, when you missed a TV speech, you missed a TV speech. A few clips of McGovern's speech aired on the nightly news later, and that was it. At the GOP convention in August, more than twenty million homes tuned in for Nixon's 10:30 p.m. acceptance speech.[98]

One might think it didn't matter much; the candidates were so different, anyway, and it's not like a raging liberal or conservative would have been likely to switch allegiances based on either half-hour speech. But it did matter. The DNC had made all these revisions not only to reform the party but also to regain control over its image. Network coverage of Chicago had shown a party rife with dissension. Four years later, the party still seemed out of control. McGovern's speech had aired absurdly late because feminists, Black activists, the young—all the new delegates—exploited procedural rules to make symbolic nominations for the vice-presidential slot. Each nomination was allotted a fifteen-minute speech.

If Carl Albert or Hale Boggs had been on the rostrum in 1972, he would have decisively shut this stuff down. Instead, the riotous nominations had the momentum of a runaway train. Finally, the VP nominations were done, and the voting began. It was a foregone conclusion that McGovern's candidate Thomas Eagleton would win, yet symbolic votes came in for Dr. Spock, the Berrigan brothers, Jerry Rubin, and Ralph Nader—even a few for Roger Mudd, Chairman Mao, and Archie Bunker. These scattered protest votes made the newly "open" party just look silly, and McGovern had lost his golden moment to reach a wide audience for an entire half-hour of free airtime.

The McGovern campaign ultimately failed for a number of reasons. The one most often singled out is that Eagleton was forced off the ticket when it was revealed that he had a history of mental problems and had received electroshock therapy. Interviewed on C-SPAN twenty years later, McGovern said that the 3:00 a.m. speech was "possibly the most costly single mistake that we made in 1972, even more costly perhaps than the vice presidential selection." He added, "All we had to do was to call the national chairman Larry O'Brien and say, 'Look, let's put the acceptance speech on now and hold all this other business until after I speak.'" McGovern described it as "the best speech I ever gave in my life." It *was* a damn fine speech, but "the whole world" was not watching.

As in 1968, the 1972 Republican convention was an extremely orderly, stage-managed event. Boring TV coverage wouldn't hurt Nixon or the GOP. They reveled in their tightly controlled self-presentation. The activist video collective TVTV (a wry acronym for "Top Value Television," making fun of mainstream TV's commercial nature) produced a brilliant documentary on the affair entitled *Four More Years*, in which they described how the networks were doing little more than airing a show that had been pre-prepared by the Republican National Committee. The Nixonettes sang cheery songs (off-key) about their man, and a demonstration coordinator gleefully declared, "The decorations alone will give us the fun we need!" It was all as canned as the Democratic convention had been freewheeling.[99]

It's clear that the conventions had one thing in common: both took TV coverage of the 1968 conventions as a crucial reference point. The GOP would present an even more tightly controlled image, and this time, with Nixon even more assured of the nomination than four years earlier, there would be less artifice in this image: the Southern Strategy had been struck four years earlier, there were no delegates to woo, no question of a groundswell of support for a liberal Republican like Nelson Rockefeller or a right-wing Republican like Ronald Reagan. TV showed the reality of a seamless, effortless Nixon triumph. The event received a scant five pages in Teddy White's book on the 1972 election.

Seeking to make an impression on the viewing public that was the *opposite* of 1968's, the Democrats did succeed in conveying a new picture of openness. At the same time, the event patently failed by conveying accommodation to the counterculture. The platform was not actually left-wing, but many home viewers understood it that way. Nixon himself had pointed to the "look of it" as one of the convention's greatest demerits. Where were the usual coats and ties and pretty chapeaux? Not surprisingly, White counted but three bearded delegates at Nixon's event.

Charles Guggenheim, who made almost all of McGovern's TV ads, found a positive angle on the openness of the convention in a four-minute ad focused entirely on its democratic nature. One interviewee, a respectable-looking young lady with a modest bouffant, observed, "A lot of people said, oh, you lost prime time by being up all night. Well, that to me was great, and every delegate that was there stayed there and stayed with it." Another interviewee singles out the fact that delegates were making peanut butter and jelly sandwiches on the convention floor because they couldn't afford to eat in the hotels, and, anyway,

"It wasn't a convention to play." Guggenheim shot this and other ads with a handheld camera to convey immediacy and authenticity, in a cinema vérité style that ultimately worked against McGovern: he was extemporaneous, whereas Nixon was tight, scripted, professional, and above all *presidential* in his ads.[100] That vérité was used in McGovern's convention-centered ad points strongly to the campaign's strong desire to spin their event as a huge success because it spoke not just to the young but also to the *sensibilities* of the young, sensibilities which could theoretically be shared by voters of all ages. That didn't play out in November. Still, McGovern leaned into his convention TV imagery about as hard as Humphrey had avoided his own four years earlier.

"Police can be a little rough."

For political parties, conventions should be a means to an end: get candidates nominated, show off a campaign platform, convey party strength and unity, and you've accomplished your mission. They are typically mostly remembered when things go wrong. In 1964, the nomination of Barry Goldwater displeased moderate Republicans (a substantial contingent in the party back then) and pleased extremists, especially those hooting in the visitors' gallery. That all came across to home TV viewers. The Democrats had their own problem that year with the Mississippi Freedom Democratic Party. No one remembers the GOP conventions of 1968 and 1972, by contrast, because they were utilitarian spectacles. The party got the job done and moved on to getting their man in office. Obviously, the exact opposite was true of the Democratic conventions of those years.

Beyond the loss at the polls, Chicago was remarkable for the bedlam that occurred not only during it but following it. The convention had direct political fallout, such as the McGovern-Fraser reforms and Humphrey's loss in November. It also led to a short but potent media war waged by Mayor Daley, which amplified the worst parts of the Chicago convention and sustained the public awareness of imagery that was also repeated in evening news stories and newspapers. The FCC received a mountain of complaint letters, undertook an investigation, and determined the networks had done no wrong that fell under their jurisdiction. The House Committee on Un-American Activities called witnesses, waged their own investigation, and issued a report, of which nothing came. The House as a whole also issued a negative twenty-nine-page staff report of which likewise nothing came. The *Walker Report* offered a solid repudiation of Daley's complaints, which was enough to slow the momentum of official investigations, although the trial of the Chicago Eight (and then Seven) remained on the horizon.

If Humphrey had won the election, it's probable that the long-term aftermath of Chicago would have been more tightly contained. The now-famous images of police and demonstrators on Michigan Avenue, of Ribicoff telling off Daley from the rostrum, of Daley shouting obscenities at him, and of him repeatedly slashing his own throat with his finger would no doubt still be with us, repeated in documentaries and history books about the 1960s. And yet, if Humphrey had won, he would not have waged a one-man war against mass media "bias." He would have had what we might describe as a "normal" antagonistic relationship with the press, like every president, a relationship of ups and downs, of difficult, occasionally even blistering confrontations with reporters, alternating with friendlier, spin-filled press conferences.

That sort of relationship simply wasn't in Nixon's DNA. Back in 1962, he had stomped off with "You won't have Nixon to kick around anymore" at his "last press conference," and the so-called New Nixon hadn't made up with the fourth estate since then. Elected president by the slimmest of margins in 1968, he owed much to a strong team of media producers and strategists but nothing to the networks, at least in his mind. The networks' failure (as he saw it) in Chicago was just business as usual. In a phone conversation with President Johnson just two days after the convention, Nixon agreed that NBC in particular had done a terrible job: "Police can be a little rough. Some of those guys are pretty tough. But on the other hand, nobody was pointing out the provocation [from the protestors]." Nixon said that Cronkite, on the other hand, "began to get it [right] the last night," a clear reference to his fawning interview with Daley. Both the current president and the next one agreed that the demonstrators were "led by the Commies," as Nixon put it, with Dave Dellinger and Tom Hayden at the helm.[101] Nixon had lunch with Cronkite just five days after the convention, but any remaining softness toward the anchorman would quickly dissipate upon his election. On November 13, 1969, Vice President Agnew made his famous speech attacking the mainstream media as a corps of liberal elitists, raising the specter of censorship and taking the war between Nixon and the "liberal media" to the next level.

For his part, Daley had stoked hostility about irresponsible reporting to defend his city and his pride. His point made, then undercut by the *Walker Report*, he lowered the volume and returned to his focus on Chicago. With his loud attacks, his complaints, and finally his own film, Daley kept his criticisms in the spotlight and amplified the convention's worst moments, helping to make the notion of politically biased news a common, widespread one, and making the ground fertile for such accusations by other political players in the future. Richard J. Daley, Mr. Democrat, had unwittingly played a role in the rise of the New Right and the ascendency of the Republican Party.

Of course, Daley was only one player among others, such as those angry TV viewers who voted for Nixon and who approved of the ways the new president exploited the notion that America's biggest problem was the liberal media. Throughout the 1970s and into the Reagan years, right-wing think tanks and activist groups helped the idea continue to grow. Later, cable news outlets like Fox News, One America News Network, and Newsmax brought the right-wing perspective to news that William F. Buckley once lamented was lacking, and also the tasteless conspiratorial sleaziness that he abhorred. All of this collectively fuels the culture wars to this day.

Conclusion From Biased News to Fake News

The 1968 convention lasted just four days. And yet so much happened, and the aftershocks could be felt for so long. In the Chicago Amphitheatre, long battles over the seating of delegates laid bare the ongoing crisis of Black disenfranchisement, the debate over Vietnam policy revealed a deeply divided political party, and excessively heavy security underscored Richard J. Daley's authoritarian impulses. Meanwhile, out in the streets, the police teargassed, maced, and beat demonstrators for four days, climaxing in a brutal showdown outside the Conrad Hilton on Wednesday night. Throughout, Mayor Daley sought to stifle network news coverage. If Daley's attacks on network news for "bias" revealed a Machiavellian politician in action, the willingness of millions to believe his attacks revealed that ours was a country full of people open to manipulation and to the idea that what they saw was actually not what they saw, a country in which a majority were willing to believe that those seventeen minutes in front of the Hilton were proof not of police brutality but of journalistic malfeasance.

The idea promoted by Daley and others was that, regardless of what those images of police beating and arresting people meant, the huge error on the networks' end was not showing *other images for context*—specifically, images of the protestors "provoking" the police. Underpinning this notion was hostility toward the counterculture, Vietnam war protestors, and, above all, toward the very idea that police brutality was a genuine problem. On the other hand, it wasn't inherently problematic to ask if TV news had told the story correctly. The awareness of media professionals as people who frame images and craft narratives is salutary, in principle. Understanding that TV journalists produce stories by including some things and leaving other things out would, in a perfect world, add up to media literacy, not reactionary anger.

TV journalists in the network era promoted the idea that their work was fair, or, rather, that that was their goal. They weren't naive about it. They understood that journalists were human beings making inter-pretations. But the *ideal* was to be as unbiased as possible. And thus, network-era news strived for balance, sometimes to a fault. We should not over-romanticize that moment. But an imperfect notion of "public service" did power the machine, coupled with a sense that the job of the national news was to highlight important stories and include images to tell those stories. Cronkite once described it as a "bulletin service" that could not go too deeply into anything. Even in a thirty-minute news show, you still got less total information than might appear any day on the front page of the *New York Times*.[1] That was part of what made live events like space launches and conventions so exciting: newscast-ers had more time to dive into issues and details. Similarly, documen-tary series like *CBS Special Reports* or *60 Minutes* allowed for more in-depth investigation.[2] But you couldn't do that every night of the week. Cronkite had originally wanted his sign-off to be something along the lines of "That's the top of the news; read all the details in tomorrow's newspaper," a humble alternative to "and that's the way it is."[3]

We might conceive of public service in the network era as a sort of complicated hydraulic system of checks and balances, with pressure coming from four levels: within the news division itself, within the broader network management system, from outside political play-ers (such as Daley, LBJ, Nixon, and the FCC), and, in a more diffuse manner, from the public. All four of these levels functioned to varying degrees throughout the 1950s, 60s, and 70s, but we see them ampli-fied during and following the Chicago DNC. The system became over-loaded, cracking apart. The news divisions upheld their usual profes-sional norms of fairness yet were roundly attacked by Daley, and also by viewers. This set the stage for attacks to come from Richard Nixon.

This was a tipping-point moment for widespread distrust of the mainstream media. Following Chicago, the timbre of viewer mail changed. Before, critical letters to the news divisions tended to finger *specific reporting* for misinterpretations or factual errors. Viewers also objected to stories that they thought included excessive violence or sexuality, or inappropriate language. There were also overtly political complaints, for example, that not enough Black reporters were featured, or, on the flip side, that the networks covered racial issues too often. Following the convention, more and more viewers wrote to Cronkite to say not "*This story* was biased" but, more trenchantly and personally, "*You* are biased."[4] Personal credibility became increasingly central to reactions against network coverage; this focus on individuals would become more and more common in the ensuing decades.

The networks pushed back in 1968, but it was an uphill battle. By the 1980s, cable had a foothold, and the era of a three-network monopoly was coming to an end. This meant the demise of *mass* media and a one-size-fits-all approach to both news and entertainment programming. Cable provided niche entertainment content: MTV for teenagers, Nickelodeon for kids, ESPN for sports fans, Lifetime for women, and so on. The 1980s also brought the decline of the Fairness Doctrine. Looking back from the divisive social media and cable news environment of the twenty-first century, it is easy to long for a "better time" and to thereby minimize the many challenges of the "balanced" approach. It is also easy to romanticize the doctrine, a relic of the era when the FCC mandated that radio and TV give "both sides" when covering controversial issues. The rationale had been that there was a scarcity of airwaves available for licensing. Airwaves were finite in a way that printing presses were not, so this technical issue superseded First Amendment concerns. To "serve the public interest, convenience, and necessity," as per the Communications Act of 1934, broadcasters could not promote only one political perspective. The result for news was a push toward moderation, and that centrist orientation served broadcasters well because it was easier to sell ads in a non-controversial environment. Why would, say, Jergens Cold Cream only want to reach prospective Democratic consumers?

Exactly "equal time" was not mandated. If a broadcaster aired a conservative commentator, it might schedule a liberal commentator on the same program, but it might also air liberal viewpoints elsewhere, as long as the schedule as a whole was politically balanced. In practice, it was simply easier and more profitable to strive for neutrality. There was probably some merit to the commonsense argument that the doctrine had a "chilling effect" on speech, though there's no strong empirical record of this.[5] At the same time, the scarcity argument was a strong one in the days before cable, satellite, internet, and social media. Further, the doctrine itself came about after World War II, in 1949, partly as a delayed response to Father Coughlin, the wildly popular pro-Mussolini, anti-Semitic, pro-Nazi radio demagogue who had stopped his national political broadcasts only when faced with the double threat of formal charges of sedition and the possibility of being defrocked.[6]

The Fairness Doctrine was conceived in part to prevent such demagoguery.[7] It was never a perfect mechanism, though it was well intentioned. Broadcasters did not care for it, but, at the same time, their professional credos and training had essentially internalized it. Network journalists didn't object to the idea of being as fair as possible, they just tended to think that they didn't need a governmental organization issuing a doctrine to hold their feet to the fire on it. The old journalistic checklist of "who, what, when, where, and why?" was understood as neutral, although "why" was potentially tricky, the spot where analysis might slip into the interpretive realm. When "why" analysis expressed the perspective of the journalist, it was explicitly labeled as such.[8]

When the FCC opened an inquiry on the doctrine in 1984, calling for public comment, "the majority of comments supported the doctrine," communications scholar Patricia Aufderheide has explained. "Supporting the doctrine were public interest groups and nonprofits ranging from the National Rifle Association to the National Coalition for Handgun Control, mainstream religious organizations, partisan political organizations such as the Democratic National Committee, conservative organizations such as the American Legal Foundation and Accuracy in Media, and corporate voices such as Mobil Oil and the Glass Packaging Institute."[9] The doctrine was not always neutrally applied—the Kennedy and Johnson administrations used it specifically to target right-wing radio extremists[10]—but this wide-ranging list of supporters suggests that a desire for "balance" in news coverage was not inherently a liberal or conservative notion. That said, the Reagan FCC's suspension of the doctrine in 1987 unequivocally opened up the doors to right-wing radio and in particular enabled the meteoric rise of Rush Limbaugh. In fact, when liberals tried to reinstate it over the course of the 1990s, Limbaugh supporters called it the "Hush Rush" doctrine.[11]

It would be reductive to chalk up network-era notions of balance to the doctrine alone. "Fairness" was a prevalent journalistic norm, and TV journalists' raison d'être in 1968 was balanced reporting. Before they got to Chicago, they were fully aware that the protestors were hoping for media attention, and also aware that any coverage they provided might be perceived as promoting the antiwar cause. In a 1970 interview, Cronkite summed up the difficulty of the situation:

> We were criticized [in Chicago] for not having told the people that the situation was getting as bad as it was up to the confrontation in front of the Hilton Hotel that night. In other words, we did not *show* the provocations. If we had done that, in this particular case, we would have been accused of fomenting the difficulty. On the other hand, not having done it, we're accused of not having shown it. I think that both sides are partly right, in that situation. But it leads to then a credibility gap. The public sees *just* the explosion in front of the Hilton Hotel. We, with our background knowledge are taking some umbrage perhaps at the way our fellow reporters are being beaten up as well as the citizens and youth on the streets, and we show it. People say we didn't show the whole thing, that quite clearly that's not the whole story, and in some way they're right.[12]

There is concern and humility here about the challenge of presenting a complex news story while knowing that you cannot possibly satisfy all viewers.

Eight years earlier, Cronkite's professional ethics were the same, but his morale was higher, and his sense that neutrality was a viable—if imperfect—ideal was stronger. In 1962, he wrote, "The greatest moments of television news have occurred when the camera simply has been turned on to watch an event in progress, when the news department's function of choice and condensation has been exercised to a minimum, or not at all. Actuality, or eyewitness reports of events as they occur: the Army-McCarthy hearings, the Kefauver Crime hearings, baseball world series, political conventions, a coronation." He added, though, that there was always an "editorial function," and that most stories needed a "voice report" or some kind of "explanation beyond the mere narrative of events."[13]

It is telling that Cronkite included political conventions in his list of events that just unrolled before the camera, requiring a minimum of interpretation. Networks spent millions of dollars on these quadrennial affairs, which required huge teams of workers, and tons of equipment. For the news divisions, it was basically the Olympics. And yet after all that work, the idea, in theory, was that the event had a built-in narrative, a big build-up to a nomination, and that the networks would just show what happened, like when a rocket was launched following several days of coverage on the ground at Cape Canaveral (fig. 31). The floor correspondents' task at a convention, then, would be to find and report all the stories that lead to that final outcome. On the other hand, Cronkite acknowledged that as early as 1960 the presence of the cameras and TV's gavel-to-gavel coverage was already changing how conventions were run. More and more stuff was happening behind the scenes so that a party's image looked better before the public. There really was no such thing as a camera "simply" being "turned on to watch an event in progress." It was an ideal that could never be achieved.

Chicago cracked all that wide open, making it obvious that network news did not just record reality but also narrated it, constructing stories for viewers from raw material. Critics of the network insisted that the cameras had been in the wrong places, that the wrong things had been shown, that the wrong people had been interviewed, and that journalists had shown monstrous bias by referring to beaten protestors not as "communists" or "terrorists" but as "demonstrators" or, more egregiously, "kids." A Manichean narrative emerged, with Daley and the police on one side and Huntley–Brinkley and Cronkite on the other. Re-

FIGURE 31. Cronkite won over Americans with his coverage of the JFK assassination and of the space program. Here, Cronkite broadcasts from a station wagon at Cape Canaveral in 1962. His NASA research ran deep, and the reporting was factual and celebratory, but not explicitly political, conveying a neutrality to which it would be difficult to return after the 1968 Chicago convention. CBS, 1962.

visiting those four days in their entirety, though, reveals a much more complicated picture. Yes, the cameras could have shown more, but it was Daley's heavy-handed censorship efforts, hand-in-hand with an electrical workers strike that the mayor exploited to the max, that had landed those cameras in front of the Hilton. Yes, the networks emphasized Daley's heavy security, but they did not emphasize the tactical errors he had made, like denying permits to protestors and atypically enforcing the park curfew. And they really underreported the police violence targeting journalists. And so, as Cronkite said, "the public sees *just* the explosion in front of the Hilton Hotel" and is outraged.

In stark contrast to the Battle of Michigan Avenue, the 95 percent of TV coverage within the Amphitheatre was almost instantly forgotten, a remarkable omission given the crises that had unfolded there, the absolute chaos, the strong protest against the war from liberal delegates, the battle over Black disenfranchisement, and the heavy-handed security. That a "police riot" had not broken out *within* the convention hall was a small miracle. Yet the fallout from the convention itself was nonetheless far-reaching, affecting both the 1968 and 1972 presidential campaigns.

In between those events, and until he finally resigned, Nixon waged his war against the "liberal" news media. "From the Nixon White House there emanated . . . attacks intended to damage the credibility not of a single journalist but of whole classes of them; to intimidate publishers and broadcast ownerships; and, almost unthinkably, to establish in American jurisprudence the legality of censorship."[14] Nixon was very hostile to print media, especially as the battle raged against the *Washington Post*'s and *New York Times*'s publishing of the Pentagon Papers in 1971, but the bulk of his high-profile attacks were against television. Newspapers were local, but the network news instantly reached a national audience. That's where the strongest impact and biggest numbers were. The fact that more Americans watched Walter Cronkite or David Brinkley or Howard K. Smith every day than read the *Times* or the *Post* fed Nixon's anxiety about negative coverage. Further, although there were all kinds of ways to harass the newspapers (and their employees), such as frivolous lawsuits or IRS investigations, the networks could be intimidated via Nixon's FCC, using the Fairness Doctrine, personal attack rules, and other regulations as weapons.

The networks were also more vulnerable to antitrust suits than the newspapers. This would change over time, but in the network era newspaper ownership was more diversified (concentrated at the local level but not yet purchased by large conglomerates),[15] while the networks held a near-monopoly on national broadcasting. In that context, TV news was understood to demonstrate commitment to public service. "'Having these stations is like having a license to print money,' CBS's chairman, William Paley, once told a CBS News employee, 'and the news department justifies it.'"[16] In a 1973 interview, Nixon's henchman Chuck Colson told journalist Elizabeth Drew, "The networks are going to be broken up one way or another in the next four or five years . . . because you have a very rapidly moving new technology in communications. You have cable, you have video cassettes, and the viewing public, . . . they're not going to be confined to three networks, and that'll be a very healthy thing."[17] Naturally, the corporations that owned CBS, ABC, and NBC did not think that breaking up their monopoly would be "a very healthy thing," and although the rise of cable did lead to an incredible diversification of TV content, the rise of politically polarized, opinion-driven, twenty-four-hour news networks has, arguably, not been healthy for American democracy. But then, Colson didn't really mean "healthy" for America. He was thinking of his boss. And his boss was out to get the network news.[18]

Following Vice President Agnew's November 13, 1969, attack on TV news for their "hostility" to the president, the Nixon administration's relationship with the media, already wobbly, spiraled. Notably, Agnew called as his "first witness" in the case against the networks "Vice President Humphrey and the City of Chicago." Agnew claimed that unfair TV coverage had both cast Humphrey's nomination in a negative light and "worked an injustice on the reputation of the Chicago police" by offering a "one-sided picture" that "exonerat[ed] the demonstrators and protestors." Agnew was, of course, more interested in Nixon's problems than Humphrey's or Chicago's, but the DNC was his argument's hook, as if to say, we all agree the networks erred in Chicago, what's next?

There was no chance that Nixon could have had a *friendly* relationship with the media, but he planted seeds in soil that had been made particularly fertile by Daley's actions in late 1968. Two contradictory strands of public opinion seemed to be irreconcilable at that moment. By August 1968, polls showed that people were increasingly souring on the war, not just Yippies and SDS-ers, but also more moderate, mainstream Americans. And at the same time, more than half of the country thought hippies and Yippies and even clean-cut McCarthy volunteers deserved what they got in Chicago, and that the media had revealed themselves as irredeemably liberal and opposed to law and order. If people could believe this line on the media after only four days of TV coverage in Chicago, they could believe it coming from the Nixon White House for six years.

Network news went on the defensive. When reporters and anchormen complained publicly that they were under siege, the Nixon administration simply denied it. But the networks were gathering receipts. A
thick, black, three-ring binder, probably created by a CBS research team
for internal reference, cataloged "Administration Attacks" from May
1969 through November 1973, and included an appendix of incriminat-
ing documents, mostly material that had come to light in the course of
the Watergate investigation. It's all there: White House internal memoranda confirming the intention behind Agnew's attacks, the planting
of anti-network complaint letters in newspapers, the harassment of reporters on Nixon's "Enemies List," and all sorts of other assault tactics.
The carefully sourced binder cites wiretaps of journalists, break-ins to
reporters' homes in which "burglars" ignored the silver chests in favor
of file cabinets, confirmation of FCC, IRS, and antitrust intimidation
tactics, and a whole mess of dirty tricks to defeat McGovern in 1972.

That year they even went after congressman Paul McCloskey, a
liberal Republican up against Nixon in the New Hampshire primary.
Nixon was obviously going to win the nomination, but why take a
chance? And so Colson sent a young aide to New Hampshire to contrib-
ute $200 to McCloskey's campaign in the name of the Gay Liberation
Front. The kid—Roger Stone—made the contribution but chickened
out at the last minute, "balked at identifying himself as a homosexual,
and said instead that he was from the Young Socialist Alliance."[19] This
sort of maneuver depended on the news media picking up a fabricated
story in order for damage to be done. The idea was you could fool the
media, not just try to censor it. The administration even created a fake
best seller. In 1971, the White House bought up copies of a book attacking the media for liberal bias, thereby "gaming the system" to single-
handedly make Edith Efron's book a best seller: "For years Nixon staffers stumbled upon boxes crammed full of *The News Twisters*."[20] No
wonder NBC News president Reuven Frank described Daley's attacks
and the incredibly harsh blowout from Chicago as just a warm-up for
the Nixon years.

During those four-and-a-half years chronicled in the CBS binder, the network news divisions stood up for their reporters and anchormen, who refused to surrender their sources or otherwise back down in response to administrations attacks. Of particular note was the crisis around *The Selling of the Pentagon,* the hour-long, 1971 *CBS Special Report* about the defense industry's public relations spending.[21] CBS correspondents and anchormen stood strong and were not petty or vindictive on the air. Behind the scenes, it was another circling the wagons moment, with all the networks up in arms over governmental attacks on CBS. On the nightly news, though, anchormen and correspondents discussed Nixon's attacks only when they seemed to be legitimate *news,* like when he made a direct, high-profile attack on the veracity of a major story they had aired. In the pre-cable news days, it would have been very strange for a journalist to fall into the sorts of on-air feuds and vendettas with public figures that are so common today. By 1974, Nixon was particularly furious with Dan Rather and sought to undercut his personal and professional credibility; Rather was under fire, but did not let it inflect his reporting. With only twenty-two minutes to do the evening news, there was no time to waste. Plus, TV journalists generally didn't hint at their own political positions on the air, unless they were explicitly delivering material labeled as commentary.

In speeches, interviews, articles, and op-eds produced when they were off-the-clock, however, they would stand up for themselves and offer analyses of what was going on. In 1969, Reuven Frank wrote an article entitled "The Ugly Mirror" for *Television Quarterly,* a journal published by the National Academy of Television Arts and Sciences. Viewers had been deluging NBC with letters saying they no longer trusted the news, and "the one crystalizing event which brought this about was Chicago." The letters also asked variants of "Why don't you show some good news?" expressing deep frustration about coverage of riots, Vietnam, poverty, and other crises. Implicit in Frank's title was his response: it wasn't reasonable to attack or attempt to censor TV, a mirror that often showed ugly things.[22] Frank seemed burned out already, and Nixon had barely been inaugurated.

CBS likewise was deluged following Chicago and on into the Nixon years with letters complaining about too much bad news. A viewer from New York City wrote to Cronkite, "You come into our homes every night, . . . and you fill us with the worst gloom. Everybody is wrong and everybody (but you) are crooks, murderers and dreadful people. We are fed up. In Russia they would put people like you in an insane asylum, and I and my friends think the sooner you are put in there the better."[23] This sort of letter existed before Chicago, but after Chicago the number went way, way up. A complaint that used to be easy to dismiss as coming from a crank was, by the early seventies, absolutely typical. Many letters by then also complained about Nixon coverage, conveying not just deep pro-Nixon feelings but also a more general concept of good citizenship. One typical letter to Cronkite suggested that "we must have trust in the president and government. . . . I for one support my President all the way."[24]

Watergate was a tipping-point moment for American belief in the trustworthiness of the government. "The segment of Americans who trusted government institutions" plummeted throughout the 1970s, "falling from a historic high of 80 percent of all Americans in 1966 to roughly 25 percent in 1981."[25] Facing tax evasion and political corruption charges, Agnew had resigned in disgrace in October 1973, and Nixon left office in August 1974. Before the president's resignation, though, many people had followed his lead, complaining that the problem was not the president or his administration but TV newsmen creating distrust and sensationalizing Watergate, a story that obviously had no merit. Nixon, often with Agnew as his surrogate, had found that attacking the media was much more effective than directly engaging with Watergate. He thereby attempted to deflect Watergate by making it into a *media* crisis, as Daley had similarly made police brutality into a media crisis a few years earlier.

In a 1970 interview, Cronkite linked the loss of faith in government and the critique of the media. He first articulated his own version of Frank's "ugly mirror" conceit, which he called the "ostrich syndrome":

INTERVIEWER: Now on television, . . . if you show a film of a student demonstration or police beating up somebody or the Black Panthers, you will be accused by one group or another saying, "Why are you showing *that*?"

CRONKITE: [nodding] People deny that something happened that they've seen on film. It's incredible, after the Chicago episode in '68. Well I think that a part of it is a real ostrich syndrome, a real difficulty in believing and not wanting to believe . . . that things are bad. I can understand that, too, to a certain extent. I can understand that if you live in a quiet community . . . or a suburb, . . . [and you feel like] you don't have any Black problem in the city, you don't have an inner city core problem, you don't have a mass transit problem, you don't have a student problem . . . I can see why you get pretty *sick* everyday of being told that this is what's happening in this country. . . . People are hungry and starving and ill-clothed and ill-housed and ill-educated and ill-medicated. I can see where you'd get *darn* sick of it. I get sick of having to report it everyday. And I know that it is a revolution, and we darn well better keep our eyes on it. I think there is this sort of ostrich syndrome of trying to bury our heads in the sand and say, . . . "It's really not that serious. Therefore somebody's trying to tell us that it is for some ulterior motive, . . . [so] then they must be lying to us."

Cronkite chalks up the frustrations he's hearing from viewers to human nature, a generous analysis, if a simple one. But then he switches gears to point at political motivations:

This crisis of confidence is *not* in the news media but is basically in the government. And it has been *translated* to news media. *Part of the Agnew trick was to do that.* This confidence was shaken in the Vietnam war, and the Johnson administration subterfuge in insinuating us into the Vietnam war, not leveling with the American people, not telling them the scope of the commitment, not telling them the danger of the commitment really. This I think is where it really began. Now, you would think that those who have the greatest lack of confidence in

the media perhaps are those who would have been Johnson supporters during that period, and now the Nixon administration supporters
certainly [are those who lack confidence in media] and so forth. But
this isn't a *rational* decision on their part. "I am going to dislike the
media because of so-and-so." It's all just part of a national mood.[26]

This is a somewhat oblique attack on the Nixon administration. They
are the ones that engineered the shift from concerns about Vietnam to
an attack on the news media. But rather than concluding that Americans are foolish or manipulable, Cronkite suggests that Agnew's "trick"
could be accomplished because of the dire "national mood." The analysis is weak sociology, but in keeping with both Cronkite's professional
norms and his square optimism.[27]

Notwithstanding all the mail Cronkite received accusing him of hat-
ing the president, the anchorman maintained that all he did was *cover*
the president. By 1973, Nixon's attacks on the press had become so
vicious that Cronkite could have been justified in lashing out, at least
off the air, but instead he mostly seemed sad, suggesting in his *Playboy* interview, "I think what he's trying to do in several cases is absolutely dead wrong. I think that the attack on the press is so antithetical
to everything that this country stands for. . . . I just don't understand
why the administration took this position in the first place. The press
wasn't that anti-Nixon in '68 or '69. I think most of the liberals in this
country would say the press was cozying up to him, if anything. And
yet, whammo, this whole explosive attack on the press."[28] Cronkite had
been seen by many as "the most trusted man in America" in the years
following his coverage of President Kennedy's assassination. When ratings of the 1964 GOP convention did not meet expectations, and CBS
management booted Cronkite from covering the Democratic convention, they received eleven thousand complaint letters in one week.[29]
The anchorman still received his share of fan mail in the 1970s, but
Nixon had succeeded in souring the milk: the country was polarized
and demoralized.[30]

Once Nixon resigned, it should have been clear to most Americans that the press had actually under-covered Watergate until fairly late in the game. The *Washington Post* had kept the story alive, and CBS was "the lone television network to pursue Watergate seriously in 1972."[31] One night in October of that year, the *CBS Evening News* gave more than fourteen of its twenty-two minutes to explaining the Watergate story. Colson phoned CBS's Chairman Paley and attacked him, and part two of the Watergate special report, scheduled to follow on another day, was trimmed down to eight minutes. This two-part coverage was notable, but Watergate wasn't a story that had frequent attention from CBS. Dan Rather correctly assessed that "the brutal truths of the Watergate story continued to be broken not by television or by the White House press corps, but by a pair of mavericks from the police beat: Woodward and Bernstein."[32] With Nixon out the door, Woodward and Bernstein emerged as heroes to liberals and villains to conservatives. Conservative think tanks and advocacy groups would tap into this, stoking distrust of the media among their constituencies. Attacks on the "liberal media" would become one important piece of the culture wars that have raged ever since.

Fifty years later, Fox News and President Trump would perfect the vilification of the "liberal media," taking it to a new extreme with the notion that any news media that wasn't pro-Trump was not so much "biased" as "fake." It's one thing to say that news is slanted, which implies that if other perspectives were included the news would be more accurate. That was the argument made by Daley and his followers back in 1968: show more footage, interview more people, and what we believe to be the true picture will emerge. It's quite another to say that facts are untrue, that photographic evidence and eyewitness accounts don't mean anything or just don't exist.

In the days before Photoshop and deepfakes, there was still the possibility of blind faith in the basic truth of photographic images. Lew Koch, a reporter and news writer for the local NBC station in 1968 and cofounder of *Chicago Journalism Review*, argued after the convention that TV cameras had fundamentally changed the relationship that police, the mayor, and other authorities had to the news media. Police missed "the old-time police reporter, the man with paper and pencil who had been on the beat and knew the score. Now it's electronic journalism, cameraman, lightman, soundman, with strange knob-twisting, lens-focusing electronic devices and a reporter with a microphone, young, seemingly brash, who police instinctively feel doesn't know what *real* police work is all about." Koch adds that a cop could take a pencil-and-paper man for a beer or a cup of coffee to tell him what was what, "but with television it all seems too final." The shift was an ontological one: "The camera could record cops as well as robbers." In Chicago's old-boy network, police and journalists had an understanding; stories might be nudged, and there was the possibility of tit-for-tat negotiations. In the new world of electronic journalism, once something was caught on film, it was real, and you could not dispute it. Koch gives a trenchant example. When Daley's "shoot to kill" comments created an uproar, the mayor said it had never happened. "But 16mm film with a magnetic sound track running in sync does not misquote; it just records—and the record is permanent."[33] The lie couldn't stick when it was so easy to show the truth.

This notion of photographic evidence seemed self-evident, though it was still tricky. After all, many Americans had seen the Battle of Michigan Avenue and still said that it was not evidence of excessive police violence. But no one denied that the event had taken place; rather, they claimed it was misrepresented (mis-filmed) by the networks. The Trump years brought a whole new meaning to the interpretation of "evidence." Rigorous investigation and re-counts found literally no evidence of widespread voter fraud in the 2020 presidential election, and yet Fox News and Republican politicians said that there was evidence, without providing it, and people believed them. Saying there is evidence had become a substitute for providing it. During and following the Trump administration, right-wing Americans, with ample Fox News and Republican Party support, dismissed any news-gathering with which they disagreed as "fake," or, failing that, simply unimportant.

The storming of the Capitol Building on January 6, 2021, was videotaped from every angle, not only by those on the scene but also by

closed-circuit television. When Trump was impeached for his incite-
ment of the insurrection, prosecutors showed the visual evidence to
Congress. Logically, you couldn't claim that automated, operator-less,
ceiling-mounted security cameras exhibited "bias," as many had regarding the networks' cameras in Chicago back in 1968. Further, much
of the smartphone footage shot at eye level was posted online by those
who took it, with taglines like "Here I am, storming the capital!"—
indisputable admission of wrongdoing, one might assume. And yet the
majority of Republicans in Congress believed (or claimed to believe) it
was not proof of anything. Later, the notion that these were all "tour-
ists" was even floated. That was both a reinterpretation of the images
and a denial of their importance. Koch's notion that "with television it
all seems too final" can't apply in an interpretive universe infused with
such bad faith.

And so, oddly enough, we look back today on the crisis in Chicago
in 1968 with a strange kind of nostalgia. That too was a moment of
misinterpretation, when most Americans thought newsmen had deceived Americans, a perception that both Daley and Nixon exploited to
the max. And yet, decades later, the notion that the Battle of Michigan
Avenue was not what it seemed has been lost, along with all the floor
battles within the Amphitheatre. The *Walker Report*'s "police riot" assessment won out. As for the chaos at the convention hall, it too has
been mostly lost to cultural memory.

Further, to most people alive today, the notion of a nominating convention as a place where battles are fought would seem far-fetched.
Conventions have become pristine showcases for political parties. Candidates are preselected via the primary process,[34] and an unexpected
floor demonstration or improvised speech is virtually unthinkable. The
online, hybrid live-recorded Democratic convention of 2020 was conceptualized as the safest way to hold a convention during a pandemic,
but it was also a spectacle of media mastery, of a party demonstrating
complete control over its own image.[35] The event was wholly unique
and yet also the logical culmination of years and years of increasingly
pre-scripted conventions.

FIGURE 32.   The Trump administration repeatedly vilified the news media as the "enemy of the people," fostering violence toward working journalists. Here, a reporter with "PRESS" written on her gasmask tries to do her job in the streets of Portland, Oregon, in the midst of street protests following the murder of George Floyd. Shutterstock, 2020.

This was a year when the conventions seemed like practically the only tightly controlled news imagery. Americans were shut at home, in quarantine, but were also out in the streets protesting the murder of George Floyd. Anchorpeople ran their news shows from their home offices. Even live entertainment shows came from home. *The Late Show with Stephen Colbert* opened on June 1, 2020, with a phony ad: "Do you miss the upheaval of the 1960s? Well now you can experience it all over again. Time Life Books proudly introduces: The Present. Featuring all the greatest hits of the '60s. Civil unrest. Police brutality. Rockets to outer space. Invasions. A corrupt and paranoid president." The first shot was of a rocket taking off, but the second was of the Battle of Michigan Avenue. More famous footage followed, of civil rights marches and campus protest, but within seconds we are back to shots of police beating people in Chicago, and then of police cars plowing into BLM protests. And finally, a shot of Nixon is followed by a shot of Trump.

Acknowledgments

Writing about political chaos, journalistic success and failure, freedom of speech, police brutality, and American elections is challenging under any circumstances, but this book was conceived and written at a particularly difficult time. This makes me exceptionally grateful to all who helped out along the way. Tim Mennel and Chris Calhoun were wonderfully enthusiastic about the work and guided the project through the nuts and bolts of publication. Tim is a rigorous editor, and the book is better for it. The University of Chicago Press's anonymous readers offered helpful feedback on the manuscript, as did Josh Braun. Derek Robertson artfully shepherded the germ of the idea for this book through its earliest appearance in print. The Stanford Humanities Center supported me with a fellowship, and I am grateful to all my compatriots at Stanford for their insights, and, in particular, to Brian DeLay, Geraldo Cadava, Ramzi Fawaz, and especially my diligent research assistant, Ali Shah. Pat Thomas was always handy with a reference, anecdote, or inspirational "yip!" and David Greenberg was a reliable expert for help with emergency queries, as was Kevin Kruse, who, if he didn't know the answer, would kindly put me in touch with the right person. Josh Berman, Clark Williams, Caroline Jack, Kevin Maher, Victoria Cain, Eric Freedman, and Fred Turner kept me afloat at key moments. A short visit as a Knight Visiting Nieman Fellow at Harvard really launched this project; never underestimate the value of a good chair in which to read.

Librarians are the best. For this project, I am particularly grateful to the staffs of the Dolph Briscoe Center for American History; the Newberry Library; the University of Illinois Chicago Special Collections and University Archives; Tufts University Digital Collections and Archives;

the Massachusetts Institute of Technology libraries; the Harvard Film Archive; the Lyndon Baines Johnson Presidential Library; Special Collections & Archives, McIntyre Library, University of Wisconsin-Eau Claire; the Minnesota Historical Society; the Harry Ransom Center; and the Chicago Film Archive.

In MIT's Comparative Media Studies and Writing program, I am thankful for supportive colleagues, in particular Shannon Larkin, Edward Schiappa, T. L. Taylor, Jing Wang, Alan Lightman, Kenneth Manning, Helen Lee, and Micah Nathan. MIT's School of Humanities, Arts, and Social Sciences propelled the project forward with sabbatical leave and significant fellowship funding for research and production costs. Leonard Rosenbaum once again delivered, and James Toftness came through with terrific assistance at the eleventh hour, as did Emma Hetrick and Suzanne Scott. A number of MIT graduate students contributed directly or indirectly to the development of this book, in particular: Mariel García-Montez, Josh Cowls, Kaelan Doyle-Myerscough, Matt Graydon, Judy Heflin, Vicki Zeamer, Sara Rafsky, and Erik Stayton. Lilia Kilburn and Evan Higgins were a delight to work with, and enabled my newfound relationship with my TV friend Joe Pera. As I wrote the first draft of these acknowledgments, it was not yet clear if my green bean arch was going to come together, but if not for Lilia and Evan, I never would have tried. (It came together.)

As always, Jonathan Kirshner was enthusiastic and supportive of my work. Ron Simon of the Paley Center for Media gets a huge thanks, not only for help with this project but also, belatedly, for help with my last. If I could, I would repay his generosity by single-handedly engineering a DVD release of *An American Family*. It was a pleasure making the rounds of academic conferences with Kathryn Cramer Brownell, Allison Perlman, Nicole Hemmer, and Oscar Winberg. Thanks also to the *Washington Post*'s "Made by History" team for being such gracious editors. Torsten Kathke's company every Wednesday at noon got me through the darkest days, and even far beyond the stars. Michael Socolow's answers to my queries were always "right on" the mark. Jordan Stokes was a ready consultant on music and sound questions; during lockdown, I often waxed nostalgic for his karaoke performance of "Anarchy in the UK." It would be impossible to overstate how delightful it was to confer with Adam Charles Hart about this project, and so many other things. He is both a brilliant scholar and a wonderful friend, the sort of fellow with whom one can freely discuss pressing issues of nomenclature, feline idiosyncrasies, and more.

Mario and Margarita Cordero, Adriana Cordero, and Geordie Grindle have long offered steadfast support. My grandmother Ethel Gallagher is long gone and probably would not have approved of this book. Nonetheless, I salute her and her cottage. Both have been a source of strength. Julie Lavelle, Martha Lewis, Liz Linder, Mary Fuller, Janet Sonenberg, Amy Herzog, Lisa Parks, Barbara Abrash, and Andrea Buffa provided lady power that undergirded not only this project, but everything else. How fortunate one is to have such good friends.

Mauricio Cordero is my anchor. Like Mandalorians, we are stronger together.

Notes

INTRODUCTION

1. Horace Newcomb and Paul M. Hirsch, "Television as a Cultural Forum," in *Television: The Critical View*, ed. Horace Newcomb (New York: Oxford University Press, 2006).

2. Consistently the ratings underdog, and therefore short on funds, ABC News did not go to a half-hour until 1967.

3. Michael J. Socolow, "'We Should Make Money on Our News': The Problem of Profitability in Network Broadcast Journalism History," *Journalism* 11, no. 6 (2010): 686.

4. "Huntley–Brinkley's Chunk of Crinkly," *Time*, April 2, 1965. There was tremendous profit in reruns, and no rerun or international syndication potential for news shows. Over the long term, then, *Bonanza* clearly beat out *Huntley–Brinkley*. See Derek Kompare, *Rerun Nation: How Repeats Invented American Television* (New York: Routledge, 2005).

5. Memo from Richard Salant to Mr. Byrne, cc. Mssrs. Cowden, Manning, Midgley, Fuchs, October 14, 1970. Sanford Socolow papers, vol./box 2014-69/1, "R. Salant Memos" folder. Dolph Briscoe Center for American History, University of Texas at Austin (hereafter Briscoe Center).

6. On MSNBC, see Joshua A. Braun, *This Program Is Brought to You By* (New Haven, CT: Yale University Press, 2015), 65–66.

7. The focus here is on "bias" in broadcasting. On print, see Michael Schudson, *Discovering the News: A Social History of American Newspapers* (New York: Basic Books, 1978).

8. Heather Hendershot, *What's Fair on the Air? Cold War Right-Wing Broadcasting and the Public Interest* (Chicago: University of Chicago Press, 2011).

9. Brian Rosenwald, *Talk Radio's America: How an Industry Took Over a Political Party that Took Over the United States* (Cambridge, MA: Harvard University Press, 2019).

10. Dan Rather and Gary Paul Gates, *The Palace Guard* (New York: Harper & Row, 1974); Susan Buzenberg and Bill Buzenberg, eds., *Salant, CBS, and the Battle for the Soul of Broadcast Journalism: The Memoirs of Richard S. Salant* (Boulder, CO: Westview Press, 1999); David M. Stone, *Nixon and the Politics of Public Television* (New York: Garland, 1985); William E. Porter, *Assault on the Media: The Nixon Years* (Ann Arbor: University of Michigan Press, 1976).

11. Rick Perlstein, *Nixonland: The Rise of a President and the Fracturing of America* (New York: Scribner, 2008), 358.

12. The TV news cameras took about seventeen minutes of footage that night in front of the Hilton. Farber notes that "although the police succeeded in clearing the Balbo and Michigan intersection in about twenty minutes, the violence went on for hours" afterward in the Chicago Loop area. David Farber, *Chicago '68* (Chicago: University of Chicago Press, 1988), 201.

13. In earlier years, no one disputed that the nation's newspapers had a fiercely Republican slant. Sam Lebovic, "When the 'Mainstream Media' Was Conservative: Media Criticism in the Age of Reform" in *Media Nation: The Political History of News in Modern American*, ed. Bruce J. Schulman and Julian E. Zelizer (Philadelphia: University of Pennsylvania Press, 2017), 63–76. On TV and anticommunism, see J. Fred MacDonald, *Television and the Red Menace* (New York: Praeger, 1985).

14. Daniel C. Hallin, *The Uncensored War: The Media and Vietnam* (Berkeley: University of California Press, 1989); David Culbert, "Television's Visual Impact on Decision-Making in the USA, 1968: The Tet Offensive and Chicago's Democratic National Convention," *Journal of Contemporary History* 33, no. 3 (1998): 419–49: "By late February [1968], surveys showed that only 32 percent of the people endorsed Johnson's war policies. . . . And for the first time, half—exactly 50 percent—thought it had been a mistake to send US troops to Vietnam." Chester J. Pach, Jr., "TV's 1968: War, Politics, and Violence on the Network Evening News," *South Central Review* 16/17, nos. 4-1 (Winter 1999–Spring 2000): 32.

15. Walter Cronkite, *A Reporter's Life* (New York: Ballantine Books, 1997), 193.

16. Douglas Brinkley, *Cronkite* (New York: HarperCollins, 2012), 349.

17. Walter Cronkite, *Vietnam Perspective* (New York: Pocket Books, 1965), n.p.

18. Cronkite's report was not pleasing to the president, but Johnson had also had a weak showing in the primaries and faced many other challenges. See Theodore H. White, *The Making of the President 1968* (New York: HarperCollins, 2010), chap. 4 "Lyndon Johnson: The Renunciation."

19. Brinkley, *Cronkite*, 369.

20. Memo from Richard Salant to Mr. Byrne.

21. "CBS Memoranda" folder, CBS News Archive papers. vol./box 2K61, Briscoe Center.

22. Theodore H. White, *The Making of the President 1964* (New York: HarperPerennial, 2010), 112.

23. Richard M. Clurman, *Beyond Malice: The Media's Years of Reckoning* (New York: Routledge, 2017), 205.

24. Rick Perlstein, *Before the Storm: Barry Goldwater and the Unmaking of the American Consensus* (New York: Simon & Schuster, 2001), 378.

25. Henry Kissinger diary entry, cited in Niall Ferguson, *Kissinger*, vol. 1, *1923–1968: The Idealist* (New York: Penguin, 2015), 609.

26. Nicole Hemmer, "Attacking the Press for Liberal Bias Is a Staple of Republican Campaigns—and It All Began in 1964," CNN Opinion, February 29, 2020,

https://www.cnn.com/2020/02/29/opinions/lyndon-johnson-barry-goldwater
-liberal-media-bias-hemmer/index.html.

27. On Buckley's idea of "The Prevailing Bias," the title of one of the episodes of his TV show, see Heather Hendershot, *Open to Debate: How William F. Buckley Put Liberal America on the Firing Line* (New York: HarperCollins, 2016).

28. Hendershot, *What's Fair*; Nicole Hemmer, *Messengers of the Right: Conservative Media and the Transformation of American Politics* (Philadelphia: University of Pennsylvania Press, 2016); Paul Matzko, *The Radio Right: Creating the Silent Majority* (New York: Oxford University Press, 2020).

29. Dan Rather with Mickey Herskowitz, *The Camera Never Blinks: Adventures of a TV Journalist* (New York: William Morrow, 1977), 75.

30. Connor, cited in David Greenberg, "The Idea of 'the Liberal Media' and Its Roots in the Civil Rights Movement," *The Sixties* 1, no. 2 (2008): 176.

31. Steven D. Classen, *Watching Jim Crow: The Struggles over Mississippi TV, 1955–1969* (Durham, NC: Duke University Press, 2004).

32. Bryan Hardin Thrift, *Conservative Bias: How Jesse Helms Pioneered the Rise of Right-Wing Media and Realigned the Republican Party* (Gainesville: University Press of Florida, 2014), 86.

33. Thrift, *Conservative Bias*, 154–55.

34. Perlstein, *Nixonland*, 16, 194.

35. White, *Making of the President 1968*, 337; "Hippie Killed by Policemen in Old Town," *Chicago Tribune*, August 23, 1968.

36. On Nielsen Ratings and demographics (the white audiences who "counted" most), see Janet Staiger, *Blockbuster TV: Must-See Sitcoms in the Network Era* (New York: New York University Press, 2000); Eileen Meehan, "Why We Don't Count: The Commodity Audience" in *Logics of Television*, ed. Patricia Mellencamp (Bloomington: Indiana University Press, 1990); Ien Ang, *Desperately Seeking the Audience* (New York: Routledge, 1991).

37. David Paul Kuhn, *The Hardhat Riot: Nixon, New York City, and the Dawn of the White Working-Class Revolution* (New York: Oxford University Press, 2020), 26, 27.

38. *Report of the National Advisory Commission on Civil Disorders* (New York: E. P. Dutton, 1968), 369. NBC's local Detroit affiliate produced *Six Days in July*, a 90-minute special, just one week after the riots. It underplays black/white conflict but, though imperfect, may be the best TV record of that moment.

39. Perlstein, *Nixonland*, 11.

40. The one-in-six figure was reported by CBS in 1978. John Schultz, *No One Was Killed: The Democratic National Convention, August 1968* (Chicago: University of Chicago Press, 2009 [1969]), 204.

41. Todd Gitlin, *The Whole World Is Watching: Mass Media in the Making and Unmaking of the New Left* (Berkeley: University of California Press, 1980), 189.

42. *Rights in Conflict: The Walker Report to the National Commission on the Causes and Prevention of Violence* (New York: Bantam, 1968), 282.

43. *Report on the National Advisory Commission on Civil Disorders* (New York: E. P. Dutton, 1968). See also Steven M. Gillon, *Separate and Unequal: The Kerner Commission and the Unraveling of American Liberalism* (New York: Basic Books, 2018).

44. Vincent Cannato, *The Ungovernable City: John Lindsay and His Struggle to Save New York* (New York: Basic Books, 2002); Hendershot, "Strikes, Riots, and Muggers: How John Lindsay Weathered New York City's Image Crisis," in *Television History, The Peabody Archive, and Cultural Memory*, ed. Ethan Thompson, Jeffrey P. Jones, and Lucas Hatlen (Athens: University of Georgia Press, 2019).

45. Ed Sanders, *1968: A History in Verse* (Santa Rosa, CA: Black Sparrow, 1997), 61. Sanders says six thousand Yippies assembled in Grand Central Terminal. The *Walker Report* says it was closer to five thousand (47).

46. David Smith, "'Whitey's on the Moon: Why Apollo 11 Looked So Different to Black America," *Guardian* (July 14, 2019); https://www.theguardian.com/science/2019/jul/14/apollo-11-civil-rights-black-america-moon.

47. Reasoner, cited in Pach, "TV's 1968," 29.

48. Adam Cohen and Elizabeth Taylor, *American Pharaoh: Mayor Richard J. Daley His Battle for Chicago and the Nation* (New York: Back Bay, 2001), 323.

49. Cohen and Taylor, *American Pharaoh*, 275.

50. Cohen and Taylor, *American Pharaoh*, 276.

51. Cohen and Taylor, *American Pharaoh*, 272.

52. Mike Royko, *Boss* (New York: Penguin, 1988), 204–6.

53. Studs Terkel, "Boss," *New York Times* (April 4, 1971); http://movies2.nytimes.com/books/99/09/26/specials/terkel-daley.html.

54. "Lyndon B. Johnson and Richard J. Daley on 13 July 1968," Conversation WH6807-01-13208-13209, *Presidential Recordings Digital Edition* [*Johnson Telephone Tapes: 1968*, ed. Kent B. Germany, Nicole Hemmer, and Ken Hughes] (Charlottesville: University of Virginia Press, 2014-); http://prde.upress.virginia.edu/conversations/4011138.

55. Cohen and Taylor, *American Pharaoh*, 470.

56. Cohen and Taylor do not rule out the importance of voter fraud in Cook County but basically say that we will never know for sure (264–79). Others are more skeptical. Paul von Hippel, "Here's a Voter Fraud Myth: Richard Daley 'Stole' Illinois for John Kennedy in the 1960 Election," *Washington Post*, August 8, 2017; https://www-washingtonpost-com.stanford.idm.oclc.org/news/monkey-cage/wp/2017/08/08/heres-a-voter-fraud-myth-richard-daley-stole-illinois-for-john-kennedy-in-the-1960-election/. See also Edmund F. Kallina, "Was the 1960 Presidential Election Stolen? The Case of Illinois," *Presidential Studies Quarterly* 15, no. 1 (1985): 113–18.

57. Cohen and Taylor, *American Pharaoh*, 450.

58. Cohen and Taylor, *American Pharaoh*, 454. Erik S. Gellman, *Troublemakers: Chicago Freedom Struggles through the Lens of Art Shay* (Chicago: University of Chicago Press, 2020), 170, 172. See also Simon Balto, *Occupied Territory: Policing*

Chicago from Red Summer to Black Power (Chapel Hill: University of North Carolina Press, 2019), 214–16.

59. Earl Bush, cited in F. Richard Ciccone, *Royko: A Life in Print* (New York: Public Affairs, 2001), 168.

60. Esther R. Fuchs, *Mayors and Money: Fiscal Policy in New York and Chicago* (Chicago: University of Chicago Press, 1992), 278.

61. Sam Kashner, "*Theeeeere's* Johnny!," *Vanity Fair* (January 27, 2014); https://archive.vanityfair.com/article/2014/2/theeeeeres-johnny. Lindsay described "a computer-dating machine set up in Central Park where a bachelor deposits his quarter and tells the machine, 'I'm sensitive, I'm single, I'm rich,' whereupon the machine mugs him."

62. Joe McGinniss, *The Selling of the President 1968* (New York: Simon & Schuster, 1969), 33.

63. Schultz, *No One Was Killed*, 55–56.

CHAPTER ONE

1. John Schultz, *No One Was Killed: The Democratic National Convention, August 1968* (Chicago: University of Chicago Press, 2009 [1969]), 57.

2. David Douglas Duncan, *Self-Portrait: USA* (New York: Harry N. Abrams, 1969), 117.

3. Reuven Frank, *Out of Thin Air: The Brief Wonderful Life of Network News* (New York: Simon & Schuster, 1991), 272. He adds that, almost as an afterthought, the networks were each given six messenger passes. Messengers could go everywhere, so correspondent John Chancellor was on the floor all week with a messenger pass.

4. *Rights in Conflict: The Walker Report to the National Commission on the Causes and Prevention of Violence* (New York: Bantam, 1968), 296.

5. Justin A. Nelson, "Drafting Lyndon Johnson: The President's Secret Role in the 1968 Democratic Convention," *Presidential Studies Quarterly* 30, no. 4 (2000), 690. Nelson shows that at the convention, "everything of major consequence required Johnson's knowledge and approval" (697).

6. Sanford Socolow interview with Dr. Ralph Engelman, August 27, 2008, Television Academy Foundation; https://interviews.televisionacademy.com/interviews/sanford-socolow.

7. "NBC Draws 106 Emmy Nominations," *Broadcasting*, May 12, 1969, 64; "An Overwhelmed Story in Miami?," *Broadcasting*, August 12, 1968, 47.

8. Bill Leonard, *In the Storm of the Eye: A Lifetime at CBS* (New York: Putnam, 1987), 115.

9. In a 1969 *60 Minutes* feature on "media bias," a reporter asks Cronkite if the news media were "used or exploited by . . . dissident elements" in Chicago. Cronkite answers, "Of course we were used," insofar as protestors did get coverage, but when asked if the actions would have happened even if the cameras had not been there, he answers yes.

10. This clip shows NBC's regular video cameras for the 1964 conventions as well as the smaller creepy-peepy, presumably the older black-and-white model; https://www.oddballfilms.com/clip/13183_8744_republican_convention4.

11. The creepy-peepy had premiered at the 1952 conventions. It had been developed by RCA/NBC, and they had dubbed it the "walkie-lookie," but some newspaper wag had come up with the new name. NBC and RCA officials were not pleased with the "vaguely naughty implication of the nickname," but it stuck. Frank, *Out of Thin Air*, 60.

12. In 1972, the video collective TVTV used the new Sony Portapak camera to make documentaries about the conventions. "Only a beefy cameraman could withstand the enormous apparatus, including scuba-style backpack to transport so-called portable television cameras. Fully equipped, they looked more like moon men. Compared with this, the lightweight, black-and-white Portapak and recorder in the hands of slim Nancy Cain . . . looked like a child's toy, which was part of the charm because no one took seriously these low-tech hippies." Deirdre Boyle, "Guerilla Television" in *Transmission*, ed. Peter D'Agostino and David Tafler (Thousand Oaks, CA: Sage, 1995), 156.

13. Louise Sweeney, ". . . And the Conventions," *Christian Science Monitor*, June 8–10, 1968, weekend issue, n.p., Walter Cronkite Papers, vol./box 2M752, "Democratic Convention" folder, Briscoe Center.

14. Susan Murray, *Bright Signals: A History of Color Television* (Durham, NC: Duke University Press, 2018), 251.

15. Jeff Kisseloff, *The Box: An Oral History of Television, 1920–1961* (New York: Penguin, 1997), 56.

16. My emphasis. The $400,000 figure comes from "Chicago Trying Hard to Keep the Lid On," *Business Week*, August 17, 1968, 24. Quotation from Lucia Monat and Guy Halverson, "And Now the Democrats," *Christian Science Monitor*, August 10–12, 1968, weekend issue, n.p. Both from Walter Cronkite Papers, vol./box 2M752, "Democratic Convention" folder, Briscoe Center.

17. By 1968, Chicago's slaughterhouse business was waning; the stockyards finally closed in 1971. One local who attended concerts there noted that "the smell was mostly gone by 1978." VBO-Phil posting, October 27, 2010; https://forgottenchicago.com/forum/read.php?1,2448,page=2.

18. Dan Rather with Mickey Herskowitz, *The Camera Never Blinks: Adventures of a TV Journalist* (New York: William Morrow, 1977), 76–77.

19. Culbert, "Television's Visual Impact on Decision-Making in the USA, 1968," *Journal of Contemporary History* 33, no. 3 (1998): 421.

20. There were also self-censorship issues. Before Tet, the networks were more inclined to report the administration's line on Vietnam. Further, they were careful about explicit footage that would elicit complaints about "bad taste." The famous footage of the summary execution of the Vietcong Nguyen Van Lem by Gen. Nguyen Ngoc Loan in the streets of downtown Saigon was both shocking and anomalous. Footage of casualties was carefully chosen, in part to spare families

from seeing nationally televised images of their dead or dying sons. On newsmen in the field, see John Laurence, *The Cat from Hue: A Vietnam War Story* (New York: PublicAffairs, 2002).

21. Daniel C. Hallin, *The "Uncensored War": The Media and Vietnam* (New York: Oxford University Press), 129.

22. Garry Paul Gates, *Air Time: The Inside Story of CBS* News (New York: Harper & Row, 1978), 253–54.

23. "TV's Top Rated Events of 1960s: From JFK to Apollo 11," *Variety*, August 27, 1969, 39.

24. Frank, *Out of Thin Air*, 271.

25. Nelson, "Drafting Lyndon Johnson," 699.

26. Adam Cohen and Elizabeth Taylor, *American Pharaoh: Mayor Richard J. Daley—His Battle for Chicago and the Nation* (New York: Little Brown, 2001), 462. Before the additional 3,200 phones were installed, there were 107 payphones already in the Amphitheatre, an impossibly small number for a political convention. In an age of mobile phones, it is hard to imagine the predicament caused by a phone installers' strike. Payphone count from "Chicago Sweats It Out," *Business Week*, July 13, 1968, 37, Cronkite Papers, vol./box 2M752, "Democratic Convention" folder, Briscoe Center.

27. Donald Janson, "Chicago Prepares for Mass Arrests," *New York Times*, August 9, 1968, clipping, Cronkite Papers, vol./box 2M669, no folder, Briscoe Center.

28. *The Guide to Chicago's Hotels, Motels, Restaurants, Night Clubs*, August 22, 1968, 16. University of Illinois–Chicago Richard J. Daley Collection, Slss1B85, Series II Democratic Party Series, Sub-Series 1 Democratic Party Papers. "Democratic National Convention [inc. photographs], 1968 [1 of 3]" folder. Items from this collection are hereafter cited by title or description, followed by UIC, Daley Collection, with Slss1 no. and other relevant detail. When all details are the same for an immediately following note, they are omitted for brevity.

29. *Guide to Chicago's Hotels*, UIC, Daley Collection.

30. Exactly how much delegates spent in 1968 is unknown, but in 1963 Chicago hosted 1,022 conventions, with 1,320,000 in attendance, spending a total of $211,000,000. In 1968 there were fifty-one more conventions held in the city, with 177,000 more attendees, but they spent $1,270,000 less. Figures from the Chicago Convention Bureau, Earl Bush Papers, box 6, "Chronological Files, 1975 [6-39]" folder, University of Illinois–Chicago.

31. Roger Mudd tells how, "in the early 1960s there was only one conveniently located film lab in Washington—Byron's in Georgetown. It was first come, first served [and] the network's motorcycle boys . . . would . . . go bombing through the narrow streets of Georgetown to reach Byron's first. Losing the race a time or two forced CBS to install in a corner closet in the bureau a small film processor." Roger Mudd, *The Place to Be: Washington, CBS, and the Glory Days of Television News* (New York: Public Affairs, 2008), 289.

32. The day before the convention, a wildcat bus-driver strike began, led by

African American drivers who were systematically discriminated against by their union. See Erik S. Gellman, "In the Driver's Seat: Chicago's Bus Drivers and Labor Insurgency in the Era of Black Power," *Labor Studies in Working-Class History of the Americas* 11, no. 3 (2014): 49-76.

33. Frank, cited in Edward Jay Epstein, *News from Nowhere: Television and the News* (New York: Random House, 1973), 153. The full memo was thirty-two pages long, and Frank had written it as a guide in particular for new NBC employees who had never worked in TV. Frank, *Out of Thin Air*, 181-82.

34. The CBS standard was that "analysis" explained without promoting a point of view, whereas "commentary" expressed the speaker's opinion. The distinction was official policy, but a bit wobbly. See Erik Barnouw, *The Gold Web: A History of Broadcasting in the United States*, vol. 2, *1933 to 1953* (New York: Oxford University Press, 1968), 135-37.

35. Reuven Frank, "1948: Live . . . From Philadelphia . . . It's the National Conventions," *New York Times Magazine*, April 17, 1988: 37.

36. Norman Mailer, *Miami and the Siege of Chicago* (New York: Random House, 2016), 10.

37. Robert Shogan, "Enemas for Elephants," *Media Studies Journal*, special issue on 1968, 12, no. 3 (1998): 54.

38. Douglas Brinkley, *Cronkite* (New York: HarperCollins, 2012), 400.

39. Brinkley, *Cronkite*, 400.

40. Cited in Eric Tscheschlok, "Long Time Coming: Miami's Liberty City Riot of 1968," *Florida Historical Quarterly* 74, no. 4 (1996): 457. When President Trump used these words to threaten protestors in the wake of George Floyd's murder in 2020, multiple news sources referred to the language as having originated with Miami police chief Walter Headley in December 1967, but the claim is unsubstantiated. H. Rap Brown's phrase "Shoot, don't loot!" was already circulating earlier in 1967, and Headley was perhaps reacting to Brown's rhetoric. Brown, cited in Bryan Burrough, *Days of Rage: America's Radical Underground, the FBI, and the Forgotten Age of Revolutionary Violence* (New York: Penguin, 2016), 41.

41. Terence McArdle, "How Three Violent Days Gripped a Black Miami Neighborhood as Nixon was Nominated in 1968," *Washington Post*, August 7, 2018.

42. Cited in Sarah Katherine Mergel, "The 1968 Republican Convention," *We're History* July 21, 2016; http://werehistory.org/1968-republican-convention/.

43. Frank, cited in Epstein, *News from Nowhere*, 16. Although Frank indicates there was no coverage, Huntley and Brinkley did mention the "Miami disturbance" on-air. Further, Abernathy asked to address the Liberty City community, and NBC complied by airing a short, filmed segment in which he called for nonviolence while also acknowledging the reality of police brutality.

44. McArdle, "Three Violent Days."

45. David Farber, *Chicago '68* (Chicago: University of Chicago Press, 1988), 212-13.

46. Jerry Rubin, cited in Martin Torgoff, *Can't Find My Way Home: America in the Great Stoned Age, 1945–2000* (New York: Simon & Schuster, 2005), 229.

47. Yippie Nancy Kurshan said, "Abbie chose this really cute pig, and Jerry was really upset with him. . . . Jerry was more hardcore political, confrontational, militant. . . . Abbie was always using humor to be more acceptable to people." Cited in Pat Thomas, *Did It! From Yippie to Yuppie: Jerry Rubin, An American Revolutionary* (Seattle: Fantagraphics, 2017), 75.

48. My emphasis. Todd Gitlin, cited in Thomas, *Did It!*, 72.

49. "Interview by Professor Andrew Stern with Walter Cronkite, CBS News," September 10, 1970, 16mm film, UARC FILM 01, box 11, Bancroft Library, University of California, Berkeley; https://californiarevealed.org/islandora/object/cavpp %3A11433.

CHAPTER TWO

1. Gary Paul Gates, *Air Time: The Inside Story of CBS News* (New York: Harper & Row, 1978), 144–45.

2. Jack Gould, "TV: Huntley and Brinkley Retain Grip," *New York Times*, August 25, 1964; https://www.nytimes.com/1964/08/25/archives/tv-huntley-and -brinkley-retain-grip-ratings-show-viewers-favor-nbc.html.

3. ABC finally advanced in the ratings when Fred Silverman brought nostalgia (*Happy Days*) and "jiggle" (*Charlie's Angels*) to the network in the 1970s. Elana Levine, *Wallowing in Sex: The New Sexual Culture of 1970s American Television* (Durham, NC: Duke University Press, 2007). ABC News was boosted in the late 1970s by the arrival of Roone Arledge. Marc Gunther, *The House That Roone Built: The Inside Story of ABC News* (New York: Little Brown, 1994).

4. ABC also aired *The Dick Cavett Show* from 1969 to 1975, which was more cerebral than most talk shows. The show's appeal was probably too limited for the network era, but it survived because it was on the underdog network where viewer numbers could be lower than they were for NBC and CBS. Heather Hendershot, "Fame Is a Bee," *Nation*, November 22, 2010.

5. Gates, *Air Time*, 235.

6. *Rights in Conflict: The Walker Report to the National Commission on the Causes and Prevention of Violence* (New York: Bantam, 1968), 160.

7. In a 1969 interview, Cronkite described CBS News as "a team effort of the entire CBS News organization," whereas NBC conceived of their program "as being more of a showcase for Huntley and Brinkley." Radio TV Reports transcript, *The David Frost Show*, Monday September 22, 1969, Channel 5, WNEW-TV New York. CBS Evening News Archive, vol./box 2K122, "Transcripts 1969–71" folder. Briscoe Center.

8. Jack Gould, cited in Gates, *Air Time*, 75.

9. David Ritz, *Respect: The Life of Aretha Franklin* (New York: Little Brown, 2014), 185.

10. Jerry Wexler cited in Ritz, *Respect*, 196.

11. Walter Cronkite Papers, vol./box 2M523, "B" folder, Briscoe Center.

12. Walter Cronkite Papers, vol./box 2M523, "B" folder, Briscoe Center.

13. Walter Cronkite Papers, vol./box 2M523, "D" folder, Briscoe Center.

14. Walter Cronkite Papers, vol./box 2M523, "B" folder, Briscoe Center.

15. Walter Cronkite Papers, vol./box 2M526, "G" folder, Briscoe Center.

16. Theodore H. White, *The Making of the President 1968* (New York: Harper-Perennial, 2010), 324.

17. Similarly, Senator Inouye was selected as keynote speaker to convey a notion of progress. He was the first Japanese American member of the House of Representatives and the Senate, a decorated veteran of World War II who had lost his right arm in battle, and the first person of color to give a keynote at a Democratic National Convention. He also supported LBJ's Vietnam policy and spoke out against the hippies and the Yippies. The choice was obviously pointed but did nothing to dilute the racial crises on display at the convention.

18. Briefing book, "Credentials" section, p. 4, Socolow papers, vol./box 2014-169/3, Briscoe Center.

19. Nick Kotz, *Judgment Days: Lyndon Baines Johnson, Martin Luther King Jr., and the Laws That Changed America* (New York: Houghton Mifflin, 2005), 205.

20. Civil rights coverage tended to center on male leaders, especially King, another factor that made Hamer's appearance unique. Aniko Bodroghkozy, *Equal Time: Television and the Civil Rights Movement* (Champaign: University of Illinois Press, 2013), 122.

21. Kotz, *Judgment Days*, 206. See also Walter Mondale, "Lectures on Public Service," Series 2000, University of Minnesota. Available at http://news.minnesota.publicradio.org/collections/special/2004/campaign/president/dnc/.

22. For example, "To one newsman, the President, when asked to comment about Humphrey, had curtly remarked, 'He cries too much." White, *Making of the President 1968*, 325.

23. Robert Caro provides a less revolting example of Johnson's intimidation tactics: "Johnson *made* the couches *in the Oval Office* softer so people would sink down, and he, sitting in his rocking chair, would be higher, towering over them" (his emphasis). Interview with James Santel, "The Art of Biography No. 5," *Paris Review* 216 (Spring 2016): 150.

24. Briefing book, "Credentials" section, p. 3, Socolow papers, vol./box 2014-169/3, Briscoe Center.

25. Much has been written on this. See, for example, Joseph Crespino, *Strom Thurmond's America*, chap. 3, "Lost in Translation" (New York: Farrar, Straus, and Giroux, 2012).

26. Goodwin, cited in David Culbert, "Johnson and the Media," in *The Johnson Years*, vol. 1, *Foreign Policy, the Great Society, and the White House*, ed. Robert A. Divine (Lawrence: University of Kansas Press, 1987), 214.

27. Johnson had a triple TV setup in his White House bedroom, in the Oval Office, at his Texas ranch, and even, at one time, in the hospital. Culbert, "Johnson and the Media," 218.

28. Culbert, "Johnson and the Media," 229. Greg Robinson estimates that Okamoto took closer to 675,000 photos. "The Man behind the Camera: The Story of Yoichi Okamoto, LBJ's Shadow," http://www.discovernikkei.org/en/journal /2018/10/11/yoichi-okamoto/. See also digitized photos at the LBJ Presidential Library (http://www.lbjlibrary.net/collections/photo-archive.html) and photos in Harry Joseph Middleton, *LBJ: The White House Years* (New York: Harry N. Abrams, 1990).

29. Culbert, "Johnson and the Media," 245.

30. LBJ's concern was for his own image: "His emotional loyalty to the Democratic party was thin. . . . Johnson felt little responsibility for its welfare and growth." Lewis L. Gould, "Never a Deep Partisan: Lyndon Johnson and the Democratic Party, 1963–1969," in *The Johnson Years*, vol. 3, *LBJ at Home and Abroad* , ed. Robert A. Divine (Lawrence: University Press of Kansas, 1994), 45.

31. John R. Schmidt and Wayne W. Whalen, "Credentials Contests at the 1968—and 1972—Democratic National Conventions," *Harvard Law Review* 82, no. 7 (1969): 1466.

32. White, *Making of the President 1968*, 324.

33. James Reston Jr., *The Lone Star: The Life of John Connally* (New York: Harper & Row, 1989), 355.

34. Negaro, quoted in John Neary, *Julian Bond: Black Rebel* (William Morrow, 1971), 206.

35. Elizabeth Gritter interview with Julian Bond, *Southern Cultures*, 12, no. 1 (2006), 87.

36. "Pacifist Rights Aide: Horace Julian Bond," *New York Times*, January 12, 1966.

37. Buckley saw the decision not to seat Bond as "imprudent" but not un-Constitutional. William F. Buckley, "Georgia Legislature Justified in Refusing to Seat Julian Bond," *Los Angeles Times*, January 21, 1966.

38. "The coffee his office staff prepared for him never quite suited the governor. One former employee recalls . . . him screaming one day, 'This is the worst goddamn coffee I've ever tasted.' . . . He liked Folger's coffee, and I remember the time he found out that a woman in the office had been buying whatever type of coffee was on sale and pouring it into a Folger's can. He was furious.'" Ann Crawford and Jack Keever, "John Connally between the Acts," *Texas Monthly*, September 1973.

39. Douglas Brinkley, *Cronkite* (New York: HarperCollins, 2012), 272.

40. Richard Campanella, *The Photojournalism of Del Hall: New Orleans and beyond, 1950s–2000s* (Baton Rouge: Louisiana University Press, 2015), 81.

41. *Rights in Conflict*, 7–8.

42. Laurence, quoted in Campanella, *Photojournalism of Del Hall*, 82.

43. Laurence, quoted in Brinkley, *Cronkite*, 401.

44. Frank and Salant, quoted in Edward Jay Epstein, *News from Nowhere: Television and the News* (Chicago: Ivan R. Dee, 1973), 17.

CHAPTER THREE

1. Daniel J. Boorstin, *The Image: A Guide to Pseudo-Events in America* (New York: Vintage, 1992).

2. Lewis Chester, Godfrey Hodgson, and Bruce Page, *An American Melodrama: The Presidential Campaign of 1968* (New York: Viking, 1969), 434.

3. "TV's Top Rated Events of 1960s: From JFK to Apollo 11," *Variety*, August 27, 1969, 39.

4. William Whitworth, "Profiles: An Accident of Casting," *New Yorker*, August 3, 1968, 37.

5. Obviously, we now clearly identify opposition to environmentalism as "conservative." That Nixon created the EPA is often incorrectly pointed to as evidence of liberalism on his part. See Rick Perlstein, "Introduction," in *Richard Nixon: Speeches, Writings, Documents* (Princeton, NJ: Princeton University Press, 2008), xlvi.

6. Whitworth, "Profiles: An Accident of Casting," 35.

7. David Culbert, "Johnson and the Media," in *The Johnson Years*, vol. 1, *Foreign Policy, the Great Society, and the White House*, ed. Robert A. Divine (Lawrence: University Press of Kansas, 1981), 227. Johnson's counsel and speechwriter, Harry McPherson, said the president "liked and trusted" fellow Texan Walter Cronkite but considered Brinkley a "smart ass."

8. Paul R. Wieck, "An Open Democratic Convention," *New Republic*, July 6, 1968, 15. Walter Cronkite papers, vol./box 2M669, Briscoe Center.

9. For a play-by-play account, see the chapter "Trompe l'Oeil," in Chester, Hodgson, and Page, *An American Melodrama*; and Rick Perlstein, *Nixonland: The Rise of a President and the Fracturing of America* (New York: Scribner, 2008), 283–85.

10. John R. Schmidt and Wayne W. Whalen, "Credentials Contests at the 1968—and 1972—Democratic National Conventions," *Harvard Law Review* 82, no. 7 (1969), 1443.

11. Abraham Holtzman, "Party Responsibility and Loyalty: New Rules in the Democratic Party," *Journal of Politics* 22, no. 3 (1960): 486.

12. On keeping legitimate Black candidates off the Alabama ballot, in defiance of the US Supreme Court, see Sheryll Cashin, *The Agitator's Daughter: A Memoir of Four Generations of One Extraordinary African-American Family* (New York: Public Affairs, 2008), 197.

13. On the national party's drive to exert authority, see Jaime Sánchez Jr. "Revisiting McGovern-Fraser: Party Nationalization and the Rhetoric of Reform," *Journal of Policy History* 32, no. 1 (2020): 1–24.

14. Norman Mailer, *Miami and the Siege of Chicago* (New York: Random House, 2016), 134.

15. The vote to remove the "white supremacy" label had been very close, and the state Democratic Party operatives in favor of the change made clear that it was a move designed to gain Black votes, since the GOP had made inroads into the state since Goldwater in 1964. "White Supremacy Rooster Taken off Alabama Emblem," *Chicago Daily Defender*, January 24, 1966.

16. Cashin, *The Agitator's Daughter*, 195.

17. Sanford Socolow briefing book, "Credentials" section, pp. 5–6, Socolow papers, vol./box 2014-169/3, Briscoe Center. See also Hanes Walton Jr., "The National Democratic Party of Alabama and Party Failure in America" in *When Parties Fail: Emerging Alternative Organizations*, ed. Kay Lawson and Peter H. Merkl (Princeton, NJ: Princeton University Press, 1988).

18. Andrew Doyle, "Bear Bryant: Symbol for an Embattled South," *Colby Quarterly* 32, no. 1 (1996): 76, 86.

19. Letter from Eugene (Bull) Connor to Mayor Richard Daley, June 24, 1968. UIC, Daley Collection, SlsslB85, Series II, Sub-Series 1, "National Democratic Convention Delegates, 1968" folder.

20. Rick Perlstein, "America's Forgotten Liberal," *New York Times*, May 26, 2011; https://www.nytimes.com/2011/05/27/opinion/27Perlstein.html.

21. Adam Bernstein, "Television Journalist Hal Walker Dies at 70," *Washington Post*, November 28, 2003; https://www.washingtonpost.com/archive/local/2003/11/28/television-journalist-hal-walker-dies-at-70/66055219-2d73-4204-baf7-aa846b0b6f52/.

22. Simeon Booker, "Ticker Tape USA" feature, *Jet*, September 12, 1968, 13. Booker noted also that "an estimated 100 Black newsmen covered the Dem confab compared to 38 covering the GOP sessions."

23. Sanford Socolow interview with Dr. Ralph Engelman, August 27, 2008, Television Academy Foundation; https://interviews.televisionacademy.com/interviews/sanford-socolow.

24. The home of Peter Hall, a Black lawyer from the Vann group, had twice been bombed. Gertrude Wilson, "Convention Sidelights from Chicago," *New York Amsterdam News*, September 7, 1968.

25. "As Blacks Cool It at Dem Meet Black Militants Disgusted with Both Parties," *Jet*, September 12, 1968, 27.

26. Chicago's Film Group made the 1969 film. Their 1966–1969 films can be viewed online at www.chicagofilmarchives.org.

27. "As Blacks Cool It," 28.

28. Valerie Bradley, "Militant Black Women Move to Forefront at Dem Confab," *Jet*, September 12, 1968, 23.

29. Gail McHenry, cited in "A Teen-Ager Takes Close Look at National Politics," *Ebony*, October 1968, 60.

30. Of these 350, 212 were delegates; the rest were alternates. By contrast, in Miami there were only 26 Black delegates.

31. Simeon Booker, "What Blacks Gained at Dem Convention," *Jet*, September 12, 1968, 18, 19.

32. Booker, "What Blacks Gained," 20.

33. Letter from Walter Cronkite to Dwight D. Eisenhower, July 8, 1968, "September 1, 1968 to September 30, 1968 General Carbon Copy File" folder, CBS Evening News collection, vol./box 2K129, Briscoe Center.

34. December 24, 1967, CBS memo from Martin Plissner to Jay Levine, Walter Cronkite papers, vol./box 2M669, Briscoe Center.

35. Bill Leonard, cited in Charles McDowell Jr. "Carnival of Excess: TV and the Conventions," *Atlantic Monthly*, July 1968, 2, Walter Cronkite papers, vol./box 2M751, "General Research" folder, Briscoe Center.

36. Eugene McCarthy, cited in Chester, Hodgson, and Page, *An American Melodrama*, 532.

37. George Katsiaficas, *The Imagination of the New Left: A Global Analysis of 1968* (Boston: South End Press, 1999), 62. Note also that the barricades built in Lincoln Park on Monday night had been inspired by the May '68 barricades in Paris. John Schultz, *No One Was Killed: The Democratic National Convention August 1968* (Chicago: University of Chicago Press, 2009 [1969]), 105.

38. The NBC News segment included interesting references to the use of both regular and underground Czech radio during the Russian invasion. On the role of the uncensored Czech press during the Prague spring, see Madeleine Korbel Albright, "The Role of the Press in Political Change: Czechoslovakia 1968," PhD thesis, Columbia University, 1976.

39. "Veteran CBS News Figure Harry Reasoner Dies at 68," *Los Angeles Times*, August 7, 1991.

40. Reasoner famously disliked Barbara Walters, which enhanced his reputation for misogyny. Douglass K. Daniel, *Harry Reasoner: A Life in the News* (Austin: University of Texas Press, 2007). See also Harry Reasoner, *Before the Colors Fade* (New York: Alfred A. Knopf, 1981).

41. Severo, "Harry Reasoner, 68, Newscaster Known for His Wry Wit, Is Dead," *New York Times*, August 7, 1991; https://www.nytimes.com/1991/08/07/obituaries/harry-reasoner-68-newscaster-known-for-his-wry-wit-is-dead.html.

42. Roger Mudd, *The Place to Be: Washington, CBS, and the Glory Days of Television News* (New York: Public Affairs, 2008), 170.

43. Sanford Socolow interview with Dr. Ralph Engelman, August 27, 2008, Television Academy Foundation; https://interviews.televisionacademy.com/interviews/sanford-socolow.

44. Socolow interview with Engelman.

45. Raymond A. Schroth, *The American Journey of Eric Sevareid* (South Royalton, VT: Steerforth Press, 1995), 64.

CHAPTER FOUR

1. John Schultz, *No One Was Killed: The Democratic National Convention August 1968* (Chicago: University of Chicago Press, 2009 [1969]), 175.

2. Ed Sanders, *1968: A History in Verse* (Santa Rosa, CA: Black Sparrow, 1997), 188.

3. Robert D. Novak, *The Prince of Darkness: 50 Years Reporting in Washington* (New York: Random House, 2007), 170.

4. Herbert Bile, cited in Frank Kusch, *Battleground Chicago: The Police and the 1968 Democratic National Convention* (Chicago: University of Chicago Press, 2008), 123.

5. Caetlin Benson-Allott, *Remote Control* (New York: Bloomsbury, 2015), 84.

6. Sanford Socolow interview with Dr. Ralph Engelman August 27, 2008, Television Academy Foundation, https://interviews.televisionacademy.com/interviews/sanford-socolow.

7. Garry Paul Gates, *Air Time: The Inside Story of CBS News* (New York: Harper & Row, 1978), 37–38.

8. Aniko Bodroghkozy, *Equal Time: Television and the Civil Rights Movement* (Urbana: University of Illinois Press, 2012), 76.

9. Letter from Anna Clark, Walter Cronkite papers, vol./box 2M532, "Vietnam" folder, Briscoe Center.

10. When Rather was slugged, the anchorman's "objectivity snapped." Walter Cronkite, *A Reporter's Life* (New York: Ballantine Books, 1997), 189.

11. Rachel Bade, John Wagner, Colby Itkowitz, and Toluse Olorunnipa, "House Judiciary Committee Abruptly Adjourns After Marathon Debate, Will Vote on Articles of Impeachment Friday Morning," *Washington Post*, December 13, 2019, https://www.washingtonpost.com/politics/house-judiciary-committee-abruptly-adjourns-after-marathon-debate-will-vote-on-articles-of-impeachment-friday-morning/2019/12/12/038962d6-1ce6-11ea-8d58-5ac3600967a1_story.html.

12. Ralph Ellison, "As the Spirit Moves Mahalia," *Saturday Review*, September 27, 1958, 43.

13. Mahalia Jackson with Evan McLeod Wyie, *Movin' On Up* (New York: Hawthorn, 1966), 119–22.

14. I have not found confirmation that DNC planners deliberately undercut Jackson; it's a reasonable guess following the reactions to Franklin's performance. Jackson herself noted, "A big orchestra is not for me. I sing better just standing flat-footed with a piano or an organ." Jackson with Wyie, *Movin' On Up*, 109.

15. Interview with Donald Peterson, 1993, Special Collections & Archives, McIntyre Library, University of Wisconsin-Eau Claire.

16. Interview with Peterson.

17. As the police told it, for "the entire fucking year" leading up to the convention, journalists had been "on the commie's side," so out on the street journalists were treated "like every other SOB." When journalists were harmed, the problem

was not the violence but the media's reporting of it: "Boy, when that slimy Rather bugger from CBS got belted by a security guy on the convention floor, they couldn't play that son-of-a-bitchin' clip enough times. I saw Rather's head flopping on the news for nights. They made it look like he got whacked a bunch of times, and he only took one little pop." Police officers, cited in Kusch, *Battleground Chicago*, 106, 147.

18. Perkins, cited in Sam Roberts, "Jack Perkins, NBC Reporter and 'Biography' Host, Dies at 85," *New York Times*, August 29, 2019; https://www.nytimes.com/2019/08/21/business/media/jack-perkins-dies.html.

19. Bernard M. Timberg, *Television Talk: A History of the Talk Show* (Austin: University of Texas Press, 2002), 91, 101; Barbara Walters, *Audition: A Memoir* (New York: Knopf, 2008).

20. Alden Whitman, "Aline Saarinen, Art Critic, Dies at 58," *New York Times*, July 15, 1972; https://www.nytimes.com/1972/07/15/archives/aline-saarinen-art-critic-dies-at-58.html.

21. Reuven Frank, *Out of Thin Air: The Brief Wonderful Life of Network News* (New York: Simon & Schuster, 1991), 237. In 1971, Saarinen was appointed head of NBC's Paris News Bureau.

22. In 2020, Fox News's Tucker Carlson defeated a defamation suit when his lawyers successfully argued that no one actually understood him as a "news" man. Michael M. Grynbaum and Nicholas Bogel-Burroughs, "Karen McDougal's Defamation Suit against Fox News Is Dismissed," September 24, 2020; https://www.nytimes.com/2020/09/24/business/media/tucker-carlson-karen-mcdougal-lawsuit.html. *Slate* nailed the story with their headline: "Judge Rules Tucker Carlson Is Not a Credible Source of News." Elliot Hannon, September 25, 2020; https://slate.com/news-and-politics/2020/09/judge-rules-fox-news-tucker-carlson-not-source-of-news-defamation-suit-mcdougal-trump.html.

23. Letter from Lois Swanston to CBS, September 27, 1968. Walter Cronkite papers, vol./box 2M532, "S" folder Briscoe Center.

24. The networks tended to reference hippies and Yippies as protestors more than the Mobe and McCarthy supporters, and on Wednesday night the newsmen didn't properly convey to viewers that the mostly clean-cut and neatly dressed anti-war demonstrators on Michigan Avenue had come from across the street in Grant Park, whereas the scruffier hippies and Yippies were a few miles away in Lincoln Park.

25. Carl Albert with Danney Goble, *Little Giant: The Life and Times of Speaker Carl Albert* (Norman: University of Oklahoma Press, 1999), 304–5.

26. John Dickerson, *On Her Trail: My Mother Nancy Dickerson TV News' First Woman Star* (New York: Simon & Schuster, 2006), 101.

27. Roger Mudd, *The Place to Be: Washington, CBS, and the Glory Days of Television News* (New York: Public Affairs, 2008), 37.

28. Dan Rather with Mickey Herskowitz, *The Camera Never Blinks: Adventures of a TV Journalist* (New York: William Morrow, 1977), 77.

29. A handheld image, "insistently gestured toward the presence of both camera and cameraperson, and that literal notion of presence became the source of its authenticity and its power as a technique." Adam Charles Hart, "Extensions of Our Body Moving, Dancing: The American Avant-Garde's Theories of Handheld Subjectivity," *Discourse* 41, no. 1 (2019): 38–39.

30. Raymond A. Schroth, *The American Journey of Eric Sevareid* (South Royalton, VT: Steerforth Press, 1995), 357. The categories are useful, but not as hard and fast as Schroth implies.

31. Schroth, *American Journey of Eric Sevareid*, 212.

32. Mudd, *Place to Be*, 158.

CHAPTER FIVE

1. Norman Mailer, *Miami and the Siege of Chicago: An Informal History of the Republican Conventions of 1968* (New York: Random House, 2016), 29.

2. Hunter S. Thompson, *Fear and Loathing in Las Vegas* (New York: HarperCollins, 1993), 161.

3. Mailer, *Miami and the Siege of Chicago*, 133.

4. Murray Kempton, "The Decline and Fall of the Democratic Party" in *Rebellions, Perversities and Main Events* (New York: Crown, 1994), 490–91.

5. Duncan worked most closely with three people. Christie Basham had started in the business in 1957 as a researcher for David Brinkley and would later produce *Meet the Press*. Raysa Bonow made her name producing feminist programming, and had earlier produced a TV special based on Duncan's book *Yankee Nomad*. Carmine Ercolano was a photographic technician for *Life*. David Douglas Duncan, *Self-Portrait: USA* (New York: Harry N. Abrams, 1969), 238–39; Bryan Marquard, "Raysa Bonow, Pioneering Producer of Feminist TV Shows; at 80," *Boston Globe*, July 12, 2011; http://archive.boston.com/bostonglobe/obituaries/articles/2011/07/12/raysa_bonow_80_pioneering_tv_executive_producer/; Haynes Johnson, "Broadcaster Christie R. Basham, 68," *Washington Post* July 17, 2000; https://www.washingtonpost.com/archive/local/2000/07/17/broadcaster-christie-r-basham-68/1b3c69a2-3b88-4c72-bfac-e679e5b2ab6a/.

6. Duncan, "Foreword," in *Self-Portrait: USA*, n.p.

7. Duncan, *Self-Portrait: USA*, 239.

8. White describes Lowenstein as "a faintly preposterous character" who, at the ripe old age of thirty-eight, reminded him "of a college football star, unable to shake off the remembered electricity of fall afternoons in the stadium and settle into the tedium of middle-aged life." Theodore H. White, *The Making of the President 1968* (New York: HarperCollins, 2010), 81–82.

9. White, *Making of the President 1968*, 86.

10. Other, less high-profile McCarthy delegates like Murray Kempton chose to express themselves in the streets instead. Kempton said dramatically, "It was the *right* to march, not the *idea* for which anyone might march, that was my man-

date; . . . the point had to be that I would do the same thing for Lester Maddox." Kempton, "Decline and Fall," 495–96. Kempton was participating in the Dick Gregory march. Since both Peterson and Gregory were stopped around Eighteenth Street on Thursday, their actions are sometimes confused. The *New York Times* reported three marches that day which were, in order: Peterson's, starting around 4:00 p.m., with thousands participating; a second march of several hundred leaving from Grant Park about an hour after Peterson's, also stopped by police near Eighteenth Street, with marchers retreating back to the park; and the third, led later that night by Gregory, in which about three thousand participated, of which some hundred and fifty were arrested, including nine delegates. It was this third action that was most heated and where marchers were heavily hit with tear gas. J. Anthony Lukas, "Thousands March: Scores Are Arrested, Some Delegates—Tear Gas Is Used," *New York Times*, August 30, 1968, https://timesmachine.nytimes.com/timesmachine /1968/08/30/issue.html.

11. "Lyndon B. Johnson and Richard J. Daley on 29 August 1968," Conversation WH6808-05-13344, *Presidential Recordings Digital Edition* [*Johnson Telephone Tapes: 1968*, ed. Kent B. Germany, Nicole Hemmer, and Ken Hughes] (Charlottesville: University of Virginia Press, 2014–); http://prde.upress.virginia.edu/conversations /4006048.

12. *Law and Order vs. Dissent* (Film Group, 1969); http://www.chicagofilmarchives .org/collections/index.php/Detail/Object/Show/object_id/2601. The next day, Sullivan went further: "The intellectuals of America hate Richard J. Daley because he was elected by the people—unlike Walter Cronkite." Cited in R. W. Apple Jr., "Daley Defends His Police; Humphrey Scores Clashes," *New York Times*, August 30, 1968.

13. Douglas Brinkley, *Cronkite* (New York: HarperCollins, 2012), 404. Daley wasn't keen on any of the networks but claimed he chose Cronkite because his wife was a fan.

14. Mike Royko, *Boss: Richard J. Daley of Chicago* (New York: Penguin, 1988), 175.

15. This same memo called out "non-action by police for on-street parking permits. CBS requested parking at 23 locations for remote trucks and other equipment and so far has received no permission anywhere. Requests went in last Monday. In Miami requests were honored immediately." The memo further noted "a general pattern of obstructionism: . . . no hard and firm refusals . . . but a lot of delaying tactics in which no answer . . . brings us closer to a deadline after which a positive answer would be of no use." [CBS's ellipses] Walter Cronkite papers, vol./box 2M669, "1968 Democratic National Convention" folder, Briscoe Center.

16. The *New York Times* later acknowledged that they had "grossly exaggerated the number of witnesses (38) and what they had perceived." Robert D. McFadden, "Winston Moseley, Who Killed Kitty Genovese, Dies in Prison at 81." *New York Times*, April 4, 2016. https://www.nytimes.com/2016/04/05/nyregion/winston -moseley-81-killer-of-kitty-genovese-dies-in-prison.html.

17. The garbage strike was not only a practical crisis but also a media and public relations crisis, as images of the city drowning in its own trash proliferated on na-

tional TV. Heather Hendershot, "Strikes, Riots, and Muggers: How John Lindsay Weathered New York City's Image Crisis," in *Television History, The Peabody Archive, and Cultural Memory*, ed. Jeffrey Jones, Ethan Thompson, and Lucas Hatlen (Athens: University of Georgia Press, 2019), 174–90.

18. Brinkley, *Cronkite*, 404.

19. Reuven Frank, *Out of Thin Air: The Brief Wonderful Life of Network News* (New York: Simon & Schuster, 1991), 283.

20. Much of the footage aired by NBC was long takes, but there was some minimal editing, and the networks did have 16mm news cameras out in the streets throughout the convention. The networks aired only a small amount of that footage.

21. Robert A. Caro, *The Passage of Power* (New York: Random House, 2012).

22. Arthur M. Schlesinger Jr., *Robert Kennedy and His Times* (New York: Houghton Mifflin, 1978), 623.

23. "Lyndon B. Johnson and Sol J. Taishoff on 6 September 1968," Conversation WH6809-01-13407-13408, *Presidential Recordings Digital Edition* [*Johnson Telephone Tapes: 1968*, ed. Kent B. Germany, Nicole Hemmer, and Ken Hughes] (Charlottesville: University of Virginia Press, 2014-); http://prde.upress.virginia.edu/conversations/4006058.

24. One week later he made similar threats in a call to *Broadcasting* editor Sol J. Taishoff, reiterating that the airwaves could not be used "just to promote" the Kennedys. Further, news had recently broken that an NBC employee had planted a bug in the Credentials Committee meeting room. Johnson surmised, "This damn microphone plant—hell, that's Gestapo. They oughtn't do things like that" and suggested there would be blowback, and "you'll have a British system overnight," meaning a public, not for-profit system. Johnson and Taishoff Conversation WH6809-01-13407-13408.

25. "Lyndon Johnson and Richard Russell on 22 January 1964," Tape WH6401.19, Citation #1477, *Presidential Recordings Digital Edition* [*The Kennedy Assassination and the Transfer of Power*, vol. 3, ed. Kent B. Germany and Robert David Johnson] (Charlottesville: University of Virginia Press, 2014-); http://prde.upress.virginia.edu/conversations/9030212.

26. David Halberstam, *The Powers That Be* (New York: Knopf, 1975), 38.

27. "Lyndon Johnson and Walter Jenkins on 6 February 1964," Tape WH6402.08, Citation #1915, *Presidential Recordings Digital Edition* [*Toward the Great Society*, vol. 4, ed. Robert David Johnson and Kent B. Germany] (Charlottesville: University of Virginia Press, 2014-); http://prde.upress.virginia.edu/conversations/9040077.

28. Print media are a separate story. See Sam Lebovic, "When the 'Mainstream Media' Was Conservative: Media Criticism in the Age of Reform," in *Media Nation: The Political History of News in Modern American*, ed. Bruce J. Schulman and Julian E. Zelizer (Philadelphia: University of Pennsylvania Press, 2017), 63–76; and Matthew Pressman, *On Press: The Liberal Values That Shaped the News* (Cambridge, MA: Harvard University Press, 2018).

29. Halberstam, *Powers That Be*, 438. Asked if the newsroom was aware that

Stanton was close to LBJ and that the president complained about negative coverage to Stanton, Sandy Socolow replies in the affirmative and offers an example. The Pentagon raised hell about a story on the cutting off of Vietcong ears by US soldiers, claiming that a GI in the story was Australian, not American. CBS spent significant time and money to zoom in on their footage, identify the helicopter, etc. to confirm that the man in question was indeed US military. Socolow did not really get at the implications of the question—did Stanton have influence?—but stood up for the integrity of the news division: they did not back down, and they proved they had been right. Sanford Socolow interview conducted by Dr. Ralph Engelman, August 27, 2008, Television Academy, https://interviews.televisionacademy.com/interviews/sanford-socolow?clip=chapter4#about.

30. Brinkley, *Cronkite*, 287.

31. Socolow interview with Engelman.

32. "Interview by Professor Andrew Stern with Walter Cronkite, CBS News," September 10, 1970, 16mm film, UARC FILM 01 Box 11, Bancroft Library, University of California, Berkeley; https://californiarevealed.org/islandora/object/cavpp%3A11433.

33. Notable controversial *CBS Reports* episodes included "Harvest of Shame" (1960), "Hunger in America" (1968), "Banks and the Poor" (1970), and "The Selling of the Pentagon" (1971). Chad Raphael, *Investigated Reporting: Muckrakers, Regulators, and the Struggle Over Television Documentary* (Urbana: University of Illinois Press, 2005).

34. There is apparently no paper archival trail confirming that Stanton pressured Cronkite about midwestern delegate interviews, although Halberstam gives one example of direct pressure over a trivial matter at the convention. Halberstam, *Powers That Be*, 428.

35. Academy of Motion Picture Arts and Sciences, "The Charles Guggenheim and Robert F. Kennedy Story"; https://www.oscars.org/news/charles-guggenheim-and-robert-f-kennedy-story.

36. The orchestra provided a steady stream of show tunes, making a painful contrast between the music ("Everything's Coming up Roses") and events. The same band had played Eisenhower's inaugural ball in 1952, and the 1956 Chicago DNC. "Democrats Sign Ike's 1952 Band Led by Bay Stater," *Boston Globe*, August 12, 1956, B38. Five months after the convention, Breese died of a heart attack on stage, moments before his signature banjo solo. "Bandleader Breese Dies During Show: Suffers Heart Attack While Conducting," *Chicago Tribune*, January 12, 1969, A14.

37. John Goodman, "An Urbanized Thoreau," *New Leader*, September 23, 1968, 23–24.

38. Adam Cohen and Elizabeth Taylor, *American Pharaoh: Mayor Richard J. Daley His Battle for Chicago and the Nation* (New York: Little, Brown, 2000), 321.

39. Daley, cited in Natalie Y. Moore, *The South Side: A Portrait of Chicago and American Segregation* (New York: St. Martin's, 2016), 50.

40. Cohen and Taylor, *American Pharaoh*, 359.

41. Cohen and Taylor, *American Pharaoh*, 395.

42. Metcalfe briefly appeared in *Olympia* and makes a cameo in Riefenstahl's autobiography. Leni Riefenstahl, *Leni Riefenstahl: A Memoir* (New York: St. Martin's, 1993), 195.

43. Matthew Wasniewski, ed. "Ralph Harold Metcalfe, 1910–1978," *Black Americans in Congress, 1870–2007* (Washington, DC: Government Printing Office, 2008), 427.

44. Metcalfe, quoted in Gordon K. Mantler, "'Organize the People': The 1975 City Council Races in Multiracial Chicago," *Journal of Civil and Human Rights* 3, no. 2 (2017): 7.

45. Cohen and Taylor, *American Pharaoh*, 464.

46. *American Revolution II (Part 1): Battle of Chicago* (Film Group, 1969); http://www.chicagofilmarchives.org/collections/index.php/Detail/Object/Show /object_id/3589. All three parts can be viewed at www.chicagofilmarchives.org. See also their *Urban Crisis* series made for the educational film market: http:// www.chicagofilmarchives.org/collections/index.php/Detail/Object/Show/object _id/689. For more on Film Group, see Jonathan Kahana, *Intelligence Work: The Politics of American Documentary* (New York: Columbia University Press, 2008), 156–64.

47. For a Lowenstein overview, see "Allard Lowenstein on *Firing Line*: A Retrospective," April 22, 1980, Program Number S0415, 942, *Firing Line* collection, Hoover Institution, Stanford University. Also, Heather Hendershot, *Open to Debate: How William F. Buckley Put Liberal America on the Firing Line* (New York: HarperCollins, 2016), 48–49.

48. Lemuel Tucker was another Black reporter who worked the convention floor for NBC in 1968. He had been hired as an NBC page in 1965. "Lemuel Tucker, TV Correspondent, 52," *New York Times*, March 6, 1991; https://www.nytimes.com /1991/03/06/obituaries/lemuel-tucker-tv-correspondent-52.html.

49. Voting at the convention moved alphabetically, but states had the option of passing, and then Bush would circle back later to everyone who had skipped on the first round. Hence, a vote from Alabama here came after a vote from Wisconsin.

50. Thompson, *Fear and Loathing: On the Campaign Trail '72*, 101. Thompson started a rumor that Muskie was hooked on the hallucinogen ibogaine.

51. In a February 1967 speech to Stanford students, Humphrey had not done well with references to the "go-go crowd" but at least had cut a terrible opener, "Greetings, Now Generation!," which appears in his typed copy of the speech but not in the transcript of the event (he made the cut spontaneously). "Stanford University Meeting: Student Panel, Stanford, California, February 20, 1967," Hubert H. Humphrey Papers, Speech Text Files, 1941–1978, Gale Family Library, Minnesota Historical Society.

52. Paul Cowan, "Chicago 1968: Moderates, Militants Walk a Bloody Route To-

gether," *Village Voice*, September 5, 1968; https://www.villagevoice.com/2020/06/01/chicago-1968-moderates-militants-walk-a-bloody-route-together/.

53. This description was slightly askew. William Davidson, a psychiatrist, had traveled with McCarthy throughout the campaign and was on hand to help with the wounded, as was the senator's brother, Austin, a surgeon. Albert Eisele, *Almost to the Presidency: A Biography of Two American Politicians* (Blue Earth, MI: Piper Company), 357.

54. David Douglas Duncan, *I Protest!* (New American Library, 1968), n.p.

55. Jerome Cavanagh, quoted in "The Fire This Time," *Time*, August 4, 1967, 13.

56. University of Mississippi, "Covering the South," April 5, 1987; https://www.c-span.org/video/?171727-6/covering-south&event=171727&playEvent.

57. See official photo held by National Archives, "President Lyndon B. Johnson and Family Watch the Democratic National Convention on Television"; National Archives Identifier: 6335394 Local identifier: A6701–31.

58. White, *Making of the President 1968*, 360.

59. Lewis Chester, Godfrey Hodgson, and Bruce Page, *An American Melodrama: The Presidential Campaign of 1968* (New York: Viking, 1969), 599.

60. Chester, Hodgson, and Page, *American Melodrama*, 591.

61. City of Chicago, *The Strategy of Confrontation: Chicago and the Democratic National Convention* (Chicago: City of Chicago, 1968), 37–38.

62. White, *Making of the President 1968*, 362.

63. George Rising, *Clean for Gene: Eugene McCarthy's 1968 Presidential Campaign* (Westport, CT: Praeger, 1997), 61.

64. Eisele, *Almost to the Presidency*, 295.

65. Eisele, *Almost to the Presidency*, 564.

CHAPTER SIX

1. David Greenberg, *Nixon's Shadow: The History of an Image* (New York: W. W. Norton, 2003), 378.

2. Bart Barnes, "Journalist Helped Usher in Heyday of Network News," *Washington Post*, June 13, 2003; https://www.washingtonpost.com/archive/politics/2003/06/13/journalist-helped-usher-in-heyday-of-network-news/6960cc59-67b1-4b01-93ff-6fef486c454e/.

3. "Lyndon B. Johnson and W. Ramsey Clark on 29 August 1968," Conversation WH6808-04-13334, *Presidential Recordings Digital Edition* [*Johnson Telephone Tapes: 1968*, ed. Kent B. Germany, Nicole Hemmer, and Ken Hughes] (Charlottesville: University of Virginia Press, 2014–); http://prde.upress.virginia.edu/conversations/4006043.

4. John P. Robinson, "Public Reaction to Political Protest: Chicago 1968," *Public Opinion Quarterly* 34, no. 1 (1970): 2–3.

5. In 1960, *TV Guide* circulated more than 7 million copies a week. By the late 1970s, it was in 20 million homes. Glenn C. Altschuler and David I. Grossvogel,

Changing Channels: America in TV Guide (Urbana: University of Illinois Press, 1992), 3. The 14 million figure comes from NBC President Julian Goodman, memo to Gen. David Sarnoff, Chairman of the Board, Radio Corporation of America, December 13, 1968, Reuven Frank Papers, Tufts University, box 2 Research and Reference files, 1943–2005, MS137/001, "TV Guide Chicago '68" folder.

6. Altschuler and Grossvogel, *Changing Channels*, xiv.

7. "Decisions, Reports, Memorandum Opinions, Orders, and Other Selected Material," *Federal Communications Commission Reports*, 2nd Series 16 (1969): 650–63.

8. Reuven Frank, "Chicago: A Post-Mortem," *TV Guide*, December 14, 1968, 40.

9. Reuven Frank Papers, Tufts University, box 2 Research and Reference files, 1943–2005, MS137/001, "TV Guide Chicago '68" folder.

10. William Boddy, *Fifties Television: The Industry and Its Critics* (Urbana: University of Illinois Press, 1990).

11. Reuven Frank, *Out of Thin Air: The Brief Wonderful Life of Network News* (New York: Simon & Schuster, 1991), 277.

12. Hubert Humphrey cited in R. W. Apple Jr., "Humphrey Greeted by Daley but Hails Party's Dissenters," *New York Times*, November 2, 1968; https://timesmachine .nytimes.com/timesmachine/1968/11/02/76901146.html?pageNumber=1.

13. Adam Cohen and Elizabeth Taylor, *American Pharaoh: Mayor Richard J. Daley, His Battle for Chicago and the Nation* (New York: Little, Brown and Company, 2000), 483.

14. The letters and address log are housed at the University of Illinois at Chicago, Special Collections and University Archives; see UIC, Daley Collection, Slss1B60, Series I Political Office Series, Sub-Series 1 Political Office Papers box.

15. Letter from Flora Phillips, Davenport, IA, April 27, 1968, UIC, Daley Collection, Slss1B60, Series I Political Office Series, Sub-Series 1 Political Office Papers box, "Chicago Riots—letter of support for mayor's actions during riots, April 1968," folder 60-9 [1 of 3].

16. Letter from Ann F. Brech, Chicago, IL, April 26, 1968, UIC, Daley Collection.

17. Letter from E. L. Culbreth to Richard Daley, August 31, 1968, UIC, Daley Collection, Slss1B66, Series I Political Office, Sub-Series 1 Political Office Papers box, "Democratic National Convention Demonstrations—correspondence and news clippings" folder, 66-2.

18. "WRAL-TV Viewpoint: An Editorial Expression of Free Enterprise in Raleigh-Durham," August 29, 1968, UIC, Daley Collection, Slss1B65, Series I Political Office, Sub-Series 1 Political Office Papers box, "Democratic National Convention Demonstrations—correspondence and news clippings" folder, 65-2.

19. Letter from S. I. Hayakawa to Richard Daley, September 9, 1968, UIC, Daley Collection.

20. Letter from Col. C. G. Dietrich to Richard Daley, September 7, 1968, UIC, Daley Collection, Slss1B65, Series I Political Office, Sub-Series 1 Political Office Pa-

pers box, "Democratic National Convention Demonstrations—correspondence and news clippings" folder, 65-1.

21. Letter from Dr. Harold S. Vaughan to Richard Daley, August 31, 1968, UIC, Daley Collection.

22. Greeting card signed only with illegible first name, UIC, Daley Collection, Slss1B68, Series I Political Office, Sub-Series 1 Political Office Papers box, "Democratic National Convention Demonstrations—news clippings sent by public" folder, 68-1.

23. Frank, *Out of Thin Air*, 285.

24. Poster created by "The Official Conrad Hilton Signpainters Herman, Eddie, Russell"; UIC, Daley Collection, Slss1B65, Series I Political Office, Sub-Series 1 Political Office Papers box, "Democratic National Convention Demonstrations—correspondence and news clippings" folder.

25. Frank, *Out of Thin Air*, 285. On independents bypassing the networks, see Gerry Nadel, "Who Owns Prime Time? The Threat of the Occasional Networks," *New York Magazine*, May 30, 1977, 33-36.

26. "Daley's Tver Blames 'Hard-Core Radicals,'" *Daily News*, September 16, 1968, clipping, UIC, Daley Collection, Slss1B65, Series I Political Office, Sub-Series 1 Political Office Papers box, "Democratic National Convention Demonstrations—correspondence and news clippings" folder, 65-1.

27. Heather Hendershot, *What's Fair on the Air? Cold War Right-Wing Broadcasting and the Public Interest* (Chicago: University of Chicago Press, 2011).

28. Mrs. and Mr. Lew Wasserman (of Universal Studios) had dropped by earlier that day for a swim (http://www.lbjlibrary.net/collections/daily-diary.html). It's unclear what time the program aired across the country. The president had a video recording system and so was not beholden to the live TV schedule.

29. Frank, *Out of Thin Air*, 285.

30. Frank, *Out of Thin Air*, 285-86.

31. See Ushijima's testimony at the Chicago hearings of the Commission on the Wartime Relocation and Internment of Civilians in 1981; https://collections.carli.illinois.edu/digital/collection/nei_japan/id/2009.

32. Henry Ushijima, "Producing the Sponsored Documentary Film," *Journal of the SMPTE* 68 (June 1959): 394.

33. The film can be seen at: https://rjd.library.uic.edu/a-new-look-at-chicago/.

34. UIC, Daley Collection, Slss1B83, Series II Democratic Party Series, Sub-Series 1 Democratic Party Papers box, "Democratic Headquarters, 1968-1971," folder. Total expenditures for the film came to just under $100,000, paid in installments. The source of the final $10,000 due to Ushijima is unclear.

35. Bonerz, who had made just a handful of TV appearances before August 1968, would go on to play Jerry the Dentist on the *Bob Newhart Show*, and following that, to find a successful career as a sitcom director.

36. Cohen and Taylor, *American Pharaoh*, 483. Daley's question was not strictly

rhetorical; he *did* plant trees to beautify the city. In his 1972 budget statement to the Chicago City Council, the mayor described "the largest tree planting program in the city's history." See "Text of the Budget Statement by Mayor Richard J. Daley, Tuesday, November 14, 1972," 6, UIC, Earl Bush Collection (hereafter cited as UIC, Bush Papers), "Bush [Chronological Files], 1972, 1970s" folder, 6–36, box 6.

37. The mayor's office issued annual print reports funded by taxpayers. Some reports were also filmed, like 1963's *A New Look at Chicago*. There are references to filmed reports in the mayor's office archival papers up until 1978. In 1960, 1,500,000 copies of a 40-page, full-color, annual report were distributed via the *Chicago Tribune* and its afternoon broadsheet, *Chicago American*. See William H. Stuart, "Heard and Seen" newsletter, May 27, 1961, issue 10, vol. 21, UIC, Bush Papers, "Bush [undated] miscellaneous" folder, 11–90, box 11. *Crisis in Chicago* was presumably also funded by taxpayers.

38. Jack Mabley, cited in Rick Perlstein, *Nixonland: The Rise of a President and the Fracturing of America* (New York: Scribner, 2008), 337.

39. Jack Mabley, "Bares Secrets of 'Red-Haters': They Think Ike Is a Communist," *Chicago Daily News*, July 25, 1960; and Jack Mabley, "Strange Threat To Democracy: Anti-Red Group Hits Leaders," *Chicago Daily News*, July 26, 1961. Edward H. Miller, *A Conspiratorial Life: Robert Welch, the John Birch Society, and the Revolution of American Conservatism* (Chicago: University of Chicago Press, 2022). Mabley took the same tactic that William F. Buckley had, condemning Welch but praising JBS members as fine, upstanding citizens.

40. Jack Mabley, "Baez Honesty Led to Rerun of TV Show," *Chicago American*, March 12, 1969. Clipping from Jack Mabley collection, Newberry Library, "Works Clippings—*Chicago American*, Jan–Apr 1969," box 8, folder 102.

41. Jack Mabley, "Objective View of Riot Films Needed," *Chicago American*, December 16, 1968. Clipping from Newberry Library, Mabley collection, "Works Clippings—*Chicago American*, Sept–Dec 1968," box 8, folder 101.

42. Max Frankel, "Introduction," in *Rights in Conflict* (New York: Bantam, 1968), ix, x.

43. Associated Press, "Dan Walker, Former Illinois Governor Imprisoned for Fraud and Perjury, Dies," *Washington Post*, April 29, 2015; https://www .washingtonpost.com/politics/dan-walker-former-illinois-governor-imprisoned -for-fraud-and-perjury-dies/2015/04/29/b3f895d6-ee94-11e4-a55f-38924fca94f9 _story.html. Walker's conviction came twenty years after his famous report, and upon his passing, the *Chicago Tribune*'s editorial board described his time as governor as "squeaky-clean." "The Passion of Illinois Gov. Dan Walker's Rage against Daley's Machine," April 29, 2015; https://www.chicagotribune.com/opinion/editorials /ct-dan-walker-governor-illinois-edit-0430-20150429-story.html. Walker's later fall from grace does not mean that corruption fueled the 1968 report.

44. "Lyndon B. Johnson and Richard J. Daley on 4 December 1968," Conversation WH6812-01-13803, *Presidential Recordings Digital Edition* [*Johnson Tele-*

phone Tapes: 1968, ed. Kent B. Germany, Nicole Hemmer, and Ken Hughes] (Charlottesville: University of Virginia Press, 2014-); http://prde.upress.virginia.edu/conversations/4005384.

45. Frankel, "Introduction," in *Rights in Conflict,* x.

46. Oral History, Victor de Grazia, Oral History Office of Sangamon State University, July 8, 1981, 10; https://web.archive.org/web/20060220074930/http://www.uis.edu/archives/memoirs/DEGRAZIA.pdf.

47. Oral History, Victor de Grazia, 9-10.

48. Oral History, Daniel Walker, Oral History Office of Sangamon State University, May 12, 1981, 30; https://web.archive.org/web/20071129175524/http://www.uis.edu/archives/memoirs/WALKERD.pdf.

49. Abbie Hoffman, cited in Frankel, *Rights in Conflict,* 87.

50. "Chicago Examined: Anatomy of a Police Riot," *Time,* December 6, 1968.

51. Unidentified policeman, cited in Frankel, *Rights in Conflict,* 237.

52. "Chicago Examined," *Time.*

53. Jean Genet, "The Members of the Assembly," *Esquire,* November 1968, 86-89. William S. Burroughs, Terry Southern, and John Sack also contributed essays on Chicago to this issue.

54. Ronald Adler, cited in Frank Kusch, *Battleground Chicago: The Police and the 1968 Democratic National Convention* (Chicago: University of Chicago Press, 2008), 25.

55. Kusch, *Battleground Chicago,* 125. Forty years later, the hatred remained strong. Interviewees described the protestors as "drugged-out animals" and "ugly, dirty little shits" (151).

56. Hank De Zutter, "How It Happened: Chronology of a Riot," *Chicago Reader,* August 25, 1968; https://www.chicagoreader.com/chicago/how-it-happened/Content?oid=872645.

57. In a 1972 investigation, Congressman Ralph Metcalfe concluded that "abusive treatment of a citizen is viewed as merely over-zealous conduct within the scope of accepted [Chicago] police behavior." Metcalfe, cited in Simon Balto, *Occupied Territory: Policing Black Chicago from Red Summer to Black Power* (Chapel Hill: University of North Carolina Press, 2019), 204.

58. Tom Freeborn, cited in Kusch, *Battleground Chicago,* 141.

59. John Schultz, "The Siege of '68," *Chicago Reader,* September 8, 1988.

60. Joseph McDonald, "Chicago 1968: *Rights in Conflict* and Rights in Conflict," *RQ (Reference Quarterly),* Winter 1969, 126. This sort of outsourcing of GPO print jobs was common, even if profanity was an issue in this case. *Keeping America Informed: The U.S. Government Publishing Office A Legacy of Service to the Nation, 1861-2016,* rev. ed. (Washington DC: U.S. Government Publishing Office, 2016), 103. The Government Printing Office was renamed the Government Publishing Office in 2014.

61. Walker later said he was the only person to write a best seller and not make a

cent—a hyperbolic statement, insofar as the book sold well but not exceptionally so. It's true, though, that government reports are in the public domain. "By law, printing plates on all government documents are [in an era before computerized production] available to private publishers. It was not the GPO that published a version of the Warren Commission report for mass-market distribution and sale, for example, but Bantam Books." James B. Adler, "Micropublishing and the Government Printing Office/Three Viewpoints, Viewpoint I: The Private Publisher" *Microform Review* 3, no. 2 (1974): 86–87.

62. Jack Gould, "Television: Covering the Siege at Miami Beach," *New York Times*, August 9, 1968.

63. Jack Gould, "TV: California Gets 3 Candidates on Air Together," *New York Times*, August 28, 1968.

64. Theodore H. White, *The Making of the President 1968* (New York: Harper Collins, 2010), 414–16.

65. On the other hand, see David L. Vancil and Sue D. Pendell, "The Myth of Viewer-Listener Disagreement in the First Kennedy-Nixon Debate," *Central States Speech Journal* 38, no. 1 (1987): 16–27; and W. Joseph Campbell, *Getting It Wrong: Debunking the Greatest Myths in American Journalism*, 2nd ed. (Oakland: University of California Press, 2016), 67–82.

66. Kathleen Hall Jamieson, *Packaging the Presidency: A History and Criticism of Presidential Campaign Advertising* , 3rd ed. (New York: Oxford University Press, 1996), 259.

67. Howard Thompson, "'A Face of War' Offers Intimate Record of 97 Days with G.I.s," *New York Times*, May 11, 1968; https://www.nytimes.com/1968/05/11/archives/a-face-of-war-offers-intimate-record-of-97-days-with-gis.html.

68. Joe McGinniss, *The Selling of the President 1968* (New York: Trident Press, 1969), 84–85.

69. Duncan worked for *Life* and *Colliers* and produced a number of Picasso photo collections. Jones later produced *Today* and *Wide World* for NBC and was nominated for an Academy Award for his 1974 documentary *The Wild and the Brave*. While not typical candidates to shoot a political campaign, they were working professionals, not eccentric choices, though it might seem that way if one knew only Duncan's photos at Khe San and Jones's dark documentary.

70. Marshall McLuhan, cited in McGinniss, *Selling of the President 1968*, 181.

71. Jamieson, *Packaging the Presidency*, 246–47.

72. Jamieson, *Packaging the Presidency*, 245.

73. Aniko Bodroghkozy, *Groove Tube: Sixties Television and Youth Rebellion* (Durham, NC: Duke University Press, 2001), 149.

74. There were two other production styles in play for Nixon media during the campaign. The hour-long town halls were tightly controlled, audience question-and-answer sessions produced by Roger Ailes and shot in very conventional studio TV fashion. On the other hand, there was *1968: A Time to Begin*, a black-and-white,

half-hour campaign film shot mostly with a handheld camera, a blatant rip-off of the Robert Drew cinema vérité classic *Primary* (1960). At the end, Nixon explains, "I'm really the most difficult man in the world when it comes to a so-called public relations firm. Nobody's going to package me. Nobody's going to make me put on an act for television. . . . I'm just going to be myself." It's the perfect conclusion of a film designed exactly to package Nixon, and it is the stylistic opposite of the psychedelic "Convention" spot.

75. R. W. Apple Jr., "Humphrey Greeted by Daley but Hails Party's Dissenters," *New York Times*, November 2, 1968; https://timesmachine.nytimes.com/times machine/1968/11/02/76901146.html?pageNumber=1.

76. "Lyndon B. Johnson and Richard J. Daley on 6 November 1968," Conversation WH6811-03-13719, *Presidential Recordings Digital Edition* [*Johnson Telephone Tapes*: 1968, ed. Kent B. Germany, Nicole Hemmer, and Ken Hughes] (Charlottesville: University of Virginia Press, 2014-); http://prde.upress.virginia.edu /conversations/4006131.

77. Jamieson, *Packaging the Presidency*, 321.

78. Storck directed and narrated *HHH: What Manner of Man*, a twenty-eight-minute biographical campaign film. He had previously worked at the Centron and Calvin companies in Kansas City, Missouri. (Centron was the company where Herk Harvey made industrial films. He is best known for his cult film *Carnival of Souls* [1962].) Storck appeared in numerous productions, such as the worker management film *Coffee Break* (Gene Carr, 1958), the VD prevention film *Innocent Party* (Herk Harvey, 1959), and the Gulf Oil training film *The Dirty Look* (Robert Altman, 1954).

79. Jaime Sánchez Jr., "Revisiting McGovern-Fraser: Party Nationalization and the Rhetoric of Reform," *Journal of Policy History* 32, no .1 (2020): 9.

80. Recall also the 1924 Democratic convention, which lasted sixteen days; votes were cast 103 times before a candidate was selected. "The convention is often called the 'Klanbake' because one of the front-runners . . . was supported by the Ku Klux Klan, . . . [and] the party's anti-Klan . . . faction failed by a slim margin to pass a platform plank condemning the Klan." Jack Shafer, "1924: The Wildest Convention in U.S. History," *Politico*, March 7, 2016; https://www.politico.com/magazine/story /2016/03/1924-the-craziest-convention-in-us-history-213708/. See also Robert K. Murray, *The 103rd Ballot: Democrats and the Disaster in Madison Square Garden* (New York: Harper & Row, 1976); and Hanes Walton Jr. and C. Vernon Gray, "Black Politics at the National Republican and Democratic Conventions, 1868-1972," *Phylon* 36, no. 3 (1975): 277.

81. Theodore H. White, *The Making of the President 1972* (New York: Harper Collins, 2010), 159.

82. Cohen and Taylor, *American Pharaoh*, 521.

83. Cohen and Taylor, *American Pharaoh*, 522.

84. Mike Royko, cited in White, *Making of the President 1972*, 165.

85. White was roundly attacked by the left for his 1968 book. See *Firing Line*,

"The Making of the President 1968," September 22, 1969. Program Number 169, Hoover Institution, Stanford University, *Firing Line* collection.

86. White, *Making of the President 1972*, 166.

87. Fred Harris, cited in Sánchez, "Revisiting McGovern-Fraser," 11.

88. Sen. George McGovern, "The Lessons of 1968," *Harper's*, January 1, 1970, 45, 47.

89. Ben Wattenberg, cited in White, *Making of the President 1972*, 161.

90. "M'Govern Endorsed by 2 on Radical Left," *New York Times*, April 24, 1972; https://www.nytimes.com/1972/04/24/archives/mgovern-endorsed-by-2-on -radical-left.html.

91. White, *Making of the President 1972*, 182.

92. Mailer had no animus against gay rights but understood them as "political suicide" for the party at the time. His stance on women's rights and birth control, by contrast, was aggressively negative: "The pride of Women's Liberation was that cunts had the right to smell as bad as any man's half-dead cigar." Norman Mailer, *St. George and the Godfather* (New York: Arbor House, 1972), 53, 57.

93. C-SPAN panel discussion, "McGovern 1972 Presidential Campaign," April 8, 1997; https://www.c-span.org/video/?80213-1/mcgovern-1972-presidential -campaign.

94. Hunter S. Thompson, *Fear and Loathing on the Campaign Trail '72* (New York: Grand Central, 1973), 288. See also Victor S. Navasky, "A Funny Thing Happened on the Way to the Coronation," *New York Times Magazine*, July 23, 1972; https://www .nytimes.com/1972/07/23/archives/a-funny-thing-happened-on-the-way-to-the -coronation-a-funny-thing.html.

95. "'Gay' People Bitter After Plank Defeat," *Washington Post*, July 12, 1972.

96. White, *Making of the President 1972*, 184.

97. White, *Making of the President 1972*, 239.

98. White, *Making of the President 1972*, 186.

99. Deirdre Boyle, "Guerilla Television" in *Transmission: Toward a Post-Television Culture*, ed. Peter D'Agostino and David Tafler (Thousand Oaks, CA: Sage, 1995), 203–13.

100. Jamieson, *Packaging the Presidency*, 322.

101. "Lyndon B. Johnson, Richard M. Nixon, and Paul Glynn on 31 August 1968," Conversation WH6808-05-13354-13355, *Presidential Recordings Digital Edition* [*Johnson Telephone Tapes: 1968*, ed. Kent B. Germany, Nicole Hemmer, and Ken Hughes] (Charlottesville: University of Virginia Press, 2014-); http://prde.upress .virginia.edu/conversations/4006052.

CONCLUSION

1. "Walter Cronkite, Interview with Ron Powers," June 1973, in *The Playboy Interview*, ed. G. Barry Golson (New York: Playboy Press, 1981), 377.

2. On 1960s network documentaries, see Michael Curtin, *Redeeming the Waste-*

land: Television Documentary and Cold War Politics (New Brunswick, NJ: Rutgers University Press, 1995).

3. Sanford Socolow, interview with Dr. Ralph Engelman, August 27, 2008, Television Academy Foundation; https://interviews.televisionacademy.com/interviews/sanford-socolow.

4. There were, of course, moments when *internal* network judgments were made about employees displaying overall political bias, as with William L. Shirer and Norman Corwin in the 1940s. Erik Barnouw, *The Golden Web: A History of Broadcasting in the United States, 1933–1953*, vol. 2 (New York: Oxford University Press, 1968), 241.

5. Patricia Aufderheide, "After the Fairness Doctrine: Controversial Broadcast Programming and the Public Interest," *Journal of Communication* (Summer 1990), 54.

6. Alan Brinkley, *Voices of Protest: Huey Long, Father Coughlin and the Great Depression* (New York: Vintage, 1982), 268; Philip V. Cannistraro and Theodore P. Kovaleff, "Father Coughlin and Mussolini: Impossible Allies," *Journal of Church and State* 13, no. 3 (1971): 427–43.

7. The doctrine was also a liberalizing revision of the 1941 *Mayflower* ruling prohibiting licensees from editorializing altogether. Hugh Carter Donahue, *The Battle to Control Broadcast News: Who Owns the First Amendment?* (Cambridge: Massachusetts Institute of Technology Press, 1989), 33–35.

8. Michael Schudson, *Discovering the News: A Social History of American Newspapers* (New York: Basic Books, 1978), 182–83. Schudson points to the premiere of *Sixty Minutes* as a tipping point for TV journalism taking an overtly critical perspective.

9. Aufderheide, "After the Fairness Doctrine," 54.

10. Heather Hendershot, *What's Fair on the Air? Cold War Right-Wing Broadcasting and the Public Interest* (Chicago: University of Chicago Press, 2011); Paul Matzko, *The Radio Right: How a Band of Broadcasters Took on the Federal Government and Built the Modern Conservative Movement* (New York: Oxford University Press, 2020).

11. Brian Rosenwald, *Talk Radio's America: How an Industry Took Over a Political Party That Took Over the United States* (Cambridge, MA: Harvard University Press, 2019).

12. "Interview by Professor Andrew Stern with Walter Cronkite, CBS News," September 10, 1970, 16mm film, UARC FILM 01 box 11, Bancroft Library, University of California, Berkeley; https://californiarevealed.org/islandora/object/cavpp%3A11433.

13. Walter Cronkite, "Television and the News," in *The Eighth Art* (New York: Holt, Rinehart and Winston, 1962), 228.

14. William E. Porter, *Assault on the Media: The Nixon Years* (Ann Arbor: University of Michigan Press, 1976), 3.

15. Raymond B. Nixon, "Trends in U.S. Newspaper Ownership: Concentration with Competition," *International Communication Gazette* 14, no. 3 (1968): 181–93.

16. William Paley, quoted in Michael J. Socolow, "'We Should Make Money on Our News': The Problem of Profitability in Network Broadcast Journalism History," *Journalism* 11, no. 6 (2010): 677.

17. Charles Colson to Elizabeth Drew, *CBS Morning News*, February 2, 1973. Cited in "Administration Attacks—CBS" binder, Sanford Socolow Papers, Briscoe Center. On Nixon and cable, see Kathryn Cramer Brownell, "'Ideological Plugola,' 'Elitist Gossip,' and the Need for Cable Television" in *Media Nation: The Political History of News in Modern America*, ed. Bruce J. Schulman and Julian E. Zelizer (Philadelphia: University of Pennsylvania Press, 2017), 160–75.

18. For a detailed account, including substantial focus on print media, see Porter, *Assault on the Media*; and, specifically from the perspective of a print reporter, Timothy Crouse, *The Boys on the Bus* (New York: Random House, 1973).

19. John M. Crewdson, "Sabotaging the G.O.P.'s Rivals: Story of a $100,000 Operation," *New York Times*, July 9, 1973; https://www.nytimes.com/1973/07/09/archives/sabotaging-the-g-ops-rivals-story-of-a-100000-operation-scope-of.html.

20. Nicole Hemmer, "From 'Faith in Facts' to 'Fair and Balanced': Conservative Media, Liberal Bias, and the Origins of Balance" in Schulman and Zelizer, *Media Nation*, 139.

21. William J. Small, *Political Power and the Press* (New York: W. W. Norton, 1972); Chad Raphael, *Investigated Reporting: Muckrakers, Regulators, and the Struggle over Television Documentary* (Urbana: University of Illinois Press, 2005).

22. Reuven Frank, "The Ugly Mirror," *Television Quarterly* 8, no. 1 (1969): 82–96. Reuven Frank Papers, box 2, Research and Reference files, 1943–2005, MS137/001, "Writings, c. 1963–1980" folder, Tufts University.

23. Letter from Beth Sayres to Walter Cronkite, April 24, 1973, CBS News Archive, vol./box 2K97, "Watergate Viewer Response" folder, Briscoe Center.

24. Letter from Mrs. M. Du Mahaut to Walter Cronkite, April 29, 1973, CBS News Archive, vol./box 2K97, "Anti Nixon Bias" folder, Briscoe Center.

25. Kevin M. Kruse and Julian E. Zelizer, *Fault Lines: A History of the United States Since 1974* (New York: Norton, 2019), 34.

26. Cronkite, interview with Stern.

27. Elsewhere Cronkite said, "Most people are good; there aren't very many really evil people. But there are an awful lot of selfish ones. And this selfishness permeates society. It keeps us from the beauty of where we could go . . ." "Walter Cronkite, Interview with Ron Powers," 385.

28. Cronkite, cited in "Walter Cronkite, Interview with Ron Powers," 390–91.

29. Gary Paul Gates, *Air Time: The Inside Story of CBS News* (New York: Harper & Row, 1978), 115.

30. Consider *The Candidate* (1972), a dispiriting film, scripted by a former Eugene McCarthy speechwriter, about the emptiness of politics, with brief McGovern and Humphrey cameos. The film conveys TV as the instrument by which candidates convey their phony public personas. The liberal film did not vilify the news

media, but it did not defend it either. That was the best you could hope for in an early seventies American film. By the time *Network* appeared in 1976, the idea of trusting network newsmen was laughable and ripe for satire.

31. David Greenberg, *Nixon's Shadow: The History of an Image* (New York: Norton, 2003), 160.

32. Greenberg, *Nixon's Shadow*, 162.

33. Lewis Z. Koch, "TV 2," in *Law & Disorder: The Chicago Convention and Its Aftermath*, ed. Donald Myrus (Chicago: Donald Myrus and Burton Joseph, 1968).

34. Elaine C. Kamarck, *Primary Politics: Everything You Need to Know About How America Nominates Its Presidential Candidates*, 3rd ed. (Washington, DC: Brookings Institution Press, 2009).

35. Heather Hendershot, "The 2020 Party Conventions Are Actually What the Parties Have Always Dreamed Of," *Washington Post*, August 17, 2020; https://www.washingtonpost.com/outlook/2020/08/17/2020-party-conventions-are-actually-what-parties-have-always-dreamed/?outputType=amp.

36. James Baldwin, "Black English: A Dishonest Argument," in *The Cross of Redemption: Uncollected Writings* (New York: Pantheon, 2010), 125.

Index

ABC (American Broadcasting Company), 40, 67, 145, 328, 351nn3–4; convention coverage, 52, 53, 65–69, 269; Daley and, 65–66, 69, 281, 282; finances, 6–7; ratings, 66–67, 351nn3–4; reputation and performance, 46, 65–67, 145, 269

Abernathy, Bob, 128

Abernathy, Ralph, 54, 107, 123, 350n43; Liberty City and, 55, 350n43; Poor People's Campaign Mule Train, 54, 123. *See also* Poor People's Campaign

ACLU. *See* American Civil Liberties Union (ACLU)

advertisements. *See* campaign ads; TV ads

"advocacy reporting," 21, 125, 129

agents provocateurs, 22, 252, 257

Agnew, Spiro T., 329; Cronkite and, 332, 333; Humphrey and, 328; and the media, 8, 22, 268, 284–85, 307, 319, 328, 329, 331–33; Nixon and, 8, 22, 54, 304, 328, 329, 331; speeches, 54, 254, 319

Agronsky, Martin, 139, 197–98

Ailes, Roger, 8, 233, 369n74; Nixon and, 8, 30, 300

Alabama, 120; Blacks in, 114–15; Black voting in, 16, 75–76, 107; civil rights in, 16, 46, 179; Daley and, 248–49; Humphrey and, 104, 106, 107; in the media, 16, 309; police, 46, 179; white supremacy in, 16, 98, 107, 108, 124, 239, 355n15. *See also* Birmingham, AL; Cashin, John L., Jr.; National Democratic Party of Alabama; Wallace, George

Alabama delegates and Alabama delegate challenge, 81, 98, 104–8, 110, 112, 114, 243

Alabama Democratic Party, 106–7

Albert, Carl, 102, 135, 153–54, 188–89, 192–95, 236, 237, 240, 244–49, 253, 254, 315; Daley and, 135, 188, 189, 249; police violence and, 188, 189; speeches, 95, 105, 109, 127

American Civil Liberties Union (ACLU), 289–91

American Revolution II: Battle of Chicago (film), 122, 244

Anderson, Eddie, 92–93, 92f

Andy Frain Services, 115, 179

Army-McCarthy hearings, 325

Aufderheide, Patricia, 323

Bailey, John Moran, 194, 195

balance. *See* "bothsidesism"; fairness, balance, and neutrality

Baldwin, James, 338

Battle of Khe Sanh, 34, 90

Battle of Michigan Avenue, 19, 38, 213, 249–50, 257, 286, 287; arrests at, 249–50; bandaging the wounded victims of, 199f, 258, 259f, 260f; Brinkley and, 183, 190–91, 197; characterizations of, 22–23, 143, 268, 336; Cronkite and, 178, 183–85, 197, 200–207, 242–44, 250, 251, 325–26; Daley and, 185–87, 193, 226–27, 265, 294, 320, 325–26; Duncan and, 212, 214, 258, 259f; footage of, 173, 178, 337; injuries, 191, 198, 260f; LBJ and, 229, 230, 257, 270, 283, 319; legacy, 336; letters to Cronkite regarding, 1, 9; Mailer and, 213, 214; and the media, 18–19, 169, 185, 191–92, 200–201, 271, 320, 324–26; National Guard at (*see* National Guard: in Chicago); overview, 183–87; police violence in, 9, 23, 24, 140, 168, 183, 186, 191–93, 216, 270, 294, 320, 335, 336; public opinion regarding, 335; responses to, 22–23; TV coverage of, 1, 22, 140, 168, 183–86, 191–92, 197, 216, 258, 260f, 265, 320, 326, 344n12; undercover agents in front of Hilton, 22. *See also* tear gas/mace; *Walker Report* (*Rights in Conflict*); *What Trees Do They Plant?* (film)